ALEISTER CROWLEY AND THE TEMPTATION OF POLITICS

Aleister Crowley and the Temptation of Politics

Marco Pasi

ACUMEN

© Marco Pasi, 2014

This book is copyright under the Berne Convention.
No reproduction without permission.
All rights reserved.

First published in 2014 by Acumen
Reprinted 2014

Acumen Publishing Limited
4 Saddler Street
Durham
DH1 3NP

ISD, 70 Enterprise Drive
Bristol, CT 06010, USA

www.acumenpublishing.com

ISBN: 978-1-84465-695-0 (hardcover)
ISBN: 978-1-84465-696-7 (paperback)

British Library Cataloguing-in-Publication Data
A catalogue record for this book is available from the British Library.

Typeset in Minion Pro by JS Typesetting Ltd, Porthcawl CF36 5BL
Printed and bound in the UK by 4edge Ltd., Essex

To my mother, Anna

Contents

Foreword ix
Acknowledgements xi
Abbreviations xiii

Introduction 1

1. An unspeakable life 5
2. Magical politics 23
3. Dangerous liaisons 65
4. The Mouth of Hell 95
5. Counter-initiation and conspiracy 117

Conclusion 137

Appendix 1: Some additional remarks on Julius Evola and
Aleister Crowley 141
Hans Thomas Hakl

Appendix 2: Key documents 153

Notes 163
Bibliography 207
Index 225

Foreword

The largest part of this book was originally written between 1993 and 1994. For a scholarly work, this is of course a long time ago. Almost twenty years are more than enough to make a book outdated with current research. This is why I had to thoroughly revise it and update it for its earlier editions: the Italian one in 1999 and the German one in 2006. When the moment came to prepare the present edition in English, I decided once again to update, revise and expand it. The result is now for me a strange mixture of old and new. If I had to start now writing on the topic of this book, I would probably do it in a very different way. But I believe that when I began working on this book, it was a pioneering enterprise and that its value – great or small it is not for me to decide – has remained intact even today. One of the reasons is that it was one of the first attempts to interpret Aleister Crowley not simply as an eccentric adventurer or even a malicious fraud, but as an intellectual and ideologist, who belonged to a particular cultural climate and had to be understood on the basis of the education he received, the ideas that influenced him, and the persons he frequented during his life. The particular angle that I chose for this research was politics, and I still believe it is one of the most interesting ones when applied to Crowley, but it could have been another as well, such as literature or art.

When I started writing my book, the most authoritative biography of Crowley was still the one by John Symonds, and scholarly literature on him was very scarce, if existing at all. Things have changed quite a bit since then, especially with the new wave of Crowley biographies that started in the late 1990s. And this is not to mention the myriad of smaller studies and articles, including scholarly ones, that have been published in the last ten years. It was impossible to integrate here all the information contained in these new publications, but I have done my best to use them and add references to them whenever they could bring something new or important to my study.

Another point of note is that in the past few years there has been a new appreciation of the importance of the scholarly study of Western esotericism in general, and of nineteenth- and twentieth-century occultism in particular. So it is today less necessary to justify one's research about someone like Aleister Crowley. My introduction still bears the traces of the wariness and the prudence one needed to show in doing research on this kind of subject, at least in Italy and especially as a burgeoning scholar, back in the early 1990s, when the first version of the book was written.

The reader will find acknowledgements related to the first edition of the book below, but I would like to thank here a few more persons who had an important role in the production of the present English edition. I would like to thank in particular the two publishers who were involved in this long (perhaps too long) process: Janet Joyce and

Tristan Palmer. They were both patient beyond what I thought was possible, and maybe even beyond what *they* thought was possible. I thank them heartily for having believed in this book, and also for having believed that this book would really be published one day, in spite of my repeated delays. I would also like to thank the translator, Ariel Godwin, and his father Joscelyn Godwin, for the work they have done and their efforts to make this English edition possible. I am happy to acknowledge also the excellent work done by Acumen editors Hamish Ironside and Gina Mance in copyediting the text before publication. I really appreciated their professionalism and the care they put into making this a better book.

Special thanks go to William Breeze and John L. Crow, for reading an early version of the translation and commenting on it. Without their suggestions this book would contain quite a few mistakes for which I would have been sorry. Apart from that, as most scholars doing serious research on Crowley and related subjects I also owe a big debt to William, who has allowed me to have access to documents from the OTO Archives that were essential for my research.

I would also like to thank Jerónimo Pizarro, Steffen Dix and Patricio Ferrari, who were particularly helpful when working again on the chapter on Crowley and Fernando Pessoa. H. Thomas Hakl has been kind enough to write an essay on Crowley and Julius Evola for the German edition of the book, and to make it available also for the present edition. It appears here as Appendix 1. A thank you also to my close colleagues at the University of Amsterdam, Wouter J. Hanegraaff, Peter J. Forshaw and Egil Asprem, not so much for specific help in the preparation of the book, but for offering such a stimulating intellectual environment that I found, as usual, most convenient and productive, when pondering about the most intricate aspects of my subject. Also a big thank you to Rosalie Basten, without whom it would be much harder to be an academic writing on such peculiar subjects as magic and esotericism.

Part of the work for the present edition took place during a research fellowship at the Netherlands Institute for Advanced Studies (NIAS) in Wassenaar. I would like to thank the Institute for providing me with an exceptional environment for research, convenient as any scholar would wish it to be.

The last thought is, as it should be, for Barbara Philipp, the companion of my life and the mother of my children, without whose patience, understanding and affection it would have been a much harder task for me to complete this book.

Amsterdam, November 2013

🙠 Acknowledgements

The starting point for this work was my dissertation for a laurea degree in philosophy, defended in the summer of 1994 at the Università degli Studi in Milan. Given its long and complex gestation period, gratitude is due to many persons. My first thanks go to Giorgio Galli, one of whose ideas was at the origin of my research. Without him – and I say this without any fear of stumbling over rhetoric – this book would not exist. His patience and intuition were a great help to me throughout its preparation, from the first shapeless draft to the final phases of revision. My gratitude to him is much greater than I can express in these few lines. Giulio Giorello, originally the second reviewer for my dissertation, followed my work through its initial phases and encouraged me on many occasions when my research seemed to be stagnating. Pietro Adamo was the *deus ex machina* thanks to whom this book was published. Besides this, he provided some important assistance during the delicate and highly significant stages of final revision. For him as well, words cannot express my gratitude. Massimo Introvigne has given me invaluable advice and was kind enough to read through my work in its original version. I also discussed parts of my work with Antoine Faivre and Jean-Pierre Laurant. Their erudition and experience were a great help to me. I owe particular thanks to Gabriele Mandel, who gave me the proper advice in a time of great uncertainty and confusion. I also discussed certain aspects of my research with Christopher McIntosh, and his friendly interest was encouraging and helpful to me. H. Thomas Hakl read an initial version of this book. His encouragement was very important, as well as the advice and materials with which he was kind enough to provide me. Heartfelt thanks also go out to Isabella Francisci, from the publisher FrancoAngeli, for editing this book with care and attentiveness. I benefited greatly from her professional advice and great patience (which I hope I did not abuse).

The OTO International, who holds the rights to Crowley's works, generously allowed me to reproduce his published and unpublished materials. Particular thanks go to William Breeze, Bill Heidrick and Tony Iannotti for their generous help in providing me with important documents from the OTO archives. Similar thanks go to Maria Babwahsingh, Martin P. Starr, Tobias Churton, Pedro Teixeira da Mota, Victor Belém, Peter-Robert Koenig, Christian Bouchet, Marzio Forgione, Dana Lloyd Thomas, David Gattegno, Laszlo Toth and Xavier Accart, for having shown me interesting trails to pursue or providing me with materials.

I am greatly indebted to the personnel at various libraries. In particular I would like to thank the former director of the Warburg Institute in London, Will F. Ryan, as well as John Perkins; Andrea Cassinasco at the Cesnur library in Turin; and François Rognon at the rue Puteaux Masonic library in Paris. The personnel at the Archivio

Centrale dello Stato in Rome, the Bibliothèque Nationale de France in Paris, the British Library in London and the Biblioteca Nacional in Lisbon all helped me and facilitated my research on various occasions. I must also thank the Equipa Pessoa in Lisbon for allowing me to consult Fernando Pessoa's unpublished documents preserved in their collection.

On a personal level, my thanks go to Marco Battarra, who showed understanding on a particularly sensitive question; Lele and Fulvio Signò, who assisted me in acquiring books from abroad; Barbara Porta and Gaetano Valenti, who hosted me in Rome during my research; Stephen Blanchard, who hosted me in London; and Claudio Ferrara for his availability. Heartfelt remembrance goes to my grandmother Pierina Porta, at whose house in Savona I spent a lovely semester writing the first version of this book. Finally, for all that I am immensely grateful to all those who have aided me, the only true debt that I can never repay is owed to my mother, Anna. There is no need to say more here; she knows why, and that is enough.

Abbreviations

ACS   Archivio Centrale dello Stato (Rome).

BNP/E3   Biblioteca Nacional (Lisbon), Espólio Fernando Pessoa. This is the collection of Pessoa's papers.

FP   Fuller Papers (Liddell Hart Centre for Military Archives, King's College, London). Collection of manuscript and typed documents connected to General J. F. C. Fuller.

OA   Ordo Templi Orientis (OTO) Archives. This collection is not directly accessible to scholars, but the organization's authorities willingly provided copies of the specific documents.

RP   Regardie Papers. Private collection of Mrs Maria Babwahsingh. The documents in this collection are not catalogued, and therefore do not have call numbers.

YC   Yorke Collection (Warburg Institute, London). The collection is centred around Gerald Yorke's legacy, and is subdivided into three parts: a collection of printed materials (simply indicated by the call number); a first collection of manuscripts (which were given by Yorke to the Library from the mid-1960s on and which, according to current usage, is referred to as "old series" and is indicated here by YC/OS, then the call number); and a second collection of manuscripts (a "new series" which joined the old series in 1984, and which will be indicated here by YC/NS, then the call number).

❧ Introduction

Why should one take any serious interest in such a bizarre character as Aleister Crowley? Even if scholars have now begun to show an interest in him and the number of serious studies devoted to him is slowly increasing, it is still easier to find books that describe him in a sensationalist manner, as a bogeyman or a charlatan or both – just as it was the case during his lifetime. Sometimes even authors who have already done courageous pioneering work in the critical and historical study of esoteric movements, and who have had to defend the subjects of their research from suspicion and from attempts at marginalization, have not held back from voicing expressions of contempt when considering Crowley. A significant example can be found in Gershom Scholem's *Major Trends in Jewish Mysticism*, a milestone in the research on Jewish esotericism. Scholem describes Crowley's use of certain Kabbalistic ideas as "highly coloured humbug" and takes a sharper tone in a later note: "No words need be wasted on the subject of Crowley's 'Kabbalistic' writings."[1]

With the emergence of new fields of research, such as the history of Western esotericism and the study of new religious movements, scholars have begun to delve beyond Crowley's personality and to study him more methodically and attentively as an author. It has been realized, in fact, that Crowley represents an essential source for the understanding of a broad category of new religious movements, ranging from neo-paganism to Satanism.[2] And with the development of the academic study of esoteric movements, scholars have begun to emancipate themselves from "conservative" positions such as that of Scholem, and have broadened their field of investigation to include authors and movements that have only entered the realm of academic research in the past few years.[3]

Being therefore convinced that an author such as Aleister Crowley should be considered as a valid and respectable subject for scholarly research, I have decided to focus on a specific aspect of his persona, namely his relationship to politics. The study of the connections between esotericism and politics, particularly in the last two hundred years, is no novelty in itself.[4] For instance, the well-known study by George Mosse on the cultural origins of the Third Reich, first published in 1964, presented the history of various German currents and movements prior to the First World War, which in certain cases may be placed in a grey zone between esotericism and politics.[5] Mosse's research in this direction was further developed, this time in a broader European perspective and with an increased interest for the specifically esoteric aspects, by the Scottish scholar James Webb.[6] Webb's assumption was that one of the characteristic historical phenomena of Western history during the last two centuries had been what he called the "flight from reason". This flight, in his view, was a reaction "to patterns of thought and society that were emerging as a product of eighteenth-century rationalism",[7] or in other words, a rejection of modernity with its rationalist and materialist aspects. The phenomenon was particularly accentuated, according to Webb, during times of social or political tension.

Although Webb's studies are today still a gold mine of information, his essential theses now seem a little dated. An approach of this kind assumes a polarity between two divergent and contrasting forces which Webb identifies as "rationalism" and "irrationalism". The clashing between these two ideological forces, according to him, is "one of the greatest battles fought in the 20th century".[8] Unfortunately, the question of how to define these two forces in historical terms, and how to identify them concretely with particular authors or movements, remains open. And when the phenomenon is subjected to closer scrutiny, we find that in many cases – even taking for granted an unambiguous definition of "rationality" – the boundaries between rationalism and irrationalism tend to become rather blurry.

More recently, Jean-Pierre Laurant and Joscelyn Godwin have presented the question in a new light.[9] Their works highlight an element that is more easily identifiable and definable in historical terms: namely, the relationship of occultist currents not so much to rationality, but rather to Christianity. This new parameter, namely the varying distance of esoteric and occultist movements from Christianity during the nineteenth century – a distance that can be partly measured by the re-emergence of thematic elements coming from the tradition of the Enlightenment – makes the analysis of the phenomenon more concrete, and offers us a clearer view of the internal and external dynamics acting upon the various currents of occultism. Crowley's case is undoubtedly better understandable in this framework than in the context outlined by Webb. In fact, as I hope to make clear in my analysis, it is impossible – or at least highly problematic – to speak of a "flight from reason" in Crowley's case, whereas it is certainly legitimate to speak of a flight from Christianity.

According to Godwin, who has studied the occultist phenomenon in England in particular, this parameter can also be connected with a possible distinction between a left-wing esotericism, with liberal and progressive tendencies, and a right-wing esotericism, reactionary and conservative.[10] An example of the first type would be Madame Blavatsky's theosophy. René Guénon's traditionalism, on the other hand, would belong to the latter type. If we accept this distinction, Crowley seems, at first sight, to fall on the left rather than on the right. But actually, in his case, things become rather more complicated. As we will see, there were two Crowleys: one was a rationalist sympathetic to the values of the Enlightenment, the other was a romantic and a reactionary. The first one had studied at Cambridge, believed in progress and rejected Christianity with the arguments of the positivist and liberal thinkers. The second one did *not* believe in progress and in the positive aspects of modern civilization, and yearned for a return to the feudal age. In this sense, it could also be said that Crowley epitomized the crisis that first characterized the late Victorian, and then the Edwardian, society. Crowley expressed this period of transition very clearly, even though the transition remained incomplete in him.

Another important precedent in studies on politics and esotericism can be found in the works of Giorgio Galli.[11] In fact, my research developed initially from his studies. Crowley's name appears in his books several times in reference to historical events whose details are not yet entirely clear (such as Rudolf Hess's flight to Britain). The present work is an attempt to offer some new elements in this direction.

More specifically about the content of this book, I may point out that my analysis focuses on two levels at the same time: the level of facts, and the level of ideas. Regarding the first level, Crowley probably holds an unusual record: the number of defamatory or simply ridiculous legends that have gathered around his person is truly staggering,[12] and one of the first tasks faced by the scholar who wishes to approach him with the necessary seriousness is to shine some light into this jumble of falsehood and truth. In Chapter 1, therefore, I will offer a brief outline of his life, thus giving the reader a clearer background for the content of the following chapters.

In Chapter 2, I will focus more specifically on Crowley's ideas. I will examine some of Crowley's texts, trying to highlight their possible political significance. Crowley did not write much explicitly on politics, but it is my conviction that his body of work is replete with fascinating political implications. I will devote ample space to his youth and to the formation of his political sensibility. In this chapter I will also touch upon the rather sensitive topic of his position with respect to the radical politics of his time, particularly Nazism.

In Chapters 3 and 4, I will seek to reconstruct events of political significance in which Crowley was involved. In Chapter 3 I will discuss in particular the relationship he had with various persons having some political influence at the time, such as the British Army general and right-wing activist J. F. C. Fuller, the British journalist and politician Tom Driberg, the *Times*'s Moscow correspondent Walter Duranty, the adventurer Gerald Hamilton and the British secret service officer Maxwell Knight. This last person turns out to be particularly interesting, because his relationship with Crowley allows me to shed some light upon the background behind Rudolf Hess's flight to Scotland in 1941.[13] Particular importance is given to the 1930 encounter between Crowley and the Portuguese poet Fernando Pessoa, which is the main subject of Chapter 4. This meeting was significant both because of the legends that took shape around it and because of Pessoa's personality. Besides being a poet, he was a political thinker and esotericist, and his ideas have a certain relevance to the subject of this book. I have also considered it appropriate to explore the interest Crowley awakened in other Portuguese intellectuals who were friends with Pessoa. This aspect had been relatively neglected by Pessoan specialists – even by those who had focused on his relationship with Crowley.

In the fifth and final chapter, I will examine the way in which Crowley has been perceived in certain circles, particularly traditionalism and the milieus of conspiracy theories. Guénonian traditionalism views Crowley as a representative of the so-called "counter-initiation", and Guénon characterized Crowley as a "shady figure" and a "puppet" in the hands of sinister and perverse forces. This point of view however was not shared by another important traditionalist thinker: Julius Evola. I will try to pinpoint the reasons for this different attitude. I will then briefly discuss Crowley's relationship with another traditionalist author, Ananda K. Coomaraswamy, during Crowley's long sojourn in the United States. Guénon's opinion of Crowley was similar to that of the "conspiracy theorists", who attributed a political role to him that went well beyond his actual influence, and probably even his intentions. The anxiety generated by Crowley's image as a dangerous subversive was undoubtedly the reason why the Italian political police kept a file on him in the 1930s, on whose curious story I will also focus in this chapter.

At the end of the book the reader will find two appendixes. One is an essay by H. Thomas Hakl on Crowley as he was perceived by the Italian traditionalist thinker Julius Evola. Hakl has been able to dig deeper into this question, and has been able to find information that brings new light to it. In Appendix 2, on the other hand, the reader will find a selection of documents that are discussed throughout the book and are of a certain interest in relation to its subject.

I hope to offer with this study a contribution to the "normalization" of Aleister Crowley as a subject of scholarly research. I believe that today, more than sixty years after his death, he can be studied for what he was: a complex, intriguing author who has left a body of work that is remarkable for its vastness and variety, and who still exerts a notable influence over several new religious movements today. The controversial aspects in the personality and activities of a man who, like Dante's Semiramis, "made lust licit in his law"[14] will certainly not be ignored or downplayed; but neither will they be used as a pretext for denying the significance of his works and ideas.

🌿 1. An unspeakable life

… one Crowley, a person of unspeakable life …
(W. B. Yeats, letter to Lady Gregory, 28 April 1900)

Status quæstionis

In this chapter, I will retrace the salient moments in the life of Aleister Crowley.[1] But first I would like to make a few remarks about sources, which are made necessary by the peculiarity of the subject. Crowley has attracted the attention of a good number of authors, and in the last sixty years a good number of biographies and monographs devoted to him have been published.

John Symonds (1914–2006), whom Crowley himself designated as his literary executor, is the author of the biography considered by many as the "standard" one. Crowley, before his death, allegedly asked Symonds to take care of the publication of his unpublished works and of preparing new editions of those published during his life, also giving him the task of making sure that his wishes concerning the revenues from the copyright would be respected.[2] By virtue of this, after Crowley's death, Symonds had the opportunity to look through all his manuscripts, original documents, diaries and letters; and his reconstruction was based on this material. Between 1951 and 1997, Symonds's biography went through several editions, often with changes and added material.[3] Practically everyone who has taken any kind of interest in Crowley has referred to Symonds's work. However, it certainly has its critics – sometimes very harsh, too, and usually from "Crowleyan" milieus.

What are the faults that these critics perceive in Symonds's biography? They mainly accuse it of being very biased, of presenting only the negative traits of Crowley's character and of having not in the least understood the meaning and goal of his work. It is true that, if a careful reader compares the sources used by Symonds and analyses the way in which he has used them, he cannot but notice how his biography is tendentious on several points, and how it shows a certain preconceived hostility toward Crowley. Perhaps it is worth giving an example. Referring to the way in which Crowley "cured" the neurosis of one of his disciples, Symonds writes:

> Crowley cured psychoses and neuroses in this wise. He saw that the mind or psyche was divided into a conscious and subconscious level; that was part of the occult tradition. The notion of the subconsciousness as a dynamic and disturbing force he took from Freud, without any acknowledgment. It would have been

difficult for Crowley to have made this acknowledgment in the light of his belief in himself as the greatest living psychologist.[4]

This remark is inaccurate to say the least; one need only flip through *The Confessions*, Crowley's voluminous autobiography, to find abundant explicit references to, and implicit acknowledgement of, not only Freud and his theories, but also Carl Gustav Jung.[5] Crowley also wrote a short essay on psychoanalysis, which was published in *Vanity Fair* in 1916.[6] It may be true that he considered himself the greatest living psychologist, but ordinarily he had no problem acknowledging ideas he borrowed from others.

The above passage is merely one of many examples of the hostility Symonds indisputably shows towards Crowley. And yet, on the other hand, the wealth of documentary material placed at his disposal still enabled him to produce so complete a reconstruction that his biography remains indispensable today for those who want to do less prejudiced research on Crowley, and to some extent even for Crowley's current followers.[7]

Symonds's most outspoken critics have undoubtedly been Israel Regardie (1907–1985) and Gerald Suster (1951–2001). Israel Regardie was a highly important figure in twentieth-century Anglo-American occultism, and was also Crowley's personal secretary and disciple from 1928 to 1931.[8] His fame is due principally to the publication of the rituals of the Golden Dawn, the magical order to which both he and Crowley belonged.[9] In the late 1960s, after having read Symonds's work, Regardie decided to write a kind of "counter-biography" of Crowley. The result was the publication, in 1970, of *The Eye in the Triangle*.[10] In this book, Regardie, taking advantage of his training as a Reichian psychoanalyst, endeavours to give a more sympathetic interpretation of Crowley, although not concealing the more negative, or even pathological, aspects of his character. Regardie's study offers many interesting insights for understanding Crowley's way of thinking, motivations and aspirations, and has helped me to understand the meaning of his magical practices by providing an "insider's view". However, apart from a few useful corrections and clarifications, it offers few factual details that are not already present in Symonds's work.

Almost twenty years later, in 1988, Gerald Suster published his book on Crowley, *The Legacy of the Beast*.[11] Suster was a very active figure in Crowleyan circles in England.[12] Much the same can be said of Suster's book as of Regardie's. Although offering no new elements of great relevance, Suster likewise seeks to give a more positive interpretation of Crowley's personality and of his magical and mystical research.

A more ambiguous position concerning Symonds's work was taken by Kenneth Grant (1924–2011), who published several studies of Crowley.[13] Grant was one of Crowley's disciples during the last years of Crowley's life, and later claimed the title of international head of the Ordo Templi Orientis (OTO), the fraternal order led by Crowley for many years (from 1925 to 1947).[14] Grant's name was associated with that of Symonds for a long time. Starting in the late 1960s, Symonds and Grant together edited for publication a good number of texts and documents by Crowley.[15] Symonds made no secret of supporting Grant's claims; in fact, in 1989, he dedicated the third edition of his biography to Grant himself, whom he styled "X°- Outer Head of the Ordo Templi Orientis".[16] Grant's works are interesting, because they are based to a large extent on primary sources that are difficult to access, but one should still approach them with scholarly reserve. He presents his personal interpretation of Crowley's work, which, valid as it may be in his own perspective, appears removed in some respects from Crowley's original intentions. From a biographical point of view, Grant adds a few new details based on his own reminiscences, especially concerning the final years of Crowley's life.[17]

Several other biographies of Crowley in English have appeared over the years. In particular, I should mention those of Charles Richard Cammell, Francis King, Colin Wilson, Roger Hutchinson, Martin Booth, Lawrence Sutin, Richard Kaczynski and Tobias Churton.[18] Cammell, like Symonds, knew Crowley personally during the last years of his life, and was fascinated above all by his poetic works. In fact, Crowley himself asked Cammell to write his biography in the late 1930s, after he had lost hope of publishing his *Confessions* in their entirety. Cammell was only able to satisfy this request after Crowley's death, and the book was not published until 1951, the same year as Symonds's biography. The final parts of Cammell's book are fascinating; he recalls his friendship with Crowley, offering some details about the last period of his life, and his judgements are certainly more balanced than those of Symonds. But, apart from that, the book follows the text of the *Confessions* (which, being then still partly unpublished, he must have received from Crowley) without adding much new information. The same goes for Francis King's book, first published in 1977. Colin Wilson's book, developing ideas presented earlier in a chapter of his classic study of occult phenomena,[19] is not really a biography, but rather an attempt at interpretation in a similar vein as that of Regardie. In my view, however, his analyses do not offer any interesting new insight for understanding Crowley; on the contrary, the book shows a rather imprecise knowledge of Crowley's works and ideas.[20] Hutchinson's biography offers some new information not found in other works, especially concerning the topic of this present work. Crowley's time in the United States is discussed thoroughly, along with his activities in pro-German propaganda, including an analysis of the file that the English police kept on him over the years.

I have already discussed elsewhere the biographies of Booth, Sutin and Kaczynski, and I may refer the reader to the review article I have written on them.[21] Here, I will merely note that all three represent a serious effort to offer a valid alternative to Symonds's biography. Sutin, in particular, delves into Crowley's psychology as perhaps no other author has done before, and offers some stimulating insights. Kaczynski's book, although often giving an overly softened, almost sanitized, image of Crowley (obviously with the intent of balancing out Symonds's preconceived hostility), is based on an impressive amount of research and is a very useful tool for the scholar, not only because it discusses some facts and events in Crowley's life that had received little or no attention from previous biographers, but also because it includes a rich apparatus of footnotes and bibliographic references. The book has been recently republished in a revised and expanded edition, which improves considerably on the first one.[22]

Only two significant biographies of Crowley have been published after my review article of 2003. The first one is by Tobias Churton. Churton, like Kaczynski, is very sympathetic to Crowley, and his book can be considered as another attempt at "setting the record straight" in presenting a more positive account of Crowley's actions, motivations and ideas. Now, as is the case with Kaczynski's book, if this means using solid evidence to correct wild or unsubstantiated claims, the intent should be appreciated. And indeed, Churton does make use of previously unpublished sources that may throw new light on some episodes in Crowley's life. But I would be less inclined to follow Churton's enthusiastic judgement when he presents Crowley as a "major thinker, as significant as Freud or Jung", or when he discusses what he considers as Crowley's "five principal achievements", which have more to do with a spiritual agenda than with a scholarly one.[23]

The second important book on Crowley that has been published after 2003 is Richard B. Spence's *Secret Agent 666: Aleister Crowley, British Intelligence and the Occult*.[24] This is not really a biography, but a monograph presenting all possible evidence about Crowley's connection to the intelligence services of various countries, especially the British. Obviously, Spence's book bears on aspects that are also relevant for the present study, and I will discuss them more specifically in the next chapters. But a few general comments are in order here. Spence basically interprets the whole of Crowley's adult life as if he had had a continuous, consistent involvement in intelligence activities. Almost any episode in his life, any travel, any apparently casual meeting with other persons, is seen in this light and interpreted accordingly. Spence, a professor at the University of Idaho, clearly has a deep knowledge of the history of secret services, since it is his very field of expertise. His book is based on a considerable amount of research in archives and exploits interesting new material. It seems to me however that he is rarely able to find the "smoking gun" of Crowley's work as a "secret agent" and is mostly obliged to recur to hypotheses and speculations, which sometimes become thin to the point of implausibility. It is true that, by its very nature, the subject is elusive and slippery, but the problem is that when a whole castle is built on a series of speculative arguments, one begins to wonder about the solidity of the whole structure. If one examines carefully the actual evidence that is available, and which Spence has so carefully collected, the picture one gets is that Crowley, on several occasions in his life, acted as an informant to British intelligence services, and that most of the time this happened out of his own initiative rather than because he was being asked. But being a voluntary informant is of course not the same thing as being an agent employed on a permanent basis by a secret service.

There is then another problem, which makes Spence's approach very different from the one I tried to adopt for the present study. Throughout his book Spence tries to argue that whenever Crowley was involved in secret intelligence operations – which seems to be all the time – he was just serving England. Even when evidence seems to indicate the contrary, all can be interpreted as a skilful game of deception and simulation played for the better interest of his home country. Ultimately, this yields a simplistic image of a politically monotonous Crowley, as if he had been stubbornly, naïvely consistent in his patriotic faith during all his life, despite all the sacrifices and the suffering that this entailed. This is of course the image that Crowley tried to give of himself in the later part of his life, namely after the First World War. The problem is that, as I will try to show in the next chapter, this does not fit either with the evidence we have, based on Crowley's youth writings, nor more generally with Crowley's personality as I have come to understand it. Crowley's psychology was extremely complex and multi-layered, and the idea of a Crowley permanently and consistently inspired by candid patriotism is simply untenable. There was indeed one part of his personality that would easily respond to the call of patriotism, and even of nationalism, but that was very far from being the whole story about him.

A few other monographs should be mentioned here, published in other languages than English: a book by Serge Hutin in French,[25] one by Ralph Tegtmeier in German,[26] and, most recently, one by Ruud Vermeer in Dutch.[27] Hutin is inclined to give a little too much credit to the more fantastic rumours that have crystallized around the figure of Crowley, but he makes an honest effort to penetrate the more enigmatic sides of his personality, making use of his erudition as a specialist in the history of esotericism. The book by Tegtmeier, a person well known in German occultist circles, is also interesting since it draws attention to the issue of politics and attempts to situate Crowley's figure in a broader cultural framework, often with pertinent observations. Vermeer's biography, taking a popular slant, adds practically nothing to the preceding ones, apart from a final discussion of Crowley's relationship to cinema, with a few pages devoted to the American underground film director Kenneth Anger (b. 1927), who took inspiration for some of his most important works from Crowley and his doctrine.[28]

In general, most of the authors cited above, with a few notable exceptions, take a fairly journalistic approach. Sources and references are often not indicated, and in most cases Crowley's scandalous behaviour takes the upper hand over the intellectual and cultural aspects. But more recently, a new trend of research on Crowley has emerged that shows a more scrupulous approach from a scholarly point of view, often making use of archives and unpublished sources. Some of the authors are, or have been, involved in the OTO, such as William Breeze (signing sometimes also with his name as international head of the OTO, Hymenaeus Beta). Breeze has prepared new editions of Crowley's works, accompanying them with very informative introductions and copious notes,[29] while J. Edward and Marlene Cornelius have published, between 1993 and 2002, the fascinating periodical of "Thelemic research", *Red Flame*. Richard Kaczynski, whose biography I have already referred to, could also be included among these authors. Beyond these circles, a few other names should be mentioned. One is the American author Martin P. Starr, who has offered with his research and his editorial work some important contributions for a better understanding of Crowley and of his influence.[30] Another is the French author Christian Bouchet, who has been one of the first authors to devote a university dissertation to Crowley. Initially, Bouchet published a short monograph on Crowley in 1988, followed in 1998 by the publication of his doctoral thesis.[31] Bouchet, who has been very active not only in French Crowleyan circles, but also in the far-right political scene, has shown a particular, if not an innocent, interest in Crowley's relationship with politics, and his books offer a fair introduction (in French) to Crowley's works and ideas.

But the real turning point in scholarly research on Aleister Crowley has been the recent publication of an anthology of essays edited by Henrik Bogdan and Martin P. Starr and published by Oxford University Press, to which I have also contributed.[32] The book is a testimony of the interest that Crowley now offers as a subject for serious scholarly research, and is in fact only the most significant example of a more general trend that has materialized in the last fifteen years.[33] Some well-known academic specialists in new religious movements and Western esotericism have contributed to the book, such as Henrik Bogdan himself, Alex Owen, Massimo Introvigne, Ronald Hutton and Hugh B. Urban, while Wouter J. Hanegraaff has written the foreword.

After this short overview of the existing literature, I would like to retrace now the essential moments of Crowley's life, focusing especially on those aspects that appear to be particularly significant for the purpose of this book. My main sources will be the biographies by Symonds, Sutin and Kaczynski.

Birth and youth (1875–98)

Edward Alexander Crowley (he adopted a Gaelic form of his name, Aleister, when he was about twenty) was born on 12 October 1875 in Leamington, Warwickshire, to Edward Crowley (c.1830–87) and Emily Bertha Bishop (1848–1917). His father owned a flourishing interest in the railway business, which had brought the family significant wealth. Both parents were members of a fundamentalist Christian sect, the Plymouth Brethren or Darbyites, characterized by extreme moral rigour and devoted to a literal interpretation of the Bible.[34] His father's parents were Quakers, but Crowley's father converted to Darbyism, and then decided to set aside his business activities in order to devote himself to itinerant preaching.[35] Young Crowley was obliged to take part in the family's daily Bible readings, and for a long time this was the only book available to him.[36] This played an enormously important role in his intellectual development: even though he gradually repudiated Christianity, he still remained always connected to the legacy of images and symbols in the Old and New Testaments, showing a predilection for the prophetic texts. In these early years of his life he was already fascinated by the evil figures in the Book of Revelation: the beast coming out of the earth and the prostitute dressed in purple and scarlet.[37] This influenced considerably the religious doctrine he later elaborated.

There do not seem to have been important episodes in young Crowley's life (if we except, of course, the peculiarity of his family's religious devotion) until the death of his father from cancer in 1887. This event marked a turning point: from the time of the funeral, as Crowley himself said, he entered into a new phase characterized by rebellion.[38] Crowley developed a strong sense of intolerance toward the religiosity and closed-mindedness of his mother and her family, as well as toward the rigid discipline of the Darbyite boarding school that he was obliged to attend. As a result of the rigorous discipline in one of these schools, Crowley's health was seriously affected. But the two immediate consequences of this physical weakening contributed to the alleviation of his moral suffering, and had great significance in his development: the doctors advised the family to take the boy out of school at once, have him study with private tutors for a while, and make him spend plenty of time out in the fresh open air. Following the first piece of advice, the family made a fatal error: one of his tutors, instead of furthering his education as an impeccable Darbyite, initiated him into various worldly pleasures, including smoking, drinking, horse racing, billiards, gambling and women.[39] The tutor was dismissed, but it was already too late. Crowley later, with a typical allusion to the biblical text, described the effect of this experience thus: "My eyes were opened and I had become as a god, knowing good and evil."[40] The second piece of advice led to his passion for mountain climbing, which he strongly developed later in life.

In his autobiography, Crowley provides an outline of his political ideas during his early twenties. I will discuss the subject more at length in Chapter 2, but here I should mention the fact that in that period he considered himself a "reactionary conservative" and a Jacobite.[41] We can already see here the signs of the romantic side of his personality.

In October 1895, Crowley entered Trinity College, Cambridge. The university experience made a profound impression on him, even if he did not obtain a degree after three years of attendance. When he enrolled and moved to Cambridge he finally felt free from the influence of his maternal family and the tutors they had imposed on him. He studied the classics with enthusiasm, both ancients and moderns, and began publishing the poems he had been writing for a while at his own expense. *Aceldama* (1898) was his first book, and was followed by, among others, *Songs of the Spirit* (1898) and *An Appeal to the American Republic* (1899). His first publisher was Leonard Smithers (1861–1907), who had also published the works of Oscar Wilde (1854–1900) and Aubrey Beardsley (1872–98).[42] During the holidays he went on long journeys abroad, especially to Scandinavia and the Alps. In 1896, at the age of 21, he inherited the conspicuous fortune left behind by his father, and thus became financially independent from his family.[43]

In this period, Crowley began to feel an attraction to spirituality and mysticism. At first, he went through a phase in which he intended to devote himself to Satanism. This lasted until the early months of 1898, when he came in contact with Arthur Edward Waite (1857–1942).[44] Waite advised him to read a classic of esotericism: *The Cloud upon the Sanctuary*, by Karl von Eckartshausen. This reading kindled Crowley's desire to become part of a "hidden community of Light ... whose sainted members watched over the welfare of mankind".[45] In the same year, Crowley met two persons who were destined to influence the course of his life considerably. The first was Oscar Eckenstein (1859–1921), a railway engineer and mountaineer; the second was George Cecil Jones (1873–1960), a chemist by profession and a member of the Hermetic Order of the Golden Dawn. I will return later to Crowley's friendship with Eckenstein. His meeting with Jones had an immediate, significant consequence: when Crowley learned from him about the existence of the Golden Dawn he asked to become a member, and his request was accepted. From this moment on, his life took a new direction. The experiences he was about to have in this occultist brotherhood would leave an indelible mark on him. Without a correct evaluation of this aspect, it would be difficult to understand the course his life took in the subsequent years.

The romantic period (1898–1906)

In November 1898 Crowley was initiated as a Neophyte in the Isis Urania Temple of the Golden Dawn in London. At this time the head of the Order was Samuel Liddell "MacGregor" Mathers (1854–1918).[46] It is unnecessary here to retrace the convoluted history of this organization; suffice it to say that at this time the Order was suffering from various internal conflicts, which would soon erupt into a dramatic crisis.[47] Crowley, who had abandoned his university studies and moved to London in the same year, immediately devoted himself with great passion to studying the Order's materials and practising the rituals in order to get past the first degrees quickly. During a ceremony at the temple, he made the acquaintance of Allan Bennett (1872–1923), an influential member of the Order who would later convert to Buddhism and become one of its "greatest propagators ... in England".[48] Bennett moved into Crowley's flat, and together they performed various experiments in ceremonial magic. Bennett suffered from asthma, and took opium, cocaine and morphine to alleviate the symptoms. Crowley also began using mind-altering substances, and it is probably in this context that the idea first arose for him to use them not for a curative or recreational use, but in order to experiment with their efficacy in bringing about mystical experiences. The consumption of drugs remained a constant throughout his life. In this period he also bought a property in Scotland, at Boleskine on the banks of Loch Ness. Originally, he planned to use it as a retreat for the practice of a series of magical rituals.[49]

In 1900 the crisis in the Golden Dawn exploded, and Crowley found himself directly involved in the events that led to the end of the Order in its original form. What actually happened was a revolt on the part of several high-ranking members, led by the poet William Butler Yeats (1865–1939) and the actress Florence Farr (1860–1917), against the authority of Mathers, who at the time lived in Paris. Crowley took Mathers's side and tried, though with very little diplomacy, to bring the rebels back into line. He was not successful: the rebel group expelled Mathers and continued the Order's activity, no longer recognizing Mathers's authority. Crowley was also excluded. After less than two years, his adventure with the Golden Dawn – at least the original version of it – was practically over. According to Crowley, he was advanced by Mathers to the level of *Adeptus Minor* during this period, although his rank was not recognized by the rebel faction. However, this has been contested by some authors.[50]

After this, Crowley began a period of world travelling and mountaineering lasting a few years. His interest in magic, still strong when he left the Golden Dawn, diminished and was replaced by a fascination with yoga and Buddhism under Allan Bennett's influence. Meanwhile, he was very prolific in his poetry: he published several works in verse, but also essays, in luxurious editions. Among the most significant works from this period are *Carmen Saeculare* (1901), *Tannhäuser* (1902) and *Berashith* (1903), the latter being his first attempt at an essay on magic.

In the spring of 1900, soon after his involvement in the conflict between Mathers and the London adepts, he travelled to Mexico, where Eckenstein joined him. Together, they climbed the country's highest peaks. After a few months, Crowley decided to go to Ceylon (today Sri Lanka) to meet with Bennett, who was living on the island and would soon convert to Buddhism. Crossing the Pacific, he visited Hawaii and then Japan before finally reaching his friend. With Bennett he began to study the texts of the Hindu and Buddhist traditions and to practise various forms of meditation and yoga. In 1902 he met with Eckenstein in Delhi. They had in view a new mountaineering expedition, more ambitious than their Mexican climbs: to reach the peak of K2.

At the time, the highest mountain in the Karakorum range still had a virgin peak, as did all the other mountains in Asia higher than 8000 metres (the so-called "eight-thousanders"). The expedition was not successful – mainly due to adverse weather conditions – but still, it was the first ever attempt to conquer this peak, reaching altitudes not attained by any previous mountaineering expedition.[51]

Subsequently, in late 1902, Crowley returned to Europe and settled in Paris. For some time he pursued a Bohemian lifestyle, mingling with artists and writers including Auguste Rodin (1840–1917), Marcel Schwob (1867–1905) and William Somerset Maugham (1874–1965).[52] In spring 1903 he left Paris to spend some time at his property in Scotland. There he met Rose Edith Kelly (1874–1932), the sister of one of his closest friends, the English painter Gerald F. Kelly (1879–1972). She and Crowley married and left on a long voyage to the Orient. On the return journey, the second of two fundamental spiritual events in Crowley's life took place (the first having been, as we saw, his initiation into the Golden Dawn). Crowley claims that, while the couple were staying in Cairo, between the 8 and 10 April 1904, he "received", from a superhuman entity, the text of *The Book of the Law*. This text would have been dictated to him directly by this entity, called Aiwass, whom he would partially identify in the years to come as his "Holy Guardian Angel". This was an event of decisive importance in Crowley's life: to mention just one example, he later began using a new calendar, the beginning of which coincided with the date of this revelation. In Crowley's view, *The Book of the Law* was to be the fundamental sacred text of a new religion, of which he himself would be the prophet: the religion of Thelema.[53] It appears, however, that Crowley did not immediately take on this role of prophet that *The Book of the Law* assigned to him. Rather, as his interest in magic gradually re-emerged after his Buddhist phase, he again felt a connection to the old system of symbols of traditional magic that he had learned in the Golden Dawn.

After returning to Europe, Crowley and his wife spent a few months in Paris before settling in Scotland. During this time in Paris, Crowley was initiated as a Freemason into a lodge of the Grand Lodge of France, an obedience not recognized by the United Grand Lodge of England.[54] In this period he published more significant works, such as the drama *Why Jesus Wept* (1904), and began releasing his earlier writings in a compilation, *The Collected Works*, in three volumes (1905–7). In the spring of 1905 he decided to attempt climbing another of Asia's colossal peaks: Kangchenjunga. This time Eckenstein did not take part, and Crowley himself led the expedition. The attempt ended in another failure; to make matters worse, one of the climbers and some of the porters died, resulting in a series of controversies between Crowley and the other members of the expedition.[55] After that, Crowley decided to remain in Asia for some time, and sent for his wife to join him. Together, they travelled across southern China on horseback. During this journey, he practised a highly significant ritual of his own invention: the *Augoeides*. Although Symonds does not explain its meaning, the ritual, which lasted thirty-two weeks, was extremely important for Crowley, who devotes many pages to it in his autobiography.[56]

It is worth noting that even after Crowley left the Golden Dawn, and throughout his Buddhist period, he still continued to work with the system of symbols and degrees that he had learned from the Order, and continued his initiatory ascent still following the Order's scheme. This is a highly important point, because Crowley's whole life – at least until the mid-1920s – was built around the scheme of degrees of the Golden Dawn. This means that each degree he "obtained" in this system marked a precisely defined phase in his life, and influenced his choices and movements. The meaning of the *Augoeides* ritual, according to him, lay in the fact that "it was necessary to complete the work of the Second Order before I could adequately take up my work in the Third".[57] The *Augoeides* was a lengthy, imaginary initiation ritual. While riding across China, Crowley *imagined* himself being in a temple and carrying out ritual gestures, the ultimate goal being initiation into a higher degree.

Having arrived at the east coast of Indochina (present-day Vietnam), Crowley and his wife continued their travels separately: while she returned to Europe by the classic route (in a ship, via the Suez Canal), he headed east, and after a stop in Shanghai, crossed the Pacific, the United States, and the Atlantic. In June 1906 he was back in England. Thus the period of his great voyages around the world was concluded.

The Logos of the Aeon (1906–19)

After returning from China, Crowley had met a British Army officer, Captain John Frederick Charles Fuller (1878–1966), with whom he had been corresponding for about a year. Fuller would, in later years, become famous as a theoretician of military tactics (especially in connection with tanks). He would then also become active in the British Union of Fascists (the party founded by Sir Oswald Mosley in the 1930s), and would be invited to Adolf Hitler's fiftieth birthday celebration in 1939. Fuller took part in a contest arranged by Crowley for the best critical essay on his work, and won.[58] Crowley published the essay, and Fuller became one of his close collaborators.

1907 and 1908 passed by relatively quietly, with the publication of some new works (*Konx Om Pax*, 1907; *Amphora*, 1908) and voyages to north Africa; but his marriage was now getting close to its end. During this period, thanks to Fuller, Crowley acquired some young admirers, mostly students at Trinity College, Cambridge. It seems clear that by now his reputation had begun to be a problem, given that the authorities of Trinity College sought to prevent his having contact with the students. One student, resisting pressure, became a disciple of Crowley's straight away, and another would become a disciple a decade later. The first was Victor Neuburg (1883–1940), later known as a poet and mentor to Dylan Thomas;[59] the second was Norman Mudd (1889–1934), then a promising student of mathematics.[60]

1909 was an important year, for two main reasons. First, Crowley found again the manuscript of *The Book of the Law*, which had been lost in the meanwhile. From this time on, his conviction that he was the prophet of a new religion grew stronger and stronger. Second, with George Cecil Jones, his old colleague from the Golden Dawn, he formed a new magical group of his own, the A∴A∴.[61] This was essentially a revised version of the Golden Dawn, largely inspired by its system of symbols and degrees, but with the introduction of certain spiritual techniques learned by Crowley during his travels in the East. Along with the creation of his Order, he began the publication of a journal, *The Equinox*, which was presented as the official organ of the A∴A∴. The editorial programme planned for the publication of one issue at each equinox, meaning two issues each year, for a period of five years. Many of the contributions in *The Equinox* were written by Crowley, but also most of his friends at the time worked on the journal with him, especially Fuller. The writer Frank Harris (1856–1931) also contributed an article.[62] In this same year Crowley divorced his wife, their relationship having increasingly deteriorated over time.

1909 was also an important year for another reason. Crowley spent the last two months of this year in Algeria with Victor Neuburg, where he carried out a series of "astral explorations" based on the Enochian system.[63] These explorations were especially important for Crowley's magical career, since they represented his "crossing of the Abyss" and consequently his achievement of the degree of *Magister Templi*.[64]

In the spring of 1910, Mathers filed suit to stop the release of the next issue (3) of *The Equinox*. He wanted to prevent the publication of the rituals of the Golden Dawn, but in the end Crowley won the case. This was an important episode, since the lawsuit had a great deal of resonance both at home and abroad, especially in esoteric circles. Crowley's name became quite well known, and through this he gained many contacts in the worlds of Freemasonry and international occultism. One of the persons who came in contact with him and went to meet him in person was Theodor Reuss (1855–1923), who had been busy with several fringe-Masonic enterprises both in Germany and elsewhere, and at the time was planning the creation of a new initiatory order. This would later become the OTO. Reuss was apparently also an agent for the German secret services.[65]

In this same year in London, Crowley organized and performed a series of rituals open to the public, *The Rites of Eleusis*.[66] Several favourable reviews were published, but a few newspapers violently criticized the performances and attacked Crowley, accusing him, his disciples and his friend George Cecil Jones of immoral behaviour. This can be viewed as the first in a long series of sensationalist attacks on Crowley, which did not even end with his death.[67] It is at that time that his "black" legend began to take shape. Crowley, despite pressure from all his friends, refused to sue the newspapers for libel. Jones sued instead, and lost the case. The price Crowley paid for the unhappy outcome of this affair and for the bad reputation deriving from it was a certain degree of isolation and rifts with many of his friends, including Fuller and Jones.

In this period, in addition to *The Rites of Eleusis* (1910), he published a collection of poetry, *The Winged Beetle* (1910), and a drama in verse, *The World's Tragedy*, with a significant preface (1910). This last work is essential for understanding his attitude toward Christianity.[68] In 1912 he had another meeting with Theodor Reuss, which was highly significant because it lead to the creation of an English branch of the OTO, of which Crowley was appointed Grand Master. Reuss also initiated Crowley to the innermost "secrets" of the OTO, namely the techniques of sexual magic. The communication of this secret was of fundamental importance for Crowley. From this time on he would spend considerable time experimenting with this new type of magic. His lovers (for some of whom Crowley reserved the title of "Scarlet Woman"),[69] as well as some of his disciples, were his "assistants" in these operations. Also in 1912, the first two parts of the important *Book Four* were published, where Crowley presented for the first time his ideas on magic in a systematic fashion.

In 1913 he published *The Book of Lies*, a collection of short and mostly enigmatic essays in which some important aspects of his doctrine were distilled. In the same year, the A∴A∴, the Order founded by Crowley, listed 88 members – quite a respectable number for such an organization. In January 1914 he performed a series of invocations in Paris, which were his first experimental application of the techniques of sexual magic. His assistant was Victor Neuburg. Also participating in at least one of these rituals was Walter Duranty,[70] who would later become a very well-known journalist in his role as Moscow correspondent to the *New York Times*. I will return to Duranty in Chapter 3.

At the outbreak of the First World War, Crowley was in Switzerland. He returned to England and, according to his version of the story, applied to work for Intelligence Services, but was rejected. By now his inheritance was almost entirely gone, and in

October he left for the United States, where he planned to meet with the American collector John Quinn to sell part of his collection of books. He intended to stay for two weeks,[71] but remained in the US for more than five years. Thus began Crowley's "American period". In these years, for the first time in his life, he experienced hardships and uncomfortable living conditions, at least in comparison to the luxury and wealth to which he was accustomed.

In the first months of 1915 he began collaborating with a German propaganda newspaper, *The Fatherland*, directed by the writer George Sylvester Viereck (1884–1962). Crowley had already met Viereck in London in 1911. The articles Crowley published in this period were violently anti-British. He also contributed various articles to the journal *Vanity Fair*. In October 1915 he left New York to tour the West Coast. On this voyage, in Vancouver, he met with his disciple Charles Stansfeld Jones (1886–1950), who had established a branch of the OTO in that city. In 1916 Crowley met the art critic Ananda K. Coomaraswamy (1877–1947) and had an affair with his wife, Alice Richardson (a.k.a. Ratan Devi), with whom he practised various operations of sexual magic. In the summer he conducted a "Great Magical Retreat" in New Hampshire. This was an important episode, because in spiritual terms it represented the central point of his sojourn in America. During this retreat Crowley initiated himself to the degree of Magus, the penultimate degree of the Golden Dawn hierarchy. Also in this period, he wrote the novel *Moonchild*, which would not be published until 1929.

In the spring of 1917, the London police stormed the headquarters of the OTO in England in reaction to the pro-German propaganda Crowley was diffusing in the United States. This appears to have been the only reaction of the British authorities to his anti-patriotic behaviour. In August of the same year, he became director of another newspaper belonging to Viereck, *The International*.[72] He held the position for eight months, until the newspaper changed owners. The material published there (articles, poetry, stories) was almost all the work of Crowley, who took this opportunity to promote his new religion.

In the spring of 1918 he met Leah Hirsig (1883–1975), a schoolteacher who became his lover and quickly took on the official role of Scarlet Woman. Apart from his first marriage, Crowley's relationship with Hirsig was surely the most important in all of his extremely varied love life.

In December 1919 he left the United States and returned to England. The American period can be said to have been a fairly homogeneous time in his life. During these five years he experienced poverty, if not true destitution. It should be noted that Crowley considered his entire sojourn in the United States as a long initiation ritual to the degree of Magus. This is a detail of more than just secondary importance, since Crowley saw the experiences of humiliation and privation that he was forced to undergo as "ordeals" necessary for completing the initiation.[73]

Wandering in Europe (1919–32)

Apparently, the British authorities gave Crowley no trouble after his return to England. However, he did not stay long in his homeland. His new plan was to found an "abbey" in which a community of disciples could put the doctrines of Thelema into practice. Magical and religious aspects aside, this was in fact also a social experiment.[74] The place chosen for realizing this project was Cefalù, in Sicily, and in March 1920 the "Abbey of Thelema" was established in a rented villa. The original core group of Thelemites was composed of Crowley himself, his Scarlet Woman Leah Hirsig and a French former governess, Ninette Shumway, née Fraux (1894–1990). The experiment lasted three years, until Crowley was expelled from Italy in 1923. During this period numerous guests visited the Abbey, predominantly from England. Moments of peace and of spiritual research took turns with altercations and conflicts, and the situation at the Abbey was often less than idyllic. In late 1921 one of the recurring crises between the residents was so serious that it attracted the attention of the local police, and led to an inspection of the Abbey.

In 1922 Crowley left the Abbey temporarily for a retreat in Fontainebleau. The purpose of this trip was to overcome his addiction to heroin, which he had begun using in 1919. The attempt failed, however; he would continue using the drug until his death. In May he went to London to try to gather some funds for the Abbey. He published a few articles in *The English Review*, a literary magazine, and managed to get a contract with a publisher to write a novel, *The Diary of a Drug Fiend*, in which he described his experiences with drugs (cocaine in particular) and the Abbey of Thelema. When the book was published it was immediately denounced by the *Sunday Express* newspaper, which accused Crowley of promoting the unrestrained consumption of drugs. Crowley also began writing his autobiography, *The Confessions*, but the plans for its publication did not go through because of the increasingly frequent attacks levied by the sensationalist press. The first two volumes would be published only in 1929. Crowley returned to Cefalù in October 1922, passing through Rome during the same days in which the fascists marched through the city.[75]

In February 1923 a tragic event took place at the Abbey: Raoul Loveday (1900–1923), a disciple whom Crowley had met on his last voyage to London, died, probably of enteric fever after drinking contaminated water. During Loveday's illness, his wife, who had accompanied him to the Abbey, complained to the British consul in Palermo regarding the living conditions at the Abbey.[76] After Loveday's death, she returned to England and held interviews with some of the same sensationalist newspapers that had already used Crowley as material, namely *John Bull* and the *Sunday Express*. As a result, the press campaign against him became increasingly more violent. On 23 April he was expelled from Italy. The day before, a new disciple had arrived at the Abbey: Norman Mudd, who in 1908 had been a member of his group of student admirers at Cambridge.

Crowley left for Tunisia, where he stayed until the year's end. Here he wrote and published (at his own expense) *Songs for Italy*, a small collection of poems satirizing Mussolini and the fascist regime. In 1924 he moved to France. There he met with Frank Harris, who at the time was living in Nice; together they developed an entrepreneurial project, which led to no practical results. He then went to Paris, where his disciples joined him. He remained in France until September 1924, when he returned to Tunisia with a new lover, Dorothy Olsen.

In the spring of 1925, from Tunis, Crowley launched the "World Teacher Campaign". In this period, the Theosophical Society, then directed by Annie Besant (1847–1933) and Charles Webster Leadbeater (1854-1934), was endeavouring to present to the world an Indian youth, Jiddu Krishnamurti (1895-1986), as spiritual master.[77] Besant had adopted Krishnamurti a few years earlier when he was still a young boy, being convinced that he possessed the characteristics of a new master of humanity. Crowley decided to block Besant's project through a press campaign, "unmasking" Krishnamurti, whom he saw as a false messiah. Crowley's purpose in this, naturally, was to present himself as the true "Master of the World". Although the campaign made some waves in the European press, it was not particularly successful.[78] Around this time, he also met George I. Gurdjieff (1866?-1949) at his Institute for the Harmonious Development of Man in Avon, close to Fontainebleau.[79]

Meanwhile, Theodor Reuss had died in 1923 without leaving any clear instructions as to who should succeed him as leader of the OTO. At the end of 1924 Crowley was recognized by two of the highest ranking members of the Order (C. S. Jones and Heinrich Tränker) as Reuss's successor.[80] Further international legitimation came in the summer of 1925, when the "German Rosicrucian Movement" (which included the German OTO and "Pansophia", a related esoteric organization) organized a meeting in Weida, Thuringia. Crowley was invited to participate and the result of this meeting was that the Rosicrucian Movement split between two sides: one that accepted Crowley as their international leader, and one that rejected him.[81] Probably the most important source of tension, apart from Crowley's bad reputation was the fact that, by this time, accepting Crowley as leader implicitly meant accepting also his religious message, essentially based on *The Book of the Law*. Clearly, some of these German esoteric groups were willing to listen to Crowley as an initiate and as a spiritual teacher, but not as a prophet of a new religion.

In the faction supporting Crowley the most prominent figures were Karl Germer (1885-1962), a businessman, and Martha Küntzel (1857-1941), a highly active figure in the world of German esotericism, who had been acquainted with Madame Blavatsky and involved in the Theosophical Society. Germer, in the years to come, would become Crowley's principal "sponsor", supporting him financially as well as organizationally. When Crowley died in 1947, Germer would inherit the position of international head of the OTO. After their meeting in Thuringia, Germer left Germany in order to work in closer contact with Crowley. Küntzel would also soon become one of his most indefatigable supporters in Germany. She is an interesting figure also because her name is connected to Crowley's alleged contact with Adolf Hitler – to which I shall return later.

In November 1925, while in Tunis, Crowley was contacted by a young student from Oxford, Thomas Driberg (1905-76). He would later become a well-known journalist, then follow a political career, and after being elected member of parliament with the Labour Party, would become its National Secretary. In those student years, Driberg combined a passion for esotericism with militant activity in the Communist Party. In 1926 he had an intense correspondence with Crowley, in which he expressed an intent to become his disciple. Although this did not come about – and in Chapter 3 we will see why – they still remained friends and often visited one another, especially after Crowley's return to England in 1932.

Between 1926 and 1929, Crowley's main residence was in Paris. In October 1928 he was joined by a new disciple with whom he had already corresponded for a few years: Israel Regardie, then little more than twenty years old. Also in this period, Crowley came into contact with another young man interested in his teachings: Gerald Yorke (1901–83). Yorke would remain a disciple of Crowley until 1932, when there was a temporary rupture; but after this, friendly relations between the two were re-established. Over the years, Yorke collected an impressive quantity of "Crowleyana", including first or rare editions of books, manuscripts and documents. This collection was later donated to the library of the Warburg Institute in London, where it is still preserved today.

In March 1929 Crowley was expelled from France. It seems that several circumstances were at the origin of this episode.[82] The expulsion made resounding echoes in the international press. Crowley, in order to obtain British citizenship for his latest Scarlet Woman, Maria Teresa Ferrari de Miramar, a Nicaraguan, and thus to be permitted to bring her into England, married her in Leipzig in August 1929. In the same month, he returned to England with his new wife and Regardie, and moved into a cottage in Kent.

He then finally succeeded in finding a publisher: a small publishing house called Mandrake, then directed by Percy Reginald Stephensen (1901–65).[83] Stephensen wrote a book on Crowley,[84] in an attempt to show that many of the rumours spread about him by the sensationalist press were unfounded, and brought out several of Crowley's works that had remained unpublished for a long time, including the novel *Moonchild* and the first two volumes of the *Confessions* (1929a). In the same year Crowley also published, at his own expense, the important *Magick in Theory and Practice*, the ideal continuation of *Book Four* and his theoretical groundwork on magic.

In spring 1930 Crowley travelled to Germany with his wife. He was now thinking of preparing an exhibition of his paintings, to be held somewhere in Germany.[85] In Berlin, he met the 19-year-old artist Hanni Jaeger (1910–c.1933) and fell in love with her. He returned to England with her, abandoning his wife in Germany. At the end of August, Crowley and Jaeger left England for Lisbon. For about a year, Crowley had been in contact with Fernando Pessoa (1888–1935), the well-known Portuguese poet. Pessoa, a great enthusiast of esotericism, was fascinated by Crowley's personality. As we shall see in Chapter 4, Crowley probably went to Portugal also with the intention of creating a branch of the OTO there, which would have been directed by Pessoa.

During his sojourn in Portugal, one of the most curious episodes of Crowley's life took place: his fake suicide. With Pessoa's collaboration, he set up a stunt to make people believe he had committed suicide by throwing himself off a cliff into the Atlantic. Then, while half of Europe's newspapers were speculating as to his fate, he quietly reappeared in Berlin. I will examine this episode in the context of his relationship with Pessoa. Some authors have hinted at some mysterious aspects of it: the source is a reference made by René Guénon in a letter to Julius Evola from 29 October 1949, in which he claims that Crowley had faked his suicide because he wanted to return to Germany in secret in order to take on a position as Hitler's adviser. I will of course return to the matter in Chapters 4 and 5.

From the end of September 1930 to the middle of 1932, Crowley lived in Berlin. Here he associated with Alfred Adler (1870–1937), Aldous Huxley (1894–1963),[86] Christopher Isherwood (1904–86) and most importantly Gerald Hamilton (1890–1970), a British adventurer who at the time had ties to the German Communist Party.[87] In late spring of 1932, Crowley returned to England.

Later years and death (1932–47)

Crowley did not leave England again after his return from Germany in 1932.[88] He was now fifty-seven years old; his health was not so good, probably due to the continual use of intoxicating substances, and he had a constant need for financial aid from his disciples. Nevertheless, despite appearances, these last fifteen years of his life do not seem to have been particularly unhappy. He still continued to write and publish books, and had a fairly active social life, at least until his final years, when the war forced him to find lodging outside of London. Cammell, who got acquainted with him in 1936, described him thus:

> When I met him, the promise and romance of Crowley's life were over; his best poetry and his best prose were written. He was bankrupt, ostracised. Publishers would not print his books, nor editors his articles. … Almost any other man would have abandoned hope in such a position, would have gone into hiding, humiliated and desperate. Not so Aleister Crowley. … His belief in his mission, real or imagined, his determination to dominate, remained inviolate.[89]

After his return from Germany, Crowley settled in London. In that period, he broke off relations with the three people who had been closest to him in the previous years: Regardie, Yorke and Germer. He would have practically no more contact with Regardie until his death, although he later mended relations – at least partially – with the other two.

In 1933 he won a lawsuit against a bookseller who had advertised *The Diary of a Drug Fiend* with a placard displaying libellous statements about him. Encouraged by this success, he decided to sue his old friend Nina Hamnett (1890–1956), who had discussed the Abbey of Thelema in her memoirs.[90] The suit took place in spring 1934 and was a disaster for Crowley. During the hearings, from accuser he turned into accused: the juiciest details of his "scandalous" private life were brought to light, and after only four days, the litigation ended with a humiliating defeat. The suit was followed with great curiosity by the press, both domestic and international.

In July of the same year, he was in court again, this time as a defendant. He was accused of having received letters that had been reported as stolen, with the purpose of using them in his lawsuit against Hamnett, even if he was found guilty and sentenced to two years' probation. In the next year (1935), unable to pay his numerous creditors, he was declared bankrupt. This can be viewed as the last "mundane" event in Crowley's life, for after this he lived in relative tranquillity, even if he still had a very active social life (as we will see in the coming chapters) and continued to publish important works. Among them we should remember *The Equinox of the Gods* (1936), in which he relates the events that led to the revelation of *The Book of the Law* in 1904, and *The Book of Thoth* (1944), in which he presents his personal interpretation of the Tarot.

In 1935 Karl Germer was arrested during a visit to Germany, almost certainly because of his connections with the OTO, which was now outlawed along with all other esoteric groups.[91] He was tortured at the Alexanderplatz prison, then sent to the concentration camp at Esterwegen. After some time he was released and, after leaving Germany, moved to Belgium. In 1940, just before the German invasion, he was arrested again, this time by the Belgian authorities because of his German nationality, and, after the outbreak of hostilities, was deported to France. He spent ten months in a French concentration camp, and was finally released. In 1941 he moved to the United States, and from then until Crowley's death, he held the office of Grand Treasurer of the OTO.

Aleister Crowley died of myocardial degeneration on 1 December 1947. After his death, other significant works came to light, including *Magick without Tears* (1954), composed in the last years of his life, where he presents the essential aspects of his doctrine in epistolary form; *Liber Aleph* (1961), a series of teachings directed to his disciple Charles Stansfeld Jones; and an edition of the *Confessions* (1969), including the parts that had remained unpublished until then.

🎱 2. Magical politics

> … my curse is
> No sooner in an iron word
> I formulate my thought than I
> Perceive the same to be absurd.
>   (Aleister Crowley, "The Sword of Song")

Crowley was a wanderer[1] not only in the physical sense, as a traveller and explorer, but also – perhaps above all – in the intellectual and spiritual sense. In him we find, for example, the influence of several Oriental mystical and religious traditions, particularly yoga and Buddhism. We find the influence of the Decadent movement[2] and of positivism, or, more correctly, scientific naturalism[3], coming in both cases from his Cambridge days. Through the curriculum of the Golden Dawn, he familiarized himself with various currents or aspects of Western esotericism, including ceremonial magic, alchemy, astrology, Rosicrucianism, Kabbalah, the Tarot. All this contributed to forming a highly complex and perhaps not always consistent whole. We should also consider the fact that, although Crowley was generally interested in politics, this interest remained always subordinate to his magical and metaphysical preoccupations. He was undoubtedly a man who lived in the present and had his own opinions about the social and political situation of his era, but for the most part he could not separate these aspects from the transcendent framework postulated by his world view. Crowley always interpreted his ideas and behaviour in the light of metaphysical considerations. He believed, in essence, that the world was ruled not by material, but by spiritual laws (or we might better say "energies"). In his view, the spiritual (or "astral") plane was the structure, and the material plane, the superstructure.[4] For these reasons, politics came not before but *after* metaphysics. If we are to find consistency in Crowley, we must search for it not in his political ideas, but in his belief that he was a master sent by the gods to bring a new religious message.

Having said this, it must be observed that in Crowley's writings, there is no lack of references to politics – both concerning the current events of his time and, from a more abstract point of view, concerning political doctrines or ideologies. During his mature age, moreover, he lived in a particular period of European history – the time between the two world wars – that was quintessentially "political". During all this period his conviction of having a new religious message for humanity remained firm, along with his decision to spread it using all the means at his disposal. How could this message, revolutionary as new religious messages so often are, not have equally revolutionary implications on the political and social level? And how could these implications have been ignored by Crowley in a time when everything seemed to have political and social significance, and "revolution" – whatever form it might take – appeared to be in the agenda of a myriad of groups and movements?

To these considerations I should add another, which is directly connected with them. Crowley lived the contradictions of his time to the fullest. As a young student at Cambridge in the years when psychoanalysis was making its first steps and Nietzsche's philosophy was beginning to gain recognition, we find in him the same inclination to explore the depths of the soul, and the same fragmentation of personality that had begun to manifest itself in different ways among generations of artists, writers and intellectuals. Nietzsche himself had predicted it, almost as a direct consequence of his philosophy: "The dissolution of morals leads, in its practical consequences, to the atomistic individual and thence to the splitting of the individual into pluralities – absolute flux."[5] These anticipations, obviously, were taken to their extreme consequences by literary modernism and the artistic avant-gardes.

All this leads us to the realization that the attempt to interpret Crowley's thought as a coherent whole is a risky operation, most likely doomed to failure from the outset – as those who have explored his works without prejudice know well. This is not only because Crowley's ideas went through some evolution during the course of his life, but also because contradictory ideas seem often to have been present in his mind. A "magical" explanation for this ambiguity could also be given; this will prove useful in Chapter 4, where I will explore the relationship between Crowley and Pessoa. In Crowley we find a Faustian desire for knowledge and experience. The true "Magus" is he who strives endlessly toward this ideal of absolute experience, putting himself to the test by undergoing ordeals of every kind. In a very important passage from *The Confessions*, he writes: "I want everything that the world holds; I would go to prison or to the scaffold for the sake of the experience. I have never grown out of the infantile belief that the universe was made for me to suck. ... This is the keynote of my life, the untrammelled delight in every possibility of existence, potential or actual."[6]

According to Crowley, one way to gain experience of reality is to step out of one's own personality and observe things through the eyes of another person. In another passage of *The Confessions*, Crowley writes:

> I did not see why I should be confined to one life. How can one hope to understand the world if one persists in regarding it from the conning tower of one's own personality? One can increase one's knowledge and nature by travelling and reading; but that does not tell one how things look to other people. It is all very well to visit St. Peter's and the Vatican, but what would be really interesting would be to know how they look to the Pope. ... My technique for borrowing other people's spectacles was to put myself in the place altogether, either by actually adopting a suitable alias or by writing a book in their names.[7]

Observing this protean aspect of Crowley's personality may help to explain the apparent incongruity of certain attitudes he displayed. As I have said, it is futile to search for consistency at all costs whereas, fundamentally, consistency is not necessarily seen as a value. It is certainly possible to trace directions of opinion and political expression that accompanied Crowley continually from youth to old age; but one should not be surprised to discover attitudes in him that run against these main tendencies.[8]

My investigation is undertaken bearing these problems in mind. Therefore I do not necessarily seek to find a consistent political doctrine, but rather to understand the way in which Crowley confronted the reality of his times, how he interpreted it and how he related to it. The political element therefore emerges as an extremely important part of Crowley's legacy – a legacy that still plays today a very significant role in those currents of contemporary religion belonging to the large area of occultism and neo-paganism.

Between mysticism and religion

Before moving on to an analysis of Crowley's political ideas, I should like first to draw attention to one particular aspect of his personal evolution, which will provide a better background for the subsequent discussion. His life in fact appears to have been divided into two distinct phases. The first consisted of a striving for mystical and initiatory achievement: a more individualistic phase, characterized by what we might call a "search for the absolute".[9] The second phase consisted of his complete identification with his religious "call". It was the mission he felt invested with as a prophet: the propagation of the religion of Thelema. In other words, in his youth he was much more focused on his spiritual development as an individual, whereas later his goal became, above all else, the spreading of the new religion he had founded. This latter undertaking, in his view, concerned the whole of humanity, not merely his own person. The passage from one phase to the other was not marked by a clear turning point. There were, however, several important stages. All in all, what we see is a gradual transition from one position to another.

Regardie, in his important monograph on Crowley that I have discussed in Chapter 1,[10] was the first to suggest a distinction of this type. As we have seen, his intent in this book was above all to trace the spiritual evolution of his former master, while also offering a psychoanalytic interpretation of his personality and behaviour.[11] But Regardie's analysis stops in 1909, when Crowley had thirty-eight years more to live, and does not cover the subsequent period. Why? Regardie claims that 1909 was a turning point for Crowley, due to two events. The first was the rediscovery of the manuscript of *The Book of the Law*, which he claims he had lost earlier. This finding, which Crowley did not consider accidental, convinced him that he was to be the prophet of a new world religion. The second event was the series of astral explorations conducted in the Algerian Sahara; Crowley considered them all together as a single ritual of initiation to the degree of *Magister Templi*.[12]

Regardie's hypothesis is that this experience in the Sahara "had a tremendous effect on the whole course of Crowley's subsequent life",[13] and influenced him in a double fashion: on the one hand it represented the achievement of an extremely important spiritual goal, but on the other hand it may have unleashed a "destructive process" which, because of the discharge of emotional energy provoked by the initiation, made some latent content emerge from his subconscious that could not be assimilated.[14]

After this, Crowley would have enjoyed a few more good creative years, but around 1914 his sources of inspiration would have dried up, and so would have ceased the development of his spiritual goals. This would be the reason for Regardie to make Crowley's spiritual biography end in those years. Here Regardie implies that, after this period, Crowley's figure would not be so interesting to him as he was in his early years. Besides his views on the exhaustion of creativity, Regardie shows an obvious preference for the Crowley who experimented with mysticism and magic, whose highest aspiration was the "Great Work"; in short, the Crowley of the Golden Dawn and of the early A∴A∴, following a trajectory of individual spiritual progress, both magical and mystical. Regardie was evidently less interested in Crowley as the prophet of a new religion.

Even if Regardie later somewhat softened his negative judgement of the post-First World War Crowley,[15] it seems to me that his distinction between the two periods still remains interesting. Obviously, for him the distinction is accompanied by a value judgement: the first period would be more positive, in terms of both spiritual development and artistic creativity, the second less so. But I would rather set aside judgements of this kind, and merely inquire as to whether we may identify differing attitudes on Crowley's part in these two separate phases – that is to say, different views on his personal goals in life, and consequently different modes of behaviour.

It is true that something happened in 1909. There was the Algerian experience that Regardie considers so important, but there was also something else. In his autobiography, Crowley states repeatedly that his first spontaneous reaction to the text dictated to him in 1904 by Aiwass, the "praeter-human" entity with whom he claimed to have established a contact, was to reject it. Not only did he initially refuse to accept the role of prophet that *The Book of the Law* seemed to prescribe for him, but he also misplaced the manuscript. Five years later he found it again, and considered this event to be a sign from the gods. The recovery of the manuscript indicated that the moment had come: he finally had to take on the task of leading humanity into a new era. But even taking this "conversion" into account, it is interesting to note that we must look ahead a few years, namely to the outbreak of the First World War, in order to see Crowley dedicating himself completely to his new mission. In fact, looking at what he wrote and published between 1909 and 1914 – for example, the *The Scented Garden of Abdullah the Satirist of Shiraz* (1910),[16] *The Rites of Eleusis* (1910),[17] *The Book of Lies* (1913),[18] the two parts of *Book Four* (1912–13)[19] and the enormous quantity of material (essays, rituals, poems, stories, reviews) appearing in the first volume of *The Equinox* (1909–13)[20] – one can see that he did not immediately develop an intense commitment to propagating the Law of Thelema. In certain works from this period there are no references at all to it, whereas it is very difficult to find anything written by Crowley after the First World War that does not relate to Thelema in one way or another. A gradual increase in his determination can be observed up until 1916, when he reached the degree of Magus. Starting from this moment, Crowley's life truly began to be identified with what he considered as his mission.[21]

In 1912, during this same period of transition, there was another important event: Crowley's second meeting with Theodor Reuss, who at the time was in the process of getting his OTO off the ground. On this occasion, Reuss allegedly "revealed" the supreme secret of the Order to Crowley, namely the techniques of sexual magic, and gave him the permission to create an English section of the Order, the name of which would be Mysteria Mystica Maxima (M∴M∴M∴).

The history of Crowley's relationship to the OTO is another key to his evolution. As we have seen, when he met Reuss, he already had his own magical Order, the A∴A∴, founded in 1909 and modelled on the Golden Dawn. It appears however that, after learning the secret of the OTO, he suddenly became an enthusiast of this new Order.[22] He devoted himself painstakingly to the diffusion of the Order throughout the English-speaking countries (which were all supposed to be part of his jurisdiction), and as time went on he dedicated more and more energy to this, until finally assuming control of the Order in 1925, after Reuss's death. He rewrote the rituals and reorganized the system of degrees. The A∴A∴, on the other hand, seems to have languished for a certain period until it disappeared as an organization proper, although apparently its activity as a network of loosely connected individual members was never completely broken off. But why did Crowley decide to devote increasingly his efforts to a newly discovered organization, of which he was not even the supreme leader, rather than the one he had himself created? Regardie has an opinion in this regard that I find quite interesting. He writes:

> Many have frequently wondered why Crowley bothered to use the Ordo Templi Orientis after he and Jones had so painstakingly formulated the A∴A∴ in 1909. The latter organization was a reformulation of the old Golden Dawn *on the level of personal accomplishment and individual experimentation with classical mystical and occult techniques*. Its goal was, in effect, that of the Golden Dawn too – the attainment of higher states of consciousness, the religious or mystical experience. ... Crowley's interpretation of the Great Work stressed above all other things a combination of Yoga and Ceremonial Magic as the operational tools by which the student could ascend to the very highest levels of spiritual attainment. The OTO, on the other hand, while teaching a form of sex-magic, was perceived by Crowley as an ideal agent for promulgating the Law of Thelema – "Do what thou wilt!" ... It almost seems as if he came to stress *the universal importance of* The Book of the Law *as against the individual attainment of higher mystical states*. [Crowley therefore] *shifted his energies from the individual to large masses*.[23]

Crowley's attitude toward his magical Orders had also changed with the strengthening of his belief that he was the prophet of a new religion. Between an individualist A∴A∴ and an OTO which, at least according to Crowley's intentions, could reach the "great masses", the latter had to be given preference. This change in attitude is a crucial and indispensable element for understanding Crowley's involvement with politics.

Did his attitude toward politics change in relation to the two phases described above? In a certain sense, it did. If in the first phase he conceived his interest in politics in an essentially *romantic* fashion, in the second phase he became a *pragmatist*, ready to sympathize with any political movement that might, in his view, help him to propagate the religion of Thelema. The process necessary for reaching this goal certainly had social and political implications, but these elements were only the means; the end remained fundamentally religious.

Attitudes

Israel Regardie and Percy Reginald Stephensen, who both knew Crowley personally and were among his keenest critics, have maintained that in many ways, Crowley's natural attitude was that of a Tory. According to Regardie, for example, this would explain the fact that he never demeaned himself by "working". This would not have been compatible with his notion of personal dignity: "In his code, the English gentleman did not work".[24] Stephensen, on the other hand, defines Crowley as an "Old High Tory" in order to explain his pro-German leanings during the First World War.[25] Crowley allegedly would have considered defeat preferable to the state of decadence into which England, in his view, had lapsed prior to the outbreak of the war.

These interpretations – however based on statements made by Crowley himself at one moment or another – seem a little too apologetic to be convincing. Surely someone who believes that the decadence of his country would justify its military defeat and possible devastation – perhaps as a necessary step towards a future revival – can hardly be considered a conservative. This resembles more the position of someone who has nothing to lose, who sees the overturning of society as the only possibility for radical renewal, and not of someone who has interests or values to defend. We must therefore not be led astray by placing undue emphasis on Crowley's "conservative" element. In his mature years this element became a little more prominent, but remained relatively superficial, as in his referring to the moral code of a "gentleman" in order to justify certain choices he made in his life.

During his young adulthood, Crowley went through a process in which he gradually freed himself from the Victorian Puritanism amid which he had spent his childhood and adolescence. This took place initially thanks to the experiences and the intellectual discoveries he made as a student in Cambridge and later as a consequence of his travels. Once this "emancipation" was complete, the person who emerged from it saw very little worth conserving in the society, customs and mentality of the England of his time.

In fact, the period of his life in which his conservative attitude seems to have been most prominent is that of his teenage years, prior to entering university. Crowley recalls his perception of politics in those days as follows:

> In those days of adolescence I had no inducement to do any political thinking. The atmosphere was one of prosperity and stability. It was taken for granted that England was the greatest country in the world and that nothing could go wrong. One heard about Ireland as a perennial nuisance; and Mr. Gladstone was regarded as a traitor, neither more nor less.[26]

In the prosperous Victorian England of the 1880s, Crowley shared a feeling of superiority and well-being with many of his fellow citizens. The British Empire was in its heyday, and as Crowley himself said, faith in its economic and military power was a widespread sentiment. Earlier on the same page, Crowley gives us to understand that this attitude matured more during the time spent at school than in his family. We have no reason to suppose that his family was particularly conservative, in the sense of approving of or identifying with the conservative party of the time.[27] Moreover, belonging to a fundamentalist sect such as the Plymouth Brethren would have brought them closer to the liberal party, which supported the interests of non-conformists, whereas the conservative party was considered to be the traditional bulwark of the Anglican "establishment". Finally, non-conformist education often lead people to develop a critical, if not necessarily hostile, attitude toward society and mainstream institutions, which in turn would naturally lead them to be more favourable toward liberal positions than conservative ones.

It is also possible that no special attention was paid to British politics in Crowley's family environment, considering that in the fundamentalist mindset of the Plymouth Brethren, religious concerns left little room for secular ones. Be that as it may, any possible disinterest in internal politics did not prevent the Plymouth Brethren, as Crowley seems to suggest, from cherishing a notion of England as the land chosen by God and being concerned about its imperialist and colonial enterprises.[28] Also, during Crowley's adolescence, sentiments of nationalist and imperialist pride were particularly widespread in English society; this may help us to understand the origin of the "patriotic", if not explicitly chauvinistic, sentiment which Crowley himself repeatedly claimed to have, and which became manifest from time to time in his life, especially in his later years.[29] But nationalist chauvinism is not necessarily synonymous with conservatism, even if at times the two may be confused with one another. It is important to emphasize this point, because Crowley's chauvinistic side may have become more apparent at times in his later years, but this should not necessarily be considered as an indicator of actual conservative leanings.

In the passage cited above, Crowley mentions the famous statesman William Ewart Gladstone (1809–98). In those days Gladstone was head of the Liberal Party, which formed one of the two poles of English politics, the other pole being the Conservative Party, with the Irish nationalists playing the uncomfortable role of third wheel.[30] The references to the "nuisance" of Ireland and to Gladstone's "treachery" point to the convoluted political situation of this period with regard to the question of Irish self-governance ("Home Rule"). At the time, Ireland was a direct dependency of the British central government and had no autonomy whatsoever. A few years earlier the Irish Nationalist Party had emerged on the scene and, thanks to recent suffrage reforms, had quickly acquired an ever-increasing number of representatives in Parliament. In 1885, after the crisis in the Liberal government, the possibility emerged of an alliance between the Conservative Party and the Irish Nationalist Party. Gladstone, convinced that the concession of some kind of Home Rule was inevitable, decided to take advantage of the situation. Manipulating the delicate balance of Parliament, he endeavoured to conceal his favourable attitude toward Irish Home Rule and at the same time to discreetly encourage an alliance between the Conservatives and the Irish Nationalists. In fact, only with the support of the Conservatives could the motion toward Home Rule break through the resistance of the House of Lords, which had a constant Conservative majority. Unfortunately, Gladstone, believing absolute secrecy to be essential for the success of his project, hid his plans from even his most faithful collaborators within the Liberal Party. When some newspapers reported, based on information rashly divulged by Gladstone's son, that in contrast to his official declarations he had suddenly "converted" to being in favour of Home Rule and was prepared to support a potential Conservative undertaking in this direction, the delicate balance on which his project had been built was upturned. His "conversion" was thought to be mere opportunism, arising from a desire to win over the Irish party in order to secure a new governmental majority for himself. The result was disastrous: the Conservatives broke with the Irish Nationalists, and some of the Liberals deserted Gladstone's party, declaring themselves opposed to any possibility of Home Rule. These events not only damaged Gladstone's reputation (he died a few years later) but also undermined the movement in favour of Home Rule and made a solution impracticable for many years to come.[31]

This context allows us to better understand Crowley's references in the passage cited, and gives us a background for another example of his youthful political intransigence against Gladstone, recorded on the same page of his autobiography. Crowley tells us that in 1892, when he was invited to go (probably with his school) to meet Gladstone in north Wales, he not only refused to go, but even wrote a poem to celebrate this refusal, obviously addressed to the statesman:

> I will not shake thy hand, old man,
> I will not shake thy hand;
> You bear a traitor's brand, old man,
> You bear a liar's brand.
> ...
> Your age and sex forbid, old man,
> I need not tell you how,
> Or else I'd knock you down, old man,
> Like that extremist cow[32]

A note by Crowley informs us that in the preceding year, Gladstone had been attacked by a cow run amok in Hawarden Park. Crowley also urged Lord Rosebery, Gladstone's successor as head of the Liberal Party and prime minister from 1894 to 1895, to rid himself of what Crowley called "red Rad fleas".[33] The Radicals formed the left wing of the Liberal Party, the group most sensitive to the question of Home Rule, and which would soon merge with the nascent Labour Party.

To these interesting views on the part of young Crowley about contemporary political issues, we can add another, dating to a slightly later period, when he was studying at Cambridge. This can be found in one of his first published works, *An Appeal to the American Republic*, a short poem in which he urges the United States to form an alliance with Britain.[34] Here we see the same kind of naïve nationalist exaltation as in the passages cited earlier. He claims that the idea of writing this poem came to him when he met two Americans on a train ride from Geneva to Paris.[35] He was inspired by the pleasant conversation he had with them. We must also recall, however, that the work was written shortly before the brief Spanish–American war over Cuba (1898), which ended in an overwhelming US victory, Cuba being converted from a Spanish colony to an independent state subject to American influence. During the war, the powers of continental Europe had supported Spain, even proposing sending an armed intervention, while Britain alone had supported the United States and made any potential European intervention impracticable. The effect of this was a relaxation of the hitherto traditionally tense British–American relations, but also an increase in Britain's political isolation from other European powers. This "splendid isolation", as it was proudly called, would remain at the basis of British foreign politics for some years, ending only with the Anglo-Russian Convention of 1907.[36] In his poem Crowley emphasized the kinship between the British and American nations, claiming that the shared Anglo-Saxon culture must be the basis for a future civilizing mission, while the great powers of continental Europe – France, Russia and Germany – are viewed with suspicion and mistrust. In view of the situation mentioned earlier, there is also no lack of references to Spain, whose subjects are referred to as "slaves of kings".[37] The war over Cuba is seen as selfless aid given by the United States to an oppressed and enslaved nation in the name of the pure ideal of liberty.[38] All in all, what Crowley writes in his poem coincides to a great extent with the vision of foreign politics that was dominant in England at the time, and does not reveal any particularly original or heterodox viewpoints.

Another point of interest in this work is the fact that, shortly after the outbreak of the First World War, Crowley republished it, touching up only a few details in order to adapt it to the current situation.[39] As we shall see, his patriotic tone displayed in these early works contrasts strongly with what he would later write while living in the United States during the First World War.

Although, as we have seen, no deviant or radical political position can be deduced from *An Appeal*, in this same period Crowley was already going through a very important phase of intellectual growth and inner development, which also had significant consequences for his political opinions. One of the fundamental moments in this evolution was undoubtedly his time at Cambridge University, between 1895 and 1898. I have already discussed the significance of this aspect elsewhere, and therefore will not dwell on it further here.[40] It will suffice to say that his Cambridge experience had lifelong consequences: it gave him the intellectual tools for developing his own personal critique, not only of Christianity but also of English society as it appeared to be near the end of the Victorian era. His intellectual education, until then more or less effectively controlled by his family, underwent an enormous acceleration. As was the case for so many other youths of his generation, university gave him the decisive impulse for the intellectual crisis that quickly led him to abandon his parents' religion and develop a more critical attitude toward his country.[41] Moreover, at Cambridge Crowley was especially subject to the influence of the scientific naturalism and agnosticism that were still dominant, in spite of the first symptoms of decline, in the late 1890s.[42] This influence remained a characteristic of Crowley's education, and in the last section of this chapter we will see how he sought to apply the criteria of scientific naturalism, which he had learned at Cambridge, to his concept of magic.[43]

But even before entering university, other influences played an important role in his intellectual development. His discovery of the Celtic tradition in those years was the first step in the development of a critical and less naïvely patriotic attitude. In the last decade of the nineteenth century, the passion for Celtic lore had become a widespread vogue, exercising its power of attraction not only in those parts of Britain where some kind of Celtic heritage could still reasonably be claimed (i.e. Scotland, Ireland, Wales and Cornwall), but also in England itself and among Englishmen such as Crowley.[44] In a certain sense, this can be considered as an epiphenomenon, along with the Decadent movement, of late English romanticism, that "romantic agony" so aptly described by Mario Praz.[45] And undoubtedly, the fascination this vogue exerted over the young Crowley brings to light the more genuinely romantic side of his character.

The growth of interest in Celtic things, moreover, had explicitly political connotations and was obviously connected to the awakening, around the *fin-de-siècle*, of nationalist sentiments in Scotland and Ireland, both demanding freedom, or at least greater autonomy, from English cultural and political hegemony. One need only consider the commitment of authors such as the Irishmen William Butler Yeats and George Russell (better known by his pseudonym "Æ") or the Scotsman William Sharp (who mostly wrote under the pseudonym "Fiona Macleod").[46] For an Englishman like Crowley, getting close to this movement – apart from its powerful romantic appeal and the charm of a fad that was then at its high point – must surely have had the effect of releasing him from that naïve adolescent view of England that I have just described.

This explosion of "Celtomania" – which became known as the Celtic Revival or the Celtic Movement – was accompanied by the rediscovery of other traditions that had been thought completely extinct. Among these was the legitimist movement known as "Jacobitism". Crowley recounts his discovery of it as follows: "Scott, Burns and my cousin Gregor had made me a romantic Jacobite. I regarded the Houses of Hanover and Coburg as German usurpers; and I wished to place "Mary III and IV" on the throne. I was a bigoted legitimist."[47]

Jacobitism was only one of many legitimist movements present in Europe at the time. Of course, most of them had very few chances to see their hopes fulfilled. Each movement had its own peculiar form: there was Portuguese legitimism, called "Miguelism"; Spanish legitimism, "Carlism"; various forms of French legitimism; and finally, this specifically British legitimism, which aspired to the restoration of the House of Stuart upon the throne of Britain, or else the re-establishment of a Scottish throne separate from that of England, which would naturally be occupied by a scion of the Stuart line. The last male member of the Stuart house to rule over England had been James II (1633–1701), who was forced to abdicate in the Glorious Revolution of 1688, giving up his throne to William of Orange. Thus the Jacobite movement came into being, taking its name from the Latin form of James, *Jacobus*. All attempts to restore the Stuart dynasty failed, ending with a bitter defeat at the Battle of Culloden in 1746, which put an end to any serious hope of a Stuart returning to the English throne.[48]

During the nineteenth century, the various legitimist movements were, as a rule, catch-alls for extremely reactionary political positions. In these circles, the French Revolution and its natural progenitor, the Enlightenment, were generally considered responsible for (or rather guilty of) the subversion of the traditional order of society. Liberalism was considered a menace, not to mention socialism. Another interesting point is that legitimist movements appear always to have been fertile territory for occultism. This is true, at least, with regard to Jacobitism, even well before the end of the nineteenth century, if we consider for instance the role that Jacobite exiles fleeing from Britain played in continental Freemasonry, and especially in France.[49]

Crowley's juvenile passion for Jacobite legitimism was anything but unique. In fact, the last decade of the nineteenth century saw a significant revival of interest in this movement in England. Various Jacobite circles were born or newly revived, and there was intense journalistic activity in newspapers and magazines. Curiously, Queen Victoria herself played a part in promoting this vogue, although Jacobite legitimists considered her a usurper. The queen felt in fact a strong connection to her Stuart ancestors and to Scotland, where she spent a good deal of time, and in 1889 she sponsored an exhibition of Stuart and Jacobite relics in London. One of the organizers of the event was Lord Ashburnham, a key figure in the neo-Jacobite movement.[50]

Not content with supporting the Jacobite cause in his country, Crowley committed himself also to another European legitimist movement, namely Spanish Carlism, and took part in some of its secret operations.[51] In fact, some Jacobite circles in those days had direct connections to the Carlist movement, which upheld the same ultra-reactionary political ideas as its British counterpart. The most remarkable episode in this collaboration was the *Firefly* affair. In 1899, off the coast of Arcachon, in the Bay of Biscay, the Spanish navy intercepted the English yacht *Firefly*, which was transporting a cargo of rifles for a planned Carlist revolt in Spain. It was subsequently found that Lord Ashburnham himself was behind the operation: he had actually chartered the yacht. Apparently Crowley was involved in these events, although he does not elaborate on them in his autobiography, preferring to remain discreet. He says only that he learned to use weapons, studied strategy and prepared for the invasion of Spain. He claims that because of his commitment, although the operation ultimately failed, he was knighted by one of the lieutenants of Don Carlos, Duke of Madrid (1848–1909), the last of the Carlist pretenders bearing this name.[52] This was no mean feat for someone who, just a year earlier, had exalted the emancipating victory of the United States over a reactionary and obscurantist Spain – especially considering that the Carlist agitations in Spain from 1899–1902 were in part due to discontent over the painful defeat in the war for Cuba!

Among Crowley's acquaintances at the time, two should be mentioned who surely played a significant role in his flirtation with legitimism and Jacobitism. The first one is Louis Charles Richard Duncombe-Jewell (1866–1947, also known as Ludovic Cameron), a journalist and writer whose parents were, like Crowley's, Plymouth Brethren.[53] The two families had been on friendly terms for years, and Duncombe-Jewell had been acquainted with Crowley since the latter was a teenager. When Crowley was spending much of his time at Boleskine, in the second half of 1903, Duncombe-Jewell was a regular presence in the house, as a sort of secretary and factotum, and probably even managed the estate when Crowley was away (for instance during his extended travels in the East between 1903 and 1904). He was of Cornish origin and became an enthusiastic supporter of the Celtic Revival. A passionate advocate for the preservation of the Cornish language, he is still remembered today for his activism, which expressed itself in the foundation of a Celtic-Cornish Society (the short-lived "Cowethas Kelto-Kernuac"), his participation in a "Pan-Celtic Congress" held in 1905, where he supported the recognition of Cornwall as one of the Celtic nations, and his contributions to various dedicated journals. It should be noted that he was also on friendly terms with some of the Celtic revivalists who were involved in the Golden Dawn, and therefore belonged to the circle of Crowley's acquaintances, such as S. L. Mathers and W. B. Yeats.[54]

Some elements in Duncombe-Jewell's biography show the typical confluence between the Celtic Revival and legitimism. We can see it in his conversion to Catholicism: not a small step considering his Darbyite background, but logical enough for someone evolving in Jacobite and legitimist milieus. Furthermore, as it was sometimes the case with the Celtic revivalists, some of his activities were more explicitly political. In the second half of the 1890s he edited *The Royalist*, a right-wing journal that, between 1890 and 1905 acted as a convenient podium for Jacobitism and other forms of legitimism, including Spanish Carlism. Interestingly enough, he was also involved in the *Firefly* affair and, in all likelihood, it was very probably him who invited Crowley to participate in the venture.⁵⁵

The second person to be mentioned in this respect is none other than S. L. Mathers. It seems very likely that the influence held over Crowley by him, as head of the Golden Dawn, played a role in these interests and activities. Mathers, who lived in Paris at the time, was actively involved in the Jacobite and legitimist causes. An enthusiast of Scottish history and lore, he had added to his family name the name of the MacGregor clan, remembered historically for their loyalty to the House of Stuart, and from which he claimed direct descent. Yeats, not yet a world-famous poet but already a fellow member and opponent of Crowley in the Golden Dawn, had been on good terms with Mathers before the schism of the Order and had been often his guest in Paris. In one of his autobiographical writings, Yeats remembers that Mathers, who also called himself the "Earl of Glenstrae", was surrounded in Paris by a small court of "Frenchmen and Spaniards whose titles were more shadowy, perhaps [than his own]", and that there was even "an obscure claimant to the French throne among the rest".⁵⁶ Although Crowley appears to have discovered the Scottish romantic tradition and the neo-Jacobite movement on his own already before entering the Golden Dawn, he doubtless found a kindred spirit in Mathers because of such interests.⁵⁷ It was certainly no coincidence that, when Crowley decided in 1899 to buy a country house where he could carry out the magical operations of Abramelin, he opted for an estate in Scotland; likewise it was surely under Mathers's influence that, also in this period, Crowley added the name MacGregor to his own name.⁵⁸ On the other hand, if Crowley really got in contact with legitimist circles and took part in their conspiratorial activities, this could only have made him appear in a favourable light to the head of the Golden Dawn. This would also explain the trust Mathers placed in him during the crisis in the Order and the subsequent schism of 1900.⁵⁹

Traditionally, the Jacobites had always had more or less direct links to the Catholic Church; James II's Catholicism had been one of the reasons for his deposition, and this inclination was even stronger among the Jacobite circles of the late nineteenth century.⁶⁰ This element was apparently not greatly appreciated by Crowley, who wrote the following concerning his legitimist involvement:

> My reactionary conservatism came into conflict with my anti-Catholicism. A reconciliation was effected by means of what they called the Celtic Church. Here was a romantic and mystical idea which suited my political and religious notions down to the ground. ... Sacramentalism was kept in the foreground and sin was regarded without abhorrence. Chivalry and mystery were its pillars. It was free from priestcraft and tyranny, for the simple reason that it did not really exist!⁶¹

Crowley preferred to remain vague about this "Celtic Church" and it seems unlikely that this movement was concretely structured as an organization.⁶² In any case, what is noteworthy is that Crowley rejected the pro-Catholic element of the Jacobite movement while supporting another: the natural sympathy of British legitimism for the Celtic tradition.

The strong link that existed between the neo-Jacobite and Celtic movements in those years can be explained by the fact that from the start Jacobitism had been especially widespread in Scotland, Wales and Ireland. Crowley, inspired as we have seen by reading two classic Scottish authors, Robert Burns and Walter Scott, was initially attracted to the Scottish tradition, but around the time of the crisis of the Golden Dawn in 1900, he began to make increasingly frequent references to Ireland. One of his poems from this period, *Carmen Saeculare*, is particularly significant in this regard. As far as we know, it is the first work in which he took a favourable position concerning Irish independence. In fact, he says much more than that; he also presents himself as being Irish! Reading this poem without knowing who wrote it, one would undoubtedly think its author was an Irishman actively involved in the nationalist cause. The work was probably composed in the summer of 1900 while Crowley was on a ship headed for New York, the first stage of the long voyage that would bring him first to Mexico and then to Ceylon.[63]

The poem is divided into four parts. In the first part, "The Exile", Crowley imagines his voyage as a form of exile. In the following verses, the tone becomes one of apocalyptic vision, seeming to echo William Blake's poems. Crowley foresees the impending ruin of England, which he calls "the ancient whore"; London will be razed to the ground and the Anglo-Saxon race will vanish from the face of the earth.[64] Thus the nation will be restored to the Celtic race, which was overrun and ousted by the Anglo-Saxons.[65]

In the second part, which bears the same title as the poem itself, the vision continues and extends to include the destinies of other nations, mostly the great Western powers of the time. England's impending doom is sealed, and a few stanzas are devoted to the downfalls of other nations. Not all of the judgement is negative; this part of the poem is interesting in that it reveals Crowley's perceptions of the international politics of the times.[66] The reference to France, for example, is significant because it touches upon the Dreyfus affair, which was a source of extremely fierce debate during those same years. Here an anti-Semitic element emerges; anti-Semitism never played a predominant role in Crowley's intellectual life, but it did surface in some ways from time to time. He congratulates France for having freed herself from the "yoke" of the Jews, and for having condemned Captain Dreyfus.[67] France is seen as the fatherland of liberty, and Crowley's view of the nation is entirely positive. Also interesting is the part on the German Empire, in which he urges the German peasants not to abandon their fields for the sordid cities in search of easier earnings, and advises the nation not to become too proud or too militarized, but above all to strive for peace. Here Crowley appears to echo – how consciously, we do not know – some of the favourite themes of the German national-patriotic (*völkisch*) movement of the epoch.[68] As we have seen, when Crowley wrote this poem, his ideas were no longer those he had expressed just a year earlier in *An Appeal to the American Republic*. The last verses of this second part, devoted to Spain and the United States, confirm this. After indicating the accession of Don Carlos to the throne as the only solution for Spain's future,[69] he then denounces the United States as the "foul oligarchy of the West". The nation that had been an archetype of civilization and democracy, the Anglo-Saxon brother of the British Empire, is now depicted as a cesspool of depravity and corruption, founded solely upon the search for individual gain and profit.[70] And to make it definitively clear which side he is now on, he rebukes the United States for having "assassinated" the bravest and best of the Southerners during the American Civil War.[71]

The third part is entitled "In the Hour Before Revolt". The revolt, of course, is that of Ireland against domination by the "saxons". But the interesting aspect here is a reference to Africa. Crowley writes:

> They [the English] boast, though their triumph Hell's gift is,
> On Africa's desperate sons:
> "Our thousands have conquered their fifties;
> Our twenties have murdered their ones."
> That glory – that shame – let them trumpet
> To Europe's unquickening ear.[72]

This passage could be easily, although erroneously, interpreted as a generic condemnation of colonialism. In fact, the reference is undoubtedly to the Boer War (1899–1902), which had just broken out in South Africa after a decade of tension between the Boer territories and those subject to British colonial authority.[73] Crowley's attitude toward this event is entirely consistent with his other viewpoints during this period. Indeed, many Irish nationalists at the time actively supported the Boer cause, based on the ancient adage that the enemies of one's enemies are one's friends.[74] Crowley, in this part of the poem, concludes that the hour of reckoning is near at hand – at least for the Irish if not for the Boers – and that Ireland will soon be liberated.[75]

The fourth part is called the "Epilogue", and here the subject returns to the United States. This part, in fact, is dedicated – significantly – to the American people (no longer to the "republic", i.e. the American state, as was the poem of two years earlier) on the anniversary of their independence.[76] Crowley appeals to the American love of liberty in order to convince them to aid the Irish, who are about to launch into a conflict comparable to what the Americans went through a hundred-odd years earlier, against the same enemy: the English. If they refuse to help the Irish, the Americans can only deserve shame and dishonour.[77]

As we know, while Crowley was writing this poem, he was at the beginning of a long journey that would take him most of the way around the world, with some periodical returns to his homeland. It is also interesting to note that during this voyage, some of the themes we have analysed continued to emerge here and there in his poetic work. Two years later, while he was in Delhi, in India, he wrote *St. Patrick's Day, 1902*: a new hymn for the Irish revolt against the "saxon" oppressor.[78] The refrain is eloquent: "Death to the Saxon! Slay nor spare! / O God of Justice, hear us swear!"[79] Here Crowley's exhortation to his Irish "brothers" becomes even more vehement. He urges them not to count on help from other European nations, no longer even the United States.[80] The battle must be merciless, to the last drop of blood, for never in the past has the "Saxon" had any mercy upon the Irish.[81]

But what prompted Crowley to take part in the Irish cause in this manner, even claiming a Celtic origin for his family?[82] What was the meaning of this attitude, apart from the romantic charm we mentioned earlier? For a young Englishman of this period, it can only have represented scorn for his homeland. Ireland certainly had not ceased to be a "nuisance" for England; Crowley simply no longer wanted to be on England's side. The fact that he switched from having a passion for Scotland, his Celtic "first love", to a passion for Ireland, can be interpreted in this way: perhaps Scotland, from a political point of view, was not a great enough "nuisance". In those years the Scottish movement was predominantly literary, and certainly did not have the breadth and resonance of the Irish movement, which also had a stronger and more immediate political significance. Crowley did not really intend to commit himself concretely to this movement for the Irish cause; but what he wrote in the works we have examined so far testifies to the birth and evolution in him of a critical attitude toward his country, albeit suffused with romantic passion. Others from his generation became socialists and extolled social reform, which in the first few years of the twentieth century was a central theme in English political and cultural debate. Crowley, instead, preferred to call himself Irish and prophesy the ruin of England as he travelled the world and experimented with exotic forms of spirituality.

But beyond the forms his romantic revolt took on during his youth, a certain aspect should be particularly emphasized, because it remains a constant characteristic throughout his life: the rejection of bourgeois values, which was naturally connected to his anti-Christian views. I will return to this point in the next section of this chapter. Crowley's anti-bourgeois revolt had probably already begun during his university years at Cambridge, but it was most likely further intensified by the events in which he found himself involved during his membership in the Golden Dawn. Perhaps not enough emphasis has been placed on the fact that it was primarily on moral grounds that the London dissident group led by Yeats and Florence Farr refused Crowley admission to the inner Order of the Golden Dawn – an event that further aggravated the conflict between Mathers and the dissidents, and accelerated the schism in the Order. Crowley, who had dreamed of becoming part of a host of the elect, a group of individuals far above the trifling preoccupations of common mortals, was denied advancement in the Order for reasons having more to do with his behaviour – in particular his sexual conduct – than with his mystical talent and knowledge of teachings and rituals.[83] This appears to be confirmed by a number of elements. His diary from the period indicates that he probably came close to getting in trouble with the police for his homosexual relationships.[84] The scandal that ruined Oscar Wilde had taken place only a few years earlier, and the accusation of sodomy was not taken lightly in Victorian England. In any case, rumours about Crowley's homosexuality circulated within the Golden Dawn. In 1911, his old Golden Dawn confrere George Cecil Jones sued the newspaper *The Looking Glass* for having insinuated that there were homosexual undertones in his friendship with Crowley in the period leading up to the schism in the Order. At that point the defence called upon another member of the old Golden Dawn to testify, Dr Edward Berridge (1843–1923). Berridge confirmed that at the time there had been a rumour circulating in the Order that Crowley was devoted to the "vice against nature", and that on one occasion, when Berridge questioned Crowley as to the reasons behind this rumour, Crowley had responded ambiguously, neither confirming nor denying it.[85] His diary from this period also shows that he was informed by fellow members that the refusal to admit him to the Second Order was motivated by his sexual conduct.[86] Quite significant, then, is the fact that Yeats, in his letter from around this time to his friend Lady Gregory (in which he informs her of the developments in the conflict with Mathers), always refers to Crowley with unmitigated contempt, describing him repeatedly as an "unspeakable" person and explaining that the London group did not accept him into the Second Order because they "did not think that a mystical society was intended to be a reformatory".[87]

It is interesting to note that Mathers had anticipated a situation of this kind in a manifesto distributed within the Second Order in October 1896, in which he stated decisively that the private life of each member was to be that person's business alone, and could not be the object of discussion or criticism on the part of other members.[88] According to Mathers, the "Wisdom of the Gods" that the Golden Dawn transmitted to its members must absolutely not be used to justify any form of "intolerance, intermeddling and malicious self-conceit" toward fellow members.[89] This attitude on Mathers's part helps to explain why he rejected the decision of Yeats and the other members of the London Temple not to admit Crowley to the Second Order, and subsequently may have initiated Crowley in Paris himself. Here we come upon one of the fundamental problems of esoteric orders and mystic societies in general: namely, the conflict between "worldly" ethics, external to the group, and internal ethics, formulated within the group and based on principles that do not coincide with those of the surrounding society.[90] In the years to follow, as Crowley's reputation became increasingly disturbing, it is probable that many members of the Golden Dawn found confirmation for their earlier suspicions and maintained that the decision to exclude him had been justified. But it is equally probable that this experience ultimately contributed to radicalizing Crowley's revolt against the values of bourgeois society in general, and against Victorian and Edwardian society in particular. We can hear an echo of this resentment more than twenty years later, when he referred to his former colleagues of the Golden Dawn as "muddled middle-class mediocrities".[91]

From this point of view, it may appear paradoxical that Crowley's anti-English and anti-bourgeois revolt took on the form – if not the substance – of the Irish nationalist activism that formed the centre of the political and literary position of his "enemy" Yeats. And a few years later, in 1912, Yeats himself must not have been particularly amused to discover that his old acquaintance, the critic David James O'Donoghue (1866–1917), had considered Crowley a sufficiently "Irish" author to include him – just a few pages away from Yeats himself – in a biographical dictionary of Irish poets which, even today, is still considered an essential standard reference in this area of study.[92]

Whatever may be the explanations for Crowley's anti-bourgeois revolt – and they are surely numerous – what is certain is that he came to identify bourgeois morals with the Victorian era, and with the particular type of religious sensibility that permeated it. His grudge against England was above all a grudge against the bourgeois and Puritan England of his youth. Observing his youthful works, we find what appears to be a fairly rapid evolution. Between the feeling of well-being, security and confidence that marked his adolescence and these later manifestations of impatience and rebellion toward his country, there appears to be a wide gap, even though only a few years separate the two. But we should remember that the general atmosphere of the nation was also changing very rapidly.

As has been much noted and emphasized, the first years of the twentieth century were a time of crisis for England.[93] Worth mentioning above all is the death of Queen Victoria in 1901. This was the end of a sixty-four year reign, characterized – albeit with various developments and transformations – by a fairly homogeneous cultural climate. The epoch was marked on the one hand by scientific naturalism and agnosticism, on the other hand by evangelicalism.⁹⁴ These two currents, moreover, were much less incompatible with one another than it might seem today, despite the heated debates over Darwinian evolution that flared up during those years. As Robert Ensor has pointed out, an element of severe evangelical moralism was unmistakably present even in agnostic thinkers and Darwinian apologists such as Thomas Henry Huxley (1825–95).⁹⁵ However, both scientific naturalism and Puritanism began to decline after their heyday of the 1870s was over, losing their hold on English society more and more as the end of the century drew near. Despite this gradual decline, which modern historians describe as the "crisis of the late Victorian era", people of Crowley's generation grew up in an atmosphere that was undoubtedly still suffused with these ideals.⁹⁶ The crisis, which initially affected only a few intellectuals, certainly did not extend immediately to all levels of society. Even in the 1880s and 1890s, as Crowley's case shows, the English schools and universities of the establishment continued imperturbably to teach the values both of evangelical piety and of unconditional faith in scientific progress. Beside these two, a third value emerged as particularly strong during the last thirty years of the nineteenth century, one to which we have already made reference: imperialistic colonialism.

In this sense, the death of Queen Victoria, accompanied by the Boer War, represented a true turning point in British history, occurring fifteen years prior to the more general and international watershed that was the First World War. What is important to realize here is that contemporary people were aware of the change. Crowley's reaction to the news of Queen Victoria's death is highly significant in this regard. He was in Mexico at the time, with his mountaineer friend Oscar Eckenstein. The representative of the local authority who sadly announced the news to the two men could certainly not expect their reaction; he must have been surprised when they immediately started dancing and shouting for joy.⁹⁷ For Crowley, as for so many other English artists and intellectuals of his generation and the preceding one, Victoria represented a foggy and suffocating epoch: "We could not see, we could not breathe."⁹⁸ In their joyful singing and dancing, we can sense the release of all the tension that had accumulated during the final decade of Victoria's reign.

The Boer War was also of no small importance; we have seen how its echoes filtered through in young Crowley's poetic work. As a result of this war, imperialist and colonialist British politics, which had dominated the preceding decades with only a few dissenting voices, began to be seriously questioned and to arouse less and less enthusiasm.⁹⁹ Moreover, it was in this war – which symbolically marked the beginning of the new century – that modern concentration camps made their first appearance, in a tragic "liberal-democratic" anticipation of what totalitarianism would be capable of in the decades to come. British public opinion was dismayed by news of the living conditions of the Boer civilians imprisoned in the camps in the period directly after the British victory. The Victorian illusion of having a mission to civilize the colonized people, the "white man's burden" as Rudyard Kipling called it, foundered amid the blood and ferocity of this war between white men over the possession of South African riches. At the same time, the certainty of being "on the right side of history", which had characterized the Victorian man, came crashing down. Kipling's dream of rule and civilization was now transformed into Joseph Conrad's nightmare of violence and extermination.¹⁰⁰

To this scenario was added the situation in Ireland, which was still far from being solved, and which, after the missed opportunity of the 1880s, continually threatened to degenerate into a downward spiral of violence and retaliation, which is in fact what happened with the tragic events of the 1916 Easter Rising.

The contradictions of this moment of crisis and transition, seem to be reflected in Crowley's works. This aspect must be kept in mind, because here a possible explanation may be found for the inconsistency of his thought and attitudes. Namely, he found himself linked in some ways to an education and an epoch that were now coming to their end, while at the same time, because of his keen sensibility, he sensed the signs of change that had begun to manifest and that would finally be obvious to everyone after the First World War. But Crowley, as we have seen, was certainly not the only person in England to feel – and hope – that an epoch was ending. London in the first years of the twentieth century was abuzz with groups and movements, heterogeneous in many ways but united, if in no other way, by the idea of societal and cultural reform and the hope for a "new era" that would bring with it the solution to the problems and general anxieties generated by the end of the epoch of faith and certainty.[101]

During the years leading up to the First World War, Crowley was close to these movements; he engaged in debate with them, and, to some extent, took part in them. Perhaps he was a member of what we might call the "esoteric" wing; but he was also in contact – or at least in conflict – with the people who have been considered the most significant representatives of this turmoil of ideas in Edwardian London, such as Gilbert K. Chesterton, George Bernard Shaw, A. R. Orage and, of course, Yeats.[102] Orage (1873–1934) was one of the central figures in the circulation of new ideas in post-Victorian London. The journal he directed starting in 1907, *The New Age*, was the essential reference point for the broadly progressive and socialist culture of the epoch.[103] In this journal, English readers discovered new trends in European art and literature, and followed debates among the various currents of English socialism. The influence of *The New Age* on Edwardian intellectual and literary circles was profound, and the greatest names in the culture of the period contributed to it more or less regularly: besides Yeats, Shaw and Chesterton, it also boasted the writings of D. H. Lawrence, H. G. Wells, Katherine Mansfield and a young Ezra Pound. Orage and his journal are recognized today for – among other things – their fundamental role in the diffusion of Nietzsche's ideas in England during those years.[104] Nietzsche at the time was a great novelty for anti-conformist intellectuals, and he was read and esteemed especially among non-Marxist socialist circles.[105] Orage also had a strong interest in esotericism and spirituality. Since his youth he had frequented various theosophical groups, and later, in the 1920s, he became one of G. I. Gurdjieff's most important and influential disciples.[106] From this point of view, Crowley's relationship with Orage and his journal, especially in the years leading up to the First World War, undoubtedly deserves further exploration.[107]

Despite all the differences between the two, Crowley and Orage had at least one element in common: a more or less radical criticism of modern bourgeois industrial civilization and its values, identified with the positivism and Puritanism of the Victorian era. Of course, there were many different opinions as to what might be a valid alternative to modernity. But very strong inspiration for these restless intellectuals, especially Yeats, Orage and Chesterton, undoubtedly came from the medievalizing, non-Marxist socialism of William Morris (1834–96).[108] Morris was part of the movement known as the Gothic Revival, which was at first principally aesthetic but later acquired increasing political overtones. It was from this movement that the aforementioned Celtic Revival originated and developed as the end of the nineteenth century drew near; in fact, we may consider the latter a branch and variation of the Gothic Revival.

Interest in medieval forms of art had revived in England around the end of the eighteenth century, especially in domestic architecture, and had lasted into the first half of the nineteenth century in civil architecture and other forms of artistic expression. In the mid-nineteenth century the movement began to acquire political connotations, initially thanks especially to John Ruskin (1819–1900), and later to Morris. Both Ruskin and Morris rejected the idea that Western civilization had truly progressed since the end of the Middle Ages, an epoch they imagined in an idealistic and nostalgic fashion. They believed that starting with the Renaissance, aesthetic and spiritual decadence had gone hand in hand with the spread of industrial production processes. From an aesthetic, but also a moral and economic point of view, the increasing industrialization of modern civilization had led society to alienation. The Middle Ages was for them an exemplary epoch, since they thought that in those times society and the individual had achieved a perfect equilibrium, which was subsequently lost. In the Middle Ages, man had not yet lost control of the means of production necessary for his work, and above all, he was not obliged to work in a repetitive and standardized manner. For this reason, Morris, like other representatives of the Gothic Revival, disputed the view of the Middle Ages as a barbaric era. Instead, he directly reversed the terms "civilization" and "barbarianism", giving them a meaning that was the opposite of the usual one.[109] Moreover, Morris identified modern civilization not only with unrestrained industrialization, but also with the hypocrisy and repression of the Victorian era. This civilization, in his view, was destined for destruction and would make way for a new era in which true sentiments and passions, liberated from restrictions and hypocrisy, would be given free rein. Morris's message obviously had a strongly revolutionary and liberating tone in the context of late Victorian society, and exercised a considerable influence over a good portion of the generation of intellectuals active in the 1890s and 1900s. It is consequently not hard to see how Nietzsche's message would have fallen on fertile ground in England, especially among those same people who had already been influenced by Morris's school. What is more, this current of medievalizing socialism was still very lively before the First World War; its most significant accomplishment was undoubtedly the theory of "guild socialism", developed in part by Arthur J. Penty and in part by Orage himself in the pages of *The New Age*.[110]

Certain passages from the *Confessions* seem to confirm that Crowley drew inspiration from the same sources as this anti-modern movement, and that he shared at least some of its ideas. At one point he calls modern civilization "the greatest of all crimes" and evinces a nostalgia for the feudal system.[111] The echo of Morris's teachings regarding the alienation of labour in factories can be heard in a passage from the poem that prefaces *The World's Tragedy* (1910) – certainly the work that expresses Crowley's disdain for Victorian hypocrisy most forcefully:

To call forced labour slavery is rude,
"Terminologic inexactitude."
This from the masters of the winds and waves
Whose cotton-mills are crammed with British slaves![112]

Crowley's position concerning "modern civilization" was undoubtedly also influenced by his travel experiences. Many times he compared the simplicity and serenity of "less civilized" peoples to the situation of Europeans, particularly his English contemporaries, placing them at a clear disadvantage.[113]

The strongly critical attitude evinced by Crowley in his youthful works did not change significantly in the following years, until the outbreak of the First World War. The Celtic element in his works appeared to retreat, even if he continued to present himself as Irish on a few occasions,[114] but it reappeared again during wartime, while he was living in America.

We do not know what opinions Crowley held in the months preceding the war's beginning. There was a widespread feeling that the tension in Europe might at any moment erupt into conflict, although few people could have imagined its potential scope. The few clues we have available for guessing Crowley's position during those months do not allow us to form a clear picture. In August 1914, just as the war was beginning, the prestigious *English Review* published a curious series of poems under Crowley's name.[115] Crowley had been contributing for some time to this magazine, in which positive reviews of his works also appeared now and then. In a brief introduction, he declares that only one poet has ever really expressed the true nature of English patriotism: the unknown author of the popular refrain "We don't want to fight, but, by Jingo, if we do, / We've got the ships, we've got the men, we've got the money, too".[116] Crowley then speculates as to what the great English poets might have written, had they had similar patriotic inspiration. In the poems that follow, he rewrites the nationalist refrain in the style of Chaucer, Tennyson and others.[117] How should one interpret this kind of *divertissement*, in a time when war rhetoric was spreading throughout all of Europe and leaving less and less room for humour? Probably, once again, Crowley wished to exhibit his heretical and iconoclastic nature without taking up an explicit position.

However, in October 1914, as mentioned above, his earlier poem *An Appeal to the American Republic* was republished in a modified version in the same review.[118] Here, it appears, Crowley wished to appeal to a more serious and reserved patriotism, although it is significant that in order to do so, rather than writing something new, he resorted to a work composed fifteen years earlier. The possibility remains that this "patriotic" publication was connected to the attempts Crowley made – or so he later claimed, after the war – to enlist in the civil service, or the secret service, in order to fulfil his wartime duty to his country.[119] In all probability, his bad reputation, already established by now, caused the British authorities to reject his application.[120] Whatever the case may be, by the end of October Crowley was on the ship *Lusitania*, headed for the United States.

In Chapter 1 I went through the most significant moments in his American period. This time of his life is surely the most controversial. His involvement in spreading pro-German propaganda has been interpreted in various ways, and undoubtedly represents a sensitive question for both the biographer and the scholar. Interpretations of these events range from accusing him of treason to attempting to exonerate him.[121]

The main character in these events, besides Crowley himself, was George Sylvester Viereck, an American writer of German origin. At the time the war began, Viereck was an author, still young but already well established.[122] Born in Germany in 1884, the son of a socialist intellectual related to the Hohenzollern imperial family, Viereck had moved to the United States with his family in 1896. During his school years he had shown precocious intelligence and outstanding literary talent. In 1907 he published his first collection of poems, *Nineveh*, in which a strong influence of the English decadents can be seen, particularly Wilde and Swinburne. This book, which met with considerable success, marked the starting point of Viereck's short-lived literary fame. In the years before the First World War, critics unanimously considered him as one of the most fascinating and promising young authors in the American literary scene, but when the United States entered the war in 1917, his propagandist activity in Germany's favour sullied his reputation.

Between 1910 and 1915, Viereck took a number of journeys to Europe, during which he met with various intellectuals and writers, mostly English. On one of these voyages, in London in 1911, he met Crowley. Around this same time Viereck also re-established some connections in Germany, the land of his birth, and published a book of impressions gathered while travelling there: *Confessions of a Barbarian* (1910). Viereck's propagandist activity can be said to have commenced with this book, a few years before the start of the war. The purpose of his examination of the situation in Germany was to make the positive aspects of his fatherland known to the United States. When the war began, Viereck, seeing the positions taken by the major newspapers – largely in favour of the Allies, especially in larger cities – decided, along with a few friends, to devote himself to balancing out the situation. It should be said however that Viereck's activities during the war were far from being a purely romantic or idealistic enterprise. It is clear in fact that he was part of a larger network of activists clandestinely subsidized by Germany in order to influence American public opinion and also, occasionally, to conduct intelligence operations. It is precisely into this network that Crowley was introduced and became active through Viereck Viereck's instruments of action were primarily his two magazines: the weekly *The Fatherland*, founded by Viereck himself a few days after hostilities erupted; and the monthly *The International*, already well known as a literary review, for which he had worked before the war. These magazines were accompanied by highly intense political activity, mostly consisting of pamphlets and texts translated from German. This pro-German mobilization, it should be remembered, was necessitated by circumstances to identify with a neutral position, since it would have been entirely unrealistic to expect the United States to come over to the side of the Central Powers. This neutral pro-German position could also appear deceptively as an authentically patriotic position, since it aimed for the defence of American interests, which on the whole were distinct and divergent from European interests. This was essentially the strategy followed by the propaganda Viereck organized. The Irish – who were quite numerous and traditionally had little enthusiasm for any American rapprochement towards England – naturally formed one of the communities most receptive to pro-German activity. The bond thus formed between German and Irish communities in the United States mirrored the bond that was forming in Europe between the German government and the Irish nationalists, since they shared a common enemy: England.

This explains why Crowley's devotion to the Irish cause may have been a significant factor in his participation in Viereck's propagandist activity. In fact, when he moved to the United States after the start of the war, Crowley introduced himself to the local leaders of the Germanophile propaganda movement as a "Sinn Feiner", and was consequently invited to work with them, writing articles for their newspapers. This provides a context for certain provocative actions taken by Crowley, such as in July 1915, when he tore up his passport in front of the Statue of Liberty and proclaimed the independence of the "Irish Republic".[123]

In this period, Crowley wrote numerous articles of a political nature, which were mainly published in Viereck's two journals, *The Fatherland* and *The International*. Besides these, a few of his articles appeared in the periodical *The Open Court*, edited by the philosopher and writer Paul Carus (1852–1919). A complete list of the articles Crowley wrote during his years in America has not yet been compiled, in part because complete collections of the two journals are extremely difficult to find. The bibliography at the end of this book lists all the political articles by Crowley that I have been able to track down.

In the late 1940s, Symonds, while preparing to write his biography of Crowley, wrote to Viereck to request information about Crowley's pro-German activities. Viereck responded:

> I believe he said he was completely or partly Irish. There were many distinguished Irishmen who refused to go along with Great Britain, including Sir Roger Casement. There were also some Englishmen who as a matter of high principle opposed the war ... Consequently, it seemed highly likely that Crowley was sincere.[124]

Attempts have been made to connect Crowley's pro-German activities to his youthful obsessions, and to situate him within various groups of Britons who chose, for idealistic reasons, to oppose England's political choices during wartime. This was not an entirely new phenomenon in England's recent history, as is demonstrated by the internal opposition movement during the Boer War, mentioned earlier. This viewpoint, however, conflicts with what Crowley himself resolutely claimed after the war's end: namely, that his activity was not *against* the allied cause, but *in favour* of it, because the articles he wrote for the pro-German press were, in his view, so stupid and excessive that they could surely have only harmed Germany's image.[125] Actually, there are two factors at play here that seem almost mutually exclusive, to the point that Crowley appears to have been unable to provide a truly coherent reconstruction of these events. On the one hand there is his possible collaboration with the British secret service in order to provide information on pro-German circles in the United States, circles he certainly frequented; on the other hand there is the allegedly negative influence of his articles on Germanophile propaganda. These are two aspects best kept separate, even if they obviously form part of the same problem. One might in fact observe that if Crowley really was working for the British secret service and acting as a double agent in the German propaganda movement, it would have been in his interest to write things that made him seem legitimate to pro-German circles. Operating publicly, albeit paradoxically, *against* Germany's interests with these kinds of publications would seem to contradict the entire purpose of the operation. Moreover, it is hard to see what advantage stood to be gained from an activity whose hidden purpose was invisible to the average reader of the Germanophile press in America – a purpose which, in fact, could not be seen by anybody except Crowley himself.

Concerning the first question, new discoveries made by the American historian Richard B. Spence seem to confirm the theory of Crowley's involvement in English espionage in America during the war.[126] Spence has found documents from the time of the First World War in the archives of the US secret service, which seem to confirm Crowley's collaboration with British agencies active in America during that period.[127] Not being able to determine from these documents exactly with whom or for whom Crowley worked, Spence hypothesizes that he was probably in contact with a cell operating in America of MI1c (Military Intelligence, Section 1c), an English spying agency also known as the SIS (Secret Intelligence Service), which became MI6 after the war. This cell was led by Norman G. Thwaites and William Wiseman. During the war, this group often competed with agencies under the command of the Naval Intelligence Division (NID), headed by Guy Gaunt (a captain at the time), who later denied having had any dealings with Crowley, even accusing him of being simply a "small time traitor".[128] On the other hand, Crowley's biographer Lawrence Sutin argues that Crowley did indeed try to establish contact with the British secret service during his sojourn in America, but they did not accept his offer of collaboration.[129] Thus, even if Crowley did not draw much attention from English agencies, his frustrated attempts may still be sufficient reason not to consider him simply as a traitor.

As long as the documents in the British archives remain inaccessible to the public, it will most likely be impossible to clear up Crowley's role in these events once and for all. Even if one concludes that he actually collaborated with English agencies, the ambiguity of his publications and of his behaviour still remains. In this regard, his later defence of himself can be viewed as only partially valid, essentially for two reasons. First, because the politically oriented articles he wrote during this period were nowhere near as stupid as Crowley would have us believe. A few of them were – as Lawrence Sutin, among others, has pointed out – a little over the top, but in general they were serious articles, with arguments that were at times paradoxical but nonetheless coherent and possibly convincing.[130] Moreover, Viereck, like most of the people working with him for the German cause in America, was by no means naïve, and knew his profession well. He would have immediately noticed any kind of false tone in Crowley's articles. After reading them, one has to admit that whatever Crowley's intention may have been, he did a fine job of serving the German – or rather anti-British – cause.

Second, Crowley's version of the story might be acceptable had he not written the other works that we examined earlier, during the fifteen years preceding the war. In fact, the position Crowley expressed in his wartime articles represented a development that was completely consistent with everything he had written and claimed for years. Had this not been the case, Viereck – who had met him in England in 1911 and was presumably familiar with what he had written before – would not have asked him to contribute to his journals. For Crowley's defence to be credible, we would have to believe that his reason for calling himself Irish and predicting England's ruin as early as 1900 was specifically to enable himself, fifteen years later, to infiltrate the German propaganda movement during the First World War. This would be a truly extraordinary case of far-sightedness, and even Crowley, despite his confidence in his magical powers, does not ask us to believe in such a prodigy, preferring to sweep his earlier writings under the rug and be silent about them.

These events present what is probably the most obvious example of Crowley's inconsistency in matters of politics, an inconsistency we continue to find, to a lesser degree, for the rest of his life. As we have seen, Ireland and the Celtic world held an attraction for him long before the start of the war. Likewise, a certain level of patriotic chauvinism, or "jingoism", can also be seen in him even during his adolescence. Therefore, it seems reasonable to believe that there was some sincerity in his pro-Irish undertakings during the war, and a great deal of insincerity in his post-war explanation of his pro-German activities. And there is also another factor that should not be underestimated. As I mentioned earlier, Crowley reported – and we have no reason to doubt this part of his story – that at the beginning of the war, his offer of collaboration was refused by the English authorities. Even during the war, it is likely that his collaboration, if it was of any use at all, did not have the significance Crowley tried to attribute to it. It is thus probable that his behaviour during those years was also motivated by pride. Crowley was certainly someone inclined to spite, and he had a tendency to hold grudges for many years against those who wronged him.

Be that as it may, Crowley stuck to his version of the story unwaveringly for years after the war. Indeed, he endeavoured to present himself as a martyr, since his reputation – to be fair, not really immaculate even before the war – had been severely damaged due to his activities: "My conscience was clear. I had been loyal to England. I had suffered for her sake as much as any man."[131] The conclusion we may draw from all this is that Crowley probably wavered from one position to the other during the course of the war. When he landed in New York, in October 1914, he had reasons, coming from both his personal story and his psychology, to be immune from those patriotic feelings that were spreading among many of his fellow countrymen back home. At least to some extent, he was being sincere when he was presenting himself as an Irishman full of resentment towards England, or as a supporter of fair play towards Germany. On the other hand, there was also another voice calling in his mind, a voice that was never completely silent in his life but that probably became more and more audible as the war went on and the intervention of the United States became more and more likely. This was the equally romantic, but dissonant voice of a loyal subject of the Empire. It is probably following the call of this voice that he made his clumsy, mostly ineffective, but repeated attempts at being of use to the British services operating in the US. Furthermore, it cannot be entirely excluded that Crowley enjoyed being involved in such a duplicitous game also for the pure sake of it. As he himself acknowledged on several occasions, and as I have also pointed out at the beginning of this chapter, it was natural for him to look at things from different perspectives at the same time, and very probably this could motivate his behaviour at an even deeper level than ideology or high-brow politics. The conclusion is that, as with many other episodes in Crowley's life, it is impossible to have a simplistic view of the events, and any interpretation of his actions as following a strictly coherent design will never be entirely convincing.

Crowley's attempt at self-justification after the war is probably also an indication of his transition from one phase of his life to another; that is, from the "romantic" phase to a "pragmatic" one. The young Crowley might have claimed that he saw no reason to justify himself, and that his homeland did not deserve his loyalty in any case. In his American articles, it was fundamentally not the victory of Germany that he championed, but rather the end of the qualities he had always detested in England. Why should he defend himself when most of his earlier works did nothing more than express the same thing? But now there was a new priority on his agenda: the diffusion throughout the world of his new "Revelation", the message of *The Book of the Law*. For this purpose, his justification, which defended a part of himself but disavowed another one, might have been necessary.

The Book of the Law

Obviously, discussing Crowley's religious message, which became synonymous with his entire personality after the First World War, also means discussing *The Book of the Law*, the text upon which this message was primarily founded. In what ways can this part of Crowley's work and intellectual legacy be revealing for our analysis?

Regardie has rightly pointed out the anti-democratic and elitist implications of *The Book of the Law*.[132] According to Regardie, in *The Book of the Law*, "there is no room … for democracy, nor the respect for the ordinary man".[133] Crowley always claimed that he was not the book's true author, and that it therefore did not necessarily reflect his personal opinions. But Regardie, although not wishing to debate the "authenticity" of Crowley's role as a medium, has shown that the concepts expressed in the book are perfectly compatible with the ideas Crowley expressed throughout his life.[134] It is true that various common elements can be seen clearly enough in the text: the anti-Christian attitude, the advocacy of sexual freedom, the elitist views.[135] But its "inspired" quality and its oracular style lend themselves to different modes of interpretation, and it might be possible to find ideas in this book that do not necessarily correspond to the ideas that Crowley consciously held. Therefore, it seems to me more worthwhile and interesting to have a close look at the commentaries on *The Book of the Law* that Crowley himself wrote, more than at the text of the book itself. These commentaries certainly express Crowley's personal, conscious views. It should also be remembered that they were mostly written in the years following the end of the First World War, especially during Crowley's period in Cefalù and his subsequent "exile" in Tunisia.[136] This was certainly a difficult time, both for Crowley and, socially and politically, for the greater part of Europe.

For the purposes of the present study, the most striking aspect of these commentaries is an attack on bourgeois values, which are naturally identified with Christianity. Considering the course taken by the young Crowley in his intellectual development, this is certainly no surprise. A letter he wrote to his friend Gerald Kelly in 1905 – to which Regardie rightly draws attention – also confirms that this element is not a projection by the Crowley of the 1920s onto the text of *The Book of the Law*, but rather something that was already well defined in him when the book was written. In this letter, Crowley declares that he has seen enough "weakness", "miscalled politeness" and "care for the feeling of others", and now wants only "blasphemy, murder, rape, revolution, anything, bad or good, but strong".[137]

Two elements are particularly interesting for us here: the question of new Thelemic ethics, as opposed to Christian and bourgeois ethics; and the question of individualism.

The first element is primarily centred around the question of sexual freedom.[138] Crowley inveighs against the "bourgeois" (i.e. Christian) concept of sexuality, and above all against marriage. All people must be allowed to pursue their own sexuality freely, without rules imposed from the outside, exclusively on the basis of their own inclinations. In this domain, absolute and unconditional individual liberty must reign. Compassion and humanitarianism (described as "the syphilis of the mind") are part of the bourgeois ethic, and must be radically eliminated.[139] In this regard, one can sense Nietzsche's influence, and indeed he is expressly cited.[140] A strong component of social Darwinism is also perceptible, very probably absorbed by Crowley during his years of study at Cambridge. The various references to the "weak", who must be exterminated by the "strong", and towards whom no compassion must be shown, are highly significant. And among the authors Crowley refers to in his commentaries we find Herbert Spencer (1820–1903), the most influential proponent of social Darwinism in England, specifically in connection with the "unfit".[141] Although ideas of this kind today are almost entirely restricted to neo-Nazi movements, in those days – especially before the First World War – they were fairly widespread among various groups, especially in progressive and leftist circles. Perfectly in line with this theory, Crowley claims that the dominance of the stronger over the weaker is not so much an ethical question as a biological one. Nature has her own rules, and humanitarian sentimentalism cannot be used for changing them, indeed it can only hinder us in seeing and understanding them. There was a time when natural selection was able to act undisturbed, and "the race, as such, consequently improved".[142] But then Christianity overturned this equilibrium, and "the unfit crowded and contaminated the fit".[143] This has been made even worse in recent times thanks to the propagation of an image of Jesus as "the pacifist, the conscientious objector, the Tolstoyian, the passive resister", put forward as a model for life.[144]

For this reason, the struggle against Christianity must be radical and merciless; no compromises can be made. Crowley then wonders whether it would not be better to directly exterminate the Christians, whom he calls "parasites of man", and also the Jews, who fundamentally belong to the same religious stock.[145] These are obviously paradoxical declarations, and it may be hard to believe that Crowley literally meant what he was saying. But they make a grim impression on a contemporary reader, who is aware of the horrors that were being prepared by totalitarian regimes in the same period as these words were written. Horrors that came to their final point of achievement a few years later in the Second World War. In any case, these passages show the clear presence of a radical component in Crowley's thought, and take on even further meaning when compared to Crowley's opinions about Nazi Germany and Soviet Russia, as we will see in the following sections and in the next chapter.

Conflicting with this idea is another that we might define as absolute individualism: "Every man and every woman is a star."[146] For Crowley, this means that every person has a personal orbit, his "True Will", which distinguishes him from all others and whose path he must follow.[147] This form of absolute individualism, which finds its ultimate basis in the verses of *The Book of the Law*, is surely one of the most characterizing aspects of Thelema. Even in his last years, Crowley strongly reaffirmed its importance through the release of his famous *Liber OZ* (or *Liber LXXVI*), which was meant to act as a Thelemic declaration of the "Rights of Man".[148] Man is proclaimed to possess the right to live, eat, think and love "as he will", each of these basic rights including particular cases that are further specified in the text. But that is not all: at the end, there is also "the right to kill those who would thwart these rights", a passage that, understandably, has become the source of some concern for contemporary Thelemites.[149]

It would be easy to interpret this aspect of Thelema from a purely anarchist or libertarian perspective, and probably this is how most readers, including Thelemites, would see it today. Things however are not so simple. Following one's own "True Will", in fact, is clearly understood by Crowley within the framework of an organicist vision, which seems to be difficult to reconcile with an idea of unlimited freedom. Quite the contrary: this vision could be easily seen as compatible with a totalitarian ideology. This is a very important point, because it explains why Crowley, despite the apparent radical individualism of Thelema, could look at contemporary totalitarian ideologies and regimes not with horror and downright rejection, as one might have expected, but with interest, or even a certain degree of fascination. Crowley's organicist interpretation of Thelema is quite evident: individuals are presented as being analogous to the parts of a greater organism.[150] The organism stays alive as long as each part performs the function assigned to it. The individual parts do not need to be happy about their roles; the important thing is that they keep performing them without rebelling.[151] Now, how can this be reconciled with the idea that every person "has the right" to do everything, in all domains, "as he will"?[152] All things naturally revolve around this idea of "right". In fact, the question of the relationship between "True Will" and free choice remains ambiguous: how can we know, at any given moment, that what we are doing coincides with our "True Will" and that we are not "rebelling" against the functions assigned to us? Obviously, only he who reaches the highest point of the initiatory journey, the "Great Work", can obtain transparent knowledge of the trajectory of his will. But for the others, whose eyes remain closed, the distinction between true will and false will remains unavoidably opaque. What is certain is that "democracy", with its "cant", is not the political regime prescribed by Thelema: "It is useless to pretend that men are equal; facts are against it".[153] Therefore there is a distinction between the "mob", who are not yet free from their prejudices, and the "aristocrats of Freedom", the "chosen".[154] It is not clear whether or not the "chosen" should aid the "mob" in freeing themselves from their condition. In one passage, Crowley states that since each one of us "is a star", the "chosen" must fight to "free" those who are not yet masters of themselves, and help them to attain the same state as the "chosen".[155] But in another passage, he also states that one must "stop meddling" in the affairs of others, and that "each individual must be left free to follow his own path".[156]

These ideas also resurface, more or less unchanged, in his later works, such as *Magick without Tears*, in which Crowley dwells in many passages upon the possible political significance of *The Book of the Law*. He states for instance that the "nauseating cult of weakness", namely democracy, is "utterly false and vile".[157] Also, equality between men is nothing but an illusion: "The Book announces a new dichotomy in human society; there is the master and there is the slave; the noble and the serf; the "lone wolf" and the herd."[158]

The anti-democratic radicalism that seems to emerge from *The Book of the Law*, and even more from Crowley's commentaries on it, has led some authors to define Crowley as a "conservative revolutionary".[159] This definition has the advantage of transcending the familiar categories of "right" and "left", which are fundamentally of little use in Crowley's case. In recent times, the label of conservative revolutionary has been applied often enough to authors and milieus that were actually not explicitly linked to this historical current, fairly heterogeneous in itself, which developed in Germany between the wars.[160]

But in what sense can one speak of Crowley as a "conservative revolutionary"? Although he lived in Germany in the early 1930s, he certainly never had any contact with the actual historical figures of this movement, such as Arthur Moeller Van den Bruck, Ernst Jünger or Ernst Von Salomon. And yet, Crowley himself seems to invite an interpretation of this type in passages from his writings, both private and public. For instance, already in 1917, Crowley reflects in his diary on the inner conflict between his "socialistic, anarchistic brain" and his "aristocrat's heart".[161] Many years later, towards the end of his life, he writes in *Magick without Tears*: "You will observe that I am advocating an aristocratic revolution. And so I am!"[162] Similarly, in a letter to John Symonds from 25 June 1946, he describes his system as "aristocratic communism".[163] Crowley was obviously trying to find an original formula, based on a kind of "third way" idea, to describe his movement; this makes it possible to categorize him within an extended notion of the Conservative Revolution.

Political radicalism and totalitarian regimes

I have already drawn attention to the kind of reading and interpretation Crowley gave to historical events. Starting at a certain moment, history is identified with the necessity for revelation and universal spreading of Thelema. This vision already appears in Crowley in connection with the causes of the First World War. In his novel *Moonchild*, written between the summer and autumn of 1916, the conviction emerges that a war of such proportions is necessary in order for the new religious message to get across. In one scene in the novel, the good magician Cyril Grey and the wise Simon Iff – both obviously alter egos of Crowley himself – discuss the war that has just begun. Grey asks Iff what, in his opinion, are the true reasons for the conflict, and Iff, revealing himself as one who carries a secret responsibility for its outbreak, answers:

> The people think it's about the violation of solemn treaties, and the rights of the little nations, and so on; the governments think it's about commercial expansion; but I who made it know that it is the baptism of blood of the New Aeon. How could we promulgate the Law of Liberty in a world where Freedom has been strangled by industrialism?[164]

The massacres and bloodbaths that take place appear therefore to be a necessary step for achieving the liberation of humanity through Thelema. The blood will forge a new kind of human being, eliminating the bourgeois chaff. Iff explains what effect the war will have on the young veterans:

> When those men come back from a few years in the trenches, they'll make short work of the pious person that informs them of the wickedness of smoking, and eating meat, and drinking beer, and being out after eleven o'clock at night, and kissing a girl, and reading novels, and playing cards, and going to the theatre, and whistling on the Sabbath! ... All Europe will be scream and stench for years to come. But the new generation will fear neither poverty nor death. They will fear weakness; they will fear dishonour.[165]

In light of this passage and what has been said in the preceding paragraphs, it is no surprise that Crowley was curious about, indeed fascinated by, the rise of radical politics and totalitarian regimes during the period between the wars. The identity of these regimes, in part, was founded upon the experiences of a generation that had fought in the front lines of the First World War.

We can now understand the significance that the emergence of this new phenomenon on Europe's political scene may have had from Crowley's point of view. He felt himself attracted to the radicalism of totalitarian ideologies principally for two reasons. The first was the one I have defined as "pragmatic". Crowley believed that if it was humanity's destiny to accept the message of Thelema as a new religion, this result could be achieved more quickly by a movement capable of reaching the masses in sufficient number. But there was also a second, more profound reason. At certain times, Crowley appears to have been inclined to believe that his message was in some ways akin to that of Nazism and Bolshevism, despite their differences. The brutality and violence of radical political movements and totalitarian regimes, in fact, matched well with the spirit of the New Aeon of Horus, the falcon-headed warrior god, and corresponded much better to certain passages of *The Book of the Law* than the liberal-democratic tradition, rather representing the despised bourgeois mentality. Moreover, these radical political movements were "new", just as the Aeon of Horus was new.

Of course, this does not mean that Crowley ever considered joining any of the political movements inspired by such ideologies. From his point of view, the current of the New Aeon was to be the driving force behind everything else, and therefore all political movements would ultimately have to submit to Thelema – not the other way round. In their exclusively political dimensions, they were missing something essential, and Crowley was ready to fill this gap.

He was fascinated at first with Italian fascism. As we saw in Chapter 1, he happened to be in Rome in October 1922 when the fascists marched on the city, and he was in Italy – in Cefalù – during the regime's early phase. He was therefore able to observe the phenomenon directly. In *The Confessions*, Crowley writes on this subject:

> For some time I had interested myself in Fascismo which I regarded with entire sympathy even excluding its illegitimacy on the ground that constitutional authority had become to all intents and purposes a dead letter. I was delighted with the common sense of its programme and was especially pleased by its attitude towards the Church.[166]

The politics of early fascism, still relatively linked to certain republican and socialist ideas at the time, was largely anti-clerical. This could only draw admiration from Crowley, who was ready to stand by any form of anti-clerical politics. Without doubt, it was above all his expulsion from Italy in 1923 that caused him to drastically change his idea of fascism and, as we shall see in Chapter 5, prompted him to write satirical poems against Mussolini. But we must also consider the fact that Crowley probably did not particularly appreciate the friendly overtures toward the Vatican that Mussolini hastened to make even prior to the March on Rome, and subsequently intensified. Crowley in fact makes reference to this, accusing Mussolini of having "almost at once" bowed beneath the pressures of the Church, and of having to "sell his soul to the Vatican".[167]

Similar observations could be made regarding the political situation in Spain one decade later, namely General Francisco Franco's revolt in 1936 and the subsequent Spanish Civil War. In June 1937, a group of intellectuals and artists, including the English poets Stephen Spender and W. H. Auden, the Chilean poet Pablo Neruda and the founder of the Dada movement, Tristan Tzara, decided to distribute among the writers and poets of Great Britain a text urging them to take a position regarding the war that was then raging in Spain. As one might imagine, the promoters' position was clearly hostile toward Franco and the insurgents, but the main idea was to prompt the greatest names in British culture at the time to express and justify their opinions, whatever they might be. The result was a strange publication, *Authors Take Sides on the Spanish War*, in which 148 British authors responded, in very diverse ways, to the demand put forward by the promoters of this initiative.[168] Among them were some very famous names, such as George Bernard Shaw, H. G. Wells, Aldous Huxley, Ezra Pound and T. S. Eliot – and also our very own Aleister Crowley, who was surely brought into the initiative by Nancy Cunard (1896–1965), an heiress from a ship-owning family who had connections in English literary avant-garde circles and was a friend (though not a disciple) of Crowley's.[169] In the booklet, the responses of the various authors were divided into three sections: in favour of the republican government (and thus against Franco), neutral, and in favour of Franco. Crowley appears in the first group, and therefore in the company of a good number of English left-wing intellectuals of the epoch. Even in that context, he did not see it fit to renounce his habitual Thelemic salutation: "Do What Thou Wilt shall be the whole of the Law. Franco is a common murderer and pirate: should swing in chains at Execution Dock. Mussolini, the secret assassin, possibly worse. Hitler may prove a "prophet"; time will judge. Love is the law, love under will."[170]

It seems obvious that, in Crowley's judgement, Franco represented a violently reactionary political and military power whose aim was, among other things, to restore the traditional values of Catholicism. In conservative circles there was a widespread idea that Spain's secular and republican government had put these values in jeopardy, but, in the eyes of the Crowley of the 1930s, this might hardly be a valid justification for causing a civil war. How distant this was from the young romantic Crowley involved in Carlist schemes! In conclusion, Franco could logically only merit the same harsh judgement given for Mussolini. But it is hard to oversee Crowley's enigmatic and potentially positive judgement of Hitler, a point that deserves a more elaborate discussion.

There is a clear contrast between Crowley's stern attitude towards the Catholic fascisms of Mussolini and Franco and his fascination with the Nazi regime of Germany and the communist regime of the Soviet Union. What Crowley liked about Nazism and communism, or at least what made him curious about them, was the anti-Christian position and the revolutionary and socially subversive implications of these two movements. In their subversive powers, he saw the possibility of an annihilation of old religious traditions, and the creation of a void that Thelema, subsequently, would be able to fill. All in all, Crowley seems to have perceived Nazism and communism as two possible, though unconscious, allies.

Moreover, at a time when Crowley considered himself as a "newcomer" in the religious field, he must have felt it only natural to ally himself with those who, for better or worse, were the "newcomers" in the political and social field, whether they be communist or Nazi. Both sides proposed radical and ambitious projects, planning for the construction of the new by way of the violent, though unavoidable, destruction of the old. This explains why Crowley, whose youthful reactionary attitudes and anti-materialism should have made him a born anti-communist, still fostered some degree of sympathy for the Bolshevik revolution. Here we can also see the pragmatic side of his personality. For him, ideology was of limited importance: what he really needed was the best means for propagating Thelema. In the two regimes – especially in their aggressive attitude toward Christianity – he perceived an element of affinity with the new spiritual movement he championed. And these were regimes that held the destiny of millions of people in their hands. He thought he should at least try to convince the leaders of the two totalitarian regimes to adopt *The Book of the Law* as a guiding text in their respective countries. In Chapter 3, I will explore some of the developments of Crowley's interest in communism and the Soviet Union. Here, on the other hand, I will rather focus on the question of Nazism. For the moment, however, I will leave aside the hypotheses – leading back to René Guénon – of Crowley as a secret adviser to Hitler. These hypotheses have found particular resonance in what we may call the literature of "Nazi occultism", beginning in 1960 with the famous book *Le matin des magiciens*, by Louis Pauwels and Jacques Bergier.[171] I will return to this point in Chapter 4, but I may anticipate by saying that, to my knowledge, there is no concrete evidence of Crowley's direct connection to the Nazi movement or regime.

The fantasist nature of Nazi–occultist reconstructions has provoked a reaction that might be termed excessive. One example is Christian Bouchet, who not only denies any direct contact between Crowley and the Nazi regime – reasonably enough – but also denies any interest on the part of Crowley in the Nazi phenomenon, which is clearly inaccurate.[172] It is known, for example, that in 1930 Crowley wrote a letter to his former collaborator and disciple J. F. C. Fuller on the subject of Nazism and Hitler.[173] As we have seen, Crowley was living in Berlin at the time, and he would spend long periods there at least until 1932. He therefore would have been in a position to observe first-hand the political developments that led up to Hitler's rise to power in 1933.

There is a letter preserved at the Warburg Institute, dated 20 January 1936, from Crowley to Oskar Hopfer (1894–1966), a friend of Karl Germer's and a member of his group of German disciples.[174] From this letter, we learn that Crowley had the idea of directly contacting Hitler to propose that he use the doctrine of Thelema to guide his party:

> It seems to me that under the present circumstances, if I understand them aright, the only means of propaganda is to address the Leader himself (Hitler. T) [note added by the typist, i.e. Kenneth Grant] and show him that the acceptance of these philosophical principles [i.e. Thelema] is the only means of demonstrating to reason instead of merely to enthusiasm, the propriety of the measures he is taking for the rebuilding of the Reich. Unless he does this the Churches will ultimately strangle him; they have an almost infinite capacity for resistance and endurance for this very reason that their systems are based on a fundamental theory which enabled them to survive attacks and restraints. They bow as much as they are compelled to bow to force and they subsequently excuse their yielding on the grounds of expediency. If the Führer wishes to establish his principle permanently he must uproot them entirely and this can only be done by superseding their deepest conceptions.[175]

This was not a fleeting idea of Crowley's, as is shown by the fact that in July 1936, after a brief correspondence,[176] he met with Viereck in London during one of the latter's frequent voyages to Europe.[177] By this time Viereck had already begun publicly showing his sympathy for Nazism; he defended it doggedly until the United States entered the war against the Axis powers in 1941. A kind of irresistible impulse seems to have led Viereck, in his adopted country, to play the same role of implacable defender and propagandist for Germany that he played during the First World War. After his stay in London, he would travel on to Germany, where he would surely have met with some representatives of the Nazi regime. Crowley would not have wanted to pass up this opportunity. It is likely that when they met, the two men discussed the political situation and Crowley tried to sound out what level of respect Viereck commanded in the Nazi hierarchy. The day after their meeting, Crowley wrote a letter to Viereck in which he got right to the point, discussing the potential fruitfulness of Viereck's visit to Germany for the diffusion of Thelema.[178] Crowley mentioned a "colleague" of his in Germany (probably his disciple Martha Küntzel), who had already tried to promote *The Book of the Law* to Hitler as a philosophical basis for Nazism. He requested that Viereck aid these endeavours using his contacts in the party, who, judging by what Crowley wrote, may have included the Führer himself. Crowley also asked Viereck to make it clear that he was the head of an "International Secret Order", which is a bit surprising, because this would have made him highly suspect to the Nazi authorities.[179] As Sutin points out, there is no reason to believe that Viereck took Crowley's request seriously and used his influence in the higher ranks of the party – if he ever had any influence – to serve Crowley's propagandist goals. But it is clear that Crowley, who in any case had little to lose in attempts of this kind, seemed to believe seriously in their possibility of success.

In Chapter 3 I will examine a letter that is similar to the ones just discussed, but which was written to a correspondent in the Soviet Union. In the letter to Hopfer – and this is an element that also recurs in other letters, as we will see – the theme of the eradication of Christianity is dominant. Understandably, for Crowley this was the indispensable condition for the worldwide diffusion of his revelation. It is not hard to imagine the results of these efforts. The leaders of the Nazi and Soviet regimes had other concerns than the diffusion of Thelema, and it is highly improbable that they even heard of it. But Crowley, at least with regard to the Nazi regime, was convinced of the contrary.

Some interesting references on this subject can be found in *Magick without Tears*. We should remember that this book was written during the final years of Crowley's life, and some parts of it were written even after the end of the Second World War.[180] From two passages in this book, we learn that Crowley was convinced of having influenced Hitler.[181] According to his version of the story, Martha Küntzel, his aforementioned German disciple and a fervent admirer of Hitler, believed that Nazism was compatible with Thelema and contacted the Führer in order to acquaint him with *The Book of the Law*. Crowley adds that Küntzel viewed Hitler as her "magical son".[182] According to him, Hitler actually adopted *The Book of the Law*, and this was the reason for his initial success. Crowley then proceeds (it should be noted that the book is written in epistolary form, and he is addressing an anonymous female disciple): "I think you have read *Hitler speaks* – if not, do so – his private conversation abounds in what sound almost like actual quotations from *The Book of the Law*."[183]

Hitler Speaks was the English title of a very famous and controversial book by Hermann Rauschning (1887–1982).[184] Rauschning, during the early 1930s, had been president of the senate of the Free City of Danzig and a member of the Nazi party. He was one of a large group of German conservatives who had seen Nazism as a tool for reforming German foreign politics and restoring Germany's status as a great power, while at the same time putting a stop to the spread of communism. When it became clear – and undoubtedly clearer to Rauschning than to many others – that Nazism had no intention of playing the role of a simple tool, but rather was an extremely ambitious, autonomous and radically revolutionary force, he began to distance himself from the party, and finally left it in 1934. Soon afterwards he emigrated to France, where he began denouncing the danger that Nazism represented for Europe and the West. And it was in France, in 1939, that he published the first version, in French, of *Hitler Speaks*.

For decades after the war Rauschning's book was accepted as a reliable source on the historiography of Nazism – until the publication in 1984 of a study by a Swiss scholar, Wolfgang Hänel, which reconstructed the scene behind the writing of the book and proved that some statements in it could not possibly be true.[185] Rauschning's book was thereafter considered to be a "fake", or rather the result of a propaganda operation, and lost its credibility as a source regarding Hitler's personality and ideas. However, the book still holds a certain interest for the scholar, at least as one of the main sources from which the mythology of "Nazi occultism" developed after the end of the Second World War.[186] It is in Rauschning's book that the image of a Hitler gifted with a medium's skills and possessing occult and demonic powers first begins to take shape. In the book one continually encounters terms such as "initiate", "magic", "occult" and "esoteric". This terminology was most probably used by Rauschning in order to make the book more exciting and more effective as a propaganda weapon, considering that this was the essential purpose of the publication.[187] Those who read the book at the time it was published, however, might well have perceived it as containing the hidden, "esoteric" doctrine of Hitler and Nazism, which appeared to be quite different and much more disturbing than the official one. All evidence seems to indicate that this was the way in which Crowley himself read *Hitler Speaks*. Consequently, the fact that this book is not considered as a reliable source for historical research today is of secondary importance here. What matters is not whether Rauschning's statements are reliable, but rather how they were perceived by those who read the book shortly after its publication and before the war's end.

Crowley, in fact, based his conviction that he had indirectly influenced Hitler on his reading of Rauschning's book. In the Yorke Collection there is a copy of *Hitler Speaks* that includes Crowley's reading notes as transcribed by Gerald Yorke.[188] In several instances, Crowley tries to connect passages of *The Book of the Law* to various statements made by Hitler in the book, as reported by Rauschning. For example, Rauschning relates that when the Nazi party gained power, those in upper management ordered their semi-official functionaries to occupy all available positions in the administration, and to take the best advantage possible of the power thus acquired: "Enjoy life and enrich yourselves."[189] Next to this passage, Crowley makes reference to a passage from *The Book of the Law* which reads: "Ye shall wear rich jewels; ye shall exceed the nations of the earth in splendour and pride."[190] In other cases, Crowley sees the connection as an opportunity to criticize Hitler for his insufficient understanding of Thelema.

In a passage where Hitler says "Do anything you like", Crowley writes: "This is where he interpreted AL [i.e. *The Book of the Law*] wrongly".[191] Crowley obviously means that if the Führer had read the sacred book of Thelema more attentively, he would have understood that there is a fundamental difference between a passing, whimsical desire and one's True Will.

Given Crowley's commentaries on *The Book of the Law* discussed above, it is no surprise to learn that he found numerous concordances between Rauschning's Hitler and his own text. But the similarity is easy to explain. Rauschning's Hitler – in many ways not very different from the real Hitler – has a deeply Nietzschean and social Darwinist mind, elements that we also find both in *The Book of Law* and in Crowley's commentaries.

Symonds – this time correctly – dismisses as "nonsense" the idea that Hitler might have known of the revelation of the New Aeon and might have taken it into consideration.[192] But Küntzel was certainly an enthusiastic follower of both Thelema and Nazism. In a letter to Crowley from November 1935 (the same year in which Germer was arrested), she makes no secret of her Nazi convictions.[193] This letter is particularly interesting in that it reveals Küntzel's delicate situation. On the one hand, she felt it her duty to explain her political beliefs to Crowley; on the other hand, the Gestapo had begun to take an interest in her because of her spiritual beliefs and her connection to the notorious English occultist. When she was interrogated by agents (who "expressed their astonishment" at the fact that she was "such a staunch National Socialist" while also being linked to Crowley), she apparently tried to explain why the philosophy of Thelema and the Third Reich could be considered as perfectly compatible. She was "firmly convinced of that Book's [i.e. of *The Book of the Law's*] immeasurable value", and explained that she believed "it would be left to the coming generation to understand it fully", because it "will be better prepared in their minds".[194] But according to her, the mental revolution that the understanding of the new Law would bring to humanity, leading also to a great step forward on the path of evolution, had been set in motion by Adolf Hitler, "the man chosen by Providence, because he was the Only [sic] one who possessed the qualities for this Great Work".[195] Moreover, in Küntzel's view, Crowley had been chosen to play a role of no lesser importance: "In the same way the Master Therion has been chosen by Providence to proclaim a Law which has for its aim the spiritual awakening of mankind, because he was the proper human instrument for Providence at the turn of the Aeon."[196]

The letter is certainly an important document for understanding how Crowley's doctrine might be interpreted in a specific historical context. But despite Küntzel's political and religious fervour, there is no direct evidence of her having ever attempted to make *The Book of the Law* known directly to Hitler. Moreover, in another letter to Crowley, unfortunately without a date (but probably written just before the war's outbreak), Küntzel laments ever having considered Hitler as her "magical son".[197] In this letter, she also confirms her double faithfulness to Nazism and Thelema, which she continues to see as perfectly compatible. Unfortunately, the Nazi regime was not of the same opinion, and treated the OTO like all the other occultist groups which, after various attacks and intimidations, were definitively declared illegal in 1937.

Thus Crowley sought to promote Thelema to the leaders of the Nazi party, and believed himself, *a posteriori*, to have exercised a certain influence over Hitler. The rise and fall of Nazism clearly held a certain fascination for Crowley. Should we conclude that this fascination translated into a clear political adherence? Things are not so simple, and the answer to the question, if posed in these terms, must be no, principally for two reasons. First and foremost, Crowley made similar attempts to persuade other political regimes to adopt Thelema, which indicates an absence of a clear ideological motivation behind these political stances. I have already mentioned his interest in Soviet Russia and communism and I shall return to this in Chapter 3. But as Sutin observed, the paradoxical aspect of these attempts is that he did not focus solely upon totalitarian regimes or radical political movements.[198] Crowley, in this same period, also sought to promote Thelema to the government of Great Britain, in this case appealing to the "principles of Liberty on which the greatness of our country has been founded".[199] Crowley, moved by his missionary spirit, was capable of emphasizing whatever aspects of Thelema were best suited to the particular situation. In addition, despite his fantasy of playing the role of "official" prophet to Nazi Germany, Crowley's patriotism had also revived, even before the start of the Second World War, and he had expressed ever-increasing reservations about Hitler and Nazism, even reaching the point of a clear and explicit condemnation of them.

This is particularly obvious, for example, in his correspondence with Germer, who, despite his experiences in a Nazi concentration camp, repeatedly tried to defend Germany's position against that of the allied powers, while international tension was growing and the situation was heading ever more rapidly toward war.[200] Crowley, as we have seen in his enigmatic response to the questionnaire on the Spanish Civil War, was possibly disposed to concede to Hitler a certain "prophetic" quality: "Of course, I have always considered [Hitler] a prophet in the Old Testament sense of the word, a more or less inspired madman who brings about the things that he prophecies [sic], or desires, by exciting mass-hysteria."[201]

Thus, according to Crowley, Hitler's "prophetic" power, though indeed existent, was dangerously close to insanity. In fact, Crowley also objected to Germer's observations, saying that they neglected a fundamental point: namely, "that a furious madman is upsetting the whole machine".[202] Contrary to Germer, according to whom Hitler had at least the merit of having overturned the Treaty of Versailles, Crowley believed that the Führer would bring nothing good to Germany: "On the contrary, ... he has destroyed all the cash and credit that remained, and has thoroughly alarmed France, England, and America".[203] Crowley observed – rightly enough – that this had led Europe into an arms race whose logical consequence could only be war. Naturally, Crowley interpreted Hitler's role in the imminent catastrophe as the direct result of the epochal passage brought about by the revolution of Thelema: "the whole thing is a function of the New Aeon".[204] In his letters to Germer, we also find the idea of the incorrect interpretation of Thelema by Hitler, to which Germer seems to have alluded in a previous letter: "H[itler] is making slaves to rule slaves. There is no room for any star in his system. His cosmos is based on the false unity of the "state" which is like Daath, not on the Tree at all. He denies individual supremacy of Godhead, and he and his will crash."[205]

Crowley's references to the philosophy of Thelema are fairly transparent here. The first sentence refers to verse II, 58 of *The Book of the Law*, in which the Thelemites are likened to kings who exercise their power over those who are not able or willing to elevate themselves from their condition of slaves.[206] According to Crowley, Nazism reduces everyone to the role of a slave. Even those who are in positions of command are subject to this condition, obviously because they are placed in a pyramid with a single man at its peak who concentrates most of the power in his hands. Moreover, according to Crowley, the implicit individualism of Thelema, represented by the maxim "Every man and every woman is a star" taken from *The Book of the Law*,[207] is incompatible with the statist, totalitarian collectivism of the Nazi regime.

This growing impatience with Nazism and Hitler seems eventually to have caused the end of Crowley's relationship with Küntzel. In one of his last letters to her, from 10 May 1939, Crowley reacts to her anti-Semitic observations by saying that her "ravings against the Jews" are "unintelligible". The following passage must have been quite shocking to Küntzel, as was doubtlessly Crowley's intent:

> Almost the whole of life in Germany above brutality, stupidity and cruelty, servility and bloodthirst, was Jewish. Germans are as far below Jews, generally speaking, as monkeys below men; but I have always been fond of monkeys and I do not want to offend them by comparing any German to one. These remarks, stated in comparatively direct language, are intended to express the general feeling of people outside Germany. There will be no second Versailles – there will be Armageddon. The Hun must be wiped out. The Hun will be wiped out.[208]

We do not know whether Küntzel ever replied to this letter. Symonds cites another letter from Crowley, probably the last, in which he allegedly writes to Küntzel that England "would 'knock Hitler for a six'".[209]

The aversion to Nazism that Crowley exhibited in the late 1930s, however ambiguous it may be, appears to be the sign of an increasing scepticism toward existing political systems. His advances toward them had failed, and war was now near, bringing with it many uncertainties about the future. In essence, neither totalitarian regimes nor democracy were the right political systems for the diffusion of Thelema. In the preface to the 1938 edition of *The Book of the Law*, Crowley writes that "ferocious fascism, [and] cackling communism, equally frauds, cavort crazily all over the globe".[210] But he is no kinder to "vacillating" democracy, calling it one of the "abortive births of the Child, the New Aeon of Horus".[211]

When the war began, it was clear which side he would stand on. The lesson of the First World War had been enough for him. We have already seen what he wrote to Küntzel; but he did not stop with that. He also published verses dedicated to Churchill, urging the allies toward victory,[212] and began bombarding English intelligence agencies with requests for employment and offers of collaboration.[213] He offered, among other things, to interrogate Rudolf Hess after his capture in Scotland in 1941 after his famous "flight".[214]

At one point Crowley observed that Hitler's ruin was due to the fact that he was not a true initiate: "Had Hitler been a less abnormal character, no great "Mischief," or at least a very different kind of "mischief," might have come of it. ... He had not undertaken the balancing regimen of the Curriculum of A∴A∴; and, worst of all, he was very far indeed from being a full initiate, even in the loosest sense of the term."[215]

For Crowley, then – and no wonder – it was on the astral plane that Hitler had lost his battle.

Magic

Before concluding this chapter, it seems appropriate to explore two aspects of Crowley's concept of magic, which at first sight may not seem directly related to the subject of this book.[216] These aspects are nonetheless central elements for our understanding of Crowley, and may provide us with some tools for grasping his world view. His particular interpretation of the esoteric tradition, which he acquired within the Golden Dawn and later developed on his own, can aid us in understanding his mentality and his mode of reasoning.

At the beginning of this chapter, I made reference to two distinct periods in Crowley's life. Without a doubt, both periods were pervaded by his true, great passion: magic.[217] Ever since he read *The Cloud upon the Sanctuary* at little more than twenty years of age, his desire was to become a member of that restricted circle of initiates described by Eckartshausen.[218] Regardie writes that "it was in this text that Crowley was first introduced to the idea of a Secret School of Adepts, of holy Saints, of Secret Chiefs of the Order to which he aspired".[219]

It is also appropriate to consider the important influence Darbyist education had on the young Crowley. One of the main elements of the Darbyist doctrine, an element shared by many Anglo-Saxon fundamentalist sects, was the belief that the "brethren" were members of a restricted community of the "holy", and that they were the only ones who were guaranteed eternal salvation.

When he discovered the Golden Dawn, Crowley believed he was now able to realize his desire to be a member of an elite. The secrecy of the Order's doctrine and ritual ceremonies, and the feeling of belonging to a community of the elect, must certainly have appealed to his romantic side. For some years after his time with the Order had ended, Crowley still gave importance to his oaths of secrecy, which obliged him not to reveal the teachings he had received. The purpose of these oaths was to protect the "esoteric" nature of these teachings: magic was not for everyone, but only for initiates. It was not "democratic", but "elitist".

Not until 1909, a date whose importance we have already seen, did Crowley begin breaking his oaths. In that year, after having established the A∴A∴, he founded its official publication *The Equinox*. This journal successively revealed all the rituals and teachings of the Golden Dawn of which Crowley had gained knowledge. For him, evidently, this represented a passage into a different view of magic and esoteric science. Magic then became wisdom for all people, something everyone could potentially use: secrets were no longer necessary.

An idea of this kind must surely have aroused hostility in those who were bound by the same oaths but still considered secrecy to be one of the fundamental elements of the magical tradition. This was the cause of his legal battle in 1910 with Mathers, whom Crowley had once so greatly esteemed as an expert on magic and supreme authority of the Golden Dawn. Two differing conceptions of magic and esotericism now confronted one another. Mathers attempted to stop Crowley from divulging the rituals of the Golden Dawn, resorting to civil justice, but after a temporary initial success, he was forced to yield in the appeals court. Thereafter, Crowley published practically all the material of the Order that he had at his disposal, naturally revised according to his own criteria.

I should add here that Crowley's breaking of his oaths was not merely the result of his "changing his mind" about the elite nature of the secrets. To view his attitudes in this way would be an oversimplification, for Crowley took magical oaths seriously. The important point is that for him, the experience of receiving *The Book of the Law* in 1904 meant the establishment of a direct connection to the "Secret Chiefs". The question of the Secret Chiefs marks the entire history of the Golden Dawn. Essentially, it was believed that some high initiates, whether incarnate or not, ruled over the destiny of humanity with special powers and boundless wisdom. This concept had been clearly adopted by the Golden Dawn from the theosophical doctrine of Madame Blavatsky, who claimed to be inspired by the teachings of mysterious secret masters.[220]

Establishing contact with the Chiefs was no simple matter: they were the ones who chose the time, the place and the person with whom to communicate. Since they were responsible for the fate of the Order – as well as, apparently, that of the entire world – anyone who came into contact with them implicitly acquired extraordinary authority. Therefore, from Crowley's point of view – clearly not shared by the "rebel" faction of 1900 – the leadership of the Golden Dawn was considered legitimate only as long as it was able, directly or indirectly, to establish a connection with these entities.

After the internal conflicts and the schism of 1900, Crowley became convinced that the contact Mathers claimed to have established with the Secret Chiefs either had been broken off or had never existed in the first place. For these reasons, starting in 1904, by virtue of his reception of *The Book of the Law*, Crowley believed himself to have an authority that Mathers could no longer trump.[221] In addition, he declared that among the instructions he had received, there had been the order to reveal all the secrets and make them public. Such was his explanation for a behaviour that might otherwise have seemed incomprehensible. This prevalence of motives that we may define as "metaphysical" (and that others might prefer to call "irrational") in Crowley's behaviour must be constantly taken into account in order to understand his psychology.

Thus Crowley, starting at a certain point in time, made the rituals and secret instructions public. We should note that there was an exception to this. Crowley never revealed the secret of sexual magic that was communicated to him by Theodor Reuss in 1912. As Symonds observes, "it was one of the few secrets he kept".[222] Even this discretion was not accompanied by any great level of enthusiasm. Near the end of his life, he wrote that he had kept this secret solely "on a point of personal honour. My pledge given to the late Frater Superior and O[uter] H[ead of the] O[rder], Dr Theodor Reuss",[223] implying that had things been different, he would also have revealed this secret.

This transition to what we might call a "democratic" conception is also noticeable in Crowley's works that are more closely linked to a theoretical development of magic, namely the second part of *Book Four* and *Magick in Theory and Practice*. The former work was written in 1912 and published in 1913;[224] the latter went through a particularly long gestation period. It was originally intended to be the third part of *Book Four*; Crowley wrote a first version of it in 1912, but did not publish it because he was not satisfied with it. He returned to it in the early 1920s, during his Cefalù period, and reworked it until he made it "a really complete treatise on every branch of Magick".[225] The book was finally published in 1930.

In his introduction to *Magick in Theory and Practice*, Crowley takes care to make his intention clear in the most unequivocal manner possible, as we can see:

> This book is for ALL: for every man, woman, and child. My former work has been misunderstood, and its scope limited, by my use of technical terms. It has attracted only too many dilettanti and eccentrics, weaklings seeking in "Magic" an escape from reality. I myself was first consciously drawn to the subject in this way. And it has repelled only too many scientific and practical minds, such as I most designed to influence. But MAGICK is for ALL. I have written this book to help the Banker, the Pugilist, the Biologist, the Poet, the Navvy, the Grocer, the Factory Girl, the Mathematician, the Stenographer, the Golfer, the Wife, the Consul – and all the rest – to fulfil themselves perfectly, each in his or her own proper function.[226]

To call this a "democratization of magic" would not be entirely inappropriate. Crowley himself seems to indicate here that his ideas in this regard have changed over time. And indirectly, he appears to confirm my division of his life into two distinct periods.

The introduction to *Magick in Theory and Practice* is highly interesting also for other reasons, as we will soon see. But first, some clarification is necessary. What I have referred to as a "democratization of magic" does not necessarily assume any reflection of Crowley's political positions, whose evolution, as we have seen, was complex and tortuous. But neither should we believe that his views on magic had no connection to his political views. Clearly, at a certain point in his life, he became convinced that his purpose was to reach the greatest number of people possible with his teachings, and not to perpetuate an esoteric tradition with a restricted number of members.

Here, there is another aspect we should consider. Crowley appears always to have been greatly preoccupied with emphasizing the "scientific" aspect of his magic, his mysticism and even his new religion. This was not a particularly unusual attitude, considering that he was effectively an heir to the occultist currents that emerged in England and in France during the second half of the nineteenth century. Here I use the term "occultism" in a specific sense to indicate a particular current that formed at a certain moment in the history of Western esotericism, ranging from Eliphas Lévi in France to the Golden Dawn in England and later offshoots or emulators.[227] One of the characteristics of this current was a particular preoccupation with the "scientific" nature of its teachings, which was by no means considered incompatible with its "occult" and esoteric aspects, but instead was viewed as indispensable, taking on different forms depending on the various authors. The spirit of the times, spurred on by the success and diffusion of positivist and scientific ideas, was exerting its power over those currents of ideas which – at least according to a fairly superficial stereotype – might be presumed the most resistant to such influences. Occultists did their best to catch up with new cultural developments, striving to have their doctrines anointed with the holy oil of credibility, gained by scientific and/or rationalist discourses.[228]

Also in the introduction to *Magick in Theory and Practice*, we find some epigraphic quotes from various authors. Among these is a long passage from James Frazer's *Golden Bough*, in which some phrases are emphasized in bold type. One of them is: "[Magic's] fundamental conception is identical with that of modern science; underlying the whole system is a faith, implicit but real and firm, in the order and uniformity of nature."[229] Here is another: "The analogy between the magical and the scientific conceptions of the world is close. In both of them the succession of events is perfectly regular and certain, being determined by immutable laws, the operation of which can be foreseen and calculated precisely."[230]

Clearly Crowley quotes Frazer's words approvingly, even if the latter might have had some difficulty accepting this unexpected application of his theory. For Crowley, a conflict with rationality arises only when the highest levels of individual initiation are reached (i.e. those levels corresponding in the systems of the Golden Dawn and the A∴A∴ to the last three degrees beyond the "Abyss").[231] At this point, the initiate can transcend the normal mechanisms of thought, and reason has no meaning for him anymore. But Crowley leaves little room for irrationality below this level of spiritual enlightenment. In the introduction to *Magick in Theory and Practice*, he writes:

> In the course of [his] Training, [the student of Magick] will learn to explore the Hidden Mysteries of Nature, and to develop new senses and faculties in himself, whereby he may communicate with, and control, Beings and Forces pertaining to orders of existence which have been *hitherto* inaccessible to profane research, and available *only to that unscientific and empirical* MAGICK *(of tradition) which I came to destroy*.[232]

These words can give one an idea of Crowley's intellectual attitude to magic, and more generally to his teachings. From what he says, one may conclude that in his view, two types of magic exist. On the one hand there is a magic of tradition, which is negative because it is unscientific and empirical, and incompatible with science because not based on definite laws, but only on trial and error. On the other hand there is Crowley's new magic, which is really scientific and against tradition. The goal Crowley set for himself was to *destroy* the first type of magic and eliminate the gap separating magic from science by making his own method prevail.

This is an important element from an epistemological point of view. Judging by his words, Crowley, rather than being interested in the *restoration* of a lost wisdom, fragments of which would be preserved in esoteric traditions, wanted to bring *progress* into magic, mysticism and religion. He was not looking backward, but forward.

There is more. In Crowley's view, science had never been able to accept magic, precisely because magic was unscientific; but in rejecting it, science had lost the possibility of investigating aspects of reality which, since they were connected to this type of magic, had been neglected and remained "*hitherto* inaccessible to profane research". But with the new Crowleyan method, there would no longer be a divide between science and magic, and even "profane" science would be able to penetrate the mysteries of existence. Interestingly, for Crowley, the appeal to science and rationality as a legitimizing means was not limited to magic, but was also present, in relation to Thelema, on the political and social level. In a curious pamphlet published in 1936 under the pseudonym "Comte de Fenix", Crowley presented the principles of Thelema as the only rational solution to the impasse in which the ruling political institutions were caught.[233]

The motto of Crowley's review *The Equinox*, and of the Order A∴A∴, was "The method of science – the aim of religion". It was a well-chosen motto; nothing could better summarize the project Crowley had in mind. In *Magick without Tears*, he indirectly gives a few indications concerning the meaning this motto had for him, helping us above all to understand what he intended with the word "religion" in this context.

As I mentioned earlier, this book is in epistolary form. The question Crowley seeks to answer in this particular letter is: "Would you describe your system as a new religion?"[234] For Crowley, the word "religion" has three meanings. One is the meaning it assumes in his motto: "'The method of science – the aim of religion.' Here the word 'aim' and the context help the definition; it must mean the attainment of Knowledge and Power in spiritual matters."[235]

In a certain sense, we might say that Crowley was thinking more of the aim of mysticism or of magic itself, and less of the aim of religion, considering that he uses terms like "Knowledge" and "Power". In any case, he is referring to religion here in a positive sense.

There is also an "etymological" meaning: the Latin word *religio* "implies a binding together ... of ideas; in fact, a 'body of doctrine'. ... A religion then, is a more or less coherent and consistent set of beliefs."[236] This is another acceptable definition of religion for Crowley. Finally, there is a third:

> ... then there is the sense in which Frazer (and I) often use the word: as in opposition to "science" or "Magic." Here the point is that religious people attribute phenomena to the will of some postulated Being or Beings, placable and moveable by virtue of sacrifice, devotion, or appeal. Against such, the scientific or magical mind believes in the Laws of Nature, asserts "If A, then B" – if you do so-and-so, the result will be so-and-so, aloof from arbitrary interference. ... For true Magick means "to employ one set of natural forces at a mechanical advantage as against another set".[237]

Obviously, out of the three meanings of the word "religion", this is the least acceptable to Crowley. There is no need here to place particular emphasis on the aspect of belief in unspecified "Beings", since Crowley also believed in the presence of preterhuman entities endowed with objective existence. The real point of conflict between religion on the one hand, and magic and science on the other, is the *attitude* of the person dealing with them. In the case of religion, one asks the entity for help, *hoping* that it will respond; whereas in magic, as in science, a particular action or series of actions will always lead to a predictable result. The magician, like the scientist, therefore possesses a certainty that the religious person can never have.

Crowley then concludes by explaining within what limits his system may be defined as a religion: "Our system is a religion just so far as a religion means an enthusiastic putting-together of a series of doctrines, no one of which must in any way clash with Science or Magick."[238] The most obvious consequence of this conclusion seems to be that religion loses its independence. Its doctrines are no longer autonomous, their status as truth now depending on what science and magic will say about them. If doctrines are confirmed by these latter, all is well; otherwise, they can be discarded without regret.

The other part of the motto pertains to "the method of science". When we consider the data about sexual magic that Crowley recorded in his diaries, we will see that in essence, this method consisted in observing the conditions of the magical practice with maximum objectivity, viewing it entirely as a scientific experiment. He later supplemented these notes with annotations concerning the results of the practice, specifically on how to tell if it had been successful; for these operations almost always had a precise goal, often a material one, for example the attainment of money or success. Finally, according to Crowley, one could examine and analyse these results in order to obtain statistics from them. This aspect was undoubtedly of great importance for him; and, in my opinion, it appears to have formed part of his overall attitude. In fact, it was a constant characteristic of Crowley's to place faith in the application of science to domains commonly considered inaccessible to it, carrying a naturalizing tendency of nineteenth-century occultism to its farthest extremes.

3. Dangerous liaisons

> Moreover, there is nobody interesting to know except saints, villains and madmen; they are the only ones whose conversation can be of any value.
> (Joris-Karl Huysmans, *Là-bas*)

In this chapter I will discuss some acquaintances of Crowley's that seem to be of particular interest for the subject of the present study. I will focus particularly on persons who had a more or less enduring connection with Crowley, and, most importantly, who were involved in one way or another in the politics of their times. In almost all cases, these persons associated with Crowley because they were attracted to the world of the occult and found his personality fascinating. This combination of the occult and the political recalls the definition of "illuminated politics" given by James Webb in his two seminal works, *The Occult Underground* and *The Occult Establishment*.[1] According to Webb, this type of thought emerges "when occult ideas are found tangled up with political and social projects".[2] In this chapter I will examine some "illuminated" characters who had connections to Crowley, leaving for Chapter 4 a more detailed analysis of the most interesting one among them: Fernando Pessoa.

J. F. C. Fuller

The first person with whom we are concerned is Major-General John Frederick Charles Fuller.[3] Fuller, who was born in England in 1878 and died in 1966, was certainly a remarkable personality. Although his name is not particularly well known outside circles of experts in military theory, he was responsible for several tactical and strategic developments that led to the use of the first tanks during the First World War and the German *Blitzkrieg* during the Second World War. Today he is counted within the canon of great war theorists, along with his friend and colleague Sir Basil Liddell Hart (1895–1970).

The son of a lawyer from Chichester, he was educated in the manner customary for the middle class of the Victorian era. He then attended the prestigious military school at Sandhurst and became an officer in the British Army.[4] His biographer, Anthony J. Trythall, tells us that even in his early youth he felt a certain attraction for the occult and the mysterious.[5] After fighting in South Africa in the Boer War, he was sent to India with his regiment in 1903. He became profoundly fascinated with Indian culture, and devoted himself to reading the main sacred texts of Hinduism and to practising yoga. According to Trythall, the fascination Indian culture held for him "developed his earlier predilection for the mystic into a full-blooded passion for the occult which he regarded not primarily as magical or supernatural but as concerned with the hidden or anterior meaning of things".[6]

While in India, in 1905, Fuller had his first contact with Crowley, who at the time was in Darjeeling planning his assault on the peak of Kangchenjunga.[7] Fuller, who in the meantime had risen to the rank of captain, wrote to Crowley because he wished to acquire some of the latter's books. Crowley had in fact arranged a kind of competition for the best critical essay on his works, and Fuller intended to participate.[8] In 1906 Fuller returned to London from India, and there finally met Crowley in person. He wrote his essay, *The Star in the West*, which won the competition and was published forthwith.[9]

During this period, Fuller also came into contact with the Rationalist Press Association and wrote a few articles for the *Agnostic Journal*. Both the Association and the journal were connected at the time to the movements of rationalist thought in England that promoted religious agnosticism, often mixed with anti-clericalism. Crowley, while a student at Cambridge, had surely come under the influence of these ideas through thinkers such as Thomas Henry Huxley; this influence was very probably the origin of his positivist attitude, as we saw in Chapter 2. In his autobiography he makes a few remarks on this direction of thought, specifically in relation to Fuller. Crowley writes that in this period Fuller "was fighting valiantly against Christianity by the side of 'Saladin', William Ross Stewart, who was the leader of one of the main branches of militant agnosticism".[10] Interestingly enough, Crowley also met three of his most important disciples during this time, through circles connected to the rationalist and agnostic movement: the aforementioned Fuller, Victor Neuburg and Norman Mudd.[11] As I noted earlier, the agnostic movement showed a certain openness toward spiritualism and mysticism. Christianity was viewed as the true enemy, especially in its established form. Consequently, certain forms of mysticism and esotericism could be seen as allies in the battle. It will therefore come as no surprise that Madame Blavatsky is mentioned with great respect in the *Agnostic Journal*, nor even that space is made for the contributions of Annie Besant, who took over the reins of the Theosophical Society after Blavatsky's death.[12]

Crowley, in his autobiography, described his intellectual relationship with Fuller as follows:

> [Fuller] was entirely at one with me on the point of my attitude to Christianity. We regard it as historically false, morally infamous, politically contemptible and socially pestilential. ... But we were absolutely opposed to any ideas of social revolution. We deplored the fact that our militant atheists were not aristocrats like Bolingbroke. We had no use for the sordid slum writers and Hyde Park ranters who had replaced the aristocratic infidel of the past. We felt ourselves to be leaders; but the only troops at our disposal were either mercenaries or mobs. ... On one point only were Fuller and I at odds. His hatred for Christianity extended to the idea of religion in general. ... It is right that we should reverence the majesty of nature and obey her laws; but he fought with me, hand to hand, week after week, about the question of Magick. He had originally intended his essay to conclude with the sixth chapter, and he had scrupulously avoided any reference to the magical and mystical side of my work; nay, even to the philosophical side so far

as that was concerned with transcendentalism. But I showed him that the study must be incomplete unless he added a chapter expounding my views on these subjects. Thus chapter seven came to be written. … By the time he had written this chapter, I had brought him to see that materialism, in any ordinary sense of the word, was thoroughly unsatisfactory as an explanation of the universe; but he was not in the least inclined to accept any theories which might involve belief of any kind in a spiritual hierarchy. In the course of our argument I had myself been made uneasy by a subconscious feeling that, watertight as my system was in itself, certain legitimate inferences might be drawn from it which I was not drawing.[13]

Certain aspects of the intellectual relationship between Crowley and Fuller merit our attention. First, there is a strong component of rationalism. Second, there is the anti-Christian element, which for Fuller was part of a refutation of all religion. Third, there is the fascination with the occult. It is interesting to note that in both men the rationalist attitude and the passion for the occult, far from being mutually exclusive, went hand in hand. Crowley claims to have breached Fuller's wholehearted materialist rationalism, but then admits having been influenced by it himself. But as we saw earlier, this interest in the mysterious and the occult was present in Fuller even before he met Crowley. Finally, there is the contempt for the masses, the conviction of being part of an elite, the opposition to "any ideas of social revolution". The intellectual portrait of Fuller given by Crowley coincides with the one given by Fuller's biographer, Anthony J. Trythall. There is an interesting passage, for example, from a letter Fuller wrote to his brother in 1906. Trythall quotes it to give an idea of Fuller's political ideas at the time:

That the masses are socialistic is not a very grave danger; for socialism is but the scum on the democratic cauldron. Socialism is anti-progressive, tending to level the higher to the lower, true democracy is diametrically the reverse, it raises: the former is but a passing phase bubbling to the surface, a cleansing, a semi-education, the latter a step in the evolutionary ladder.[14]

Fuller became a highly assiduous collaborator of Crowley's, taking part in the founding of the journal *The Equinox* in 1909, as well as in the editing of the first few issues.[15] He also joined the Order Crowley created in 1909, the A∴A∴, with the magical motto "Per Ardua Ad Astra". Their friendship lasted until 1911. In that year, as we have seen, George Cecil Jones made his unfortunate attempt to defend himself from insinuations published in *The Looking Glass*. Crowley, despite the entreaties of his friends (Fuller above all), refused to sue the journal for defamation or to defend himself against the first of what would become an extremely long series of personal attacks. Jones, on the other hand, decided to take legal action to defend his reputation; but he lost his suit.

Following this event, several of Crowley's friends deserted him, including Fuller.[16] In the latter's case, the motive appears to have been twofold: first, his belief that Crowley had conducted himself in a dastardly manner and had betrayed his friendship with Jones by not suing *The Looking Glass* himself; and second, the fact that Fuller's reputation as an officer in the British Army might have been put at risk if he had continued associating with Crowley after all that had taken place.[17] After some six years of friendship and close collaboration, Crowley and Fuller had parted ways. Fuller left the A∴A∴, but remained a lifelong friend of another member of Crowley's Order: Meredith Starr, whose real name was Herbert Close (1890–1971). We do not know whether Starr remained in contact with Crowley after Jones lost his suit. Trythall describes him thus: "a mystic, writer, poet, herbalist, homoeopath and self-described 'constructive psychologist' with whom he was to have a close and life-long friendship quite outside his military life".[18]

It is worth examining Fuller's career and experience subsequent to his break with Crowley. During the First World War, he worked with a group that had been created within the British Army for the purpose of studying the use of armoured tanks in battle. In 1917 he was responsible for developing the tactics to be used in the battles of Arras (April) and Cambrai (November) which, although not decisive victories for the Allies, offered the possibility of evaluating the overall potential of this new weapon. Fuller's ideas were then exploited in the Battle of Amiens (August 1918), in which tanks played an enormous role; strategically, this marked the end of the war. On Fuller's contribution to the First World War, Trythall remarks: "There is no doubt whatever that Fuller's was the driving intellectual force behind the development of the tactics and organization of the Heavy Branch and the Tank Corps in France in 1917 and 1918, often in the face of strong military opposition."[19]

After the war, having attained the rank of lieutenant-colonel, Fuller was employed by the War Office to lay the foundations for an autonomous body of tank-based troops; he also began writing books and articles on military history and theory. But in the meantime his interest in the occult had not vanished, despite his break with Crowley. Trythall writes:

> In quite extraordinary contrast to all this professional activity, ... were Fuller's revived and continuing interest in and contact with the world and underworld of the occult at this time in his life. ... In April 1923 he published an article in the *Occult Review* on "The Black Arts" ... Two years later he actually published a very learned little book on *Yoga* which he defined as leading to mastery over the Unknowable.[20]

Fuller also sought to connect his passion for the occult with his studies in military theory. The result was a book, *The Foundations of the Science of War* (1926), that provoked considerable bad humour among his superiors.[21] The publication of this book did not have good effects on Fuller's military career. Despite all the recognition he had enjoyed since the end of the war, there was still friction between him and his superiors, due in great part to his impatient and not very diplomatic personality. According to Trythall, the delusions Fuller had on the professional level may partially explain his political choices during the 1930s. His dislike of democracy and the "masses" deepened, and the sympathy for Germany he had fostered in his youth, and which had disappeared during the war, re-emerged. He saw democracy as an "illness" of the times; what was needed, he felt, was "authority", meaning the control of the "masses" by an elite.[22]

In 1933 Fuller retired from the army and began dedicating all his time to journalism and to his studies in military theory. At the same time, however, he began to take a closer interest in politics. The first group with which he was involved was New Britain. This is a highly significant detail, and I will investigate this group further in Chapter 5, in reference to the interest that conspiracy theorists took in Crowley. The New Britain movement was founded in 1933 by Dimitrije Mitrinovic (1887–1953), a Bosnian Serb who had moved to London in 1914 as a member of the Serbian legation.[23] Previously, he had studied art history in Munich and had befriended Wassily Kandinsky and the other members of *Der Blaue Reiter* group. In 1927 Mitrinovic founded the Adler Society in London and was responsible for introducing Adler's ideas and work to an English audience.[24] He was an eclectic visionary who combined concepts borrowed from Rudolf Steiner's Anthroposophy with Adlerian psychoanalysis, along with theories on the role of the Slavic people and the Aryan race in history. The New Britain movement had its origins in the New Europe Group, which had been created in 1931 also under Mitrinovic's initiative, and which was closely linked to the Adler Society in London.[25] A related initiative was the Eleventh Hour Group, which shared most of the ideas of its parent New Europe Group, and was based on the idea of clubs created by individual citizens "in any house, town or village" in order to face the impending economic, social and political crisis of the 1930s "before it is too late".[26] While the New Europe Group continued its activities even after the Second World War and well into the 1950s, the New Britain movement was dissolved around 1935. As is the case for other, similar movements, it is difficult to place New Britain within any political category: "the organization was pledged to a functional society, guilds, social credit, the welfare state, a European federation, Rudolf Steiner's Threefold Commonwealth, and a restored Christianity".[27] The movement rejected capitalism, but also communism and fascism, and belonged therefore to the complex galaxy of "third way" movements that were active in Europe in the 1930s. And, as it was often the case with these movements, the rejection of communism and fascism did not exclude an occasional flirting with either of the two, or even both at the same time. New Britain published a journal with the same name, to which Fuller contributed.[28] But what is even more interesting is that Crowley was also in contact with Mitrinovic – a contact that appears to have awakened a certain degree of suspicion in conspiracy theory circles.[29] In Crowley's diary from his stay in Berlin in 1930, reference is made to a meeting with Mitrinovic.[30] The two also had some friends in common, since Mitrinovic collaborated closely with A. R. Orage (whose relationship with Crowley I have mentioned in the previous chapter) and contributed regularly to his journal *The New Age*.[31]

When a fascist party founded by Sir Oswald Mosley appeared on the British political scene, Fuller joined it, leaving New Britain. According to Trythall, Fuller believed that Mitrinovic's movement "lacked organisation; fascism, on the other hand, he concluded as early as February 1934, had 'come to stay'".[32] Mosley, descended from an aristocratic Staffordshire family, was an active member of the Labour Party for a few years (1924 to 1930), and was even appointed to a ministerial position during that period. In 1932 he founded the British Union of Fascists (BUF).[33] Mosley allegedly modelled his political movement on the example of Italian fascism, and the key point of his program was the struggle against the widespread unemployment that affected England in the early 1930s. Mosley admired Fuller greatly, and the two men collaborated and maintained close contact for many years. Had Mosley led the government, Fuller would have been his minister of defence.

Although Fuller, after his break with Crowley, tried to maintain a respectable distance from the latter and from his various activities, their old friendship appears to have caused some perplexity in British fascist circles. In the review *The Fascist*, an article was published that stigmatized Fuller for this reason. Fuller considered suing the review, but at his lawyer's advice – and with the agreement of Mosley himself – he let the matter drop.[34] From the historian's point of view, one could regret that Fuller took his lawyer's advice, since the judiciary proceedings in such a suit would undoubtedly have led to some very interesting testimonies concerning his relationship to Crowley, the causes of its ending, and the reasons why Fuller felt it necessary to defend himself against any undue connection of his name with that of his old comrade.

During this time, and surely in connection with his activity in the BUF, Fuller's anti-Semitic stances, which had already begun to manifest themselves in the previous years, became increasingly conspicuous.[35] Webb describes Fuller's ideas about the Jews as a peculiar kind of "magical anti-Semitism":

> The Jew, he wrote [in the pages of Sir Oswald Mosley's *Fascist Quarterly*], hoped "to gain world domination under an avenging Messiah as foretold by Talmud and Qabalah." As a former member of a magical order – Crowley's Astrum Argentinum – Fuller knew all about the real significance of the Cabala. But now he alleged that "the Jews attack by Magic and Gold".[36]

Webb rightly points out the paradox of someone who dedicates many years to the study of the Hebrew esoteric tradition and at the same time develops such anti-Semitic tendencies. However, we should keep in mind that such attitudes were very widespread among the "illuminates" of the time.

Beginning in 1934, Fuller paid several visits to Germany, during which he met with Hitler and other central members of the Nazi party, including Rudolf Hess. Considering Hess's attraction to the occult world, it would be interesting to know whether there were opportunities for him to converse with Fuller at leisure, and, if so, what subjects they might have touched upon. In 1935 Fuller went to Ethiopia to follow, as a journalist, the war Italy had declared on that nation. During the voyage he stopped in Rome, where he was received for a private meeting with Mussolini. Naturally, Fuller was opposed to the sanctions the League of Nations had imposed upon Italy as a result of the war. In Ethiopia he also met Italy's foreign minister, Galeazzo Ciano, as well as Pietro Badoglio. Beginning in 1937, Fuller made various trips to Spain, again as a journalist, in order to follow the Spanish Civil War. In April 1939, a few months before the outbreak of the Second World War, Fuller was invited to Germany to attend Hitler's fiftieth birthday celebrations – the only Englishman there aside from Lord Brocket.

When the war broke out, the BUF's activities began to be closely monitored. In May 1940 several members of the party were arrested, Mosley among them. Fuller, however, was spared, apparently by intervention from Churchill, who had admired the general since the First World War. Fuller did not reciprocate this admiration; he grew to loathe Churchill viscerally, above all because of his decision to push the war forward to the point of Germany's "unconditional surrender", excluding from the outset the possibility of a negotiated peace. Fuller believed the Soviet menace was much more serious for Europe than was the Nazi one, and that the total destruction of Germany would eliminate the only barrier against Bolshevik expansion into Europe.

During the war, Fuller continued cultivating his interest in the occult, publishing articles in the *Occult Review*. Trythall comments: "It is further evidence that his interest in the occult was a deep and continuing one and that it ran parallel to, *and often supported*, his military and political thinking."[37] After the war he continued to devote himself to his studies of military history and theory, publishing several more books until his death in 1966.

Both Trythall and Symonds agree that after 1911, Fuller refused to rekindle relations with Crowley, despite the latter's repeated attempts in this regard. Indirect contact between the two took place when a friend and colleague of Fuller's, Captain F. H. E. Townshend, paid a brief visit to the Abbey of Thelema in the spring of 1921.[38] Townshend, on holiday in Sicily, heard tell of Crowley's community in Cefalù and went to find it. Captivated by Crowley's ideas, he wrote to Fuller describing the meeting and telling of his intention to stay for a while at the Abbey.[39] Fuller hastened to send a telegram, and then a letter, in the attempt to dissuade his friend, who in fact did leave Crowley, moving on instead to Taormina, where he finished his holiday. One can deduce from Townshend's letters to Fuller the fervour with which the latter had warned his friend to keep his guard up against Crowley's captivating power. As for the many letters Crowley wrote to Fuller after 1911, they always remained unanswered. As I have already mentioned in the previous chapter, one of these letters, which is not extant, would be particularly interesting, because we know that in it Crowley expressed his opinions regarding Hitler.[40] Considering Fuller's political trajectory, which led him as far as attending the Nazi dictator's fiftieth birthday party in 1939, one cannot help but be curious about this letter.

Even if it is true that the relationship between Fuller and Crowley ended in 1911, there are still some points worth mentioning here. First, it is undeniable that Crowley, during the years of their friendship, exercised an influence over Fuller that was not really extinguished even after their parting. Fuller himself, in fact, acknowledged that his meeting with Crowley had been a decisive event in his life. Clearly, it was not just Crowley who continued admiring Fuller after the end of their friendship. Fuller's admiration for Crowley was also still very strong even many years after they had stopped seeing each other. C. R. Cammell met with Fuller in the mid-1940s and reported his judgement on Crowley: "I have heard an eminent personage, General J. F. C. Fuller, a man famous in arms and letters, one who has known the greatest statesmen, warriors, dictators, of our age, declare solemnly that the most extraordinary genius he ever knew was Crowley."[41] And a few years later Fuller made the following remark to Edward Noel FitzGerald (1908–58), who had been a friend and follower of Crowley's in his last years: "Crowley was a genuine avatar, but I don't think he knew it, but I do think he senses it in an emotional way."[42] Second, as we have seen, even after Fuller split with Crowley, he maintained a close friendship with an old friend from his period in the A∴A∴: Meredith Starr, Crowley's ex-disciple, to whom I will return later. Concerning the correspondence Fuller kept up with Starr, even after the Second World War, Trythall writes that Fuller's letters "show his continuing interest in the occult and are yet more evidence that his Edwardian association with Crowley had made a deep and indelible impact upon him".[43] Finally, as a third point, it appears highly interesting that Fuller worked with Mitrinovic's political movement, New Britain, in the early 1930s – because we know that Mitrinovic and Crowley were in contact and met at least once in 1930.

These circumstances will appear even more interesting in Chapter 5, where we will see how the connection between Crowley and Mitrinovic's group drew considerable interest among the English "conspiracy theorists" of the mid-1930s.

Tom Driberg

Thomas (better known as Tom) Driberg was a fairly well-known figure in British politics and journalism, especially after the end of the Second World War. He was born in 1905 in Crowborough, Sussex, and died in London in 1976.[44] As an eccentric, homosexual, anti-conformist and rebel, Driberg's life was marked by his rejection of the bourgeois conventions of his time and reflects a complex, many-faceted personality. He is interesting for us here because he was a friend, and for a certain period a potential disciple, of Crowley. In the third edition of his biography of Crowley, published in 1989, John Symonds added a chapter entirely devoted to the Crowley–Driberg relationship.[45] It is easy to understand why Symonds had avoided this subject in the earlier editions of the book: as we shall see, Driberg, despite all his anti-conformism, did not want the true nature of his relationship with Crowley to be divulged, surely fearing repercussions upon his political career. Symonds had to wait until after Driberg's death to add that chapter to his book.

Driberg was born into a middle-class family and had a difficult childhood. He was expelled from various schools due to his homosexuality. Very early on, around the age of fifteen, he joined the Communist Party of Great Britain (CPGB). In this same period, he also appears to have taken an interest in Catholicism. In 1924, nineteen years old, he enrolled at Christ Church, Oxford, ranking third from the top in the entrance exam for classical studies. It was around this point that his first contact with Crowley took place. In November 1925, Driberg wrote a letter to Crowley, who at the time was in Tunisia with his current Scarlet Woman, Dorothy Olsen. As we saw in Chapter 1, Crowley had been involved in his "World Teacher Campaign" in 1925, and had attended a meeting in Weida, Germany, where he succeeded in getting himself recognized as the international head of the OTO and as a spiritual guide to various personalities in German occultism. It is not necessary for us to go over all of the correspondence that developed in the months following Driberg's first letter; Symonds has already done this, with plenty of quotations.[46] Nevertheless, I will linger upon certain interesting aspects of this correspondence.

For what reasons would the young and restless Oxford student have written to the notorious magician living in exile in Tunisia? Like so many other young men who came into contact with Crowley, such as Victor Neuburg, Norman Mudd, Raoul Loveday, not to mention Israel Regardie and Gerald Yorke, Driberg was seeking a spiritual master, a "guru", a guide who would help him walk on the path of inner development. In his first letter, from 15 November 1925, Driberg wrote that he was interested "in the development of latent spiritual powers" and that for this reason he had joined the Theosophical Society.[47] Apparently he was not particularly satisfied with this experience, because he asked Crowley whether he could help him reach this "development" in a faster and more direct manner than was available through theosophical teachings.

Driberg was inspired to write to Crowley after reading the latter's novel *The Diary of a Drug Fiend*, which had been published three years earlier; it described the Abbey of Thelema in Cefalù in rather idyllic terms. At the beginning of the third part of the book, a note informed the reader that the place described in the novel actually exists, and that "the training there given is suited to all conditions of spiritual distress, and for the discovery and development of the 'True Will' of any person".[48] Those interested were invited to contact the author. What Driberg did not know when he wrote to Crowley was that by then the Abbey no longer functioned, as a consequence of its founder's expulsion from Italy. However, Abbey or no Abbey, Driberg hoped finally to make contact with a master possessing effective techniques for spiritual development.

After this first letter, Crowley and Driberg continued to correspond for several months. At the beginning of 1926, Driberg planned to visit Crowley in Tunis.[49] The young student would have arrived around the middle of March. At the last moment, however, he was forced to cancel his trip due to an unforeseen illness. He wrote to Crowley on 16 March, expressing his great regret at this circumstance and promising that this only meant the voyage would be postponed.[50] This was only the first of many appointments with Crowley missed by Driberg.

After this episode the correspondence between the two continued. Driberg probably hinted at his activity in the Communist Party, which must have awakened Crowley's interest. In fact, in a letter from 15 July 1926, the young student gave the magician some explanation of his political decisions:

> It is of course Lenin's character and achievements primarily that have attracted me to him: and I joined the Communist Party partly because it was the one party which had the sense to see that the 19th Century Liberal-Democratic idea was a sham, and that the majority could always be led and controlled by an intelligent and clear-sighted minority.[51]

Crowley probably agreed with one part of this statement: namely, that the Liberal-Democratic idea was deceptive and that "an intelligent and clear-sighted minority" should always rule over the majority. However, he could not possibly have accepted the accompanying premise, namely that the Communist Party alone had understood these "truths". From Crowley's point of view, *The Book of the Law* showed that Aiwass, well before Lenin, had understood them perfectly well in 1904.

The rest of Driberg's letter is even more interesting:

> You say that you rely on me to put you in touch with the real leaders – *do you mean the political leaders or what?* If so I can introduce you to Bob Stewart, a leading member of C[ommunist] P[arty]. I am afraid I don't know any of the Theosophical leaders, except (by correspondence) a Miss Debenham, who is connected with the Society of the Divine Wisdom, which professes to adhere to the pure teaching of HPB. ... I am ready and indeed anxious to take any steps you may think best to make your person and teachings as widely known as possible and deem it a very great privilege to be allowed to help: do you want any communication made to the press – either in the form of new (publicity) or serious articles (propaganda)? We can discuss details when we meet.[52]

Crowley was obviously more interested in making contact, through Driberg, with the "true" heads of the British Communist Party than with those of the Theosophical Society. What Crowley meant by "true" leaders was not very clear to Driberg, and even less so to us, since we do not have Crowley's original letter. Did Crowley believe there were secret powers behind the Communist Party? Be that as it may, he intended to push forward with his campaign as "Master of the World", and in order to do this he had to make himself known as much as possible, making contact with movements that were already in place, whether they were political, like the communist movement, or "spiritual", like the Theosophical Society. Driberg – who, we should not forget, was only a 21-year-old university student at the time, however enterprising he may have been – initially appeared very well disposed to help with Crowley's requests. But as we will see, after the first missed meeting in Tunis, another hindrance would force Driberg to miss their second appointment.

Between the spring and summer of 1926, Crowley left Tunis and settled in Paris. In principle, this should have made a meeting with Driberg easier, since the latter would not have had to make the long voyage from England to Tunisia. From Driberg's subsequent letters we learn that the two in fact agreed to meet in Paris, probably around the first of August. But once again something at the last minute prevented Driberg from going to see Crowley. The nature of this obstacle is not clear, but we do know that Crowley, after waiting in vain for his would-be disciple and receiving no communication from him, resolved to write to one of Tom's two older brothers, James, who had been in contact with Crowley earlier, around the time of his younger brother's missed voyage to Tunis. On 10 August, James responded to Crowley:

> Dear Sir,
>
> I beg to thank you for your telegram and letter. As I am not in sympathy with my brother Tom's various activities, I am not kept very much in touch with his movements. I have made inquiries and I understand that he is at present staying with his mother in Sussex. I fail to understand why he did not keep his appointment with you, and also why he did not notify you that he was unable to keep it. I can only apologise for the fact that a person bearing my name has been guilty of such discourteous behaviour.
>
> Yours truly,
> James Driberg[53]

Probably at the same moment James was writing his letter, Tom was also writing a letter to Crowley:

> Dear Sir Aleister,
>
> I am writing this in the hope that it will reach you: I sent another letter the other day, but I am sending this one by a different channel. I was unable to visit you as I had promised owing to circumstances over which I have *no control*. I am afraid you must be terribly disappointed in me but these are the first chances I have had

of getting a letter to you. I have no time to say more than that, I am at least safe and well, and will try to write later on. I do hope you will get this.

Yours fraternally,
Thomas Driberg[54]

All this leads us to believe that Driberg's mother (his father had died when he was fourteen years old), or someone else in the family, had discovered Crowley's letters and collected some information about him. We may assume that Tom's mother had forbidden his meeting with Crowley, perhaps even keeping him at home and preventing him from communicating with the outside world.

We do not know when or where Driberg and Crowley finally met, or whether Driberg introduced Crowley to any of the leaders of the British Communist Party.[55] What we do know, however, is that they became friends and met regularly during the 1930s and 1940s, until Crowley's death.[56] We also know that at least for a certain time, Driberg continued to see Crowley as a spiritual master rather than merely a friend. John Symonds, among the many papers to which he had access in his role as Crowley's literary executor, found the following note:

Do what thou wilt shall be the whole of the law.
 I, Thomas Driberg, in the presence of The Beast 666 solemnly pledge myself to the Great Work: which is to discover my own True Will and to do it.
 Love is the Law, love under Will.

Witness my hand,
Thomas Driberg[57]

This was surely a fairly compromising document for a Labour Party member of the British Parliament. Such, in fact, was Driberg's status when Symonds found this note, a few weeks after Crowley's death. Symonds magnanimously handed the document over to an extremely embarrassed Driberg, who – we can be sure – destroyed it immediately.[58]

After leaving Oxford, Driberg moved to London and began devoting himself to journalism in the late 1920s, writing for the *Daily Express*. In this period he began to frequent London's literary circles, making contact with T. S. Eliot and Aldous Huxley.[59] His activities in the Communist Party also continued, but it appears that with the passage of time, his beliefs began to change. Evidence of this is given by the fact that near the end of the 1930s he was recruited by MI5 (Military Intelligence, Section 5), a branch of the British secret service, to give information on the Communist Party. Driberg's contact there was Maxwell Knight, another remarkable character and another friend of Crowley's, who will have his own section later in this chapter.[60] Knight, at the time, was head of Section B5(b) of MI5, the purpose of which was to maintain surveillance over subversive political groups on both the extreme right and the extreme left, and above all to identify any potential "external" infiltrations – that is, linked to foreign secret services – in these groups. According to Knight's biographer, Anthony Masters, Driberg did not consider his role as an informer for MI5 to be a demonstration of "disloyalty" toward his party; but in any case, "he needed Knight's help to conceal his promiscuity which was increasing and might well have become too conspicuous ... So Driberg received protection while Knight received information."[61]

Driberg's role as a double agent continued for some years, but was suddenly ended in 1941. Anthony Blunt, a member of the notorious "Apostles' Club", is thought to have been responsible. The Apostles were one of Cambridge University's "historical" groups.[62] Within this group, during the second half of the 1920s, a subgroup of communist students formed, including Blunt, Kim Philby, Guy Burgess and Donald MacLean.[63] Blunt, like his friends, became a Soviet spy and gained entrance to the British secret service in the early 1940s. When he exposed Driberg's role as an informer in 1941, the latter was immediately expelled from the party without any official explanation.[64] This episode did not mark the end of Driberg's political career, but was rather, in a certain sense, its beginning: in 1942, after his expulsion from the Communist Party, Driberg ran for Parliament as a leftist independent and was elected. In 1945 he became a member of the Labour Party, and served almost continuously until 1974, also holding a position as the party's president from 1957 to 1958. In 1974, two years before his death, he was made a peer of England, with the title of Baron Bradwell.

His expulsion from the Communist Party in 1941 had no effect on his relationship with Knight, given that "he remained an MI5 agent as well as a close personal friend [of Knight's]. When he became an MP in 1942 he was able to pass on to Knight interesting information on the public and private lives of various Members of Parliament."[65]

Masters also claims that Driberg, after his election to Parliament, secretly resumed contact with the Communist Party, for which he played more or less the same role he had played for MI5, passing on background information about Parliament and the lives of its members. Knight also appears to have been aware of this.[66]

Despite Driberg's attempts to conceal the nature of his relationship with Crowley, which surely would have compromised his image as a politician, it is obvious that he was at least initially attracted to Crowley's occult teachings. It is difficult to establish whether or not this relationship was merely a youthful infatuation without further developments. What is certain is that Driberg continued to associate frequently with Crowley until the latter's death.[67] Moreover, it was Driberg who put the secret agent Maxwell Knight in touch with Crowley, thus contributing, as we will see, to the creation of a potentially highly explosive mixture.[68]

Walter Duranty

The Englishman Walter Duranty (1883–1957) was for many years – between 1922 and the end of the 1930s – the Moscow correspondent for the *New York Times*.[69] During this period he was "widely recognised as the top authority on the Soviet Union", and for more than a decade, his articles and reports from Moscow would appear on the newspaper's front page.[70] He was a war correspondent on the western front during the First World War, a Pulitzer Prize winner, and was also friends with William Shirer, another famous journalist and Berlin-based correspondent who, after the Second World War, published an equally famous book on the history of the Third Reich.[71]

During his time in Moscow, Duranty must have formed important contacts in the higher echelons of the Soviet Communist Party. One episode is particularly significant in this regard. Duranty is often mentioned as the first Western journalist to interview Stalin, even though in fact he was the second. Events went as follows: in November 1930 a rumour was spread that Stalin had been assassinated. To give greater credit to the official refutation of this news, the Soviet dictator decided to grant an interview to a journalist chosen from among the Western correspondents present in Moscow. The one chosen was Eugene Lyons, a correspondent for the United Press and a fervent communist. Duranty might have been chosen in his place, but unfortunately he had the bad luck to be out of the country at the time, and thus missed out on what could have been a once-in-a-lifetime opportunity. But as soon as he heard of this windfall, he hurried back to Moscow and prostrated himself before the Soviet press officer, declaring that since he was the Western correspondent with the most years of service behind him, it would be wrong not to grant him an interview as well. Evidently he knew how to strike the right tone, because not even a week after Lyons's interview, Duranty was also given the privilege of personally meeting and interviewing the elusive dictator. His article, less inclined to adulation than Lyons's interview and written in a much more penetrating and vibrant style, remains impressed upon the collective memory as the first interview with Stalin, while Lyons's article has fallen inexorably into oblivion.[72] According to Sally Taylor, Duranty's biographer, the publication of this interview was a turning point in his career. It "marked the beginning of his true international celebrity, and he became one of the best known journalists in the world".[73]

Still more significant is the fact that Duranty appears to have played a certain role in the United States' decision, in November 1933, to recognize the Soviet Union diplomatically – a fact of enormous political importance. The Soviet leaders had been waiting a long time for this recognition, by virtue of which their regime could undoubtedly obtain a certain degree of international legitimization. Duranty accompanied Soviet foreign minister Maxim Litvinov to Washington, where he had the decisive meeting with Franklin D. Roosevelt. Apparently as a reward for his help, Stalin granted Duranty another interview in Christmas 1933, this time on the initiative of the dictator himself.[74]

The unquestionable sympathy Duranty enjoyed with the communist leaders, along with the favour and admiration with which he described the results of the Soviet revolution, have led some authors to foster suspicion as to his intellectual honesty. For example, in his essay on the relationship between Crowley and Russia, W. F. Ryan states that Duranty, "alone among Western journalists, ... seemed to have *carte blanche* in the Soviet Union, which he described sympathetically for his paper, without apparently causing himself any problems in the West. One has to assume that he was paid by more than one master."[75] Duranty made no secret of his admiration for both Lenin and Stalin. In his articles he often praised the achievements of Stalin's five-year plan, in a period during which the West was struggling with a massive economic, but also social and political, crisis. Thus, as Taylor observes, "his stubborn chronicle of Soviet achievements made him the doyen of left-leaning Westerners who believed that what happened inside Soviet Russia held the key to the future for the rest of the world".[76]

Duranty, like Crowley and Driberg, had also studied at Cambridge, where he had earned his BA degree in classics. After leaving university, he had moved to Paris in the years immediately preceding the First World War, and there had led a carefree Bohemian life, supporting himself by teaching Latin lessons.[77] It was in this period that he met Crowley. The future journalist was still far from becoming famous, and it appears that fairly often he had to sleep by the banks of the Seine, being unable to pay for a room. Duranty and Crowley shared at least two things in common: a habit of smoking opium and the favours of a woman called Jane Chéron. They were both Chéron's lovers, without this having any repercussions upon their friendship. Later on Duranty married Chéron. Duranty, however, must have also been interested in Crowley's magical activity if it is true that, as we hinted in Chapter 1, he took part in a series of invocations known as "Paris Working", which Crowley and his disciple Victor Neuburg carried out in January and February 1914. In his *Confessions*, Crowley remains strangely discreet on the subject of Duranty. He refers to him in at least two passages – but without giving his name.[78]

Highly significant, however, is the fact that between 1929 and 1930, Crowley and Duranty were in contact once again. At the Warburg Institute, there are three letters from this period which are particularly interesting: two from Crowley to Duranty, and one from Duranty to Crowley. At the time, Crowley had recently been expelled from France and had returned to England with his secretary (Regardie) and his current Scarlet Woman, Maria Teresa Ferrari de Miramar. This was also the period during which Crowley was in contact with Fernando Pessoa. A few months later, Crowley would be in Berlin, where he would meet Aldous Huxley, Alfred Adler, Dimitrije Mitrinovic, Christopher Isherwood and Gerald Hamilton. This period, in short, seems to have been particularly thick with meetings and initiatives on Crowley's part.

In November 1929, after the two men had evidently lost touch for some time, Crowley wrote a long letter to Duranty in which he made reference to the current situation in Russia and spoke of his intent to travel there himself soon. His motivations for this are particularly interesting to us:

Dear Wally:

Do what thou wilt shall be the whole of the Law.

It is a long while since I heard from you. You never seemed to be in Paris at the same time that I was. How is everything with you? I should like to know something of your plans because I have an idea of running out to Moscow in the course of the next 2 or 3 months. I have not seen it since the war, and I should very much like to get a first hand notion of the new régime. Most of the fanatic bourgeois nonsense appears to be exploded. What I really want to know is what life is like from the purely poetical standpoint. I have also ideas which I should like to put before the Soviet. ... I ... want to get the USSR to adopt a state religion. ... My attitude is, to put it briefly, the following: The Russian temperament, perhaps more than any other in the world, demands something in the nature of spiritual debauch. Complete forgetfulness of the pain of existence in artificial ecstasy. This is a national characteristic and does not depend on Christianity at all. As you know, all sorts of little Messiahs are always springing up spontaneously in Russia, and getting very often a wide and important following. The success of any movement depends more on its extravagance than any other qualities. Of course the powers that be may say, and very rightly, that this indulgence, whether in alcohol or piety, is very bad for the people. That is no doubt true, but we have got to face the facts, and in the present stage of evolution of the Russian temperament, we

cannot expect them to think like Ray Lankester.[79] It consequently seems to me that the next step in their evolution is to give them the ecstasy for which they crave, without attaching it to any absurd theories such as Christianity or any other mystical cult. I had Russia particularly in mind when I wrote the Gnostic Mass. In this ceremony we have every opportunity for the enjoyment of those states of consciousness which will alleviate the pain of the realization of the futility of material existence. But there is nothing in the ritual which is not scientifically accurate. And the element which produces fanaticism and other socially dangerous states of mind are eliminated. It is not only impracticable but dangerous to sit on the safety valve. I do think the authorities ought to realize that nothing tends to foster counter-revolutionary sentiment more than depriving the people of the natural outlets for their pent-up energies. The Romans knew perfectly well what they were doing when they accepted the popular demand for bread and circuses. It is certainly not sufficient to assure the material comfort of the people. There is another type of hunger which must be satisfied or trouble immediately results. The adoption of my Gnostic Mass would, I feel sure, serve to wean the people from their superstitious beliefs and give them something to look forward to (on occasions when they feel like blowing off steam) without filling their minds with subversive ideas. You will understand, of course, that this proposal of mine is based on purely philosophical and psychological grounds. I make no pretence to understand the economic and political situation in Russia or in any other country. It is emphatically none of my business, and I should not dream even of forming an opinion of such matters. The most I can say is that I regard the present régime in Russia as the greatest social experiment ever attempted, and I should not like to see it destroyed by mistaken judgment as to the national temperament. The danger seems to me that the optimism of the authorities as to the possibilities of enlightening the people may lead to their overthrow and the temporary failure of the whole plan. We have already seen how attempts to apply the doctrines of Marx too strictly have been defeated. At least partially! Modifications have had to be introduced. I am thoroughly agnostic on such points. It seems to me that no doctrine of any kind is universally applicable. I wish you would let me have your ideas on these matters, and if possible those of any important persons with whom you may be in touch. In particular, are you going to be in Moscow all winter?
Love is the law, love under will.

Yours ever,
[Aleister Crowley][80]

This is certainly a fascinating document. Crowley was obviously following the development of the political situation in the Soviet Union with great interest, and probably hoping to see whether, with the upheavals following the revolution, a void would be created which might be filled with his newly proposed religion. And it is certainly interesting to learn that Crowley saw the Bolshevik revolution in quite a positive light. But the most striking thing about this text is the fact that Crowley did not want to suggest that the Soviet regime should adopt Thelema in its entirety as a religious and philosophical system, but rather only the Gnostic Mass, which was only one of the ritual aspects of

Thelema.[81] There was certainly a close "historical" link between Russia and the Gnostic Mass, given that Crowley had written the ritual itself during his trip to Russia, in 1913. But the fact that he suggested solely this aspect, and not the whole of Thelema, remains a curious aspect, even more so because later, when he made similar advances toward Nazism, he would rather be thinking of Thelema as a whole. Perhaps Crowley thought that the simple practice of the Gnostic Mass would be accepted more easily by the Soviet authorities and would then serve as a "Trojan Horse" for introducing the philosophical and doctrinal aspects of Thelema. But he also emphasized the more specifically "practical" aspect of the ritual: namely, as a means for producing an altered state of consciousness. This would enable people to release tensions which, having accumulated for an overly long period, might otherwise explode with dangerous consequences. Far from being an ardent prophet or a fervid missionary, Crowley appears here to have cold-bloodedly defended a theory of social control by means of religion. This sounds almost paradoxical, since it was directed toward the representatives of a political doctrine whose goal, at least in theory, was the emancipation of the masses from this same form of control. But Crowley seems to have foreseen this objection, and appeals to a realistic view of things: perhaps one day the Russians will not need any religion, but as long as they have not yet developed to that point, it is just as good to satisfy their needs in the manner that offers the best guarantee of success. One should also note the importance attributed to the alleged "scientific" nature of the ritual in question, which distinguishes it from old religious practices based on "superstition". This brings us back to the "rationalist", or "naturalist" element of Crowley's thought that I have already discussed in the previous chapter.

It is interesting to note that these points, in relation to the Russian situation, may have been on Crowley's mind for quite some time. In fact, he had already taken an interest in the Soviet Union for several years.[82] For instance, after his expulsion from Italy, in 1923, he intended to write to Trotsky.[83] Furthermore, we find similar arguments to those in his letter to Duranty in an earlier text, a typewritten essay which, according to W. F. Ryan, was written around 1925:

> Until education has operated without interference for centuries Russia must always lie at the mercy of a madman ... The solution of this difficulty [i.e. how to make the Revolution work] is the introduction of a new religion, constructed skilfully on sound psychological principles. Two objects must be kept well in mind (a) the religion must be orgiastic in character, to afford a safe outlet for the instinct of enthusiasm (b) its doctrines must be based upon sound science and psychologically therapeutic, so that the morbid need of the people may be gradually eliminated from their root-consciousness ... Firstly let there be a proclamation by diverse subtle methods of the arrival of a Spiritual Saviour of the Russian people (see Manifesto enclosed) [alas, not apparently extant]. It is well that this saviour should be a non-Russian, incapable of interfering directly in any way with the internal government of the country [i.e. Crowley himself]. Next, let his "Law" be proclaimed and the existing government adhere officially to it ... This new Rite will produce in Europe and America the utmost religious consternation and the old faiths will crumble into dust at the touch of the Reality of the new Formula of Truth.[84]

Here we see the same two themes: the idea of giving an outlet to natural needs through ritual practices that lead to some form of altered consciousness; and the scientific nature of his new religion, which is being proposed as a solution to the problem of emancipation of the masses from superstition. Of course, the *spiritual* revolution hoped for by Crowley would then follow the *political* revolution, automatically spreading beyond Russia, presumably throughout the world. We must not forget that this text was apparently written during the period when Crowley was most intensively occupied with his "World Teacher Campaign", which we saw connected to the beginning of his relationship with Driberg. Now the requests Crowley made to Driberg to introduce him to the "true" leaders of the British Communist Party make more sense: Crowley was probably looking for a channel through which he could gain important contacts in the Soviet Union.

Duranty, writing from Moscow, answered Crowley's letter on 8 January 1930:

My dear Crowley,

I am sorry to have been so slow in answering your most interesting letter but have been terribly busy, on the one hand, and expected to be going to England on the other. So I thought I would see you. But things are happening here too quickly and now I don't expect to get abroad before the end of February. I don't know whether you remember a young man named Sturgis[85] who apparently was with you at Kephalu [sic]. Anyway I met him in Berlin recently (and I may say he has the highest regard for you) and he also was all thrilled about the idea of giving the Bolsheviks a substitute for the god they have spurned. Having got as far as Berlin he was all hot up to come [to Moscow], but I could not encourage him, and did not. Your suggestion of course is much more interesting, but at least ten years too soon in my opinion. They are too damn busy. Incidentally, the 5-day week – your pet child, as you call it – has not been abandoned in the least (there is nothing so lousy as the news in the English papers about Russia) and is going strong everywhere, especially in the big towns. This, however, you see, is a practical measure which is where the difference comes in. What I mean is that anyone who has not been here lately cannot understand how completely what you call the "spiritual" is eliminated from Russian life at present. I don't say for a moment it has ceased to exist, or won't come back – perhaps all the stronger from repression – but for the time being the Kremlin won't hear of it. And what the Kremlin won't hear of doesn't count. For instance, you say "We have seen how attempts to apply the doctrine of Marx too strictly have been defeated at least partially". That was perfectly true some years ago. But it is not true today. Stalin is now applying 100% Marxism, but more generally and in my opinion with greater chances of success than Lenin was able to do. All of this doesn't alter the fact that it would interest you tremendously to come here and would interest me very much if you came, so what about it?

Yours,
wd.[86]

Duranty placed emphasis on the effectiveness and radical nature of Soviet anti-religious politics, which had left little room behind for any spiritual element, be it traditional or modern. This would seem to offer little hope for the success of Crowley's plans. But the surprising thing here is that Duranty – who, as we have seen, was profoundly aware of the current state of affairs in the Soviet world – was not hastening to discourage Crowley. On the contrary, the fact that Duranty even invited Crowley to join him in Moscow, is particularly intriguing. It is also worth noting that this letter was written only a few months before Duranty's first interview with Stalin. There is no doubt that by this time, Duranty had already established good relations with prominent members of the Soviet regime.

Crowley responded to Duranty's letter on 11 February 1930:

Dear Wally:

Do what thou wilt shall be the whole of the Law.

Thanks so much for your letter. I have delayed answering it till now because I wanted to check up with one or two things here. I am very glad indeed of what you tell me, especially about the five day week. We are all rather rejoicing about the sacrilegious outrages, and only hope it is true. We wish something could be done to stamp out the Christians here. They are becoming a perfect nuisance. ... But I should like very much to give another look at Russia. It seems to me that the old stories about eyewash must be completely false as apparently the Soviets are trying to run Russia as a tourist country. It would really be a good thing if a large number of independent people travelled round the country on their own. But at present the general impression is that anyone would be liable to be thrown into prison and tortured for any or no reason as soon as he crossed the frontier. I think it is up to the Soviets to make it impossible for the Mail to publish the rubbish it does, and this seems to me the way to do it. I am hoping to get my big business through this week, and if so I might take a little holiday in your direction.

Love is the law, love under will.

Yours ever,
[Aleister Crowley][87]

Crowley's complacency in observing the destruction of Christianity by Soviet politics is noteworthy. He was hoping that a spiritual current in harmony with Thelema might arise in Russia subsequent to this destruction. The most curious aspect of this is that Crowley's hopes were not as completely unfounded as they might appear to us today. In fact, his ideas had not come too early, but rather too late. Bolshevik religious politics immediately following the revolution had tended to favour (or at least tolerate) native Russian minority and dissident religious groups and movements, such as the flagellants (*khlysty*) or the castrati (*skopcy*), since at the time the real enemy of the regime that had emerged after the revolution and civil war was the dominant Orthodox Church.[88] In this situation, heterodox sects could function as allies in the eradication of the Church from Russian society. Today it is obvious that these politics were simply a means to an end, because as soon as the primary goal was achieved, the regime turned in a more generally anti-religious direction. Around 1927–8, the government began tracking down and persecuting the members of these various sects as well. Thelema, which of course already had the disadvantage of not being an indigenous Russian religion, could not have gone very far in the Soviet Union, but it is still fascinating to consider the idea that Crowley's proposals might, in theory, have met with some interest.

In any case, as we will see in the next chapter, instead of going to Russia, Crowley went that year to Portugal, to meet with Fernando Pessoa. It is not known whether or for how long contact between Crowley and Duranty continued after this exchange of letters. I have found no other documents giving information on their relationship after 1930. Crowley's opinion of the Soviet Union during the subsequent years, however, deserves some consideration. In Chapter 2 we have found interesting comments on the current political situation in Crowley's correspondence with his disciple and collaborator Karl Germer. This interest becomes increasingly conspicuous towards the end of the 1930s, when the downward spiral leading to the Second World War was accelerating ever more sharply. Although most of Crowley's comments relate to Germany and Nazism, probably due in part to Germer's nationality, there is also some discussion of other countries. In a letter from 29 December 1939, Crowley expresses his ideas on the pact of non-aggression between Germany and the Soviet Union (the famous Ribbentrop-Molotov Pact), which had been signed in August of that year and had left Poland open for invasion by Hitler on the one hand and Stalin on the other:

> The Nazi–Soviet pact was a magical error unexampled in history. It simply proved that the gang [of the Nazis] has no idea of any principles. It was the desperate tactics of a cornered gangster [i.e., Hitler]. Nor did I ever believe in the power of Russia as a striking force. Are the Soviets really less corrupt and crazy than the Boyars? Does a Jacuerie [sic] turn a shiftless ignorant proletariat into a skilled and disciplined organism of scientific habit of mind? Rubbish. German troops would have wiped out Finland in a week. And it proves how small is the Nazi margin that they allowed the USSR to seize the Baltic at all. At what a cost in prestige?[89]

After showing relative enthusiasm for the anti-Christian politics of the Bolsheviks in his correspondence with Duranty, Crowley had become more disenchanted near the end of the 1930s, as his own country stood on the brink of a merciless war. After the ambiguity of the preceding years, the time had come for him to make a definite choice. Crowley was now confirmed in his conviction that the Russian revolution had not fundamentally transformed the social and cultural conditions of the Russian people. He found evidence of this in the war that had recently broken out, but time, and the final outcome of the war, would ultimately prove how wrong his judgement was.

Gerald Hamilton

Gerald Hamilton was perhaps the most remarkable among all the personalities described so far, to the point of rivalling even Crowley himself. Tellingly, John Symonds wrote a book about Hamilton as well, based on conversations he had with him and full of anecdotes from his adventurous life.[90] Nor is it any surprise that Hamilton and Crowley found themselves at ease with each another as soon as they met, and began to associate frequently. Hamilton has even been described as one of Crowley's most significant political contacts. Christian Bouchet, for instance, mentions their meeting in the early 1930s and their friendship as evidence of Crowley's faithfulness to the Irish cause, since Hamilton was, among other things, a Sinn Feiner.[91] The relationship between Crowley and Hamilton is certainly of interest, but I do not believe Bouchet's hypothesis to be correct. When the two men associated with each another, it was certainly not with the goal of helping Ireland to obtain independence. Crowley does not appear to have been concerned with Ireland after the First World War; and as we have seen, after he returned to Europe from the United States in 1919, he claimed that he had only taken Ireland's side during the war in order to act as a provocateur and spy on circles with connections to Germany.

Hamilton does not really seem to have been more consistent than Crowley from a political point of view. In his life, he oscillated between apparently incompatible positions, and it is not always clear whether his convictions were inspired by sincere adherence or by simple opportunism. If his name is remembered today, it is mostly due to literature. He was, in fact, the main source of inspiration for the colourful Mr Norris, the main character of a famous novel by Christopher Isherwood.[92] Isherwood was a good friend of Hamilton's. He met him in Berlin, where he resided from 1929 to 1932, and later they got acquainted with Crowley, who was also living there at the time.

Isherwood was very much aware of Hamilton's tendency to easily change his political ideas. In a later autobiographical novel, *Christopher and His Kind*, where he remembers the time he spent in Berlin, Isherwood observes that Hamilton "felt no embarrassment in changing his convictions ... At one time or another, he was a pacifist, a crusader for Irish independence (no matter what that might cost in the blood of others), a near-Communist, a right-wing extremist, a critic of the Vatican's foreign policy, a devout Catholic."[93] And so, once again, we are dealing with a many-sided, if not downright ambiguous, personality; one that is difficult to place within any clearly defined category.

In *Christopher and His Kind*, Isherwood emphasizes Hamilton's "Irishness".[94] Hamilton stood by the Irish cause, was friends with Roger Casement (1864–1916) and helped him with his plans for revolt against British domination during the First World War. According to Isherwood, this did not represent treason against Britain, because as an Irishman, he had every right to defend his homeland. It should be noted however that Hamilton's family, which was of aristocratic descent, did own property in Ireland but were certainly not in favour of Irish independence.[95] In fact, they were Protestants and fervent loyalists. Hamilton offers a few amusing anecdotes in this respect in his autobiography. During a long period spent in China, lasting almost two years, Hamilton, then twenty years old, became seriously ill. During his illness he was cared for by a Catholic nun to whom he promised he would convert to Catholicism if he survived. Once recovered, he kept the promise and was baptized as a Catholic. His father, upon hearing the news, declared that it would have been all very well for his son to become "a Parsee or a Buddhist, or a damned Fire-Worshipper", but that he could never accept him as a Catholic.[96] Indeed, Hamilton was immediately disinherited. By no means discouraged by this inconvenience, he continued living a carefree youth, travelling about Europe, thanks to an allowance given to him by an aunt. The young Hamilton, thanks to family relations and personal connections, was received into many of the royal courts of Europe. He was the guest of Tsar Nicholas II at Tsarskoye Selo, was introduced to Kaiser Wilhelm II at a reception in Berlin, obtained private audiences with Popes Pius X and Benedict XV; and so on. Thus he had free access to the highest echelons of society, and was able to establish connections to the most prominent political figures of the time. Just like Crowley, he spent his younger years in a fever of continual movement, squandering the substantial amount of money placed at his disposal.

In 1913 he met Roger Casement; this connection would have an important influence upon his life. Fascinated by this revolutionary figure, and possibly having even fallen in love with him, Hamilton asked to become a member of Sinn Fein. When the First World War broke out, he, like Crowley, left England, initially going to Italy. Once Italy entered the war, he relocated to Spain. As an Irishman, he stood by his perceived right to remain neutral rather than siding with England. He offered his services to Casement, who at the time was in Berlin with the purpose of seeking support from the German authorities for the Irish cause. Casement invited Hamilton to join him there. Hamilton claims that he intended to accept the invitation, but before he could reach the German capital he was forced to return to London urgently to stabilize his financial situation. Once in London, however, he was arrested and charged with treason. Apparently it was not possible to find hard evidence against him, but he remained in prison for the duration of the war.

After the end of the conflict he was released. His experience in prison had marked him deeply. He began to occupy himself with social problems and to work with international organizations fighting famine and aiding impoverished children. But in the mid-1920s, further events led to his being incarcerated once more, this time in Italy under the accusation of fraud. By now he could no longer use his ancestry to his advantage; hence his involvement in shady business. The Hamilton/Mr Norris of a thousand sly dealings began to emerge, often mixing financial intrigues with political ones. It was this personality that Isherwood portrayed so vividly in his novel. He recalls this aspect in his memoir:

> Aside from Gerald's temperamental extravagance, which drove him to run up bills he knew he couldn't possibly pay, his wrongdoing seems to have been almost entirely related to his role as a go-between. If you wanted to sell a stolen painting to a collector who didn't mind enjoying it in private, to smuggle arms into a foreign country, to steal a contract away from a rival firm, to be decorated with a medal of honor which you had done nothing to deserve, to get your criminal dossier extracted from the archives, then Gerald was delighted to try to help you, and he quite often succeeded. All such transactions involved bribery in one form or another. And then there were Gerald's operational expenses. And certain unforeseen obstacles which arose – probably with Gerald's assistance – and had to be overcome, at considerable cost. All in all, a great deal of money would pass from hand to hand. The hands in the middle were Gerald's and they were sticky.[97]

At the time Isherwood met Hamilton, during the winter of 1930–31, the latter was the representative of the London *Times* in Germany, one of the few respectable jobs – if not the only one – that he ever held. This was also the period in which Hamilton met Crowley.

As we can see from Crowley's diary, he and Hamilton met in October 1931.[98] What we read in the diary is in agreement with the account given later by Hamilton:

> One of the bright interludes at this time was my acquaintance in Berlin with Aleister Crowley, who at that time was exhibiting in a Berlin gallery some of the pictures he had painted. After visiting the gallery I called at his house together with an English friend, Christopher Isherwood, whom I was seeing very often in Berlin at that time.[99]

So it was through Hamilton that Crowley was introduced to Isherwood. It appears that the three men, along with the poet Stephen Spender (also a close friend of Isherwood's), spent many evenings together in various homosexual hangouts in Berlin. Isherwood does not say this explicitly in his memoir, but there is a passage that most likely refers to Crowley: "[Among Hamilton's acquaintances in Berlin] I remember a man, he was connected with French counter-espionage, whom Christopher met through Gerald; he had the most evil face I have ever seen in my life".[100] There can be little doubt that this man was Crowley, and it is interesting to note Isherwood's comment about his connection to the French secret service, which sounds a bit surprising, considering that Crowley had been expelled from France not long before. However, it would suggest at least that there was a connection between Crowley and the secret service of some country. As we will see in the next section, the British secret service evaluated the possibility of using Crowley for some operations during the Second World War, but then abandoned the idea, apparently because the German secret service had already identified Crowley as a collaborator of the English secret service. This information had been acquired from an "agent" who had lived with Crowley during this period. This "agent" could not possibly be any other than Hamilton himself.

We know that in the first months of 1932 Hamilton lived in Crowley's apartment as a paying guest.[101] Symonds notes that, during this period, Crowley was collecting information on Hamilton.[102] The situation therefore seems to have been slightly grotesque: Crowley was passing information about Hamilton to the English secret service, while Hamilton was passing information about Crowley to the Germans.[103] There is another detail to add to all this. Isherwood writes of the unidentified, evil-faced man being connected with the French secret service – and in his novel, *Mr Norris Changes Trains*, Norris himself (Hamilton's alter ego) is also in contact with the French secret service. In the novel, Norris comes into contact with the German Communist Party (something the real Hamilton actually did), but is in fact double crossing them: he is sending information about the party to the French secret service, while seeking to put the service in contact with a prominent German political man, Baron Kuno von Pregnitz, in order to pass on important state secrets. At the end Norris is discovered and has to flee Germany. These details, fictional as they may be, show us an interesting pattern. In this case we may, in fact, conclude that there was a definite involvement in activities of espionage on the part of Crowley and of some of the persons who associated with him during his Berlin period. We do not know to what level his contacts went, and all in all it seems improbable that he was ever more than a simple informer. Hamilton, however, independently from whatever ideas can be gleaned from the Norris character in Isherwood's novel, seems to have made a business of murky operations, and was most certainly involved on higher echelons.

At the beginning of 1933, when Hitler became chancellor, Hamilton decided to leave Germany. In his autobiography, he explains that Nazism went entirely against his personal views, but his decision must also have been influenced by the fact that, most probably, the atmosphere in an increasingly Nazified Germany would not have been very congenial to his sly business undertakings. Another significant complication was the very close relationship he had established with the German Communist Party. After leaving Germany and settling in Belgium, he was invited to serve on an international committee opposed to fascism and the war, and was chosen as the British delegate for the congress to be held in Shanghai in the autumn of that year. While in that city, he met a person whose adventurous and rambling life was a match for his own, not to mention Crowley's: Ignácz Trebitsch Lincoln (1879–1943).[104] This encounter is particularly interesting because on a number of occasions René Guénon associated Trebitsch Lincoln's name with that of Crowley.[105] I will return to the relationship between Crowley and Guénon in Chapter 5. The traditionalist thinker saw both Crowley and Trebitsch Lincoln as emissaries of what he referred to as the "counter-initiation", which was in his view responsible of the widespread process of subversion of traditional values. It is not known, however, if Crowley and Trebitsch Lincoln ever met or even knew of each other.[106]

During his return from China, surely thanks to his contacts in the Communist Party, Hamilton was invited by the Soviet authorities to travel through Russia. He thus enjoyed the privilege – certainly not a common one – of having been cordially received in Russia both by the Tsar and by the Soviets.

At the outbreak of the Second World War, Hamilton returned to England, where he lived more or less stably until his death.[107] His political convictions had gone through another change, and his sympathies for the left had now turned toward the right. During the war he was openly opposed to Churchill's politics of "unconditional surrender" and favoured a separate peace with Germany – a position which, as we have seen, led to the imprisonment of several key personalities in British politics. But Hamilton did not limit himself to declaring his intent; he also endeavoured to act concretely with the help of his connections, in order to bring England into negotiations with Germany. Through the embassy of a neutral country, he got in contact with Cardinal Maglione, Secretary of State to the Vatican. A brief exchange of messages took place, but Hamilton's project was destined to be short-lived. He was once again discovered, arrested and immediately incarcerated according to the same ad hoc regulation that had permitted the arrest of Mosley and other activists of the pro-German right. It is quite probable that one of the persons responsible for his arrest was Maxwell Knight, the British secret service agent whom we have already encountered in relation to Driberg, and whom I will discuss further in the following section. Hamilton, as unlucky as he was incorrigible, thus became the only British citizen to have been imprisoned for political reasons during both world wars.

Not surprisingly, during his imprisonment Hamilton met and got along splendidly with Oswald Mosley, Archibald Ramsay and Barry Domvile, all personalities from the English radical right whom we shall encounter again later on.[108] He describes his incarceration as something of a homecoming. Once again, however, Hamilton must have conducted himself with extreme caution, because no conclusive evidence was found against him, and he was released in January 1942.

There is no need here to dwell on Hamilton's life after the Second World War. I will just mention another singular aspect of Hamilton's turn toward the right: his association during this period with Nesta Webster (1876–1960), who had published a series of books on the international Jewish–Masonic conspiracy between the two wars and was highly active in political groups of the extreme right.[109] In Symonds's book of conversations with Hamilton, we find the following passage:

> While Gerald was making me a cup of coffee, I sat and read the *Observer* – the review by A. J. P. Taylor of Alan Moorehead's book on the Russian Revolution.
>
> In discussing this book, Mr Taylor dismisses the view that Lenin was a German agent, paid with German gold to start a revolution. "In any case", he wrote, "the idea that German money caused the Russian Revolution is about as convincing as the theory, propagated by Mrs Nesta Webster, that the French Revolution was a conspiracy of Freemasons."
>
> When Gerald returned to the room, I told him of Mr Taylor's summary dismissal of Nesta Webster's opinions. Gerald did not agree with Mr Taylor. His expression became serious. I remembered that he had mentioned Mrs Webster's name to me in the past.
>
> "What is she like?" I asked. "Isn't she a hunchback?"
>
> Gerald exploded. "On the contrary! She is very *tall*. I said she is a cripple, not a hunchback." He went on to say that she lived in Draycott Avenue with her daughter who ministered to her needs, and that he was frequently in her flat.
>
> "What did you talk about?" I asked.
>
> "The subversive influences at work today," replied Gerald.
>
> "Political, I take it?"
>
> "Yes, political."
>
> "What a pair you must make!"
>
> Gerald did not deign to reply to this remark.
>
> I asked, "What sort of government would she like?"
>
> "Obviously a very right-wing government. She suffered, of course, from all the restrictions put on her during the war. ... She was known to be heartily opposed to the war, but her activities weren't of such a nature as to warrant her internment".[110]

It is likely enough that, speaking of "the subversive influences at work today", these conversations did sometimes turn to Aleister Crowley, about whom Hamilton certainly would have had plenty of anecdotes to tell Webster. After all, she had indeed paid some attention to Crowley in her writings, as a representative of the dark forces of subversion.[111]

Maxwell Knight

The name of Maxwell Knight (1900–1968) is linked to some of the most important counter-espionage operations carried out in England during the second half of the

1930s and the first years of the Second World War.[112] As we have seen, the purpose of the section of MI5 that Knight led for several years, the B5(b), was to keep an eye on extremist and subversive groups, especially with regard to possible infiltrations of these groups by foreign agents. Knight's strategy consisted in sending his own particularly well-trusted spies to infiltrate these groups. He achieved significant success in 1938, exposing a network of spies in the employ of Moscow operating under the cover of the British Communist Party; and again in 1940, with the notorious "Kent–Wolkoff affair", which merits a brief digression.

Tyler Kent (1911–88), an American citizen, was an employee of the United States embassy in London, and was responsible for transcribing the embassy's secret messages and documents into a ciphered code. He had been transferred there from the Moscow embassy in October 1939. There are reasons to believe that during his service in Moscow he was recruited by the Soviet secret service, even though he did not hold communist beliefs.[113] Kent thought it was supremely important for the United States to stay out of the new conflict in Europe, and he probably considered his activity as a Soviet agent as a way to contribute to the isolationist cause. His position at the London embassy made it possible for him to make copies of the secret documents that he was only supposed to convert into code.

Among the documents that Kent copied, some were of a particularly explosive nature: the strictly confidential letters exchanged between Churchill and Roosevelt immediately following the outbreak of the war. At the time, Churchill was not yet prime minister and Roosevelt was campaigning to be re-elected as president. American public opinion was, in the great majority, opposed to US entry into the war, and Roosevelt had set up his campaign in accordance with this opinion. In his correspondence with Churchill, however, the president revealed that he was quite favourable to the possibility of US involvement in the war.

This exchange of letters also continued after the spring of 1940, when Churchill became prime minister. Kent believed, surely with good reason, that exposing this correspondence would irremediably damage Roosevelt's chances at being re-elected, and that his defeat would prove a great boon to the isolationist party. Kent had connections in England's extreme right, which was very much in favour of making peace with Germany and forming a British–German alliance against the Soviets. The exposure of the Churchill–Roosevelt correspondence would also have proved beneficial to these groups, since it would have caused difficulties for Churchill's government, which refused to consider any form of negotiation with Germany.

Thanks to the infiltrations performed by his agents, Knight managed to follow the movements of Kent and his contacts. On 20 May 1940, with the permission of US ambassador Joseph Kennedy, he had Kent arrested, along with two others with whom he had plotted to use the correspondence: Anna Wolkoff, the daughter of Russian exiles and a catalyst of the extreme right in England; and Archibald Ramsay, the aristocratic founder of the Right Club, a political group that spread anti-Semitic ideas and promoted the idea of a negotiated peace with Hitler. The discovery of this conspiracy gave Churchill's government a pretext for shutting down all extreme right-wing political groups suspected of having pro-German sentiments. In May 1940 most of the members of the British Union of Fascists, including Oswald Mosley, as well as the members of The Link, another pro-Nazi and anti-Semitic organization, were incarcerated.[114]

The outcome of the Tyler Kent case was covered up to prevent undesirable political repercussions.[115]

All these events are of a certain importance, because they shed some light on the extreme right in Britain at the time the war broke out. It was presumably among these circles that Rudolf Hess hoped to find interlocutors when he made his solo flight in May 1941. These same circles included members of the British aristocracy and adherents to world conspiracy theories. We will return to this point in Chapter 5 when we examine the role attributed to Crowley by conspiracy theorists.

Knight was deeply fascinated by the occult world. In the mid-1930s he met writer Dennis Wheatley, who was not an occultist, but who did write novels in which magical and diabolical elements were often present.[116] A very close friendship developed between Knight and Wheatley, lasting until Knight's death.[117] During the war Wheatley also worked for the British secret service. Both Knight and Wheatley believed in reincarnation and discussed the subject of astral projection.[118] It was Wheatley who introduced Crowley to Knight. Wheatley, for his part, had met Crowley through Tom Driberg. The connections between these persons are complex, especially considering that Knight also knew Driberg and used him, as we have seen, as an informer within the Communist Party.

Masters, in his biography of Knight, cites an interesting story:

> Knight told his nephew, Harry Smith, that he and Dennis Wheatley went to Crowley's occult ceremonies to research black magic for Wheatley's books. "They jointly applied to Crowley as novices and he accepted them as pupils," Smith told me. "But my uncle stressed that his interest – and also Wheatley's – was purely academic."[119]

Another person with whom Crowley was in contact during this period was Ian Fleming, the author of the famous series of James Bond novels. Fleming, who was fascinated with the occult world, also knew and often met Knight and Wheatley.[120] At the beginning of the Second World War, Fleming was recruited to the NID (Naval Intelligence Department), the information service of the British Navy. Undoubtedly the most fascinating aspect of the connections between Crowley, Knight and Fleming concerns their role in the affairs behind Rudolf Hess's mysterious flight to Scotland in 1941. This remains one of the most obscure and intricate episodes of the entire Second World War. The fact that aspects still considered "sensitive" must lie behind this event is made evident by the care the British government has taken, even up to the present day, to keep most of the documents relating to the affair inaccessible. At the same time the British government has never deviated from the official position that Hess decided to undertake his flight simply because he was prey to an insane and confused exaltation. While there is an enormous literature on the affair, the book by the historian Rainer F. Schmidt can now be considered as one of the most complete reconstructions of the events.[121]

For quite some time, the hypothesis had already existed that the British secret service played a significant role in the events behind Hess's flight.[122] British historian John Costello has shown that Hess's flight was effectively the result of a British secret service operation aimed to make certain members of the Nazi regime believe that there were individuals in Britain, especially among the aristocracy, who were prepared to lobby for a negotiated peace.[123] Hitler needed this peace in order to be able to turn all Germany's power against the Soviet Union. Unfortunately Costello does not discuss one very important aspect of the question: namely, who in the British secret service was responsible for planning and implementing this operation up to the point of Hess's flight. The answer to this question appears to be provided by Anthony Masters's biography of Knight: not only were Knight himself and Ian Fleming involved, but Crowley as well. Masters writes: "Ian Fleming, then in the Department of Naval Intelligence, was fascinated by Knight's mysterious persona, and was to involve him in an extraordinary adventure whose components – The Link, Aleister Crowley and Hess – were to make an explosive mixture."[124]

As we have seen, The Link was an extreme right-wing organization that counted eminent British aristocrats among its members, and had been outlawed following the Tyler Kent affair in 1940. Before the organization was prohibited, its head was Admiral Sir Barry Domvile. Masters continues:

> It was Domvile and The Link that gave Fleming a brilliant, if audacious, idea. Having gone to Knight and studied Domvile's file, he suggested it might be possible to lure one of the Nazi leaders to Britain if The Link could be reborn for the occasion. The two of them built up a fictitious picture of The Link being driven underground but still retaining a membership influential enough to overthrow the Churchill government and negotiate peace with Germany.[125]

According to Masters, Fleming turned to Knight and not to his superior John Godfrey because he knew that the latter would never have approved such a risky operation. Knight, however, had a reputation for enjoying great independence from his superiors, especially given that he was a friend of Desmond Morton, Churchill's private secretary, who for Knight represented a guarantee of direct access to the prime minister. Also, Knight had a record of great success in his infiltration operations thus far.

> The next step was to look for a gullible Nazi leader and, to Fleming, the best candidate seemed Hitler's deputy, Rudolph Hess, who was not only anxious for peace to prevent Germany taking on the onerous task of attacking Russia, but was a student of astrology and the occult. Knight's thoughts turned at once to Crowley. He had him in mind for some time as a potential MI5 agent, but because of his eccentric personality he was considered just a little too much larger than life to be successful. Yet here was a top Nazi leader who believed in the occult and here was Crowley, the artful perpetrator of occult practices. Somewhere, Knight thought, there must be a link.[126]

Ultimately, however, it was decided that Crowley could not be used for an operation of this type. We have already seen one of the reasons that made his involvement seem less than desirable: "the Germans already knew, via a German agent who had lived with Crowley in Berlin, that Crowley had been passing information on Communism in Europe to the SIS".[127] As we saw, the German agent was none other than Gerald

Hamilton, and this refers to the period when he and Crowley were living together in Berlin in the early 1930s.

Fleming, however, devised another system for luring Hess into the trap. Via a connection in Switzerland, he made contact with a German astrologer who was working for the British secret service, and asked him for help in infiltrating the same occultist circles frequented by Hess. The astrologer succeeded in establishing contact with Hess and in giving him false information regarding the existence in Great Britain of an influential group of potential allies for Germany and conspirers against Churchill.

Around the end of 1940, Knight withdrew from Fleming's initiative, needing to devote his attention to the other cases his section was working on. Fleming continued his operation, however, deciding to use the name of the Duke of Hamilton to lure Hess. Douglas Douglas-Hamilton, Duke of Hamilton, was a Scottish aristocrat who, as master of ceremonies at Buckingham Palace, had direct access to King George VI at the time. The intent was to make Hess believe that the duke was disposed to discuss conditions for a negotiated peace between Britain and Germany. Hess, with his flight to Britain, intended to meet with the duke, believing the latter could help him in his mission. The duke, after the outbreak of the war, had been a member of the Anglo-German Fellowship, an association promoting friendship and cultural exchange between England and Germany. A fair number of the association's members came from British high society. In the 1930s the duke had often travelled to Germany, in particular attending the Berlin Olympic Games in 1936; on this occasion, he probably met with Hess. During these voyages the duke also met Albrecht Haushofer, son of the geopolitician Karl Haushofer and later a member of the anti-Nazi resistance in Germany.[128] There was apparently a relationship of confidence and esteem between the two, interrupted only by the force of events when war broke out. However, a month after the war began, the Duke of Hamilton was one of the first members of British Parliament to publicly express his opinion in favour of a negotiated peace with Germany.[129] It is now certain that around the end of 1940, Hess, now convinced that he could play a prominent role in the heretofore frustrated attempts by the Nazi government to contact some representatives of the British establishment and discuss conditions for a negotiated peace, asked Haushofer to write to the Duke of Hamilton and suggest a meeting with him.[130] The letter, however, was intercepted by British secret service agents, who contacted the duke. They told him to respond to the letter favourably, and if necessary to meet with Haushofer, certainly not in order to encourage any kind of peace with Germany but rather to obtain whatever information might be useful. It is certain that the British secret service intended to take advantage of the opportunity offered by Haushofer's letter; the question is whether this same letter, and consequently Hess's interest in meeting with Haushofer, were the result of a broader operation on the part of the secret service, as Masters seems to indicate – or whether the letter was merely a coincidence that the secret service exploited when they saw it coming their way. Research thus far has failed to answer this question, especially since certain documents are still kept under lock by the British government.

One should also be prudent about the intrinsic credibility of Fleming's role in these events, as told by Masters. But assuming that the secret service *did* play a part, and that they acted *without* informing Churchill or the government of the operation,[131] the possibility of Fleming's involvement – as well as Knight's – is far from being excluded.

And Crowley? Masters concludes his reconstruction as follows:

> Once Hess was in captivity, MI5 and MI6 congratulated themselves on a brilliant coup (although it was badly handled as a propaganda weapon) and Knight breathed a sigh of relief. The incredible plan had worked, largely as a result of Fleming's persistence. Crowley still waited in the wings and Knight now had no intention of allowing him on stage. Fleming was not so cautious and he suggested to Godfrey that Crowley might see Hess in prison and try to extract information from him about the influence of astrology on the Nazi leaders. It could have produced some interesting results but Godfrey turned the idea down out of hand. Ruefully, Fleming wished he had taken the proposition to Knight, but as Knight was now so much more cautious, he would have been unlikely to have received cooperation from him either.[132]

Knight's "caution" was motivated by a dangerous false step in his career. In May 1940 he had ordered the imprisonment of Ben Greene (1901–78), a cousin of the author Graham Greene (1904–91), believing him to be pro-Nazi on the basis of tendentious reports from one of his infiltrating agents. Ben Greene, however, was merely a Quaker pacifist who had been active for some time in the Labour Party and had worked for humanitarian associations aiding people displaced by the war. His strong anti-war opinions had nothing to do with any form of pro-German sentiment. The case risked turning into a scandal, and Greene had to be released. It was a bad blow for Knight, who until that time had enjoyed only successes. This explains his careful behaviour at the time of Hess's flight.[133] Fleming, on the other hand, was in favour of employing Crowley to interrogate Hess.[134] The subsequent events are recounted in a biography of Ian Fleming written by John Pearson:

> For many years he had been fascinated by the legend of wickedness which had attached itself to the name of Aleister Crowley. ... When the interrogators from British Intelligence began trying to make sense of the neurotic and highly superstitious Hess he got the idea that Crowley might be able to help .... He seems to have had no difficulty in persuading the old gentleman to put his gifts at the disposal of the nation, for a brief formal note sealed with cabbalistic signs arrived, through the "usual channels", for the Director of Naval Intelligence [i.e. John Godfrey, Fleming's superior].[135]

A copy of this "formal note" is in the Yorke Collection. The letter bears the date 14 May 1941, four days after Hess's arrival, and was written at Torquay, a seaside town in Devon to which Crowley had retreated after the outbreak of the war:

> Sir,
>
> If it is true that Herr Hess is much influenced by astrology and Magick, my services might be of use to the Department, in case he should not be willing to do what you wish.

Col. J. F. C. Carter ..., Thomas N. Driberg ..., Karl J. Germer ..., could testify to my status and reputation in these matters.

I have the honour to be,
Sir,

Your obedient servant
Aleister Crowley.[136]

Thus Crowley appears to have played, or at least may have played, a role in the Hess affair; certainly not a major role, but a role nonetheless. This would also have been in line with the patriotic attitude Crowley endeavoured to show during the years of the Second World War.

Crowley's possible role in relation to the Hess affair has also been discussed by Giorgio Galli, who examines the influence of esoteric culture on some members of the Nazi regime's elite.[137] On the basis of some hypotheses that take this element into account, he offers an explanation for some of the controversial episodes of the Second World War. According to Galli, Hess's flight was decided upon by the "esoteric" current of the party, with Hitler's support, the purpose being to establish contact with influential members of British society who shared at least a part of this esoteric culture and might therefore play a role in the making of a peace treaty between Germany and Britain. It was necessary for Hitler to secure Germany's western front before he could launch his attack on the Soviet Union. Galli also takes Aleister Crowley's position into consideration, if not as a possible direct intermediary between Hess and the British establishment, then at least as someone who may have played some sort of role in the events.[138] This hypothesis, of course, is primarily based on the assumption that "esoteric" circles that had significant social and political influence existed in Great Britain at the time; and, secondarily, on the idea that esoteric ideas shared by these circles and some members of the Nazi elite might have led the former to become more open to Germany's aspirations. In general, authors who have occupied themselves with these events have not attributed any great significance to the esoteric element. But as we have seen, it was anything but absent. Its role merely appears to have been a little less "fascinating" than Galli believes. If Masters's version were confirmed in all its details, then the esoteric element would be reduced to playing the role of a decoy: a bait to attract a credulous and ingenuous Rudolf Hess. Crowley himself, far from offering the Nazi regime a "contact point" for getting through to Britain's high society, was ready to put his esoteric expertise at the disposal of his country, in the role of a simple consultant. His esoteric knowledge had become like any other type of knowledge: a tool to be used for reaching a particular goal.

❧ 4. The Mouth of Hell

His attempts to apply the law of Thelema in politics and economics etc. were childish.
(Gerald Yorke, in a letter to Henri Birven, referring to Aleister Crowley)

Every time he had to concretize his political thought, he did so in a childish and vague form. (João Gaspar Simões, *Vida e Obra de Fernando Pessoa*, referring to Fernando Pessoa)

Fernando Pessoa's political mysticism

In this chapter I will examine one of the most mysterious and enigmatic episodes in Crowley's life: his journey to Portugal to meet with Fernando Pessoa (1888–1935).[1] Why is this episode and more generally Crowley's relationship with Pessoa so significant? To begin with, there is the interest that Pessoa's personality holds for anyone investigating connections between politics and esotericism during the first half of the twentieth century. Unfortunately, Pessoa's political and esoteric works are not yet available in English.[2] Most of Pessoa's esoteric writings are fragmentary in nature, and most remained unpublished for a long time after his death.

Fernando Pessoa is considered today as one of the great authors of modern times. He was an author whom critics discovered only little by little, and it is hardly surprising that for many decades, the exceptional quality of his poetic work outshone his other writings, such as those dedicated to political and esoteric matters. Pessoa published only a very small part of his writings during his life, mainly in journals with limited circulation.

Only some years after his death in 1935, with the increasing publication of the writings he had left behind, did Pessoa's figure begin to acquire the renown he now holds in the landscape of European literature. Once Pessoa's "other interests" came to light, however, some critics reacted with a certain unease. Italian writer and Pessoa specialist Antonio Tabucchi observed in 1979 that among the factors that had thus far prevented "a satisfying systematisation of Pessoa as an 'intellectual'", one should not underestimate

> the discomfort of critics when faced with a personality as disconcerting as Pessoa: which speaks to the prejudices and inhibitions of all those critics who examine Pessoa as a poet while forgetting that he was also a political man and a

philosopher ... relegating him to the heterogeneous, composite and ill-defined category of the "bad guys" of the twentieth century.[3]

Pessoa's "disconcerting" nature evidently arises from his political activity (which always took place strictly outside any institution or party). This activity even led him to write a "Defence and Justification of the Military Dictatorship in Portugal", in support of the regime that had seized power following the *coup d'état* of 28 May 1926, paving the way for Salazar's regime.[4] Pessoa's esoteric side could also appear "disconcerting" to some critics, at least initially; he left behind hundreds of pages bearing reflections on alchemy, magic, astrology, occultism, Kabbalah, Rosicrucianism, Templarism – in short, practically every aspect of the Western esoteric tradition.

Paradoxically, this same "disconcerting" nature is the reason why Pessoa is a significant figure for the present study. With his anti-bourgeois attitude, his anti-materialism, his messianic vision of the history of Portugal and his idea of a mystical regeneration not only of the individual but also of the entire nation and race, Pessoa expressed ideas that fall within the paradigm of the "illuminate thought". This makes his relationship with Crowley particularly interesting for us.

In Chapter 1, I mentioned another reason why the meeting between the two men deserves attention. René Guénon, in a letter to Julius Evola dated 29 October 1949, mentions Crowley's fake suicide, staged with Pessoa's assistance at a place near the town of Cascais known as the Boca do Inferno ("Mouth of Hell"). According to Guénon, Crowley intended to make the world believe he was dead, so that he could go to Germany and serve in secret as Hitler's "occult" adviser.[5] I will tackle this point at the end of this chapter.

I cannot engage here in a thorough discussion of Pessoa's esoteric ideas. A complete, critical edition of his esoteric writings is still lacking, and there is still much work to be done with regard to an evaluation and interpretation of these texts.[6] It should also be remembered that the archive of Pessoa's papers at the National Library in Lisbon still contains a great quantity of unpublished material. Here, in any case, I will offer a brief and synthetic overview of these aspects of Pessoa's work.

António Quadros, one of Pessoa's best-known critics, noted that "all of Fernando Pessoa's political thought is based not on a commonplace socio-political idealism, nor on the influence of ruling ideologies, but rather on the myth of Portugal as Fifth Empire".[7] The myth of the "Fifth Empire" is a recurrent theme in the Portuguese literary tradition, going as far back as the sixteenth century with Luís de Camões (1524–80). It is based on a specific interpretation of Daniel's famous prophecy. Daniel, interpreting a mysterious dream of King Nebuchadnezzar, describes four earthly kingdoms – Nebuchadnezzar's current kingdom and the three that will come after it – followed by a fifth kingdom, which will be set up directly by God and "shall never be destroyed".[8] The prophecy has naturally been interpreted in many different ways, depending on time and place. In seventeenth-century England, for example, it inspired the political and religious movement of the Fifth Monarchists. In Portugal, above all due to the writings of a Jesuit missionary and priest, Father António Vieira (1608–97), the prophecy soon came to be linked to another myth; that of Sebastianism.[9] According to the Sebastianist myth, the Portuguese king Sebastian (1554–78), who was defeated and slain in the battle of Al-Ksar el Kebir (1578) during a military expedition into

Morocco, did not actually die, but would return one day and restore Portugal to its imperial destiny. The origin of this myth can be explained above all by the significance this defeat had for Portugal's history. Almost all the country's young noblemen died in the battle; and the death of Don Sebastian left a dynastic gap open that enabled King Philip II of Spain to expand his hegemony over Portugal. Portuguese independence was finally regained in 1640. Similar "sleeping King" myths also exist in the traditions of other European countries. At the other end of the continent, in Romania, we find another example: the myth inspired by the figure of Stephen the Great, Voivode of Moldavia, which sparked a movement similar to Portuguese Sebastianism between the two world wars.[10]

Pessoa was not simply an eccentric whose inspiration was stirred up by these myths. Both the Sebastianism and the Fifth Empire myth had been a lively presence in Portuguese popular tradition and literature for centuries.[11] For Pessoa, however, the myth was not merely a literary theme but also a political tool. With it, he proposed to awaken the national sentiment of the Portuguese people in order to lead them back to a lost and mourned imperial splendour.[12] In his poem *Mensagem* especially, Pessoa reshapes the two myths, adding elements from the Rosicrucian tradition and the Arthurian cycle, and presenting them in a very sophisticated form.

Pessoa also dedicated himself to politics in a more direct and immediate way, writing magazine articles, debating fiercely with his adversaries, publishing pamphlets and writing works that analysed the Portuguese political, social and cultural situation.[13] As Tabucchi points out, Pessoa during his life occupied "a place in the Portuguese culture of the time that was more that of an intellectual than a poet: he was a cultural operator, as we would say today, next to being a ferocious and contradictory polemicist".[14]

Perhaps the best-known such episode in Pessoa's career as a "cultural operator" was the publication of his pamphlet in favour of the military dictatorship in Portugal, noted above. It is worth observing that the title of this pamphlet, *O Interregno*, suggests that Pessoa considered the dictatorship as a necessary but transitory condition preceding actual national regeneration, which would come with the advent of the prophesied Fifth Empire.

Moreover, the Empire Pessoa had in mind was not based upon military expansion or territorial conquest. Rather, it was based on a "spiritual" and "cultural" influence over the world.[15] Pessoa, for all that he had never held a particular sympathy for democracy, was never a proponent of totalitarianism. In a sort of memorandum written in March 1935, a few months before his death, he defined himself as a "conservative of the English style, that is, liberal within conservatism, and absolutely anti-reactionary".[16]

In touching now briefly upon Pessoa's esotericism, it is especially necessary to observe that a distinction between his political and esoteric interests may well be purely instrumental. To a certain extent, Pessoa did not consider these two fields as belonging to different realms.[17] As we have seen, a myth of national spiritual regeneration was at the basis of his political ideas, while an ambition for individual spiritual regeneration was at the basis of his interest in esotericism.

This contiguity between politics and esotericism can be seen very plainly in Pessoa's attitude toward the Jewish question. In the early 1920s he founded a publishing house, "Olisipo", with the purpose of giving new impetus to the Portuguese culture of the time, which he saw as stagnating and provincial. The enterprise was short-lived – Pessoa only managed to publish a few books – but among the various notes left over from this project, there is a list of titles that Olisipo was intended to publish.[18] This list includes works by Shakespeare, Aeschylus, Edgar Allan Poe, Greek lyricists, Coleridge – all of which were to be translated and edited by Pessoa. In addition, there are also works by Pessoa himself and his friends, such as the poets Mário de Sá-Carneiro (1890–1916) and António Botto (1892–1959); and the philosopher and esotericist Raul Leal (1886–1964). Among the titles listed, there is one that cannot help but draw our attention: *Protocolos dos Sábios de Sião*, the notorious *Protocols of the Learned Elders of Zion*.[19] As it is known, this text claimed to reveal the Jews' plan for world domination; it was created in the early twentieth century in circles connected with the Tsarist secret police, as an anti-Semitic propaganda tool. The Nazi regime later made use of the alleged revelations contained in the text to justify its racist politics. Pessoa gives the initials of the person who was supposed to edit the translation of the *Protocols*: A. L. R. These initials are quite mysterious; they do not match any of the various heteronyms Pessoa is known to have used, nor those of any of his better-known friends. It is hard to resist the suspicion, however, that the initials refer to Pessoa himself.[20]

But this is not all. Yvette Centeno, a scholar who has been mainly occupied with Pessoa's esoteric writings, brought to light various previously unpublished fragments in her book *Os Trezentos*.[21] These fragments were probably intended as part of a greater work that was never completed. It would be no easy task to give a comprehensive interpretation of these texts, but some elements are absolutely unequivocal. Pessoa's starting point was a statement made by a famous German industrialist and statesman of Jewish origin, Walter Rathenau (1867–1922). Rathenau had very important ministerial positions in Germany during the First World War and after, and was assassinated by right-wing extremists in 1922 for his supposed role in causing Germany's defeat.[22] In a journal article published in 1909 Rathenau had claimed that Europe was ruled by three hundred men, and this had become a common trope in the contemporary literature of conspiracy theories.[23] For Pessoa, these "three hundred" were an occult group of individuals who were ruling the world, or seeking to rule it. They were bearers of decadence, because with their influence they sought to destroy Europe's true traditions, which were based on three fundamental elements: Greek culture, Roman order and Christian morality.[24] In relation to this, Pessoa spoke explicitly of a "Jewish invasion", which was manifested above all in our epoch's tendency toward materialism.[25] Pessoa also distinguished between "Judaism" and "base Judaism", and claimed that the three hundred identified neither with the former nor with the latter, since they were not necessarily Jewish, but in any case exploited base Judaism as a tool for bringing about decadence and dissolution.[26]

As regards the more specifically esoteric Pessoa, Centeno wrote that "his preoccupation with the occult world was not an accidental episode near the end of his life, but something long-lasting that emerged in him very early on".[27] His first contacts with the occult took place in the mid-1910s, when he was employed to translate theosophical books.[28] During the same period he also had experiences with spiritualism, which he quickly abandoned. His interest in the occult, thus awakened, grew as the years passed, going through various phases. For example, one of the most obvious characteristics of his esoteric reflections is the component that we may define as neo-gnostic.[29] Pessoa had a dualistic vision according to which the material world is satanic and negative, while the spiritual world – which more than anything else was the world of symbols – is divine and positive.

In a famous letter to the critic Adolfo Casais Monteiro, dated 13 January 1935, Pessoa outlines three possible paths to realization through esotericism: the path of magic, the path of mysticism and the path of alchemy.[30] Magic – because it acts through the manipulation of matter, albeit in an indirect fashion – is satanic and dangerous, the work of sorcerers. Mysticism, although safer than magic, is far too slow. Alchemy was Pessoa's preferred path; this was a purely interior alchemy, not acting upon matter. It is worth noting that this letter was written by Pessoa a few months before he died; it represents the result of a lifetime of reflection upon esotericism, passing through several phases of development.

This refutation of the "magical" path suggests that Pessoa, near the end of his life, had taken distance from Crowley's ideas – ideas by which he had most certainly been significantly influenced in earlier years.[31] Astrology was also particularly important for Pessoa, and for a certain period he considered the possibility of practising as a professional astrologer, even opening an astrological studio in Lisbon. It was astrology, as we will see, that gave Pessoa occasion to come into contact with Crowley.

The magician and the poet

Thus far, insufficient attention has been paid to the many analogies that make Crowley and Pessoa look close to each other. The use of so many pseudonyms, or rather "heteronyms", which forms a fundamental part of Pessoa's psychology and artistic creativity may be compared to certain aspects of Crowley's character. Let us recall the passage from the *Confessions* that I quoted in Chapter 2: "I did not see why I should be confined to one life. How can one hope to understand the world if one persists in regarding it from the conning tower of one's own personality?"[32] Crowley, with the purpose of having experiences he could not have had while being simply himself, pretended to be other persons, becoming the Russian Count Vladimir Svareff or the Persian Prince Chioa Khan (it is interesting to see that his alter egos were almost invariably aristocrats). In both Crowley and Pessoa, we find the same desire to stray from the original identity at times when this identity, for one reason or another, proves insufficient. Both men seem to have wanted to break past the epistemological barriers with which Western culture had surrounded them, and to bypass a necessarily uniform and consistent personality. As an example, Pessoa wrote the following in an article published in 1915: "Let us – us young people – work at least to perturb souls and disorient spirits. Let us cultivate mental disintegration within ourselves, like a rare flower."[33] But in both Crowley and Pessoa, this process of disintegration never took place without a certain form of self-irony, which prevents us from taking either one of them too seriously. In this game of multiple personalities, there was always a certain element of jest.

Other analogies also come to mind, such as the neo-pagan and anti-Christian element; the sense of mission propelling both men, one as the prophet of a new religion, the other as the bearer of a national awakening; and their political ideas. Both had sympathies for authoritarian regimes. But most importantly of all, their "esoteric" backgrounds were similar. In the field of esotericism, they most certainly spoke the same language. Madame Blavatsky's theosophy, alchemy, Eckartshausen's Christian mysticism, Arthur Edward Waite's Masonic and Rosicrucian speculations – all these, and several others, were sources and interests they both shared. Consequently, if Crowley and Pessoa fell to discussing occult materials during their time together – as they very probably did – they would have been in a position to understand each other perfectly.

Both Crowley's biographer, John Symonds, and Pessoa's, João Gaspar Simões, have devoted some space to the meeting that took place in 1930, each biographer naturally approaching it from the point of view of his respective subject.[34] To these reconstructions there has more recently been added the publication of the complete correspondence between Crowley and Pessoa, together with other documents related to their meeting.[35] Originally, these documents were not donated to the National Library in Lisbon along with the other papers in the Pessoa collection; they were retained by Pessoa's family, and were therefore inaccessible to researchers for a long time. Their publication has cleared up certain obscure points, and marks an important step in the study of the relationship between the two men.

There does not seem to be any mystery in the way contact between Crowley and Pessoa was established. Pessoa followed the "esoteric scene" in Europe, and especially in Great Britain, with interest; he kept up on the news and ordered books from abroad. As a result, Aleister Crowley's fame must have reached him.

In March 1929, as we know, Crowley was expelled from France, along with his secretary, Israel Regardie, and his current Scarlet Woman (soon to be his wife), Maria Teresa Ferrari de Miramar. The news echoed throughout Europe. Crowley returned to England and moved into a cottage in Kent. In that same year he published the first two of the six projected volumes of his *Confessions*. Pessoa, learning of this publication, ordered the two volumes directly from the Mandrake Press publishing house. He received them in late November 1929 and responded with a letter on 4 December, accompanying his payment by cheque.[36] In this letter, besides asking to be sent any forthcoming volumes of the *Confessions* upon their publication,[37] Pessoa asked the publisher to inform Crowley of the incorrectness of his horoscope:

> If you have occasion to communicate, as you probably have, with Mr. Aleister Crowley, you may inform him that his horoscope is unrectified, and that if he reckons himself as born at 11h.16m.39s. p.m. on the 12th. October 1875, he will have Aries 11 as his midheaven, with the corresponding ascendant and cusps. He will then find his directions more exact than he has probably found them hitherto. This is a mere speculation, of course, and I am sorry to inflict upon you this purely fantastic intrusion into what is, after all, only a business letter.[38]

Pessoa was referring to Crowley's astrological chart, which appeared at the beginning of Volume I in this first edition of the *Confessions*.[39] Mandrake Press passed the letter on to Crowley, who responded from his cottage in Kent on 11 December: "I dare say your guess is accurate enough. I don't bother with directions. I do very little astrology, except pure genethliacal and transits. I should be very glad if you would let me have some information about my present situation."[40]

A few days later, apparently before even receiving Crowley's response quoted above, Pessoa spontaneously sent Crowley three of his books, containing poems in English that Pessoa had published at his own expense some time earlier. The books were *35 Sonnets*, *English Poems I–II* and *English Poems III*.[41] Crowley wrote another brief letter to Pessoa on 22 December:

> Thank you very much for the three little books. I think they are really very remarkable for excellence.
> In the Sonnets, or rather Quatorzaines, you seem to have recaptured the original Elizabethan impulse – which is magnificent.[42]

A small detail in these last two letters stands out as being of a certain importance. In both letters, Crowley addresses Pessoa as "Care Frater". With this, he appears to have intended to indicate a spiritual affinity between himself and his correspondent, much as if they belonged to the same initiatory order. We might recall here that the members of the Golden Dawn called each other "*fratres*" and "*sorores*".

Before continuing with these letters, let us turn for a moment to the biography of Pessoa written by João Gaspar Simões, and to that of Crowley written by John Symonds. It is interesting to see the motivations that the two authors give to Crowley for his voyage to Lisbon.[43] Gaspar Simões writes:

> Correspondence between the two was established; Pessoa sent Crowley his *English Poems*, and one fine day the magician announced to his new admirer on the western edge of Europe that he was coming to Portugal, specifically to meet this astrological prodigy face to face. ... The announcement of this unexpected visit caused [Pessoa] great apprehension. Crowley, the poet naturally knew, was a magician – a demonic and satanic magician, no less.[44]

And here is Symonds's version:

> At the end of August, [Crowley] decided that it was time he withdrew into another Great Magical Retirement. Like the sage Lao-tzu on his Magical Retirement, he took a young maiden (Hanni) with him. On Friday, 29 August, Crowley and Hanni stole away together to Southampton with tickets to Lisbon in their pockets and little else. ... Crowley sent Pessoa a cable to say he was on his way.[45]

Here we anticipate a little, but merely to show that according to both Symonds and Gaspar Simões, Crowley decided to go to Lisbon in a fairly extemporaneous way, almost as if he wanted to surprise Pessoa: "one fine day ...". Now, however, as we return to the correspondence between the two men, which began nearly a year prior to their first meeting, we see that things did not happen so casually and were not the result of a sudden whim.

Before sending his letter of 22 December, in which he thanked Pessoa for sending his English poems, Crowley added a handwritten note to it. This postscript is highly significant, because in it, for the first time, Crowley reveals his intent to meet Pessoa in person. The text of this postscript, which does not appear in the copy of the letter preserved at the Warburg Institute (and was therefore inaccessible to me when the first edition of the present study was published), first came to light with the aforementioned publication of the complete Crowley–Pessoa correspondence. Crowley wrote: "I have, indeed, taken the arrival of your poetry as a definite Message, which I should like to explain in person. Will you be in Lisboa [sic] for the next three months? If so, I should like to come and see you: but without telling any one. Please let me know by return of post."[46]

Why did Crowley place so much importance on the arrival of Pessoa's English poetry? What is the meaning of this reference to a mysterious "Message"? These questions remain unanswered, although I will later formulate a hypothesis as to the motives Crowley may have had in mind when meeting with Pessoa. Curiously enough, one of Pessoa's most famous poems, and one of the few that were published in book form during his lifetime (in 1934), is entitled *Mensagem*, meaning "Message".

On 6 January 1930 Pessoa responded to Crowley's two letters of 11 and 22 December:

Carissime Frater:

I thank you very much indeed for your letters of the 11th. and the 22nd. December, particularly so for the second one, and especially for the written addendum to it. ...

I shall be in Lisbon, for all practical purposes, during the next three months. ... If, however, any month of these first three of the year will serve your time and intention, I should very much prefer to meet you here *in March* – at any time within March. I shall not leave Lisbon at all in that month, and I have both the present month and February taken up by matters, of no importance in themselves – either absolutely, or relatively to the present one –, which deliver me over to an extraneous attention which I should not like to be clogged with when listening to you.

Apart from this, astrological reasons would counsel me to suggest March ....

Furthermore, there is a vague possibility that I may have to go to England in the end of February. If so, I would inform you in full advance and (unless there be some reason I cannot foresee for the place of meeting to be Lisbon) you would be spared the trouble of coming to Portugal. ...

I shall, of course, tell no one at all about your visit. Was your warning connected with the receipt by you of a booklet (in French) by Raul Leal? He is a friend of mine (so to speak, for I am altogether apart from any sort of friendship and from every sort of intimacy); I translated to him some pages, here and there, of the first volume of your "Confessions", and he asked me for the address of the publisher, so as to send you his book to their postal care. He now tells me, on my return to Lisbon, that he has received a letter from you, and is going to write to you a long one "on occult matters". With this, of course, I have no connection, as I have no connection with anything. Please do not take this as a reflection of any kind on Leal, whom I really like and whose splendidly intense metaphysical ability I appreciate. This is a mere statement of fact and, so to speak, a non-juror's note.

...

Yours fraternally,
Fernando Pessoa[47]

As we can see, Pessoa took Crowley's handwritten postscript quite seriously. Besides not wishing any "extraneous attention" to distract him from his visitor, he also brought in astrological considerations concerning the best time for their meeting, and even considered the possibility of this meeting taking place in England rather than Portugal.[48] Meanwhile, Crowley's salutation of "Care Frater" to Pessoa was reciprocated by a "Carissime Frater" from Pessoa to Crowley. However one may choose to interpret this letter, at this point it is clear that Crowley's decision to go to Portugal was in fact not so extemporaneous; indeed, Pessoa had been expecting the visit for months.

Interestingly, we also find the name of Pessoa's friend and fellow esotericist Raul Leal being mentioned here. As we will see later in this chapter, Leal was fascinated by Crowley's personality and teachings, and was very keen on meeting him when the latter went to Portugal. Pessoa seems to have thought that Leal might be involved in Crowley's "Message", and preferred thus to take distance from him, perhaps being afraid that Leal's eccentricity might jeopardize his relationship with Crowley. This was perceptive enough, because as we will see later, when Crowley met Leal in Lisbon, he did not have a very positive impression of him.

Crowley responded to Pessoa, dating his letter in a peculiar manner according to his own personal calendar, from which we deduce the date to be 14 January 1930:

Care Frater

… I quite agree with you about March. I have many matters to put in order.

But it would be still better should you be in London in February. Our meeting there should elucidate some points in dispute in my mind about the Message*, so that proper plans may be made. I shall expect to hear from you as soon as you know your own plans.

…

*I did not say, or mean, "warning".[49]

Crowley's added note is interesting, because it shows he took notice of Pessoa's apprehension in relation to his "Message". He made it clear that Pessoa had no reasons to be concerned: his "Message" was not a warning and had nothing to do with Raul Leal. We now know that it just referred to his plans for the spreading of his magical and literary work through the help of Pessoa, which was one of the things that motivated him when he decided to travel to Portugal.

Pessoa waited a while before responding to this letter. On 25 February, he wrote:

Care Frater:

My writing you so late implies only that not till the very verge of yesterday was it certain to me that I would not go to England.

I shall not leave Lisbon – unless for an occasional short voyage to Evora, from which four hours can recall me – until the middle of the year, and even then I may not leave.

If, therefore, you wish to come over, or think it within Fate to do so, you have but to give me a slight advance notice and I shall be here to see and hear you.[50]

The possibility of meeting in England, which Crowley seems to have preferred, had faded; but Pessoa reconfirmed his availability for a meeting in Portugal.

After this letter, the correspondence continued casually until May, but plans for a visit did not take a more concrete form.[51] Then, after a few months' pause, on 28 August, Pessoa received a telegram announcing Crowley's arrival in Lisbon by ship.[52] This was indeed a sudden acceleration of events, but, after examining these letters, it becomes clear to us not only that Crowley and Pessoa had been intending to meet for several months beforehand, but also that there was a *specific motive* for this meeting. What was this motive?

During my research at the Warburg Institute, I came across an unpublished document that may shed some light on these events. At first sight it appears to have nothing to do with Crowley's voyage to Portugal: it is a typewritten text by Crowley about Gerald Yorke.[53] It is one of those documents in which the petty side of Crowley's personality shows itself mercilessly. As we saw in Chapter 1, in the early 1930s Crowley broke up with two of his most important disciples and friends: Gerald Yorke and Israel Regardie.[54] Crowley took "revenge" on them, writing "statements" in which he insulted them and accused them of betrayal. Crowley circulated his statement on Regardie among their common acquaintances.[55] He might have done the same for the one on Yorke, although we do not know this for sure.

In the text on Yorke, Crowley, summarizing the history of his relationship with his ex-disciple, devotes some space to the events of August 1930. He claims that upon returning from Germany near the end of the month, he found that his wife, Maria Ferrari de Miramar, had disappeared. Some of his friends informed him that Yorke had received her as a guest.[56] Further on, Crowley writes: "I had no time to investigate these rumours at the moment, as I was obliged to leave immediately for Lisbon in order to establish there a headquarter for the Order under Don [sic] Fernando Pessoa."[57] By the "Order", Crowley doubtless meant the Ordo Templi Orientis.

Thus, going by what is said in this letter, the aim behind the meeting between Pessoa and Crowley must have been the creation of a Portuguese section of the Order that would be led by Pessoa.[58] This seems to be confirmed by another document, a letter Crowley wrote to Pessoa during the first days of the former's stay in Portugal. Crowley suggests to him that they arrange a meeting for discussing various questions: "I have very much to say to you besides the questions of translations and publishing. There is in particular the scheme of putting the Work of the Order on a world-wide basis of close organisation".[59] It therefore appears evident – and confirmed once and for all – that the relationship between Crowley and Pessoa also had implications that were "esoteric", if not specifically initiatory. Crowley and Pessoa met several times during his first visit to Portugal, but in his diary Crowley does not provide any details of the content of their conversations.

It is difficult to say how Pessoa reacted to Crowley's proposals of collaboration in relation to the Ordo Templi Orientis. Judging by what we know of his personality and his apparent resistance to direct involvement in any organization, whether political or esoteric, it is probable that he did not pursue the matter further. However, at least in the ideal sense (if not in the concrete sense, which cannot be excluded *a priori*), this aspect is connected to another element: Pessoa's interest in Templar traditions.

The Ordo Templi Orientis was inspired by this same tradition, passed down via the Masonic Templarism that had spread throughout continental Europe in the mid-eighteenth century.[60] But the OTO was not the only group to draw inspiration from Templar ideas. Near the end of the nineteenth century there was a revival of interest in the neo-Templar tradition, and besides the OTO, we might also mention the racist Ordo Novi Templi (ONT), founded by Lanz von Liebenfels around 1907, and the ephemeral Ordre du Temple Renové (OTR), founded in 1908 by René Guénon along with a few other members of the Parisian occultist milieu of the time.[61] But beyond these, the most mysterious is undoubtedly the OTP: Ordem Templária de Portugal. There are numerous references to this Templar order in Pessoa's esoteric writings. However, as far as we know, the OTP was not a concrete, existing organization, but merely the fruit of the Portuguese poet's fantasy.[62]

The information Pessoa gives on this order appears somewhat contradictory. In his letter to the critic Adolfo Casais Monteiro, Pessoa also devotes some space to the OTP. As I said, the letter was written in January 1935, and this is an important detail, because Pessoa died in November of the same year:

> As to "initiation" or lack thereof, I can tell you only this, for I do not know how to answer your question: I do not belong to any Initiatory Order. The quote, the epigraph to my poem *Eros e Psique*, from a passage (translated, since the *Ritual* is in Latin) of the Ritual of the Third Degree of the Templar Order of Portugal, indicates simply – this is a fact – that I was permitted to leaf through the Rituals of the first three degrees of this Order, which has been extinct or dormant since circa 1888. Were it not dormant, I would not have quoted this part of the Ritual, because one must not quote passages (indicating the source) from rituals that are being used.[63]

In this letter, Pessoa claims not to belong to any order of initiates. He also claims that the OTP has been extinct, or "dormant", since 1888. But that year was also the year of Pessoa's birth. A few months earlier a friend of Pessoa's, Augusto Ferreira Gomes (whom we shall meet again shortly hereafter), had dedicated a book of poems significantly entitled *Quinto Império* to Pessoa, with these words: "To Fernando Pessoa, born in the right year".[64] What was this supposed to mean? Why was 1888 the "right" year? According to a certain interpretation of a prophecy by Bandarra (pseudonym of Gonçalo Anes, 1500–1556), the "Portuguese Nostradamus" who played an important role in the earliest formulations of Sebastianism, King Sebastian was to return in that year.[65] Pessoa apparently saw the coincidence of this date with his year of birth as a "sign" of his leading role in the national revival of Portugal.[66] In this same year, the Templar Order of Portugal had become dormant. But here a problem arises: two months after writing this letter to Casais Monteiro, Pessoa wrote a memorandum, cited earlier,[67] in which he describes his "initiatory position": "Initiated, through direct communication from Master to Disciple, into the three lesser degrees of the (apparently extinct) Templar Order of Portugal."[68]

What was the truth? Was the OTP extinct, or only apparently so? Was Pessoa initiated or not? Might he have been initiated at some point during the two months that passed between writing the letter and writing the memorandum? The mystery may be cleared up by a fragment published by Teresa Rita Lopes, in which Pessoa confirms that he was initiated to the "three lesser degrees" of the OTP.[69] Here he explains that there is a certain difference between "being initiated" and "belonging" to an Order, and that therefore his two statements (cited above) are not contradictory. Unfortunately, this fragment does not tell us much about the nature of this Order.

Whatever may have been the nature of the Templar Order of Portugal, Pessoa cannot have been unaware of the fact that Aleister Crowley was the international head of another neo-Templar order. It becomes then tempting to think that Pessoa's ponderings on the OTP were somehow connected to Crowley's visit to Portugal; and this hypothesis appears even more likely when we look at the structure and degrees of the OTP, as Pessoa presents it.

What these degrees show us is an unequivocal Crowleyan influence: they are taken, without any variation, from the degrees of the A∴A∴.[70] At this juncture it is worth noting that, between the degrees of the Golden Dawn and those of the A∴A∴, there was not perfect equivalence: Crowley introduced some modifications of his own. Thanks to these modifications, we can be certain that the model Pessoa used for the OTP structure was Crowley's A∴A∴, and not the Golden Dawn in its original form. In fact, it becomes clear that most of the notions Pessoa had of the Golden Dawn were acquired through Crowley, and therefore filtered through his interpretation of it.

We should also bear in mind that Pessoa, besides the *Confessions*, had at his disposal another major work by Crowley: *Magick in Theory and Practice*.[71] In the book there is an entire appendix dedicated to the system and degrees of the A∴A∴.[72] But in Pessoa's texts, we also find other typically Crowleyan themes, such as the "knowledge and conversation of the Holy Guardian Angel" or the principles of Thelema.[73]

I will give here only an example of Crowley's influence on Pessoa, citing an annotation from Pessoa's posthumous fragments. It is an undated typewritten text in English. Remember that for Pessoa, English was more than a second language: between the ages of eight and eighteen, he had lived in South Africa and attended English schools. He used English not only in his part-time work for commercial enterprises in Lisbon, but also as a language for self-reflection.

> There is apparently something degrading in such a formula as "Do what thou wilt shall be the whole of the Law", but it so happens that this formula can be understood in many senses, the thing being to have the right one. As in Masonry there are many understandings of the Order and its Symbols, so in this, and all the more in this because it stands higher and has therefore more space below it for the arbitrariness of understandings.
>
> In immediate appearance, the formula is a simple call to licence in all ways. But, if it be understood that Will means the soul's true Will, the whole is changed, for the soul cannot rightly desire that which is its own bondage, as licence is.
>
> The formula, in its essence is, Find out what you are; Find out what that which you are wants; Do what you want as such as you are.[74]

Even if Crowley's name is not mentioned, it is obvious that Pessoa is here referring to Thelemic doctrine. Moreover, his comment regarding the precept of "Do what thou wilt" is in complete agreement with what Crowley himself always said about it, so much so that Crowley himself might have easily subscribed to this interpretation. As we have seen, "Do what thou wilt" for Crowley had nothing to do with licentiousness. According to him, the goal was to discover the direction of the force he calls "True Will", and then follow it, instead of hindering it, as he claims often happens to normal human beings. This is supposed not to have anything to do with the satisfaction of ephemeral desires. Pessoa's passage testifies to the attention with which he must have studied certain aspects of Crowleyan doctrine. A deeper study of Pessoa's esoteric texts would undoubtedly lead us to conclude that Crowley's influence over Pessoa was far more profound than critics have cared to admit until now.

The suicide stunt

The principal source for what Crowley did during his stay in Portugal remains his diary from this period.[75] From this we learn that Pessoa made a favourable impression on him from their first meeting. On 2 September, the day of his arrival in Lisbon, Crowley notes that "Pessoa met us: a *very* nice man".[76] We have less information, however, on the impression Pessoa had of Crowley.

Then came Crowley's faked suicide. On the night of 16 September, Crowley and Hanni Jaeger, the German girl who had accompanied him to Lisbon, had a violent scene in their hotel room.[77] The next day, Jaeger left Crowley, who then informed Pessoa of the situation. Crowley managed to track her down two days later (19 September), but could not convince her to stay with him in Portugal: she had decided to return to Germany alone, and the next day she left Lisbon for Berlin. Meanwhile, it appears, the idea of staging his suicide emerged in Crowley's mind.

According to Symonds, the idea came to Crowley only after Jaeger left. He quotes the following passage, which according to him was written by Crowley in his diary on 21 September: "I decide to do a suicide stunt to annoy Hanni. Arrange details with Pessoa."[78] However, this sentence does not appear in Crowley's diary, and, supposing that Symonds attributed it to the diary by mistake, it is unclear what its real source might be.[79] Even if Crowley elaborated his plan further on 21 September (he wrote, among other things: "Developed plan to utilise local scenery", obviously referring to the Boca do Inferno), the diary does not say explicitly that the purpose of the set-up was to put pressure on Crowley's young companion – with whom, despite her departure, he was already reconciled anyway. Moreover, it appears that a similar idea had surfaced in Crowley's mind on at least two other occasions. In August 1923, when he was living in Tunis after his expulsion from Italy, he planned a fake suicide modelled on that of the legendary Empedocles, the intent being to draw public attention to the "unjust" measures taken against him by the Italian government and to protest the attacks against him by the scandal-hungry British press.[80] And then in March 1929, while he was in the process of being expelled from France, he had another plan for a suicide stunt, which he proposed to journalist Francis Dickie (1890–1976), who however refused to collaborate.[81]

Whatever Crowley's motivations may have been, in the late afternoon of 25 September, the journalist and writer Augusto Ferreira Gomes (a friend of Pessoa's, as we have seen) happened to be walking by chance (as he later claimed) past the Boca do

Inferno, a chasm in an inlet near Cascais where the waves pound constantly below a tall, overhanging cliff. It was, in fact, a favourite place for suicides and for the disposal of inconvenient corpses.[82] As he passed by, Ferreira Gomes came upon a letter, weighted down by a cigarette case to keep the wind from blowing it away. It was, in fact, the farewell letter that the notorious British adventurer Aleister Crowley had written to his last companion: "An I 4 ☉ in ♎ / L.G.P. / I cannot live without you. The other 'Boca do Infierno' [sic] will get me – it will not be as hot as yours! Hjsos! Tu Li Yu".[83]

On 27 and 28 September, two articles appeared in the Lisbon daily paper *Diário de Notícias*.[84] The second article stated that, according to the International Police, Crowley had crossed the border into Spain on 23 September. The plot began to thicken: how could it be possible that Crowley left Portugal on the 23rd and Ferreira Gomes found the letter only two days later? The article also included an interview with Pessoa, who was interrogated as a friend of the missing person. Pessoa claimed that he had seen Crowley twice in Lisbon on 24 September, the day after the latter had supposedly left Portugal – and the day before his presumed suicide.[85]

On 5 October, Ferreira Gomes published a special report in the *Notícias Ilustrado*, to which he regularly contributed: "O Mistério da Boca do Inferno".[86] The article gave an account of how the letter was found and of the initial investigations, a brief and sympathetic description of Crowley's career (for which Crowley himself must have provided the information) and another long interview with Pessoa, who repeated what he had said a few days earlier, adding a few astrological considerations.

The news quickly travelled outside Portugal: on 30 October the French illustrated magazine *Détective*, which had already published a report on Crowley's expulsion from France in 1929, came out with Crowley's face on the cover and an interview with Ferreira Gomes. The British press, of course, covered the case as well. Interest in the event remained alive for several weeks. On 16 December, the Portuguese illustrated *Girasol* published an article with a new, chilling hypothesis: "Aleister Crowley foi assassinado?" ("Was Aleister Crowley Assassinated?"). The article contained a new interview with Pessoa, who claimed that he knew nothing of Crowley's fate and that he was sure some British detectives had come to Portugal to investigate the case, but had not reached a solution. At the end of the interview Pessoa mentioned an article in the daily *Oxford Mail* from 15 October in which it was stated that a medium in London, during a spiritualist séance, had found out that Crowley had in fact been assassinated by "an agent of the Roman Catholic Church".

But what did Crowley actually do? In fact, while the papers and their readers around Europe were still puzzled about his destiny, he had already reached Berlin, where he soon arranged an exhibition of his paintings, and very probably threw himself again into the arms of Hanni.[87] We know that he and Pessoa continued to exchange letters for a certain period, either directly or through the mediation of Crowley's associates, such as Germer and Regardie. Pessoa therefore, despite his statements to the press, knew quite well what had become of the British occultist. On 1 October, Crowley wrote in his diary: "Wire from Pessoa. 'Letter cigarette case identified Crowley's discovered evening 25th place coast Mouth Hell police investigating doubt suicide though nothing definite ascertained.'"[88] On 13 October: "Accounts of 'O Misterio da Boca do Inferno' in *Notícias Ilustrados* [sic] arrive."[89] So Pessoa also sent Crowley the articles on his case that had appeared in Portugal.

The relationship between Pessoa and Crowley also has an interesting appendix. After the Boca do Inferno affair, Pessoa translated a poem by Crowley, namely the *Hymn to Pan* (*Hino a Pã*). The poem had been originally published in *Magick in Theory and Practice*, which as we know was one of the books by Crowley that Pessoa owned. We do not know whether Pessoa translated this poem spontaneously or whether he did so at Crowley's request. However, he did send the poem to his friend and future biographer Gaspar Simões, who was a key figure in the most important Portuguese literary journal at the time: *Presença*. Pessoa had published several of his poems there, and would publish still more, thanks to Gaspar Simões. On 6 December, Pessoa wrote to him:

> I am sending you, as a simple curiosity, a translation I did from English of a true "magic poem" – the *Hymn to Pan*, which constitutes the *preface* to the treatise *Magick* by Master Therion. *This poem is not meant for publication*, but only for you to read. I also beg you that you do not show it to too many people. I do not say that you cannot publish it, but the point is that for that purpose the authorization of Master Therion would be necessary; and Master Therion has disappeared.[90]

Gaspar Simões, aware of Pessoa's fertile imagination and apparently not aware of the "Boca do Inferno" affair, at first thought that "Master Therion" was one of Pessoa's alter egos. Pessoa, in a subsequent letter, was forced to explain that

> Master Therion is not my heteronym; it is simply the "supreme name" of the English poet, magician, astrologer and "mystery man" whose common name is (or was) Aleister Crowley, and who also took the name of "The Beast 666". ... After writing you, I reflected upon what I had said, namely that the poem should not be published. After all, I see no reason not to publish it, if you find it interesting.[91]

Thus, although Pessoa initially did not intend to make his translation of the *Hymn to Pan* public, he later changed his mind. Gaspar Simões decided to publish the poem in his journal, but the matter evidently took some time, for on 5 October 1931 Pessoa wrote to him to ask for news of the poem:

> I am writing you ... because I want to know with certainty whether the next issue (by the way: when will it come out?) will include my translation of the *Hymn to Pan* by Aleister Crowley. Crowley, who went to live in Germany after his suicide, wrote to me a few days ago and asked me about the translation – or rather, about the publication of the translation. I had written to him a few months ago, saying it would soon be published in *Presença*. You have led me to put myself in a pinch with this declaration. See now, don't put me on the bad side of a magician! But seriously, if there is any reason not to publish it, please tell me frankly.[92]

A year after the event, Pessoa could finally reveal that he was in contact with Crowley, doing so with his unmistakeable sense of humour. Now there was no longer any need to feign ignorance about the magician's fate. This letter also shows that Crowley and

Pessoa remained in contact for a good deal of time after the Boca do Inferno affair. The *Hymn to Pan*, in Pessoa's Portuguese translation, was finally published in number 33 of *Presença*, which was issued between late November and early December of that year. This must have calmed the worried poet, who had been so keen on keeping the promise he had made to Crowley a few months earlier.

What interpretation can we give of the (actually quite successful) Boca do Inferno set-up? As we have seen, Crowley had thought about such a stunt before, and it had always been in moments of acute stress. On the basis of the available evidence, it seems evident that the primary purpose of the stunt was just personal publicity, combined with the thrill of being on the front page of the international press. He was then short of money, and very probably thought that such a sensational stunt would at least help boosting the sale of his books, which was one of the very few sources of income that were still open to him at that stage in his life. At the same time, there were certainly other factors playing a role. It is quite possible that, as Symonds suggest, Crowley also intended to make an impression on his girlfriend Hanni, after things had turned sour during their stay in Portugal. And then, we should also not forget his love of hoaxes and pranks for the sheer sake of them. This was a drive that continued throughout his life: the pages of the *Confessions* are strewn with accounts of pranks, often highly amusing ones, that Crowley played upon friends, acquaintances and strangers. In this regard he and Pessoa were certainly on the same page: Pessoa loved deception and trickery just as much as Crowley. Finally, it should also be mentioned that both men were voracious readers, as well as authors, of detective novels and stories.[93] For them, nothing could have been more exciting than being involved in a case so mysterious, and so well-tailored to their respective personalities, as the Boca do Inferno affair.

But what of Guénon's "chilling hypothesis" that the staged suicide was intended to allow Crowley to disappear for a while so that he could serve as Hitler's secret adviser? Here is what René Guénon wrote to Julius Evola from Cairo on 29 October 1949:

> To return to Crowley, what you tell me reminds me of the story from 1931 (at least I believe this was the correct date) [it is not, as we know]: he went to Portugal, and suddenly disappeared; his clothes were found on the seashore, leading to the belief that he had drowned; but it was only a simulated death, so that people would no longer watch him and try to find out where he had gone. In fact, *he had gone to Berlin to function there as a secret adviser to Hitler*, who was then starting out; and this probably gave rise to certain rumours about the "Golden Dawn", but in reality it was only Crowley, because the man who was his "colleague" at the time, a certain English colonel named Etherton, no longer had any connection to this organization.[94]

Guénon had also alluded to this topic in another letter, many years earlier. On 4 September 1938 he had written to his Romanian correspondent Renato Schneider: "What is true is that at the beginning of the Hitler affair, there was not only Trebitsch-Lincoln, but also Aleister Crowley and a certain Colonel Ettington."[95]

First of all, it is important to keep in mind that Guénon considered Crowley either a charlatan or an agent of the "counter-initiation", if not both at the same time. I will return to this in the following chapter. This can help us to better understand and interpret Guénon's statements. We may also observe that if Crowley had wanted to disappear in order to fulfil a secret political role in Germany, he certainly chose a bizarre way of doing so. He was undoubtedly aware of the fact that his staged suicide would echo throughout the entire European press, as indeed it did. He was actually so well aware of this outcome that he did his best to organize the event in the most striking manner possible. All evidence indicates that Crowley really did not wish to disappear from the public scene, but on the contrary, that he wanted to be on the front pages of all the newspapers, surrounded by that aura of romanticism and mystery of which he was so fond. It was indeed a very loud request for attention and consideration. It does not seem to be the best game plan for someone wanting to gain a very discreet, delicate position in service to the future German dictator. Needless to say, there is not the slightest evidence that might confirm Guénon's "hypothesis". Neither in Crowley's diaries from that time nor in the things he occasionally wrote later about Nazism do we find anything to suggest that he had had any personal contact with Hitler or with other members of the Nazi party – before or after his faked suicide in 1930.

This being said, however, I should also add that we still miss some documents that might shed further light on Crowley's activities in Germany at the time. In fact, while the portion of his diary for the Portuguese trip has now been found and published,[96] we still miss a collection of his memoirs from the Berlin period (from 1930 to 1932), which was originally kept together with that part of the diary and is even listed along with it in the index of the Yorke Collection at the Warburg Institute. This text was called *Love and Adventures in Berlin*.[97] It may have contained details that are not mentioned in the diary. Moreover, the Berlin period is also interesting regardless of Guénon's hypothesis; during this time Crowley's connections to members of the illuminate underground appear to have thickened. Curiously, it was in this same period that Crowley began to attract the attention of the *Revue Internationale des Sociétés Secrètes*, a Catholic anti-Masonic periodical. But I will return to this in the next chapter.

The shadow of the magician

During his sojourn in Portugal Crowley was not only in contact with Pessoa. There appear to have been two other persons especially – both close friends of Pessoa – who took an interest in the English visitor. One was Augusto Ferreira Gomes, whom we have already encountered; the other was Raul Leal, one of the authors whose works Pessoa intended to release through his publishing house in the early 1920s.

Ferreira Gomes, born in Lisbon in 1892, was a writer and journalist, as we know, and also possessed graphic talent. He was probably Pessoa's closest friend in the last years of the poet's life. In 1934, a year before Pessoa's death, Ferreira Gomes published *Quinto Império*, a collection of poems inspired by the Sebastianist myth. Pessoa wrote a preface to the book, and Ferreira Gomes dedicated it to him, with that strange sentence relative to the year of his birth.[98] Ferreira Gomes, like Pessoa, was interested in esotericism: Gaspar Simões described him as a "fellow occultist" of Pessoa's, and according to António Quadros, he was a "poet greatly dedicated to the study of astrology, Kabbalah and prophecy".[99] In 1938, three years after Pessoa's death and a good eight years after the Boca do Inferno affair, Ferreira Gomes published a poem dedicated to Aleister Crowley in the Lisbon-based literary review *Mensagem*.[100] The fact that one of the players in the faked suicide would publish something relating to Crowley so many years after the event leads one to believe that the latter's exploits in Portugal must have left quite an impression on the cultural elite that had surrounded Pessoa – particularly on an elite so very attracted to esotericism and occultism. This becomes even more evident when we consider the case of Raul Leal.

Leal, born in Lisbon in 1886, was of aristocratic origin and abandoned a career as a lawyer to dedicate himself full-time to literary activities.[101] For a certain period he lived as an exile in Spain due to his monarchist views. He was certainly an eccentric character: like Crowley, he had his own personal religion, Paracletianism, and called his system of thought Transcendental Vertiginism; in it, the influence of late-nineteenth-century Decadent occultism seems quite apparent, particularly that of Joséphin Péladan (1858–1918). In 1923 Leal was at the centre of a scandal caused by his pamphlet *Sodoma Divinizada*, in which he presented his theories relative to esoteric and spiritual homosexuality. An association of Catholic university students published a manifesto in favour of censoring immoral works, citing Leal's pamphlet as a prime example; the latter was withdrawn from sale. At this juncture Pessoa came to his friend's aid, publishing *Aviso por Causa da Moral*, in which he derided the censorious attitudes of the students and vigorously defended Leal from their outrageous insinuations.[102] In the following years, Leal remained connected to Pessoa out of sincere gratitude for his moral support on this occasion.

As regards the relationship between Crowley and Leal, there is a copy at the Warburg Institute of a letter from the former to the latter written on 22 December 1929.[103] In this letter, Crowley thanks Leal for sending him his book. How did the two manage to come into contact? Through Pessoa, of course. As we have seen earlier, from Pessoa's letter to Crowley dated 6 January 1930, Pessoa had translated some pages from the first volume of the *Confessions* for Leal, who did not know English.[104] Leal was so fascinated that he asked Pessoa for the address of Crowley's publisher in England in order to make contact with him. He subsequently sent a letter together with his book, containing a poem in French: *Antéchrist et la Gloire du Saint-Esprit*. We also learn from Pessoa's letter that after he received Crowley's response, Leal intended to write a letter to Crowley on "occult subjects". And on 15 January 1930 Leal wrote indeed a long letter to Crowley, in which he tried – in a rather confused way – to present the main points of his mystical and esoteric system.[105] There, Leal also expressed his admiration for Crowley and his ideas, of which he had gained knowledge thanks to Pessoa:

> ... I have recognised that you are a superior individual from a terrestrial and astral point of view, whose doctrines are very close to mine, despite the convictions that you have of being profoundly integrated into the Empire of the Beast (Antichrist-Reason: 666). I therefore have the highest consideration for your opinions, and it is for this reason that I ardently desire to know what you think of my poem.[106]

Among the essential elements in Leal's vision was the conviction of being the personification of "Enoch", the prophet (whom Leal also identified with Hermes Trismegistus) who, according to his "Paracletian" conception, would herald the end of the present era and the beginning of the "Third Divine Kingdom", namely the Kingdom of the Holy Spirit. Here Leal was obviously drawing upon a very old Western tradition whose sources can be found in the apocalyptic literature of the first centuries of the Christian era; this tradition underwent a strong revival in the Middle Ages under the influence of Joachim of Fiore (c.1130–1202), and became popular again in both literary and esoteric milieus in the nineteenth century.[107]

It is likely that Leal's conviction of being the prophet of a new era was not particularly congenial for Crowley, considering that he had the same convictions regarding himself. And neither of the two seemed ready to accept the idea that this new era might have more than one prophet. This fundamental incompatibility between their respective doctrines, of which Leal does not seem to have been fully aware when he wrote his letter, probably influenced Crowley's personal opinion about Leal, which as we will see was not very positive. But this incompatibility is after all also the flip side of their similarity, which Leal was not mistaken in pointing out. Besides the messianic and millenarian element, Leal emphasizes "*folle luxure*" (mad lust) as the highest and purest state of existence. This state can be reached only "through a progressive intensification of the life of the senses, which must become more and more profound and more and more bestial".[108] This "life of the senses" is something that "we will ultimately deify, identifying it even with the creative fury of God, a delirious, mad, vertiginous fury".[109] This "Dionysian" element (not lacking in late Romantic and Decadent flavour) is certainly also present in some aspects of Crowley's work, and must undoubtedly have been what struck Leal, who believed he had found a kindred soul in his spiritual search. Later in his letter, Leal also mentions the polemic over *Sodoma Divinizada* and makes some interesting remarks about the Templars, whom he considered "the audacious precursors of Paracletianism".[110]

But the most interesting aspect of Leal's letter is in its conclusion. Leal reveals to Crowley that his "initiation into the Occult World was only done directly by God and by myself".[111] Leal recounts his experience with a Brazilian esoteric group, the Sociedade Esoterica da Comunhão do Pensamento, based in São Paolo. Leal claims that he was excluded from this group before he was even initiated to it, because its members sensed that his spiritual power was out of the ordinary and were afraid of it.[112] He therefore found himself in a position in which he was unable to receive an external initiation from a master. This led him to formulate a request:

> I hope that our relations may become more and more fraternal and intense: so that if one day you have the desire to carry out my initiation, which up to the present has only been in outline form, I will promptly follow your esoteric indications. You will thus be Master of the High Initiation of the holy Prophet of God and Death.[113]

Leal, in a very interesting letter to João Gaspar Simões from 23–24 July 1950, gives some further information on his relationship to Crowley.[114] At the time, Gaspar Simões's biography of Pessoa had just come out, and Leal's purpose in writing the letter was to point out some inaccuracies he had seen in the book about himself. From this letter we learn that Crowley responded to Leal's long letter, expressing "duma forma muito curiosa" (in a very curious form) his desire to meet him personally as soon as an opportunity presented itself.[115] When Crowley came to Lisbon he asked Pessoa to arrange a meeting with his friend; the meeting took place at Leal's apartment. During the meeting – Leal writes – "I spoke a great deal about magic and occultism with *Master Therion* (666) (in French, of course), and at a certain point he told me *that I should leave Portugal because it was much too small a world for me*."[116]

Crowley's diary confirms that he met Leal on 9 September. The entry is highly intriguing: "To Lisbon: lunch with 4000 scudos. Met Leal: don't like him. There's something very definitely wrong about him. At night Initiation."[117] So we learn that Leal, unlike Pessoa, did not make a good impression on Crowley. But there is a much more important element here: the reference to the initiation that took place that evening. Judging by the context, it seems evident that Leal was initiated by Crowley on this occasion. This would not be surprising, given that Leal had expressed his desire to be initiated by Crowley in his letter. And yet there is another detail that remains obscure in this entry, but which is of the utmost importance: was Pessoa present at the meeting? Crowley says nothing about this, but Leal's letter to Gaspar Simões seems to confirm it. Leal states, in fact, that Pessoa came to his apartment specifically to introduce him to Crowley. Did Pessoa stay there with them the whole time? Was he present at Leal's initiation? Was he also initiated? Conclusive evidence about this point does not seem to be available in the extant documents, but I consider it quite likely that Pessoa was also initiated that same night, or that he was at least involved in some form of ritual. There are reasons to support this hypothesis. We saw that, in documents dating from a later period, Pessoa claimed explicitly, if enigmatically, to have been initiated into a neo-Templar order. We also saw that Crowley, at least in one occasion, claimed that the primary motive for his trip to Lisbon was the expansion of his Order (be it the OTO or the A∴A∴) in Portugal with the help of Pessoa. But there is also another text by Pessoa that seems to bring new light to the matter. This is a private note that has only been recently published. It reads thus:

> To feel the opposition of the middle is the beginning of the impulse toward victory. This was given to me by the Master Therion with authorization from above. Creating a disanalogy between myself and the one who encircles me: this is the first step and the beginning of the awakening.
>
> Dissatisfaction: this is the starting point. Honour to the Master who gave me, through the irony of what happens, the truth that exists so that it does not happen.
>
> Thus I am what I am, and will have to be it separately. The high lesson of the mockery of others hosts stars in its future.[118]

The text is quite enigmatic because of the use of a poetic and metaphoric language. But it seems clear that Pessoa claims to have received some important esoteric insight directly from the Master Therion (i.e. Crowley). Did this involve also a form of initiation? This is not stated explicitly, but can be surmised by the fact that Pessoa does not seem to refer to some intellectual knowledge or teaching, but to an inner transformation, which has enabled him to "feel the opposition of the middle" (whatever this may mean). Furthermore, Pessoa reiterates the word "Master" in the text, which seems to indicate that he did not use it only because of Crowley's pseudonym, but also because he really regarded Crowley as a spiritual master. Interestingly, Pessoa claims that Crowley even had an unspecified authority from above ("autorização superior"). If we compare this document with the other note Pessoa wrote at the end of his life, where he claimed to have been "initiated, through direct communication from Master to Disciple, into the three lesser degrees of the (apparently extinct) Templar Order of Portugal",[119] things begin to make sense. There seems to have been no other figure in Pessoa's life whom he may have called "Master" in an esoteric sense. It is therefore very likely that the "Master" Pessoa is referring to in this note is none other than Crowley himself. If this is so, then this would indeed be a confirmation that Pessoa was initiated by Crowley during his trip to Portugal, and it seems logical to think that this happened during that night of 9 September at Raul Leal's apartment.

Intriguingly, in his letter to Gaspar Simões Leal remains silent on the subject of the initiation that he received from Crowley that night. All he says is that, some time afterwards, he went to Crowley's hotel to meet with him again and give him one of his books, but that he did not find him there.

By this time Crowley was in fact already involved in his faked suicide affair: "on this occasion the *truly magical* 'set-up' at the Boca do Inferno occurred, and I never saw him again, only learning later from Fernando [Pessoa] that he had finally written to him from Germany".[120] In the remainder of the letter, Leal offers some "esoteric" reflections on Crowley's magical system in relation to his own, reminiscent (though with a little more detachment) of the ideas expressed in his letter to Crowley from twenty years earlier. On the whole, Leal's letter to Gaspar Simões confirms that he attributed considerable importance to his meeting with Crowley.[121]

Crowley, however, was not the only interesting personality who went to Portugal in 1930. In a singular coincidence, that same year saw the arrival of another member of the illuminate underground: Hermann Keyserling (1880–1947). Descended from an aristocratic Baltic family, and a relative of the "Mad Baron" Roman Ungern von Sternberg (1885–1921) who had gathered a Mongol army to fight the Red Army during the Russian Civil War, Keyserling has been described as "the most influential guru of Central Europe between 1918 and 1933".[122] In Vienna, during the first years of the 1900s, he had met Houston Stewart Chamberlain (1855–1927), the author of *The Foundations of the Nineteenth Century*, a book of racist theory that strongly influenced Nazi ideas. Keyserling does not seem to have shared Chamberlain's racist ideas, but remained on good terms with him until Chamberlain's death in 1927. In 1920 Keyserling founded a "School of Wisdom" in Darmstadt, where he taught his own synthesis of esoteric and metaphysical teachings. The school did not last long; it ceased activity in 1927, following various internal conflicts. Keyserling's relationship to Nazism during the 1930s was somewhat ambiguous. James Webb writes that "in 1934 he was claiming to have been one of the prophets of the Third Reich, but he was later summarily denounced by the Nazis themselves", due to which he underwent "a brief period of persecution".[123]

On 15 April 1930, Keyserling arrived in Lisbon. He intended to give a series of lectures in Portugal.[124] The nation's daily papers gave some coverage of his arrival. Most probably, Pessoa himself attended Keyserling's lecture held on 16 April, entitled *A alma duma nação* (*The Soul of a Nation*). One of Keyserling's ambitions was to "capture the inner experience of the countries he visited", and an initial result of his research had been a book which, published in 1919, achieved notable success: *The Travel Diary of a Philosopher*.[125] Now, evidently, the time had come to capture the soul of Portugal.

In the collection of Pessoa's papers, Pedro Teixeira da Mota has found a letter in French that Pessoa wrote to Keyserling.[126] It is evident that Pessoa was not pleased with the manner in which such a foreign visitor intended to interpret the "inner experience" of his homeland. Hence, this letter, in which Pessoa tried to present his own vision, based on the idea of a triple national soul, also inspired by the Sebastianist myth.

We do not know whether the letter ever reached Keyserling, but it is a fascinating document – every bit as fascinating as the circumstances that led two of the major representatives of the illuminate underground, Crowley and Keyserling, to visit Portugal within a few months of each other, both coming to the attention of another great illuminate: Fernando Pessoa.

5. Counter-initiation and conspiracy

> An occult tactic guides, to a single end, the most decisive international conflicts; Jewish finance secretly arms militarism; while on the other hand the Jewish–Masonic ideology of liberalism and democracy prepares convenient battle arrays.
> (Julius Evola, in his introduction to the 1938 Italian edition of *The Protocols of the Elders of Zion*)

> But in a while suspicion grows.
> "This fellow, now, by Jove, who knows?
> Perhaps he too is in the Plot.
> I like Scotch Whisky: he does not.
> He prefers Job to Second Kings.
> We disagree on many things."
> (Aleister Crowley, "The Suspicious Earl", in *Konx Om Pax*)

In this chapter I will tackle a subject that has hitherto been almost completely ignored by scholars of Crowley: namely, the interest that conspiracy theorists and traditionalist circles took in him. I use the term "conspiracy theory" to indicate those theories that spread throughout Europe especially between the late eighteenth and mid-twentieth centuries, postulating the existence of an international conspiracy arranged by an unknown and mysterious elite, the purpose of which is to gain power over the whole world.[1] As Joscelyn Godwin has pointed out, "conspiracy theory is anathema to the historian, but indispensable to the history of occultism".[2] This is undoubtedly true, given that conspiracy theories have so often germinated and developed in esoteric and occult circles. As for traditionalism, I refer here to the current of esotericism that is often traced back to René Guénon (1886–1951), and that sees Julius Evola (1898–1974) and Ananda K. Coomaraswamy (1877–1947) as two of its main figures.[3] Of course, conspiracy theory and traditionalism must not be confused with one another; these are two essentially different cultural phenomena. But there can be no denying that between the two there exists a kind of "grey area", in which they share certain traits. The essential idea of conspiracy theory is that history and reality are not entirely visible, and that consequently, what cannot be seen *directly* is also of fundamental importance. To this is added another element: in this dimension that is not directly observable, obscure forces are at work, and their purpose is the perversion and subversion of the positive order of things. It is possible to perceive some faint traces of this negative action, but not to observe it in the full complexity of its design and development, because it naturally tends to mask and hide itself. Belief in the existence of these subversive forces can in certain cases degenerate into a form of paranoia. A classic example of this is the case of Nesta Webster, whom we encountered earlier as an acquaintance of Gerald Hamilton, and who was probably the most influential conspiracy theorist author of the period between the two wars. Webster appears to have had a tendency to see agents of the international conspiracy practically everywhere, "so that she would only open her front door with a loaded revolver in hand".[4] This belief in the subversive action of occult forces appears to have had many things in common with the notion of "counter-initiation" devised by Guénon and further developed, in various forms, by other representatives of the traditionalist current. This explains why the image of Crowley produced by conspiracy theorists is remarkably similar to the image we find in René Guénon's writings.

The missionary of gnosticism

In all major European countries, the first half of the twentieth century saw the flourishing of a whole genre of writing dedicated to international conspiracy theories involving Jews, Freemasons and, after 1917, Bolsheviks. The belief was that this mysterious international organization had infiltrated, or was trying to infiltrate, all the key positions of power: big business, government, and communications media. The tentacles of the conspiracy were reaching in all directions.

We must not make the error of assuming that ideas of this type were spread only in Germany in the period between the two world wars. In fact, this phenomenon first began during the French Revolution, and spread throughout all of Europe, though it found particularly fertile ground in Germany after the defeat in the First World War. According to Norman Cohn, the idea of a worldwide conspiracy, at least in its modern form, can be traced to the Abbé Augustin Barruel (1741–1820) and his *Mémoires pour servir à l'histoire du jacobinisme* (1797–8).[5] Cohn observes that, in the eyes of Barruel, "the French revolution represented the culmination of an age-old conspiracy of the most secret of secret societies".[6] This "most secret" society had supposedly infiltrated Freemasonry and brought it under its power. The Freemasons were therefore secretly responsible for the subversion of the traditional order of society.

There seems to be a strong link between conspiracy theories and Western esotericism. The easiest way to see it, is as a simply empirical, historical link, which emerges from the realization that quite often persons who believed in conspiracy theories also associated with occultist circles, and vice versa. But a more thorough analysis would also need to investigate the ideological elements shared by conspiracy theories and esotericism. To mention one example, it is hard not see an analogy between the "secret Masters", or "Mahatmas", described by H. P. Blavatsky and other Theosophists, and the assembly of conspirators that is an unavoidable ingredient of any conspiracy theory. In both cases a small group of individuals, often endowed with extraordinary powers, is secretly ruling or planning to rule the world. The difference lies only in a small but significant detail: for Theosophists their influence on the world is positive, whereas in conspiracy theories it is usually negative.

Among the various persons connected to Crowley, we have already encountered several who had an interest in esotericism and conspiracy theories at the same time. Two prime examples among them are General Fuller and Fernando Pessoa. Crowley, despite the fact that the legitimist circles he frequented in his youth had clear leanings towards conspiracy theories, did not believe in a Jewish–Masonic conspiracy.[7] However, he did believe in something quite similar: namely, the existence of the Secret Chiefs. This belief was quite common among esotericists at the time, and had its immediate origins in theosophical teachings, in this case also mediated through the Golden Dawn. Beginning at a certain time – more or less around the initiation to the degree of Magus he claimed to have received in 1916 – he believed himself to be one of these Chiefs.

Just as conspiracy theorists would interpret any significant event in terms of their conspiracy schemes (everything that happens, if relevant, must support the conspiracy theory as a whole), so Crowley interpreted wars, revolutions and other large-scale events as proof of the work of the Secret Chiefs, whose goal was to destroy the current order of things and replace it with the new order of the Aeon of Horus.

Crowley may not have believed in a Jewish–Masonic conspiracy, but this did not prevent authors of conspiracy theories from believing that he was involved in such a conspiracy, and sometimes even that he was one of its key players. It is not hard to understand the motives of conspiracy theorists. Jewish–Masonic conspiracy theories proliferated quite often in conservative Christian circles, especially Catholic (such as in France and Italy), or Orthodox (as in Russia). Crowley, with his anti-bourgeois revolt, his anti-Christian agenda, his extreme sensuality and his vision of the end of a traditional social and moral order, could hardly pass unobserved. Moreover, some of the connections he had, as we have seen, could only have increased suspicion about him.

Generally – and this is a constant in all countries where such beliefs were widespread in the period between the two world wars – worldwide conspiracy theories were cultivated in circles of the extreme right. We should not underestimate the political significance of the milieus in which conspiracy theories flourished. In the third chapter I have mentioned the Tyler Kent affair in relation to Maxwell Knight. At the time, Kent frequented radical right-wing circles in England. In these circles, conspiracy theories were particularly popular, and Kent's attempt to publish the Churchill–Roosevelt correspondence could have done serious damage to the allied cause, because it might have offered hard-core evidence that such high-level conspiracies did indeed exist and had far-reaching historical consequences. With the Nazi regime in Germany, conspiracy theories were promoted to the status of state doctrine, and *The Protocols of the Elders of Zion* became one of the top-selling books, second only to Hitler's *Mein Kampf*. For these reasons, it seems worth investigating further the role that authors of conspiracy theories attributed to Crowley.

Various European magazines that distributed information about the alleged Jewish–Masonic conspiracy showed interest in Crowley and the OTO during the interwar period. Among them were the English *The Patriot*, the German *Der Judenkenner* and the French *Revue Internationale des Sociétés Secrètes* (*RISS*).[8] Here, I will focus on the articles that appeared in this last magazine in the first half of the 1930s.[9]

The *RISS* was founded in 1912 by Monseigneur Ernest Jouin (1844–1932), curate of the church of Saint-Augustin in Paris.[10] Jouin, who had already been involved in the anti-Masonic cause for several years, founded the review after having acquired an impressive collection of Masonic and occultist works. In 1913 he also founded the *Ligue Franc-Catholique*, reserving for himself the position of president-for-life. Its purpose, naturally, was to study the subversive influences at work in society. Jouin neatly summarized the threefold nature of subversion: "Israel is the king, the Mason is his chamberlain, the Bolshevik his donkey."[11]

Jouin was also among those who, in the period between the two world wars, placed faith in the truthfulness, if not the authenticity, of *The Protocols of the Elders of Zion*. He published an initial translation of the *Protocols* in the *RISS*, and later, in 1920, republished them as the first volume of a collection entitled *Le péril judéo-maçonnique*. In this collection, over the following years, a whole series of studies and "documents" were issued, intended to give proof of the satanic activity of Jews and Freemasons. Jouin's research must evidently have been judged as highly meritorious by the Holy See, which conferred various honours upon him. He was made a prelate by Pope Benedict XV, nominated as an apostolic proto-notary by Pius XI in 1924, and died "with papal benediction and approbation of his work".[12] As Cohn remarks, these recognitions "must certainly have added to the prestige of his publications".[13]

The *RISS* was divided into two sections, which were sold separately and were distinguished by the colours of their covers: the grey section, a weekly, was dedicated to "Judeo-Masonry"; the pink section, a monthly, was dedicated to occultism. In fact, the contents of the two sections often overlapped, but the grey section generally covered materialist, liberal and modernist influences on society, attributed specifically to so-called "Judeo-Masonry", whereas the pink section was dedicated to the forms of neo-spiritualism that manifested above all through occultism, theosophy, spiritualism and Eastern religions, behind which the direct influence of evil could be seen.[14]

One of this journal's favourite themes was the revival of Léo Taxil's anti-Masonic "revelations".[15] These revelations had been based on the alleged memories of a repentant "Luciferian" woman by the name of Diana Vaughan, but Taxil later, with an extraordinary *coup de théâtre*, had confessed having entirely invented both the character of Vaughan and her memories. His retraction had divested his revelations of all their credibility. Despite this, some of the more hot-headed enthusiasts of the anti-Masonic cause had immediately begun explaining away the retraction, suggesting that Vaughan had been a real person but could not appear in public because she had been assassinated by Luciferian Freemasonry with the complicity of Taxil himself.

All this had occurred in the last decade of the nineteenth century. By the time the *RISS* began to take up the case again, in the late 1920s, Taxil's revelations were considered as discredited even by anti-Masonic groups. Jouin brought these revelations back to the forefront with the aid of some new "documents", and also gave the most extensive coverage possible in his review to a new "case" that shook the anti-Masonic world: the story of "Clotilde Bersone". Bersone was allegedly a repenting adept of "Satanic" Freemasonry (an appreciable upgrade from Vaughan's "Luciferian" Freemasonry), and her adventures were narrated in a novel, *L'Élue du Dragon*.[16] As was the case for the *Protocols*, the fact that a document was very unlikely to be authentic did not prevent the editors of the *RISS* from believing in it, or at least using it as a convenient tool for their purposes.[17]

In February 1929 mention of the OTO and A∴A∴ began to appear in Monseigneur Jouin's review.[18] The first article in which Crowley's orders were mentioned had however nothing to do with Crowley himself; it was a polemic against the Equestrian Order of the Holy Sepulchre.[19] In this article we find the standard "theorem" of the *RISS* with regard to Freemasonry:

Now is the time to cease concealing certain facts, which cannot appear as a revelation to anybody. It is time to remind all people that behind the political Masonry of the Grand Orient and the symbolic Masonry of the Grand Lodge, as well as behind the so-called regular Lodges of England and America, there are in fact background-Lodges, or Higher Sects, little known and consequently all the more formidable: the true Synagogue of Satan, obedient to a Supreme Occult Power.[20]

This passage contains the key for understanding the interest taken in Crowley by the *RISS* and by conspiracy theorists in general. They claimed that behind "normal" Freemasonry, there were High Sects (*Hautes Sectes*) or High Lodges (*Hautes Loges*), which in turn were governed by obscure and diabolical forces. The conspiracy therefore did not make *direct* use of regular Freemasons, but acted through secret lodges, which in their turn governed all regular international Freemasonry and coordinated its movements.

Obviously, at least two conditions would be necessary for this theory to be true. The first would be the existence of these secret lodges. The second would be their effective power within the variegated world of Freemasonry. The *RISS* preferred not to linger too much upon proving the second condition, but there seemed to be no lack of evidence concerning the first. Where could a good example of these High Lodges be found? The author of the quoted article had no doubts: "One of the mechanisms of this masonic underground is the A∴A∴, whose identity we will study further on, and the OTO".[21] Even if Crowley's name was not yet being mentioned explicitly, with this article the *RISS* had begun targeting the orders he was leading at the time. It would only be a question of time before he would also enter the firing line.

The journal returned to the issue in March, with the article "La querelle des Hauts Grades", by Roger Duguet.[22] A section of it was dedicated to the "Satanist" Aleister Crowley. Duguet took on "regular" Freemasons, who defended themselves from anti-Masonic campaigns by claiming that, although there were indeed Masonic bodies influenced by occultism, these bodies were "irregular" and therefore had no influence over true Freemasonry. To this argument, Duguet responded that the only "regularity" he could acknowledge as a good Catholic was the spiritual authority of the Pope. No "regular" recognition, spiritually speaking, could come from other sources than the pontificate, whose authority came from the investiture of St Peter by Jesus Christ. Consequently, since all Freemasons were irregular in any case, it was legitimate to postulate the influence of persons such as Aleister Crowley over Freemasonry: "In short, like it or not, an Aleister Crowley exists; he is a Mason and chief of a branch of Masonry, just as regularly Masonic as Calvinism is Protestant without being Lutheran."[23] It would be pointless to insist on the inanity and captiousness of this reasoning, which deals with the phenomenon of Freemasonry using categories of Catholic theology that are wholly foreign to it. The premise – namely, that no legitimacy exists outside of the Church – is in fact identical to the conclusion, and this says a lot about the kind of arguments that could be found in this literature. Probably, most of the readers of the *RISS* did not need to have sound, convincing arguments to be persuaded of the dangerous nature of Freemasonry in the first place, because they were already convinced of it. But some were not so easily persuaded, and this, as we shall see, was the case with René Guénon.

After this article, two others were published: "Atlantis et Amis de l'Atlantide", also appearing in March, and "Encore Atlantide", appearing in May.[24] These articles did not refer directly to Crowley either, but rather to the review *Atlantis*, directed by the French esotericist Paul Le Cour (1871–1954). The main focus of this journal was, among other things, the study of the traces of the famous lost continent. The first of these two *RISS* articles was intended to point out a possible connection between the review *Atlantis* and the A∴A∴. In fact, according to the author, the letters in the name of Crowley's Order stood for "Adeptes d'Atlantis" (Adepts of Atlantis). This interpretation had not been invented by the *RISS*,[25] but was nonetheless entirely fantastical; the name of the A∴A∴ had nothing to do with Atlantis.[26] The result was that Paul Le Cour, director of the review *Atlantis*, protested vigorously against the *RISS*, to the point that the latter retracted their allegations. These events have another interesting aspect: Guénon was also highly interested in the review *Atlantis*, albeit for different reasons. Thus, to his great disappointment, he found himself mentioned – in a rather specious manner, as was often the case with the *RISS* – in the first of the two articles, together with his friend Louis Charbonneau-Lassay (1871–1946), the renowned scholar of Christian symbolism.[27]

In this period, as we know, a highly significant event took place: Crowley's expulsion from France. He appears to have left Paris on 17 April 1929 and returned to England. The event caused resounding echoes in the European press, and the *RISS* naturally took interest in the expulsion as well. In May, an article appeared in the journal devoted entirely to Crowley.[28] The other articles had been published thus far in the Masonic section; this one was published in the occultist section. The author, A. Tarannes, indicated Crowley as a successor, by way of Theodor Reuss, to the Satanist Freemasons with whom Clotilde Bersone had been supposedly involved. The article repeated various sensational rumours about Crowley that could be found in the press, including the accusation that he burned women alive and drank the blood of children. Given the general anti-Semitic tone of the journal, Tarannes also did not miss the opportunity to emphasize the fact that Crowley's secretary and disciple, Israel Regardie, was a "*judéo-américain*" (an American Jew).[29]

But perhaps the most interesting aspect of this article is the fact that the author compared Crowley to Julius Evola. In February 1929, Tarannes had published a long article on the Italian traditionalist thinker,[30] in which the latter was defined as a "Satanist". It was especially the ideas that Evola had expressed in his *Imperialismo pagano*[31] that had scandalized Tarannes. Now Tarannes commented on Crowley's 1923 expulsion from Italy, and recalled how Crowley's wickedness was not tolerated in Italy, "because, as we have seen in the case of Evola, Mussolini's regime can in principle tolerate a certain kind of Satanism, provided that this occultism be itself marked with the fascist stamp".[32]

In June, the *RISS* published an article on Crowley that had appeared earlier in the English review *The Patriot*.[33] The article concluded thus: "According to Crowley's opinion, Christianity is played out, a new era will begin, evidently the era of the Cult of the Serpent, the sexual cult, 'redeemer of humanity'! – the Power of Illuminism and of Judeo-Masonic domination."[34] From this we can see that the *RISS* contributors were at least aware of the strong sexual and anti-Christian component of Crowley's new religious message, and had therefore some good reasons, from their perspective, to target him in their articles.

After another article by Tarannes appearing in July, in which Crowley was once again linked with Bersone's Satanic Masonry, and an anonymous article published in December, the interest of the *RISS* in Crowley seemed to wane for a while. In fact, his name was not to be seen in the review again until May 1931, when a special issue came out, also with English and German versions. The title was "Les Missionnaires du Gnosticisme" (the Missionaries of Gnosticism), and the author was Lesley Fry, a fairly well-known name in French conspiracy theorist circles.[35] Fry subsequently republished the article as an appendix to her book *Léo Taxil et la Franc-Maçonnerie*.[36]

"Les Missionnaires du Gnosticisme" proves that, on occasion, the *RISS* collaborators knew how to do thorough and well-documented research. The subject of the article is the OTO. Drawing upon unpublished documents, Fry goes over a few points in the pseudo-Masonic career of Theodor Reuss, who had been the international head of the Order prior to Crowley (and who, at the time the article was published, had been dead for eight years). Interestingly enough, she also publishes some manuscripts by Reuss, in which he outlines his ideas for a new era, which would follow the end of Christianity and would be characterized by emancipation from the concept of sin. The article concluded with a note signed by Monseigneur Jouin:

> Let us make no mistake about it, Russia, at this very moment, is becoming a wasted, gangrenous corner of earth whose cancer is invading the world. Why? Because of secret societies, whose members, being disciples of Reuss and Crowley, are those innumerable cesspit men who bear the name of Bolsheviks and Judeo-Masons.[37]

Evidently, Jouin, along with his collaborators in the *RISS* and other conspiracy theorists, attributed a very specific role to persons such as Crowley. It was certainly a "political" role, since Crowley was considered one of the instruments, if not one of the masterminds, of a world conspiracy whose main purpose was the subversion of traditional social order and the destruction of Christian values.

Subsequently, Crowley's name appeared again in three other pieces in the *RISS*, which were published between June 1931 and October 1932. It is actually inaccurate to describe these as articles: all three consist of various excerpts from Crowley's works translated into French.[38] In this case, the sources used by the *RISS* appear to have been limited to *The Equinox* vol. 3 no. 1, which had been published in 1919, and *Magick in Theory and Practice*, published in 1930. It is worth noting that the French translation of these excerpts appeared in the *RISS* practically without any comment. Perhaps the editors of the *RISS* thought they would speak for themselves. In any case, as we will see shortly, this was one of the reasons why Guénon considered their publication suspicious in the first place.

The file at the Archivio Centrale dello Stato

English and French conspiracy theorists were not the only ones to take an interest in Crowley in the 1920s and 1930s. In the same period, the intelligence services of various countries also followed his movements and activities. I have already mentioned the file kept by the British police, discussed especially by Roger Hutchinson in his recent biography of Crowley.[39] But the Italian police, around the mid-1930s, also took an interest in him. As a testimony to this, we have a curious file preserved at the Italian Central Archives of the State in Rome.

This file is in a folder that mainly contains documents on Zionism, communism and Freemasonry. The file is labelled "Crowley Alistair Eduard A.",[40] and contains documents dated from September 1935 to June 1936. Why did the Italian police feel a need to keep an eye on Crowley during this period? Over a decade had passed since his expulsion from the country, and he had never since returned; moreover, he had been living "quietly" in England since 1932. An analysis of the documents in the file will help us answer this question.

It appears that at the origin of this interest in Crowley there was an exchange of letters between a Jesuit priest, Joseph Ledit (1898–1986), then a professor at the Pontifical Institute for Oriental Studies,[41] and an anonymous English correspondent. In one document this correspondent is indicated as "M". Ledit was an expert in matters relating to the spread of communism in Europe, and was on the front line of the cultural battle against communism led by the Vatican in those years.[42] He possessed, among other things, an impressive archive in which he collected information on this subject. From the file, and from other files from the same period preserved in the Italian Central Archives, we learn that he was in contact with prominent Italian police officials, such as Guido Leto (1895–1956), then director of the Division of General and Reserved Affairs of Public Security, with whom he exchanged information.[43]

But who was "M"? From the same files, we learn first of all that she was a woman, because one of the documents refers to her as an "*informatrice*" (a woman informer) of Father Ledit. We also learn that she was deeply involved in the fight against Bolshevism, and had a high regard for the Italian fascist regime; she had in fact even published a book about Mussolini. Finally, we learn that she was a close collaborator of the right-wing political activist John Baker White (1902–88),[44] which makes us assume that she was British or at least residing in Great Britain. After the publication of earlier versions of the present book[45] other authors have tried, unsuccessfully, to solve this mystery and give a name to "M". Richard B. Spence, for instance, has suggested that the best candidate would be Maxwell Knight, who was also known as "M" among his MI5 colleagues;[46] while Tobias Churton has proposed the name of Baker White himself, without realizing that the file of the Italian secret police includes a letter *from* Baker White *to* "M", clearly indicating that they were two distinct persons.[47] Both authors also mention the possibility that "M" might hide the name of conspiracy theorist Nesta Webster, who was indeed a woman and was in contact with Baker White, but never wrote a book about Mussolini. All these hypotheses are actually incorrect, because we have a much better candidate for "M". There is in fact enough evidence to come to the conclusion that "M" was Gertrude M. Godden (1867–1947), right-wing political activist and author of a series of anti-communist books in the 1920s and 1930s.[48] Most importantly, she was also the author of a book on Mussolini, published as early as 1923.[49] This was certainly one of the earliest monographs on the Italian dictator to be published in English, if not the very first. She seems however to have been forgotten by historians and we have in fact little biographical information about her.[50]

The file of the Italian police contains three letters from Godden to Ledit, in which the former asks for information on various movements and groups, undoubtedly involved, in her view, in subversive activities.[51] In the third of these letters, Godden also asks Ledit for information on Crowley. The interesting thing is that in the other letters, Godden mentions Dimitrije Mitrinovic and his movement, New Britain. I have already discussed Mitrinovic and New Britain in Chapter 3, in relation to J. F. C. Fuller. It will be remembered that for a certain period, namely between 1933 and 1934, Fuller had been involved with Mitrinovic's group, and that Crowley had also been in contact with Mitrinovic. It is entirely possible that it was this link that sparked Godden's interest in Crowley. But more generally, the impression we receive from the letters is that Godden was collaborating closely with John Baker White and his organization, the Economic League, and that some of her investigations were conducted on his behalf. More precisely, it seems likely that Godden was involved, directly or indirectly, in a secret unity called "Section D", for which Baker White also worked.[52] The unity was part of a larger structure, which had been created by Sir George Makgill (1868–1926), a Scottish novelist and political activist who seems to have had close ties with the higher echelons of the conservative party and the secret services. The structure was organized in cells so as to facilitate its clandestine operations. It functioned as a private intelligence service, and its purposes were similar to that of the Economic League: the fight against subversion and communism through infiltration, intelligence and propaganda. There are good reasons to believe that, after Makgill's death in 1926, Baker White took control of the section he had been working in, and combined its clandestine activities with those of the more public Economic League.[53]

There are at least two points that are particularly significant here. The first one is that Makgill seems to have been particularly interested in the activities of Aleister Crowley and of his occult organizations. According to Baker White, Makgill had "devoted a considerable amount of time to unmasking the cult of evil of which Aleister Crowley, alias 'the Beast', was the centre".[54] The investigation on Crowley had been carried out by one of Baker White's contacts in the group, an unnamed person referred to as "H". Apparently, soon before being victim of a mysterious accident, "H" "had uncovered a blackmail plot, involving two well-known politicians, connected with Crowley's activities in the island of Cefalu".[55] It is easy to think that one of the two politicians might be Tom Driberg, who as a left-wing activist and an associate of Crowley would be an obvious target for someone like Baker White. But then the hint, if intended, would also be patently incorrect because, as we have seen, Driberg never was in Cefalù (which by the way was also not an island). The second point of note in relation to the activities of Section D, is that Maxwell Knight was also very probably involved in it,[56] which creates the strange impression that many of the key characters in our story were connected through multiple, variable networks of political influence and action. Makgill's interest in Crowley, in any case, creates an interesting background for Godden's investigations and for her correspondence with Ledit. As Richard B. Spence has noted, the important point to keep in mind is that, after the First World War and especially in the 1930s, Crowley was increasingly perceived by the police and the secret services of various countries as being involved in left-wing radical movements.[57] Therefore, he was suspect not only for his esoteric activities and his amoral behaviour, but also for more specific political reasons, even if these reasons were not necessarily well-founded and missed an important aspect of Crowley's position. I believe my analysis in Chapter 2 has shown that there was indeed a strong radical component in Crowley's thought, but also that he was hardly interested in political activism per se, and that he was quite ready to move along a broad spectrum of political ideologies in order to affirm his own religious message.

From Godden's letters, we learn that between 1935 and 1936 she was particularly busy researching Dimitrije Mitrinovic's movement. She also mentions the French movement L'Ordre Nouveau, which was connected to New Britain.[58] Another interesting element is that in the first two letters, she makes reference to the psychologist Alfred Adler and to the "Adler Society". Godden points out that there is a connection between Adler and Mitrinovic's group. The connection was indeed close, for in 1927 Mitrinovic founded the English section of the Adlerian Society and made efforts to distribute Adler's works throughout England.[59] Another important element is that Crowley knew Adler. The two had met twice in Berlin, in August 1930 and again in August 1931.[60] Most intriguingly, in August 1930, Mitrinovic's name is mentioned in Crowley's diary on the same day as Adler's name.

Evidently Godden considered Mitrinovic's movement to be part of what she perceived as a network of subversive forces. The fact that Crowley and his OTO were believed to be in some way connected to New Britain can only have aggravated her suspicions. Godden consequently wrote to Ledit to ask whether he could provide her with any useful information. When mentioning the possible connection between New Britain and the OTO, she adds concernedly that this "makes it quite dangerous stuff to handle!".[61] The letter proceeds with a very interesting statement: "I expect you have the OTO – in its esoteric and exoteric name, C.C. fully documented?". We do not know why Father Ledit, whose special interest was Bolshevism and the religious situation in the Soviet Union, would have had the OTO "fully documented". But a further reference leads us to understand that Godden did not know whether or not Crowley's main headquarters was still in Cefalù. She therefore likely thought that if there was still a Crowleyan base in Italy, Ledit would certainly know. In any case, Godden continues: "Can you tell me anything of the last ten years, and especially the 1935–1936 movements of the world famous Abister (or perhaps Aleister) Crowley – *and his many alias names*? *This is urgent.*"[62]

It is likely that Ledit did not even know who Aleister Crowley was, but to satisfy his correspondent, he decided to turn to his police contact, Guido Leto. The latter saw the urgency with which this question was asked and contacted the General Chief of the Italian Police, Arturo Bocchini (1880–1940) in person. Bocchini, in turn, sent the request on to the police commissioner in Palermo. Since Crowley's Italian residence had been in Cefalù, the commissioner was logically the appropriate officer to address with a request for information.

This explains the presence of another document in the file: a letter from the Palermo police commissioner to Bocchini. The letter is dated 6 June 1936, and chronologically, is the last document in the file. From various elements in the letter, we gather that Bocchini, after receiving it, passed it on to Leto, who in turn informed Ledit of its content. At this point, Ledit probably wrote back to Godden, giving her the information supplied by the commissioner.

But what was this information? The commissioner began by giving biographical details about Crowley. They are more or less correct, apart from the spelling of some words.[63] But then the interesting part begins:

> [Crowley] lived for about five years in a villa in the vicinity of Cefalù, and was expelled from the Kingdom following Ministerial ordinance on 13 April 1923, it having been confirmed that rites were taking place in his villa based on obscene and perverse sexual practices, in which three foreigners participated who were living with him as if married, besides other foreigners who came there from time to time.

Obviously Crowley did not spend five years in Cefalù: he arrived there in the early months of 1920 and was expelled in April 1923, which makes less than four years. But we also learn indirectly that the reason for his expulsion was the "obscene" behaviour of the villa's denizens. Since the documents directly relating to Crowley's expulsion have not surfaced yet, this information is highly intriguing.[64] The letter proceeds to list the reports on Crowley and his community that were sent by the Palermo prefecture to the Minister, which unfortunately are not in the file. According to the commissioner's list, the first of these reports (there are three in all) is from 25 July 1922, and therefore well before the expulsion. This would suggest that the behaviour of Crowley, his concubines and his disciples attracted the attention of the Italian authorities for quite some time before actually provoking action. Furthermore, judging by the commissioner's statements, interest in the Abbey did not entirely vanish after Crowley's expulsion,[65] considering that the "Political Police Division ... indicated that defamatory statements regarding conditions in fascist Italy were being distributed from Crowley's house in Cefalù, statements that were being collected by the special espionage service of the British Foreign Ministry and were published by some newspapers."[66]

And so the Abbey of Thelema had been perceived as a centre for anti-fascist propaganda! But the commissioner then hastened to add that "the aforementioned notice was unfounded because, after Crowley's departure, only one of his two women remained in Cefalù – a French citizen – who lived in poverty and had no relations with anybody".[67] These rumours regarding alleged anti-fascist activities at the Abbey of Thelema continued to 1927, long after Crowley's expulsion.

Crowley did in fact spread "anti-fascist" propaganda, but in his own way. While he was in Tunis in the summer of 1923, he began writing satirical poems about fascism and Mussolini, who appeared to be directly responsible for his recent expulsion from Italy. These poems were collected and republished the same year with the title *Songs for Italy*.[68] A single quotation is enough to give an idea of the content of the work:

Blackshirts
How practical to wear a shirt
Whose colour will not show the dirt!
How excellent a point of art
To wear a shirt to match my heart!
Helpful its hue for those who lurk
At night, with knives to do their work![69]

In the Yorke Collection at the Warburg Institute, there is a copy of *Songs for Italy* with a handwritten note by Gerald Yorke and various notes glued to the blank spaces on the pages. Among these notes is a letter from Norman Mudd to the editor of a French daily paper, the *Quotidien*, in which he writes:

> [Crowley] has, in the last few months, written a number of poems and sonnets against Mussolini, whom he regards as the mad mongrel cur of Europe. I have the honour to enclose herewith a copy of these poems, and suggest that you should print them in the *Quotidien*, with a French translation and, if necessary some words of introduction. The vigour of these poems and the bitterness of their contempt and irony should make them very effective in helping to rid Europe of this desperate danger.[70]

Crowley, through his disciple Mudd, sought to present himself as the victim of a repressive and freedom-killing regime. But as we have seen, he had not been so shocked, at least initially, by fascist methods and ideas. This naturally makes his sudden anti-fascist enthusiasm less than convincing. It is interesting to see, in any case, that a few years later the Abbey of Thelema was still considered connected with "defamatory statements regarding conditions in fascist Italy".

In the same folder that contains the file on Crowley, there is another interesting file, entitled "Massoneria in generale" and containing a single, typewritten, seventeen-page document.[71] The text begins as follows: "Masonry and Judaism: two powers which, by reason of their international character and the political aspirations that arise from them, must necessarily be, and are, implacable enemies of every internally strong nation-state with a good sense of itself and its own honour."[72]

This passage appears emblematic. It continues:

> [Freemasonry and Judaism] ignore the concept of "Fatherland" and ... by the strength of their own international connections, continually endeavour to oppose the aspirations and efforts of peoples when those aspirations do not agree with the principles of internationalism, unconditional tolerance, pacifism and consequently Marxism in general upheld by these groups.[73]

It should be kept in mind that this report was written in the context of a collaboration between the German and Italian police, according to an agreement between the two countries signed in 1936, foreseeing the exchange of information on "sensitive" subjects – such as Freemasonry and Judaism.[74] Further on, in fact, the author writes: "If I am preoccupied above all with Masonry, it is because I believe that, given the equal situation in Italy and in Germany, there will be complete agreement about the way to confront such problems."[75] Everything here leads us to conclude that this report was read at a meeting between the representatives of the two police forces.

The report is based on two theories: the infiltration of Freemasonry by Judaism in order to make it an instrument of political influence upon society; and the existence of an international coordination of all Freemasonry worldwide (also throughout the various rites and obediences).[76] Freemasonry is consequently depicted as an effective international instrument, used by Judaism and supported by Marxism and Bolshevism.[77]

These are undoubtedly some of the basic ideas on which most of the conspiracy theories of that period were constructed.

But this report on Freemasonry is also directly related to our subject, which is why I refer to it. Just as Freemasonry is a tool of Judaism, the report continues, so in turn it needs its own tools in order to influence all of society, since the number of actual Freemasons is limited. One of these tools is the press; another is a host of organizations, such as the "Lega dei Diritti dell'Uomo" ("League of the Rights of Man") and the Rotary Club; yet another instrument consists of the "avanguardie della massoneria" ("vanguards of Masonry"), formed by the "pansophic and occultist lodges and by theosophy, which, via the *Ordo Templi Orientalis* [*sic*] and the 'Droit Humain' lodge, are in close connection with the high degrees of French Masonry".[78] Crowley's Order was therefore given quite some importance in the context of worldwide subversion. It was there that Crowley and his organization took on political importance in the eyes of the Italian police and, in all probability, of the German police as well. Unfortunately, the author of the report does not explain the manner in which the OTO and the other "logge occultistiche" ("occultist lodges") were supposed to exert their disintegrating influence on society; all that is clear is that they formed part of the same mask supposedly covering a single demon face: the face of Jewish world domination.

Here, then, in a semi-official Italian police document from that period, we find the same arguments, based on the existence of phantom "High Lodges", that had been developed over the years in the *RISS* and in other conspiracist publications. The author of the report attributes responsibility for the French Revolution, and even the First World War, to Freemasonry. If the Masons had been capable of producing so much destruction in the past, what else might they and their "vanguards" achieve in the future?

Traditionalism

It should be no surprise that traditionalist authors tend to evaluate Crowley in a negative light. One of the key features of traditionalism is an essentially negative view of modernity. Secularization, liberal democracy, materialism, relativism, feminism, socialism, evolutionism: all these are aspects of modernity that traditionalists, albeit with various nuances and differences between them, see negatively. From the traditionalist point of view, we live in an age of decadence, drawing near to the end of time. Perfection is not an ideal to be found in an ideal future, as modernity "ingenuously" believes with its "myth" of progress; instead, perfection lies in a primordial past. Step by step, we are moving farther away from that distant time, increasingly subject to degradation and involution. This degenerative process is inevitable since it is intrinsic in the nature of the temporal cycles of the cosmos, but it is also encouraged by the action of the so-called "counter-initiation", together with anti-traditionalist forces that have historically taken on diverse forms. Although the intellectual stature of authors such as Guénon and Evola is undoubtedly superior to that of the average conspiracy theory author, it is the shared notion of "occult powers" working to subvert the traditional spiritual and social order that allows us to make an ideological comparison between them. Traditionalism, however, has a metaphysical conception of time that is generally missing from conspiracy theories, which tend to be preoccupied more with the negative influences at work in society than with the grand cyclical chronologies typical of traditionalist thought.

As we have seen, in many respects Crowley did not have a "traditionalist" and antimodern outlook. On some points, there was surely a certain ambivalence – I have discussed the legitimist tendencies of his youth, and his criticism of Western civilization – but in general, his mental structure remained that of a positivist and of a "modern" person. Moreover, the spiritually and socially subversive aspect of his proposed religion would certainly hold no appeal for traditionalists – no more than for adherents of theories of worldwide conspiracy.

The two traditionalists who appear to have been most interested in Crowley are undoubtedly René Guénon and Julius Evola.[79] Let us begin with Guénon. As it is known, after frequenting Parisian occultist circles in his youth, Guénon developed a severely critical attitude toward all forms of occultism and new spirituality, particularly those originating in Anglo-Saxon countries. One of his favourite targets was the Theosophical Society, on which he wrote a sharply critical work also containing references to the Golden Dawn and the OTO.[80] Guénon claimed that the Theosophical Society, besides playing an anti-traditionalist role, had been used by British intelligence services, for instance in India, to further the interests of counter-initiation. The kind of relationship Guénon established between politics and occultism forms a pattern that Crowley also fits, considering his alleged relationship to these same intelligence services.

We have already encountered references to Crowley in letters written by Guénon. Everything leads us to believe that Guénon followed Crowley's activities with a certain curiosity. In order to find further references in Guénon's writings, we should turn for a moment to the articles that the *RISS* devoted to Crowley. Guénon was an assiduous reader of this anti-Masonic journal, with which he was involved in an open polemic at the time. The argument began well before the *RISS* took any interest in Crowley; namely, when Guénon collaborated, between 1913 and 1914, with another anti-Masonic review, *La France antimaçonnique*.[81] Essentially, Guénon contested the extreme conspiracist theses of the *RISS*, which, as we have seen, were based on the notion that "High Lodges" were secretly controlling regular Freemasonry. Guénon logically pointed out that it would be impossible to steer the entire phenomenon of Freemasonry into a single direction, or to attribute an unequivocal influence on society to it. However, in his evaluation of the *RISS* he embraced a conspiracy theory of his own, believing that agents of the counter-initiation were hiding behind the review. By all appearances, the interest in Crowley shown by Jouin's review, and the publication of extracts from Crowley's works, was extremely suspect in Guénon's eyes.

As we have seen, in March 1929 the *RISS* contained an article entitled "Atlantis et Amis de l'Atlantide", in which Guénon and Louis Charbonneau-Lassay were mentioned, along with Paul Le Cour and his review. The *RISS* insinuated that there must be some kind of synergy between the three authors, because Guénon was cited a little too often in the pages of Le Cour's review, albeit polemically, while Charbonneau-Lassay had published a few of Guénon's sharp attacks here and there in his review. As soon as Guénon found out about the *RISS* article, he wrote to Charbonneau-Lassay to tell him about it. In a letter from 30 March 1929, he explained to his friend that, as usual, the anti-Masonic review had seen connections between things that had nothing to do with each other.⁸² The connection made between Crowley's magical Order and Le Cour's review had indeed no foundation. Guénon was certain of this, declaring that he knew much more about the A∴A∴ and the activities of its head than the collaborators of the *RISS* did. Curiously, however, Guénon appears to have accepted the entirely fantastical interpretation of the name of the A∴A∴ as "Atlantean Adepts", which leads us to suspect that even his sources of information were hardly impeccable. Crowley, in any case, is described as a "highly dubious" character. Above all, he is "a trickster and a conman", rather than being the representative of any real "occult power".⁸³

But Guénon also had an opportunity to take a public position with regard to the interest of the *RISS* in Crowley. In a review essay from July 1929, published in *Le Voile d'Isis*, Guénon wrote:

> The *Revue Internationale des Sociétés Secrètes* … has published some documents on the OTO, whose current head, at least for the English-speaking countries, appears to be Sir Aleister Crowley, recently expelled from France …. These documents are naturally accompanied by a tendentious commentary, in which the OTO is presented as a "High Lodge" and Aleister Crowley as a successor of the "Illuminati" that are the subject of *L'Élue du Dragon*; this is a great deal of honour paid to the more or less suspect fantasies of individuals without warrant or authority!⁸⁴

In October of the same year, Guénon returned to the question, again in *Le Voile d'Isis*:

> It is very difficult to remain serious when any importance is being given to the mystifications of Aleister Crowley. Surely one must believe that this person's lucubrations are in perfect accord with the theses upheld by the *RISS*; but what this journal does not make known to its readers is that the OTO (Ordo Templi Orientis) and its head are not recognized by any Masonic organization and that, if this self-styled "high initiate" were to present himself at the entrance of even the smallest Lodge of Apprentices, he would be immediately shown to the door with all the respect due to his rank!⁸⁵

With this last sentence, Guénon incurs in an amusing mistake. He does not appear to have been aware of the fact that in Masonic terms, Crowley was actually a fellow brother, having been initiated into a lodge of the Grand Lodge of France in 1904 – the same obedience into which Guénon himself had been initiated in his youth!⁸⁶ Crowley was certainly not a "regular" Freemason in terms of the regularity of the Grand Lodge of England, but from this point of view, Guénon was no more regular than him. In any case, according to Guénon, the *RISS* committed the error of believing Crowley's "boasting", attributing an importance to his statements that they did not actually have. But the most interesting aspect of this story is that, according to Guénon, the *RISS* overestimated Crowley not out of naïveté, but out of malice. More precisely, Guénon believed that Monseigneur Jouin's review was "in cahoots" with Crowley, and that all this was part of some counter-initiation plan. This, at least, is what can be deduced from a passage in a letter from Guénon to Renato Schneider, dated 5 November 1936: "Be that as it may, the large collection of documents published by ex-collaborators of the *RISS* has given me, in an unexpected fashion, the opportunity to have proof of their connivance, which I had suspected for a long time, with Aleister Crowley."[87]

Guénon was clearly referring to Lesley Fry's book, *Léo Taxil et la franc-maçonnerie*, which I have already mentioned.[88] Unfortunately, he does not explain in what consisted the proof he was referring to consisted of. He was most likely simply thinking of the republication, in this same book, of Lesley Fry's article "Les Missionaires de Gnosticisme", which had originally appeared in the *RISS*.[89] It is hard to know, however, why the simple republication of an article might now offer further "proof" of the connivance Guénon mentions. All we can say is that, if Crowley knew about the *RISS* articles, and especially the copious translations of his writings, he probably considered them as free publicity. On one point, Guénon was probably right: that the *RISS* was taking Crowley very seriously. But the connivance between the two seems to be no more than the fruit of his fantasy.

But there is an important question we have not yet asked: what did Crowley know of all this? Some documents indicate that he knew about the articles in the *RISS* and of Guénon's polemical reaction. The first document is a letter to Crowley from Henri Birven (1883–1969). Birven was a German esotericist who had founded a review of esoteric studies, *Hain der Isis*, and had contacted Crowley because he, like so many other German occultists at the time, viewed Crowley as the spiritual master of a new era.[90] He was fascinated with Crowley and intended to do everything possible to spread his ideas in Germany, especially by means of his review. At the same time, however, he wanted explanations regarding the defamatory rumours that surrounded Crowley, both inside and outside occultist circles.

Birven wrote the following to Crowley on 21 October 1929 (we should remember that Crowley was in England at the time): "Guénon says, in a polemic with the *Revue Int[ernationale] des Sociétés Secrètes* (*Voile d'Isis*, October 1929), that if you were to present yourself at the least apprentice lodge, you would be turned away at the door with all the honours due to your rank. (!) This is idiotic, but it also proves that people do not know you."[91]

On 29 October Crowley wrote back to Birven: "Thank you for your letter of the 21st, which reached me this evening in the country. Monsieur la Guenon's monkeying amuses me. What a wheeze!"[92] This was one of Crowley's typical jokes, which is impossible to render in the English translation: in French, "guenon" (without the accent on the "e", as in "Guénon") means female monkey. Unfortunately, this kind of wordplay was not the kind of clarification Birven was expecting from Crowley with regard to his reputation; and a few months later, in fact, their correspondence ceased. But what interests us here is that Crowley knew of Guénon's opinions and indirectly responded to them in such a jocular way.

As for the *RISS*, Birven's letter referred to it, but this does not mean that Crowley necessarily knew about the articles. There is however a letter written by Israel Regardie to Gerald Yorke on 20 May 1930 that very probably refers to the French magazine. Both Yorke and Regardie were still disciples of Crowley at that time, and Regardie was his personal secretary: "666 [Crowley] appears anxious to get hold of that Froggy magazine *La Revue des Sciences Secrètes*. Did you order it from Watkins?"[93]

It is quite likely that Regardie made a mistake and wrote "sciences" in place of "sociétés". At the time, there does not seem to have been any review bearing the title mentioned in the letter.⁹⁴ For what reason would Crowley have been so "anxious" to have this review if not to take a look at the articles that were being published about him?

The other aspect of Guénon's interest in Crowley relates to the question of the latter's alleged connection to Hitler and Nazism, which I examined in Chapter 4. The letters in which this connection is mentioned – namely the one to Renato Schneider from 4 September 1938 and the one to Julius Evola from 29 October 1949, come from a period long after the *RISS* polemic. The interesting thing is that over time, Guénon's opinion of Crowley seems to have slowly changed. During the polemic with the anti-Masonic review, he tended to downplay Crowley's negative influence, while in the letter to Evola the tone appears rather different.⁹⁵ Regarding the Golden Dawn and its value as an initiatory group, Guénon writes:

> Only very much later did Crowley enter the scene, as he did with many other things; even if this was only a case of fairly insignificant pseudo-initiations (perhaps this was not completely the case for the *Golden Dawn*), his introduction into it brought in truly sinister influences, making it into something much more dangerous.⁹⁶

Here Crowley, much more so than in the polemic with the *RISS*, is portrayed as a downright agent of counter-initiation.⁹⁷

We now come to Evola. In certain ways the Italian traditionalist thinker can be considered much more of a "conspiracy theorist" – in the true sense of the term – than Guénon. The question of the subversive influences of Judaism and Freemasonry is known to have played an important role in his work, especially in the period leading up to the end of the Second World War. His divergence from Guénon on this question – especially in regard to the role of Freemasonry – is also known.⁹⁸ Having only a superficial knowledge of his work, one would therefore guess that his evaluation of Crowley would be even more negative than Guénon's. And yet, as we will see, this was not the case.

The first question we must ask is: when did Evola first become aware of Crowley as an author?⁹⁹ We know that the latter, for a certain period, was in touch with the same Italian occultist circles that Evola later entered. These connections were mainly formed through Reuss's international Masonic network. In this way, Crowley got in contact with Eduardo Frosini (1879–?) and Arturo Reghini (1878–1946). Frosini, a very active man in fringe Masonry, created the Italian Philosophical Rite (Rito Filosofico Italiano) in 1909 together with Reghini. This was, in essence, an attempt to create a form of Freemasonry based on esoteric and nationalist ideas, inspired above all by the Pythagorean tradition, therefore contrasting with the rationalist and internationalist tendencies of mainstream Freemasonry in Italy. There is no room here to go into the intricate story of this Masonic initiative, which had a rather troubled existence.¹⁰⁰ The interesting thing here is that among the reciprocal recognitions that took place between the various fringe Masonic powers, there were exchanges between Reuss and Crowley's OTO on the one hand, and Frosini and Reghini's Italian Philosophical Rite on the other. Crowley, in fact, received a diploma from the Rite in October 1913, while Reghini and Frosini were written into the "Golden Book" of the OTO.¹⁰¹ There is no indication that their contacts went any further than this, although Reuss and Frosini must surely have written letters to each other. There are no documents attesting to further contact with Crowley after the aforementioned diploma. As far as we know, after Reuss died in 1923, Crowley did not try to re-establish contact with the Italian representatives of the Order.[102]

Evola, of course, was not involved in all these events, and, considering his anti-Masonic bias, it is doubtful that Reghini would have mentioned them to him during the time of their collaboration. It is still more doubtful that he would have mentioned Crowley's name. Renato Del Ponte, however, has noted that in a 1928 issue of the review *Ur*, directed by Evola, a reference appears to a book by "a certain Master Therion", which, as we know, was one of Crowley's aliases at the time.[103] The author who made the reference – most likely Evola himself – appears not to have been aware of the Master Therion's true identity.[104]

The second – and again indirect – connection between Crowley and Evola is found after the Second World War, namely in Guénon's letter cited previously. From the context, we can assume that Evola had asked Guénon for his opinion of a whole list of persons in the European occultist and esoteric world, including Gustav Meyrink (1868–1932) and Giuliano Kremmerz (pseud. of Ciro Formisano, 1861–1930).[105] From Guénon's responses it becomes apparent that while Evola attributed a certain value to their teachings, Guénon tended to see them predominantly as "sinister" and dangerous figures. The two traditionalist authors clearly differed in their opinions of occultism as seen in its specifically historical sense. From Guénon's point of view, the lack of "initiatory regularity" condemned the activities of occultists from the outset. And if a "valid" initiation were actually present, it only made their activities all the more dangerous, as in the case of Bô Yin Râ (pseud. of Joseph Anton Schneiderfranken, 1876–1943).[106] Naturally, this difference in views also pertained to magical practices in general, which Guénon considered rather unfavourably, while Evola attributed positive value to them.[107]

It is certainly significant that Evola, in a new edition of the articles from the reviews *Ur* and *Krur* (published in three volumes in 1955 with the title *Introduzione alla Magia*), included a translation of a text by Crowley.[108] Intriguingly, this text consists of some parts of *Liber Aleph*, which at the time was still unpublished, as is duly stated in Evola's introduction.[109] This poses a problem: through what "Crowleyan" channels did Evola acquire this unpublished text? The biographies of Crowley by Symonds and Cammell had already been published by this time. From these books, Evola would have been able to obtain information about Crowley's life and works; but in order to obtain an unpublished text, he would have had to make contact with Crowleyan circles. H. T. Hakl, in his essay included in the present book as Appendix 1, finally brings an answer to this question. But another interesting aspect is the unsigned note with which Evola prefaces the translation of Crowley's text:

> In the "amphitheatre" of contemporary magic, the Englishman Aleister Crowley is a figure of the highest rank. According to common opinion he belongs more to the "black" or even Satanic side of things, which appears to have been the image he desired, even calling himself "The Great Beast 666". In fact, this was for the most part merely a façade: the truth is that Crowley simply followed the line

of the "left hand path", for which he was particularly well qualified. His life was extremely varied and complex ... and it is even believed that he had a secret hand in some recent political movements.[110]

Of course, the last sentence is a veiled reference to Guénon's letter, which I have mentioned earlier. Evola then proceeds to describe the Law of Thelema and its principles, with evident first-hand knowledge, and presents a comparison between Crowley's Magick and Tantra, in terms of the sexual aspect and the use of mind-altering substances. According to Evola, it is easy to find "elements of traditional magical doctrine" in Crowley's works.[111] This is obviously quite different from Guénon's evaluation. Evola shows a decided interest in Crowley's teachings. Despite the reference to Crowley's political implications, it was his operative magical side that truly interested Evola. Crowley's possible involvement with Hitler and Nazism would certainly not have met with Evola's immediate disapproval, as appears to have been the case with Guénon. The counter-initiatory or charlatan element that Guénon saw in Crowley appears absent in Evola's case. Evola would later return to writing about Crowley on various occasions, not changing his opinion and eventually further developing the views expressed in the note cited above.[112]

Finally, it seems appropriate in this context to point out Crowley's relationship to another important traditionalist author: Ananda K. Coomaraswamy. Their relationship appears to have been only of biographical significance. The Anglo-Indian art historian never mentions Crowley in his writings, and Crowley only mentions Coomaraswamy with reference to personal events, not in relation to his ideas.[113] The two met during Crowley's period in the United States, and often met each other over a period of time covering the spring and summer of 1916. According to Crowley, it was Coomaraswamy who approached him, due to his reputation as an expert in Eastern doctrines.[114] This was just before Coomaraswamy began working for the Museum of Fine Arts in Boston; his encounter with Guénon's ideas, which took place in the early 1930s, was still a long way off. Unfortunately, concerning their relationship we only have Crowley's side of the story. Crowley states that he had an affair with Coomaraswamy's second wife, the English singer of Indian songs Ratan Devi (pseudonym of Alice Richardson, 1885–1958), who became pregnant by him. Crowley accused Coomaraswamy of causing his wife to have a miscarriage by making her go on a long sea travel despite serious complications in the pregnancy. Crowley's judgement of Coomaraswamy is extremely harsh and injurious, including racist undertones in reference to the latter's half-Asiatic origins.

A possible political dimension to the Crowley–Coomaraswamy relationship has been suggested by Richard B. Spence.[115] He observes that Coomaraswamy had Indian nationalist sympathies and connections. During the First World War the loyalty of the different parts of the Empire was a primary concern for British authorities, and Indian nationalism clearly was a potential threat to its stability. This may have given good reasons to English intelligence services in America to keep an eye on Coomaraswamy's activities. If, as Spence argues, Crowley was regularly working for the English services during his American period, then he might have passed information about Coomaraswamy to his contacts. However, it must be said that Spence's suggestion is mostly speculative, and not based on hard evidence.

In Coomaraswamy's correspondence with Guénon, which began in the mid-1930s, no reference to Crowley is to be found.[116] It is therefore likely that Guénon never knew of Coomaraswamy's earlier relationship with the English occultist.

It is interesting to note that Coomaraswamy spent a long period in England before moving to the United States. Here he became immersed in the same Edwardian cultural milieu that I have described in reference to Crowley. For example, he was in contact with A. R. Orage and the group of authors associated with the *The New Age*, to which he also contributed.[117] In a certain sense, then, Crowley and Coomaraswamy were exposed to the same intellectual influences, which they naturally assimilated according to their respective sensibilities. This most likely provided the common ground for their encounter, until personal reasons pushed them apart, leaving – at least for Crowley – a strong sense of resentment. But while Crowley's criticism of modern civilization was part of an extremely ambitious project of religious renewal, the ideas that Coomaraswamy first developed in the context of Edwardian England would later be integrated, after he discovered the works of Guénon, into a traditionalist doctrine that would not render these ideas superfluous, but would rather give them completeness and consistency.

❧ Conclusion

One of the conclusions this study does not reach, and against which the reader must be warned, is the idea that Crowley's doctrine was inherently linked to an extreme right-wing or pro-Nazi political ideology. It is true that analogies and connections do exist between the doctrine of Thelema, as Crowley presented it, and certain elements of the radical politics of the interwar period. Nevertheless, the differences between the two are no less significant. First of all, Thelema presents itself as a universalistic message, despite its elitist component. It does not postulate intrinsic differences between people on the basis of their birth, sex or ethnicity. For all that Crowley may have had some idiosyncrasies in this regard, it appears that he more or less consistently endeavoured to keep these personal attitudes separated from the universal value of his religious message. It should therefore be emphasized that, even if it is not too difficult to find sexist or racist statements in Crowley's writings, there does not seem to be an intrinsic anti-Semitic or racist component in Thelema.

Certainly, there is a substantial difference between those who have discovered their True Will and those who remain "asleep", not knowing their existential trajectory; but this is true for all doctrines of an initiatic or gnostic type, to which Thelema obviously appears to be related. Surely, the motto "Do what thou wilt" can be more easily interpreted by Thelemites today as the basis of an anarchist or libertarian doctrine than of a totalitarian one. Perhaps this would not correspond entirely to Crowley's vision, but in this context his personal interpretation of Thelema should be considered as just one among others: certainly the most authoritative, but not necessarily the only one.

Thus far, there has been no study of the political orientation of members of movements or groups with Crowleyan inspiration. Nothing allows us to state that one type of political vision is more widespread in these circles than any other. Given the vastness of the phenomenon, my personal knowledge of these circles is extremely limited. However, it seems to me that no single specific political orientation appears to stand out. In any case, before drawing conclusions it would be best to wait until thorough sociological research in this area has been done. And yet, even once such analysis is available, it will still be difficult to grasp the "Crowleyan" phenomenon in its entirety. For the organized and structured groups that have a claim to Crowley's legacy in some form are one thing; another thing is Crowley's larger, and more impalpable, cultural influence, which spreads over a significant part of contemporary, occult-oriented new religiosity, but expands even further, touching phenomena such as popular culture and contemporary art. To ascribe a precise political value to this influence would seem misguided in my view. As I have observed, *The Book of the Law* is an inspired text that, like any other religious text, allows for multiple interpretations. No criteria exist for attributing pre-eminence to one hermeneutic choice over another. Here as well, Crowley's interpretation, closely related to his times and to the historical context in which he lived, remains only one among many other possibilities.

To this it must be added that among the largest and most organized Crowleyan groups, for which societal acceptance becomes increasingly important as the size of membership grows, certain "inconvenient" elements of Crowleyan doctrine may be safely kept in the background, even if they can never wholly disappear. This is the case, for example, with Crowley's anti-Christian attitudes, which seems to have been taken up in Crowley's own virulent terms only by a small number of groups inspired by his ideas. This does not exclude the existence of Crowleyan groups where a radical political element is present and made explicit.[1] However, it appears that among the various groups of Crowleyan inspiration, such cases remain exceptional and limited.

I thought it necessary to point this out, because one of the risks run by this study is that its conclusions might be seen not as relating particularly to Crowley and his personal ideas, but to all the many and diverse contemporary movements that have been inspired by his doctrines.

I will now more concretely discuss the contribution that I believe can be ascribed to this study. As we have seen, Crowley often felt the "temptation" of politics, in various ways depending on the time. In Chapter 2, I suggested that it is possible to distinguish two main phases in Crowley's life. The first one was what I described as the "romantic" one, the second as the "pragmatic" one. I believe that this distinction offers us a key to understanding Crowley's relationship to politics and the motivation behind some of his choices and behaviours, which might otherwise appear simply extravagant, or dictated by a compulsive need for "transgression".

An initial individualistic and romantic phase, therefore, contrasts with a second phase in which Crowley's primary interest was the diffusion of a new religion, of which he considered himself a prophet, a priest and a missionary at the same time. In his multiform personality, we can consider one thing to have been certain and steadfast, beginning at the end of the First World War: his conviction of having a message for humanity, a message humanity could not refuse to listen to. As this conviction prevailed in his mind – and we have seen the stages of its progression – he had a growing desire to find appropriate channels for reaching the greatest possible number of people. It is particularly easy to accuse him of having sought publicity at all costs; his very life appears to have been one long, desperate quest for publicity. This desire, however, can also be seen from the perspective of his sense of mission, which in my view was, at least to some extent, genuine and disinterested.

During the first part of his life, Crowley was a *seeker*. He climbed mountains, travelled the world and joined an esoteric brotherhood with the ambition of following a mystical and spiritual path. After the First World War he became a *teacher*; he had all the answers, and wanted not only disciples but *masses* to convert. It was probably this same desire for "masses" that drove him to hold views that were often completely outside of reality. This is the sense in which we can understand his musings on the influence of *The Book of the Law* over Hitler, or his attempt to get the Soviet Union to adopt the religion of Thelema. And yet this seemingly absurd project can also be interpreted as a form of "pragmatism", by which I mean Crowley's absolute mental autonomy from any political ideology. For him, there seemed to be no difference between Nazism and communism; the important thing was to reach the masses.

This last consideration seems important, because on the basis of his intellectual education and youthful reactionary attitudes, the natural consequence should have been an attitude of extreme anti-communism. Moreover, while I have pointed to Crowley's rationalist side, it is equally true that throughout his life, in keeping with the typical ideology of occultism, he was radically opposed to materialism. This should have also led to an opposition to communism. But this was not the case. In my view, this can be explained precisely by the "pragmatic" attitude that he developed in parallel with his messianic convictions.

I have devoted some space in this book to the analysis of Crowley's rationalism in order to show, at least indirectly, the limited validity of the stereotype that sees occultists as being gripped by absolute irrationalism. It is no more possible today to draw a clear line between rationalism and irrationalism in this respect. The equation "right wing = irrational = esotericism", which has been so widespread among left-wing intellectuals after the Second World War, does not seem to offer a correct framework for interpreting the relationship between esotericism and politics. Crowley's example, in my view, is a clear indication of this.

The problem of the ideological relationship between Thelema and totalitarianism forms a highly sensitive question. It is important to recognize that *certain* aspects of the Thelemic religious message, as Crowley himself presented them, seem to be in agreement with certain aspects of an elitist and, occasionally, totalitarian ideology. But I have tried to show that these aspects were not peculiar either to Crowley or, for example, to Nazism; rather, they pervaded to a certain degree English intellectual circles, especially progressive ones before the First World War. The implications of social Darwinism, for example, were discussed not only in radical political circles but also, and primarily, in scientific ones, and were even considered respectable enough before the horrors of Nazism led to a universal, uncompromising condemnation of these ideas.

As for Crowley's personal relations, I have investigated a select few that help us better understand certain obscure or insufficiently known episodes in his life. It is interesting to note that many of the persons with whom he was in contact had radical political views, and were on the "wrong" side – that is, the losing side – during one or other of the two world wars, if not both. Besides Crowley himself, the list includes Gerald Hamilton, J. F. C. Fuller, P. R. Stephensen, George Sylvester Viereck and Frank Harris. During the Second World War, however, Crowley was wise enough to avoid taking the side on which his intellectual history might have so easily placed him.

The manner in which Crowley was viewed in certain circles – the primary subject of Chapter 5 – undoubtedly speaks to a certain interest of conspiracist groups in his persona. We can identify a kind of self-referentiality in these groups, which looks almost like a game. When these groups were attributing a political import to Crowley's statements and actions, which in fact they never had, they were simply going along with Crowley's own game. In this context, the case of René Guénon, admittedly distinct from that of conspiracy theorists in the strict sense, seems particularly interesting. Guénon rebuked the *Revue Internationale des Sociétés Secrètes* for attributing a role to Crowley that he did not have, but then fell into the same trap by imagining improbable scenes of collaboration between Crowley and the *RISS*, or even between Crowley and Hitler, thus paving the way for more conspiracist speculations, whose end is most likely not yet in sight.

In conclusion, Crowley remains a figure that can be adequately understood only when placed within the historical context in which his intellectual education took place, and in which his proposed religion was developed. If my study has been able to offer some new elements in this direction, then its primary goal will have been achieved.

Appendix 1
Some additional remarks on Julius Evola and Aleister Crowley
Hans Thomas Hakl

It is no simple task to find something interesting to add to Marco Pasi's well-balanced and highly detailed discussion of the connections between Crowley and Evola. It seems certain now that they never met each other, even though Crowley lived in Sicily for three years and was not forced to leave his Abbey in Cefalù until 1923 (when Evola was already 25 years old). A meeting would therefore easily have been within the realm of possibility, especially when we consider Evola's family roots in Sicily, as well as the interest in occult matters that was growing in him at the time. But the fact that in June 1928 Evola was still unaware of Crowley's pseudonym, "Master Therion", and even more the fact that he did not mention Crowley in the chapter on contemporary esoteric currents ("'Magic' in the Modern World") in his book *Maschera e volto dello spiritualismo contemporaneo*,[1] published in 1932, seems to me sufficient proof that they did not know each other personally. Even in the revised second edition of this same book, from 1949, Evola says nothing about him. Crowley does not emerge until the third revised edition of 1971. It is known that Crowley never once mentioned Evola in his writings, and none of Crowley's previous biographers have written a single line about the Italian author. Nor is anything on this subject to be found in the world's largest collection of Crowley documents, located at the Warburg Institute in London.

Even if I am personally inclined to believe that Evola encountered Crowley's name in the late 1920s (I will explain this point further on), the first documentary (albeit indirect) proof that Evola knew about Crowley is still René Guénon's letter to Evola from 29 October 1949, mentioned by Pasi – written some two years after Crowley's death. The reason for this rather surprising lack of knowledge, or perhaps just lack of interest, on the part of Evola, may simply be attributed to his lack of knowledge of the English language,[2] besides certain other "hidden" reasons to be discussed below.

In connection with this, Pasi raises a very interesting question which has puzzled other scholars as well. How did Evola, in the third volume of *Ur* published in 1955, manage to include passages from Crowley's *Liber Aleph*,[3] which was not officially published until 1961[4]? This question remains unanswered, and even recognized experts on Evola have no explanation for it. Who can have given Evola copies of this Crowleyan manuscript, completed in March 1918, if not someone from the circle of closer or more distant acquaintances surrounding the late English magician? Unfortunately, Evola hardly ever kept the letters he received from his numerous correspondents. In the few extant letters, no reference to this is found.

One person with whom Evola was definitely acquainted, and who also knew Crowley personally, was Gerald Gardner, the founder of the modern Wicca movement. Evola first mentioned Gardner, who had visited him in Rome "several years ago", in an article called "La congrega delle streghe" published in the Neapolitan paper *Roma* on 21 November 1971.[5] In an interview with Gianfranco de Turris and Sebastiano Fusco in December 1973,[6] he also mentions Gardner, albeit not in particularly effusive terms. But the contact appears to have been a one-time affair. Gardner wanted to know whether there were still remnants of an ancient tradition of witchcraft in Italy, which Evola dismissed as absurd. It therefore seems improbable that Gardner would have brought along a copy of Crowley's manuscript or sent it later. For that, we would also have to assume that Gardner had already visited Evola prior to 1953, which is very unlikely. Why should Evola have waited until 1971 to publish his article on Gardner and witchcraft? Incidentally, Evola is not mentioned in any biography of Gerald Gardner so far published.

From my researches, there essentially emerge two persons who could have given Evola a copy of Crowley's manuscript. The first, Dr Heinrich Wendt, a Heidelberg judge, has been described as a most knowledgeable expert on the "history of initiation in the present and recent past".[7] In 1949 he sent Crowley's *Book of the Law* to Evola, asking him for his opinion on it. In a letter from 18 December 1949 to Dr Herbert Fritsche, who had taken over the patriarchate of the Crowleyan Gnostic-Catholic Church after the death of Arnoldo Krumm-Heller in 1949, Wendt reports Evola's answer as follows:

> Regarding the "Book of the Law" the "findings" are not so favourable. If the story of its origin is true, then it did not result from a conscious intervention from "above", but rather comes from influences (wandering and even "syncretistic" influences) from the intermediate world. 50% of the text does not consist of "mysteries" but of dross, various other things are woven into the rest of it, and Crowley's personal "complexes" may themselves have played a part.[8]

Dr Heinrich Wendt might, in theory, have also had the manuscripts of the *Liber Aleph*, and might also have sent them to Evola.

The second person, however, seems more likely to have given Evola a copy: Dr Henri Clemens Birven.[9] He knew Crowley personally, and in 1930 published some of his writings in German translation.[10] He also had a connection to Evola. Birven was initially very impressed by Crowley, and visited him in London for three days in July 1929. Crowley then visited him in Berlin in April 1930. But Birven became ever more sceptical – due to his own "painful" experience with Crowley and the negative reports he received from France, for example from Joanny Bricaud, Patriarch of the Gnostic Catholic Church. And so, as Marco Pasi writes, he broke with Crowley around the end of April or beginning of May 1930. However, he did continue to value Crowley's writings, or at least parts of them.[11] There is no doubt that Birven knew of the *Liber Aleph*; he published excerpts from it in "Die Werke Aleister Crowleys", a series of essays in the journal *Oriflamme*, the organ of the Swiss OTO.[12] Although it cannot be proven that he knew of this book before 1955, it can be assumed – the reason being that he knew Crowley's enthusiastic disciple and translator Martha Küntzel, at least since 1932 when she visited him together with Gerald Yorke in Berlin; she had translated the *Liber Aleph* into German, along with other works by Crowley. Birven could even have known her already in 1928, as we can see from his letter to Crowley dated 15 April 1928,[13] in which he suggests that he might support Küntzel during her translations.

However, it is not known whether, or if so when, Henri Birven personally met Julius Evola, or even when they began corresponding. In any case, Birven was in contact with Evola in 1960. In his book *Pforte der Unsterblichkeit*, published in that year, Birven writes:

> But since in the meantime the Italian author Julius Evola, in the third volume of his *Introduzione alla Magia quale Scienza dell'Io*, Rome 1955 ... has said what is necessary in a comprehensive essay [on C. G. Jung] ..., we will limit ourselves in the following to essentially summarizing the remarks of Evola, *to whom we have promised a translation of his essay*.[14]

This contact, however, is very likely to have existed already in 1953, considering that in his book of that year, *Lebenskunst in Yoga und Magie*,[15] Birven writes:

> In J. Evola, in the domain of "magic as a metaphysical attitude", Italy possesses a scholar and author of the highest rank. Like us, he is a representative of "magical idealism". Between 1927 and 1929 he published three volumes of a journal, *Ur* (later *Krur*), which are an "Introduction to Magic as Science of the Self". The essays therein are among the most valuable materials ever produced in this domain. *A reprint of this series is forthcoming*.[16]

Who, if not Evola himself, could have informed Birven in 1953 (or even earlier) that a reprint of the issues of *Ur* was being planned, which then became reality in 1955? And since Birven gladly boasted about his knowledge of Crowley, a conversation, or at least a correspondence, regarding Crowley is definitely conceivable. In such an exchange, the subject of the *Liber Aleph* could also have come up. We will recall that Evola, in his Foreword to his partial translation of Crowley's *Liber Aleph*, also mentions the year 1953.

Certainly, all these reflections are only indications and not proof, but at least it does not seem implausible that Evola may have received his copies of Crowley's manuscripts from Birven. But in the end, the question is not yet solved. Unfortunately, Evola only ever mentioned Birven's name once, in a private note from 3 August 1970, in which he indicates that he has heard no news from him in the last few years. He was also aware of Birven's valuable library.[17] Birven, by contrast, mentions Evola often in his books – always in an entirely positive light – and even cites long passages from several of his books, often including his earlier works.[18] This might even allow us to conclude upon a contact possibly going back quite far, considering that a large number of Evola's works from the 1920s and 1930s were very hard to find by the 1950s. On the other hand, Henri Birven, as a great bibliophile, would surely have had sufficient ways and means to acquire these books, and Evola may have been helpful to him in this regard as well. However, I do not believe that their acquaintance dates back to the 1920s or 1930s,[19] even though Birven did read René Guénon's periodical *Le Voile d'Isis*[20] at that time, and may even have obtained access to Guénonian circles. Birven loved France, and had an excellent command of the French language. A contact with Evola through such circles is therefore entirely conceivable.

I would like to add something more to this, which is not greatly important but appears not to have been noticed thus far: the Italian translation in *Ur* III does not correspond precisely to the English text of the *Liber Aleph* as it was published in 1961 by the Thelema Publishing Company in West Point, California. First, the succession of the text is completely different – even though the *Ur* volume only published excerpts from the *Liber Aleph* – and second, the Latin headings of the individual sections are more or less different from those in the American edition. For example, what was "De arte mentis colendi" ("On the art of cultivating the mind") in the English version becomes "De arte mentis colligendae" ("On the art of concentrating the mind") in Evola's version. In the "Ultima thesis de amore" the last sentence is missing from the Italian version, and the third, fourth and fifth paragraphs of the Italian "De motu vitae" appear in the English version under the heading "De morbis sanguinis". Either there were two slightly different versions of Crowley's text, or else Evola made these changes himself. But why should he have done this?

In the aforementioned German translation of the *Liber Aleph* by Martha Küntzel, not published until 2003,[21] the content, progression and chapter headings correspond very closely to the American edition of 1961, which once again raises the question of whether Evola had a variation of the text.[22] Perhaps Hymenaeus Beta, Frater Superior of the OTO, gives the correct answer in his "Prolegomenon zur zweiten Auflage", the foreword to this edition of Küntzel's translation.[23] Here he informs us that Crowley, "over the years, made significant changes" in the *Liber Aleph*. So Evola's manuscript could have been an earlier version of the text, which does not make the puzzle of its origin any easier, but rather supports the conclusion that Birven supplied the manuscript, because Birven had already broken off relations with Crowley as early as 1930.

It is interesting, in connection with this, that Birven's aforementioned German excerpts from the *Liber Aleph* are not reproduced in Küntzel's translation, but are linguistically far poorer. Also, the order in which his four excerpts appear is not the same as in the American, and therefore also the German, editions. When, and by whom, these excerpts were translated remains unclear, and in fact it may have been Birven himself – despite his poor knowledge of English.[24] In any case, these translations were published only after Birven's death. Since Evola's excerpts in *Ur* III and Birven's in *Oriflamme* unfortunately concern different chapters, no clues can be drawn from them as to whether Evola used the same manuscript as Birven. So the question as to their origin must remain unanswered.

Merely for reasons of completeness, I would like to refer to two other articles by Evola about Crowley, which are not mentioned by Marco Pasi and have not yet been republished in any of the many collections of Evola's journalistic writings: "L'uomo più perverso del mondo – Credevo di conoscere ogni malvagità disse un giudice al satanico Crowley" ("The most perverse man in the world: I thought I knew of every vice, said a judge to the Satanist Crowley"), in the Neapolitan paper *Roma*, 17 April 1954;[25] and "Parliamo di Crowley: La 'Grande Bestia 666' – Maghi e streghe sono in mezzo a noi" ("Let's talk about Crowley: 'The Great Beast 666' – Magicians and witches are in our midst"), also in *Roma*, 14 May 1959. In the second article Evola mentions J. F. C. Fuller's *Star in the West* and John Symonds's first two books on Crowley,[26] which probably also formed the background for Evola's fairly comprehensive articles.

* * *

Although the possibility of direct contacts between Evola and Crowley can most probably be excluded, we do find a report from the political division of the Italian police from 7 April 1930 which alleges, at least, an indirect connection. The report states: "Jules Evola is known in the occultist centres of Paris as a member of the order 'Ordo Templi Orientis', a Satanist sect whose grand master Sir Aleister Crowley was banished from Italy, America ...".[27] Evola is also accused of portraying himself as a dedicated fascist – without actually being one – in order to recruit members among the fascists for his secret Order.

Aleister Crowley had in fact taken over the OTO *de facto* (even if he could not produce any document of appointment) after the death of its founder, Theodor Reuss, in 1923. He had met Reuss at some point between 1910 and 1912. In 1912 Reuss appointed him as head of the Order's British section.

Are we to believe this report of Evola's membership in the OTO, coming from an anonymous informant? If so, then it is even possible that Evola knew Crowley personally, given that the latter lived in Paris from 1926 to 1929. And yet, there is no real proof that Evola was actually in Paris during that time. Evola only rarely divulged biographical information about himself, considering such matters to be unimportant in comparison with his spiritual work; therefore we must rely on reports from his contemporaries, which unfortunately are lacking in this case. Only in 1930, when the Italian police began to keep an eye on him, do we begin to have better information about his movements.

Piero Fenili, perhaps Evola's most knowledgeable critic, considers Evola's membership in the OTO to be entirely possible.[28] I personally, however, would exclude this possibility. In the first place, a very important fact should be noted here. As Peter-Robert Koenig, an expert on the history of the OTO, has kindly informed me, Evola's name does not appear on any of the OTO membership lists known to him, nor in the lists of correspondents compiled after Crowley's death. This makes any connection between Evola and the OTO highly improbable. The membership lists of the OTO under Theodor Reuss are missing, but since Reuss died in 1923 and Evola was still primarily involved in artistic and philosophical activities at this time, such an early membership in the OTO – especially without any mention of it being made later – seems hardly believable to me. Evola was also simply not the type to join orders of which he himself was not the leader,[29] and would most likely have written something about Crowley or the OTO if interesting information had been available to him. But as we know, he did not write about them until 1954. If we do not assume that Evola simply feigned ignorance of Crowley in the June 1928 issue of *Ur*, there was not much time available between then and the above mentioned police report of April 1930 for Evola to become a member of the OTO. Therefore, this "connection" between Evola and Crowley does not seem to be likely.

The source of this membership rumour, however, still remains unexplained. It is possible, maybe even probable, that the informant had received information from Paris, namely from the circle surrounding Monseigneur Jouin and his *Revue Internationale des Sociétés Secrètes* (*RISS*); or perhaps he was simply a reader of the *Revue*. This journal's specialty was conspiracy theories, in which Jews, Freemasons and Illuminati were portrayed as "adherents of Satan", holding the "threads of world history", so to speak, in their hands. No number of the *RISS* directly mentioned Evola's membership in the

OTO, but he is the main subject of two articles, and, like Crowley, is defined explicitly as a "Satanist" – the same term used in the police report.[30] In a third essay, "L'OTO – Expulsion de Sir Aleister Crowley", by the same A. Tarannes who had written the two articles on Evola, Crowley and Evola are even mentioned in the same breath. And after discussing the accusation of Satanism levelled against Crowley, the author goes on: "because, as we have seen in the case of Evola, the Mussolini regime deals very harshly with a certain Satanism".[31] Also, in this essay – suspiciously similar to the police report – reference is made to Crowley's numerous expulsions. Also, for a second time, Evola is mentioned together with Crowley in this article. Here the alleged Tantric initiation rites of "the Satanist Evola" are described in connection with the terrible "black masses" that Crowley supposedly held. If, as it appears, the *RISS* was the main source of information for the police report, then this latter certainly loses still more credibility.

But here, a question must be answered once and for all: is it conceivable that Evola could have heard nothing, absolutely nothing, about these negative reports concerning himself in the *RISS*? If he knew about them, however, then he must also have known of Crowley's name by 1928 or 1929. So why does he not mention him? Was it simply a matter of his reputation, for the sake of which, very understandably, he did not want his name in any way connected with Crowley's? By this time he had enough difficulties already, as we will see. Or did he have another motivation? Did he really have something to hide, as some people will claim? Unfortunately, these questions cannot be answered. All we can assume is that he must have heard about the reports in the *RISS*, as he has been in personal contact with René Guénon since 1927 at the latest.[32] Guénon kept a very careful watch on the *RISS*, and continually attacked it in his own essays. Would he, or someone from his circle, not have informed Evola about this? In addition to all this, Evola himself was fluent in French.

Unless new documents emerge, these questions must remain unanswered. In any case, to construct from this an argument that Evola and Crowley were in touch with one another is, in my opinion, far too great a leap; and besides, there is no proof of it.

But there is another report from the political division of the Italian police, which also may point to an indirect connection between Evola and Crowley, albeit a more distant one. This report, dated 3 March 1930, discusses alleged contacts between Evola and the German "Illuminati". And here, at least theoretically, Theodor Reuss, with his connection to Crowley, comes into play once again. In Germany there was a group known as the "Weltbund der Illuminaten", whose origins are unclear but which may have been founded around 1895 by Theodor Reuss.[33] This "international alliance" (Weltbund) was connected at best ideally, but certainly not historically, with the Order of the Illuminati led by Adam Weishaupt, which ceased existing in 1793 with the death of Johann Joachim Bode. The well-known German spiritist and esoteric writer Leopold Engel is said to have joined this Weltbund in 1896, and to have quickly risen to a position of leadership. Reuss and Engel, however, soon quarrelled with one another, but were reconciled some time later before finally going their separate ways in 1902.

After this point, Reuss appears not to have concerned himself with the Weltbund any further. In 1903 Engel issued a new charter for an Order of the Illuminati in Dresden. In 1924 this Order was forced to close due to lack of membership. But in 1926 we find a new registration at the district court of Berlin-Tempelhof that again mentions a "Weltbund der Illuminaten". Engel died in 1931, and in 1933 the Order was dissolved.

APPENDIX 1   147

Nothing has yet been found to indicate that Evola had any contact with Leopold Engel or his Order of the Illuminati. But not even Crowley was apparently initiated into this Order; his relationship to Reuss was established around 1910 at the earliest, at which time Reuss was no longer involved in the group, which was then under the sole leadership of Leopold Engel; and independent contacts between Crowley and Engel's Illuminati group are equally impossible to prove. Despite this, Crowley described himself in 1918 as "Custos of the Illuminati" – but this may have been a decorative title, not based on any regular succession.

What, then, is the actual text of the aforementioned (second) police report, which also only cites a "reliable source"?

> The position of the journal *La Torre*, edited by the occultist and philosopher Baron Julius Evola (former editor of *Il Mondo* and still friendly with numerous anti-fascists) is to be observed. Evola, with his journals, first *Krur* and now *La Torre*, has started a kind of propaganda for German imperialism. This began with the secret journey to Austria and Germany that Evola claims to have made[34] ... and during which he had occasion to meet several persons from the religious political sect of the "Illuminati", an imperialist sect whose seven-man council allegedly includes the crown prince and Frau Krupp. This sect, which has political and intellectual connections to the Swiss sect of the Steinerians ... has made efforts to find a general agent in Italy ... in the service of German imperialism, in the defence of which the "Illuminati" in Germany have founded the "stahlhelm" [*sic*]. Evola is allegedly in contact with the "stahlhelm" via the Steinerians, and perhaps at the same time with the seven-man council and the council of the "Illuminati".[35]

Furthermore, Evola is described as a spy and a propagandizing agent of the Illuminati and Steinerians in Italy.

How can we judge this document? First it must be understood that Evola was in dire straits, politically and personally, at this time. Following his critique of Mussolini's "populism" in his journal *La Torre*, fanatic and potentially violent adherents of "Il Duce" had conspired against him, so that for a while he could only leave the house with a small group of bodyguards (who were also fascists, but agreed with Evola's criticism). *La Torre* was subsequently banned by the regime after its tenth volume. Therefore Evola surely had a good number of personal enemies who were ready to speak out against him. In his intellectual autobiography (which unfortunately makes little mention of external events), *Il cammino del cinabro*, he himself writes of additional "entirely base defamations ... conflicts and personal aggressions" at that time.[36]

The first thing we must investigate in this police report is Evola's alleged secret trip to Germany. According to Evola's aforementioned autobiography, however, his first journey to the north took place only in 1934.[37] Two of his main destinations then were Berlin, where he spoke at the Herrenklub and at the Lessing-Hochschule, and Bremen, where he attended the Second Nordic Thing at the invitation of Ludwig Roselius, the coffee merchant and "inventor" of decaffeinated coffee (Kaffee Hag).[38] In addition, there is an (admittedly unsatisfactory) statement made in another document from 4 June 1934 – also from a police office – to the effect that Evola had never been to Germany before that time. According to the document, although he had set off full of enthusiasm, he returned entirely disappointed by the spiritual positions of the Nazis. Specifically, these positions were oriented only around day-to-day political necessities. Spiritual viewpoints counted for nothing at all.[39] This report is unsatisfactory because it is apparently based on statements made by Evola himself, who can hardly have had any desire to own up officially to his "secret journeys" – if indeed he had actually taken them.

There is no way, however, that 1934 can have been the year of his first trip to Germany, because on 8 January 1933 Evola interviewed Dr Friedrich Everling on behalf of the *Corriere Padano*[40] in, according to the article itself, "an ultra-modern Café on the Kurfürstendamm" in Berlin. The location is also designated as Berlin at the top of the article. Most importantly in this case, Friedrich Everling was a parliamentary member of the group centred around Dr Alfred Hugenberg, which was closely connected with the Stahlhelm. Incidentally, Everling's statements met with complete approbation from the Italian interviewer. Evola must therefore have forgotten his 1933 trip when writing his autobiography, because he definitely travelled to Germany again in 1934; it is confirmed that he attended the Second Nordic Thing, which took place that same year. This error, however, surely has nothing to do with the alleged "secret" journey, which must have taken place before the date of the police report, namely before February 1930. The question of whether this journey really took place or is purely fictional unfortunately cannot be answered, since there are neither witness reports nor any other indications to confirm it.

In the police report, Frau Krupp and the German crown prince are mentioned as members of the seven-man council of the Illuminati. We can definitively exclude the possibility that they presided over Reuss's and Engel's Order of the Illuminati. But it is likely enough that contact took place between the Order of the Illuminati and the "Steinerians". Rudolf Steiner himself knew Theodor Reuss, and was briefly a member of his Memphis Misraim Order, but not of his OTO, as Peter-Robert Koenig points out.[41]

The Reuss–Engel Order of the Illuminati also certainly had nothing to do with the Stahlhelm. This paramilitary organization was founded in 1918 by reserve officer Franz Seldte, and used its clout to support the Deutschnationale Volkspartei (DNVP); its members included many Mussolini fans, incidentally.[42] This group's ideological position was nationalistic, and often anti-Jewish and pro-monarchist. The Stahlhelm was in very close contact with the Herrenklub, a conservative circle where Evola also spoke during what was probably his first visit to Germany; Evola was on excellent terms with the club's leader, Heinrich Baron von Gleichen,[43] as well as with the "Junkers" (great landholders) east of the Elbe.

There is no doubt that Evola had connections to the Stahlhelm; we know this from his interview with Friedrich Everling.[44] Evola was politically most sympathetic with those ideas, which, under the name of Harzburger Front, formed the basis for a political movement in 1931. The Harzburger Front had originated mainly from the initiatives of the aforementioned "press tsar" Alfred Hugenberg.[45] In it, the Stahlhelm, the Alldeutsche Verband, the DNVP and also the NSDAP worked together. The conservative powers centred around Hugenberg had hoped they might influence Hitler and pull the strings controlling him, which soon turned out to be a complete illusion. Even at the rally celebrating the founding of the Harzburger Front, Adolf Hitler and Joseph Goebbels showed how far removed they were from the other participating organizations, declining to join in the general luncheon and leaving early instead of attending the Stahlhelm parade.⁴⁶

Hugenberg, from 1909 to 1918, was chairman of the board of directors of Friedrich Krupp AG, and was extremely well connected in the world of big industry. This offers an acceptable explanation for the mention of Frau Krupp in the secret report by the Italian police, since it is established that Hugenberg was on the best of terms with the Krupp family. And there is also an explanation for the mention of the "crown prince" in the document. According to John A. Leopold, Hugenberg's biographer, Crown Prince Wilhelm, the eldest son of Kaiser Wilhelm II, was also present at the Harzburger Front's founding ceremony; and besides him, at least two more of Wilhelm II's sons were present, namely Princes Eitel Friedrich and Oskar.⁴⁷ But another prince, August Wilhelm of Prussia, was also one of the dominant personalities in the Harzburger Front. The Front was formally unified only on 11 October 1931, and the Italian document is dated 3 March 1930; but we may assume that the Front was the result of years of informal collaboration beforehand. All the aforementioned princes were members of the Stahlhelm, except for the crown prince, who was not allowed to become involved in politics. Prince Oskar of Prussia was also a member of the "Bund der Aufrechten", whose aim was to restore the monarchy; Dr Friedrich Everling also collaborated with this group.

It is unknown, and still remains entirely unclear, how and when Evola came into contact with the members of these political movements.⁴⁸ It is equally unclear whether this happened merely through correspondence (Evola did speak German) or through a "secret" visit to Germany. It is entirely plausible that, as the document claims, he may have received help from Steinerians. Evola's magical group, *Ur*, included several devout anthroposophists, such as the poet Arturo Onofri and the physician Giovanni Colazza; Evola was very close friends with both. Giovanni Colazza, who undoubtedly exerted a strong influence over the *Ur* group and over Evola himself, had also studied directly under Rudolf Steiner, and was this latter's great confidant. Evola's lifelong friend Massimo Scaligero (pen name of Antonio Sgabelloni), who later also became an anthroposophist, cites a statement in his autobiography made by one of the co-founders of the anthroposophical movement in Italy, Olga de Grünewald, according to whom Rudolf Steiner once went to Rome specially to meet Colazza there, because the "spiritual world" had advised him to do so. Colazza is even said to have been the second person in the anthroposophic hierarchy after Steiner himself.⁴⁹ He also allegedly belonged to the innermost circle of the twelve disciples that surrounded Steiner, and took part in the latter's inner rituals.

I have found no indication that the Anthroposophical Society had any connection to the Stahlhelm. Rudolf Steiner certainly had some German nationalistic tendencies – as did many other Germans and Austrians after the First World War. He rejected the judgement that Germany was the single guilty party, and saw the Treaty of Versailles as a forced peace that was going to make life impossible for the people of central Europe.⁵⁰

Some facets of the report from the Italian police are therefore true, but a great deal of misrepresentation and distortion of facts subsequently grew out of them. However, this has nothing to do with the Illuminati in the strict sense. It is far more a question of the political organizations with which Evola had doubtless sympathized from the late 1920s onward. When we consider the first police report and assume the *RISS* as its possible source, we can very easily see a connection with that journal in this case as well. According to *RISS*'s conspiracy theory, it was precisely the "Illuminati" and "Freemasons" who were responsible for political developments, and above all the drive for expansion, in Germany. In the police report the "Illuminati" mentioned were not the "Weltbund der Illuminaten" of Reuss and Engel; rather, the word "Illuminati" (like "Freemason") was simply used as a codeword for an alleged power hiding in the background, working to strengthen Germany and so-called "Pan-Germanism". Here it is also worth mentioning that in an unsigned article in the *RISS*, Aleister Crowley was apostrophized as a "follower of the Illuminati".[51]

The police accusations discussed here, moreover, are not the only ones made against Evola. As an example: in a police report from 24 February 1930[52] he is described as an "anarchic Indologist", a mystical anarchist, a student and agent of "Krisna Murthi" [*sic*] and even a "red Jewish agent", belonging to the 3rd International and the "International of Zion". He is also suspected of being an American agent, having infiltrated into fascism only a few months previously. All in all, he is a "dangerous person in every regard". He is also accused of being a pederast, the document's inevitable conclusion being: "He is surely a degenerate". With such a multitude of accusations, it is easy enough to doubt the seriousness of the research carried out by the police.

* * *

Thus we have established that a personal acquaintance, or even merely a connection, between Crowley and Evola through membership in the same esoteric groups cannot be proven, and is in fact highly unlikely. I will conclude by discussing a possible spiritual affinity. Evola is rebuked, for example by Italian Pythagorean traditionalist circles responsible for the journal *Politica Romana*, for having evaluated Crowley far too positively – even calling him an "initiate"[53] – suggesting a fear that these sympathies might have been at the root of Evola's political course, which was without doubt pro-German and consequently could have been directed against Italian traditionalism.[54] Since Evola, as we know, was accused many times of being a Satanist and always remained an outsider, a certain sympathy for a fellow "Satanist" and outsider is entirely understandable. But what was truly decisive for Evola's positive evaluation was something totally different: certain statements from Crowley in which Evola, rightly or wrongly, discerned genuine initiatic and magic elements.

However, I have not been able to identify an effective influence of Crowley over Evola. Evola seems to have taken an interest in Crowley only after the latter's death, and to have studied him only superficially (apparently mostly from secondary sources). And it was not only Crowley's showmanship and theatrical demeanour that marked a difference between the two, but also – in my view – their opinions. Here is not the place for a thorough analysis of the differences between the world views, political ideas and theories of magic held by the two men, but a few points are certainly worth making. Here, unfortunately, I must sacrifice exploration of the finer nuances in favour of brevity.

"Modernity" was common to their understanding of magic in the sense that for both Evola and Crowley, the higher development of the individual was placed at the centre, and great importance was placed upon personal experience as opposed to simply handing on inherited knowledge. Hierarchical, theological and moral aspects counted for nothing in this regard. And both developed their world views based on high intelligence and comprehensive education rather than mere belief. But their premises, in my view, were diametrically opposed. Evola saw himself as a traditionalist seeking to realize, here on earth, a world of Platonic ideas that was timelessly present in the transcendental realm, while Crowley imagined himself as the founder and missionary of the entirely new Law of Thelema. Evola pessimistically saw humanity evolving ever downward, while Crowley expected and proclaimed the advent of a new, liberated age. Evola had arrived at his world view primarily through synthesis and study. For Crowley, on the other hand, what lay at the basis was something he described as a revelation, which he supposedly obtained in 1904 through his first wife.[55] For Evola, the study of tradition was reserved for a spiritual elite, while Crowley, despite his elitist and often misanthropic views, thought more "democratically" to bless the entire world with his teachings, and consequently expected to be recognized by it.

Evola's magic was founded primarily on philosophical principles from the German romantics, solipsism and French personalism, as well as the ideas of Otto Weininger and Carlo Michelstaedter, which he brought into synthesis with Far Eastern teachings and with his natural magical talent and intuition.[56] Crowley's main magical sources, by contrast, were Éliphas Lévi and the Order of the Golden Dawn, although philosophical influences from Hume, Berkeley and Nietzsche can also be identified.[57] They both worked very pragmatically, but Evola placed enormous value in the so-called continuity of consciousness, and with the exception of some drug experimentation in his youth, always remained "actively" conscious. Crowley, on the other hand, had nothing against giving himself over to "passive" ecstasies and letting himself be taken over by "demons". The goal of magic for Evola was fundamentally an integration into the transcendent, in order to lend a "higher value" to man. For Crowley, magic also served for the "knowledge and conversation of the Holy Guardian Angel", but this was certainly not its only purpose. Gaining a material advantage, or holding influence over another person, could also be the goal.

They both saw sexuality as the most effective method for realizing the goal of their magic, and were greatly inspired by Tantrism, although for Crowley this only took place through a Western filter. For Evola, "ascesis" was central, and a special requirement for his sexual magic. For him, orgasm was to be prevented, and the erotic power of the woman over the man broken. Human sexuality was ultimately to be overcome and converted to a higher form of duality (androgyny). For Crowley, however, orgasm was the driving force for the implementation of his magical ideas, although for him as well, the "True Will" was superior to a passive abandoning of oneself to lust.

Only in their political and social ideas can I see certain external commonalities. Pasi, in the present book, has discussed Crowley's viewpoints, and above all his relationship to Germany, with particular thoroughness. The efforts of both Evola and Crowley to influence current political events in their favour is something that unified them and at the same time doomed them. Their youths, with strict Christian upbringings and subsequent rebellions, were also not too different. Evola then, as we know, came to his traditionalist world view under the influence of René Guénon, and finally postulated an "organic" state in the Platonic sense. However, if we grant more than a merely ephemeral value to Crowley's diary entry from 29 May 1923, we see something surprising. The entry reads as follows:

> I have been asking Ethyl about Political Wisdom.⁵⁸ ... I'm certainly not an anarchist, for the family is the smallest and so [the] vilest unit of government: nor a Socialist, for the State is the largest and so the least human unit. I suppose then, that – with Ethyl as without – I want a Patriarchal-Feudal system run by initiated Kings.⁵⁹

However, Crowley's jotted down opinions are not always to be taken literally. One of his specialties (with which I actually sympathize) was to tease his readers with ironic, sarcastic or simply humorous statements. The reader who falls for such things at least has the chance to learn something new.

As one can see, the spiritual relation between the two esotericists only goes so far. In the end, we can only sum it up thus: if one can indeed place Evola and Crowley in relation to one another at all, then – in my view – they can only be placed "side by side" and not "joined together". Or in the common analogy of two circles, one might speak of points of tangency, but only of a very small amount of intersecting space.

Acknowledgements

For important information and documentation, as well as criticism, I would like to thank the following persons, without whom this appendix could never have been written: Annemarie Aeschbach, Dr Piero Fenili, Peter-Robert Koenig, Dr Marco Pasi, Prof. Renato Del Ponte, Dr Gianfranco de Turris and one person who does not wish to be named.

✣ Appendix 2
Key documents

The Crowley–Pessoa Correspondence

Letter from Fernando Pessoa to the Mandrake Press. Published in part in John Symonds, The King of the Shadow Realm, *p. 445. Original preserved at the Warburg Institute, YC/OS, E21. Typescript.*

The Mandrake Press,	Apartado 147
41, Museum Street,	Lisboa
London, W.C.1.	4th. December, 1929

Dear Sirs:

I am much obliged for your letter of the 22nd. November, and for your courtesy in so speedily sending me the two books I had referred to. I am enclosing a cheque value £2.7.0, in payment of your invoice in that respect. Please acknowledge receipt at your convenience.

I was not in Lisbon when the books arrived and this is why I am remitting with one week's delay. I am often away from Lisbon for some time, and this will explain some similar delay – not likely to extend over a fortnight – in any future remittance you may similarly not receive in what seems to you decent postal time. Please send me each volume of the Confessions as soon as it is issued, and in the same manner as you sent this, *registering the parcel always*, and sending me by separate unregistered letter (or simple postcard) a notification that you have sent the volume.

If you have occasion to communicate, as you probably have, with Mr. Aleister Crowley, you may inform him that his horoscope is unrectified, and that if he reckons himself as born at 11h.16m.39s. p.m. on the 12th. October 1875, he will have Aries 11 as his midheaven, with the corresponding ascendant and cusps. He will then find his directions more exact than he has probably found them hitherto. This is a mere speculation, of course, and I am sorry to inflict upon you this purely fantastic intrusion into what is, after all, only a business letter.

Yours faithfully,
Fernando Pessoa

* * *

Letter from Aleister Crowley to Fernando Pessoa, Warburg Institute, YC/NS, 13. Carbon copy of typescript.

Fernando Pessoa, Esq.,   Ivy Cottage,
Apartado 147,   Knockholt, Kent
Lisboa, Portugal   Dec. 11th. 1929.

Care Frater:

Do what thou wilt shall be the whole of the Law.

    The Mandrake Press have forwarded to me your letter to them of the 4th instant, so that I may answer the last paragraph.

    The time of my birth is not quite certain. In no. 10 of the first volume of the Equinox, I took 0.3 of Leo as rising. But subsequently, I thought that the time might be a little later as I suspect that Herschell [*sic*, i.e. Uranus] and Saturn are within the first and seventh houses, respectively.

    I dare say your guess is accurate enough. I don't bother with directions. I do very little astrology, except pure genethliacal and transits. I should be very glad if you would let me have some information about my present situation.

    Love is the law, love under will.

Yours fraternally
[Aleister Crowley]

* * *

Letter from A. C. to Fernando Pessoa, Warburg Institute, YC/NS, 13. Carbon copy of typescript. The postscript at the bottom, which is handwritten, does not appear in this version (which is a carbon copy of the original sent to Pessoa), since it was evidently added after the letter had been typed. It does appear, however, in the original received by Pessoa, reproduced in Miguel Roza (ed.), Encontro "Magick" de Fernando Pessoa e Aleister Crowley *(Lisbon: Hugin, 2001), p. 78.*

Ivy Cottage,
Knockholt, Kent,
Dec. 22nd, 1929.

Care Frater:

Do what thou wilt shall be the whole of the Law.

    Thank you very much for the three little books. I think they are really very remarkable for excellence.

    In the Sonnets, or rather Quatorzaines, you seem to have recaptured the original Elizabethan impulse – which is magnificent.

    I like the other poems, too, very much indeed.

    Love is the law, love under will.

Yours fraternally,
[Aleister Crowley]

[I have, indeed, taken the arrival of your poetry as a definite Message, which I should like to explain in person. Will you be in Lisboa for the next three months? If so, I should like to come and see you: but without telling any one. Please let me know by return of post. 666]

* * *

Letter from Fernando Pessoa to A. C. First published in John Symonds, The King of the Shadow Realm, *pp. 446–7. Original preserved at the Warburg Institute, YC/OS, E21. Ms.*

Apartado 147
Lisboa
6th. January, 1930.

Carissime Frater:

I thank you very much indeed for your letters of the 11th. and the 22nd. December, particularly so for the second one, and especially for the written addendum to it.

I have just returned to Lisbon, so my "return of post" is inevitably somewhat late, though I am writing immediately.

I shall be in Lisbon, for all practical purposes, during the next three months. Even when I am absent from here, it is only to stay in Evora, which is only four hours away, by train. I can therefore always return to Lisbon at very short notice. The point is that I have that notice in good advance, and even then, that it do not reach Lisbon just when I have left, so I find it only on my return, which may mean anything up to a fortnight, the purpose of an advance notice being thus nullified.

If, however, any month of these first three of the year will serve your time and intention, I should very much prefer to meet you here *in March* – at any time within March. I shall not leave Lisbon at all in that month, and I have both the present month and February taken up by matters, of no importance in themselves – either absolutely, or relatively to the present one –, which deliver me over to an extraneous attention which I should not like to be clogged with when listening to you.

Apart from this, *astrological reasons* would counsel me to suggest March; and it is indeed the very lapsing of the direction, which makes January and February impeding months, that will make March a propitious one, especially to meet you, the underlying solar direction (pro. ☉ [Sun] ✶ [Sextile] ♆ [Neptune]) being remarkably attuned to the circumstance.

Furthermore, there is a vague possibility that I may have to go to England in the end of February. If so, I would inform you in full advance and (unless there be some reason I cannot foresee for the place of meeting to be Lisbon) you would be spared the trouble of coming to Portugal.

By the middle of February I shall be able fully to inform you about all this.

I shall, of course, tell no one at all about your visit. Was your warning connected with the receipt of a booklet (in French) by Raul Leal. He is a friend of mine (so to speak, for I am altogether apart from any sort of intimacy); I translated to him some pages, here and there, of the first volume of your "Confessions", and he asked me for the address of the publisher, so as to send you his book to their postal care. He now tells me, on my return to Lisbon, that he has received a letter from you, and is going to write to you a long one "on occult matters". With this, of course, I have no connection, as I have no connection with anything. Please do not take this as a reflection of any kind on Leal, whom I really like and whose spendidly intense metaphysical ability I appreciate. This is a mere statement of fact and, so to speak, a non-juror's note.

I hope to send you in the course of the present month the rectified nativity and the directions reckoned from it for the present time. When away from Lisbon I had no ephemerides or data.

I am registering the letter only that I may be the surer that it will not be likely to go astray.

Yours fraternally,
Fernando Pessoa

* * *

Letter from A. C. to Fernando Pessoa, first reproduced as a plate in França (1987). Now also in Pessoa and Crowley (2010: 314). Ms.

Ivy Cottage	die ♂
Knockholt	☉ in 24° ♑
Kent	An I 4

Care Frater

Do what thou wilt shall be the whole of the Law.

I was very pleased of your letter dated Jan 6.

I quite agree with you about March. I have many matters to put in order.

But it would be still better should you be in London in February. Our meeting there should elucidate some points in dispute in my mind about the Message*, so that proper plans may be made. I shall expect to hear from you as soon as you know your own plans.

Love is the law, love under will
yrs fraternally 666.

* I did not say, or mean "warning".

* * *

Letter from Fernando Pessoa to A. C. Warburg Institute, YC/OS, E21. Ms.

Apartado 147,
Lisboa, 25th. February 1930.

Care Frater:

My writing you so late implies only that not till the very verge of yesterday was it certain to me that I would not go to England.

I shall not leave Lisbon – unless for an occasional short voyage to Evora, from which four hours can recall me – until the middle of the year, and even then I may not leave.

If, therefore, you wish to come over, or think it within Fate to do so, you have but to give me a slight advance notice and I shall be here to see and hear you.

My astrology is in slight means, but I hope to have your nativity rectified in no more than a few days.

Yours fraternally,
Fernando Pessoa

The "Crowley Alistair Edward A." file

File preserved at the Central State Archives (Archivio Centrale dello Stato) in Rome (ACS, PS, AAGR, 1903–49, RG, b. 1, fasc. 20). Here I reproduce the entire contents of the file, with the exception of the Italian translation of the three letters from M. (Gertrude M. Godden). It should also be noted that the three letters are not present in the file in their original version, but are typewritten copies, probably made by their addressee, i.e. Father Joseph Ledit.

The three letters from M. to Father Joseph Ledit

Sept. 25 1935

Did you follow at all the very remarkable English group calling itself *New Europe* and *New Britain* and connected with a certain Dr Adler – the Adler Society, – the International Society for Individual Psychology. I had to investigate them a year or two ago. Lately I came on some startling European connections which might be of very grave import politically but not with any "psychological" reference. There is a connexion [sic] with a Mittel-Europaische Press dienst in Vienna. There is an intimate connexion with a serbian [sic] whose name I can give you if necessary. "Dr Adler" is I believe now in America. I think those responsible for the safety of prominent individuals and European peace might investigate the whole group. There is Paris contact through the Serb. I add 3 of their notice papers. The Colonel Delahaye was in the English War Office (!!).

* * *

April 20 1936

Enclosed copy speaks for itself – coming from that very practical worker Mr. Baker White I attach great importance to it.

Have you any information re *Dim Mitrinovic* (? the key man of a very large organization) or Ernest Beernink, O [sic] Köllerström, – Chelomsky, Philippe

Mairet, Mittel-Europaische Pressdienst, Opera ring Vienna, Dr Alfred Adler, founder of the "International Society for Individual Psychology", Vienna. – Dr Victor Bauer, Babenberger str. 9. Vienna.

[The following is the text of the enclosure referred to in the letter, which reproduces a letter from J. Baker White to G. M. Godden]

The Economic League
April 16 1936

Dear M.

I would be glad if you would take on a special commission for me, which is to investigate the present activities of the New Britain Group in general and of Mitranovic [sic] in particular. I am also anxious to know what part Valerie Cooper and Vivian Slade are at present playing in the movement.

I have of course a great deal of information that you have collected for me in the past, but what I want is a really up to date picture of the situation, and as soon as possible. I would like to know who is leading the Movement, besides the above-mentioned, and what appears to be the present scope of its influence. I would be pleased to pay for the work done on the usual basis.

Yours sincerely,
J. Baker White

* * *

May 28 / 36

I have been very occupied and latterly with the special urgent investigation into the group calling itself

XI Hour / New Britain / New Europe / New Order

In France, *l'Ordre Nouveau*: M. Emile *Pillias. Can you throw any international light on this*? I am inclined to link it up with "OTO" – *Ordo Templi Orientis* – which makes it quite dangerous stuff to handle! I expect you have the OTO – in its esoteric and exoteric name, C.C. fully documented?

Can you tell me anything of the last ten years, and especially the 1935–1936 movements of the world famous Abister (or maybe Aleister) [the text between parentheses is clearly added by Ledit, or by the person who typed this copy of M.'s letter on Ledit's behalf] Crowley – *and his many alias names*? *This is urgent.* He has published verses in Paris under the name of H.D. Carr. He deluded Burns and Oates into publishing anonymous Marian Verse. One of his publications is the "Equinox". He writes as Frater Perdurabo of the A∴A∴. He has run occult schools. He has been in Sing Sing (pro German). His "temple" (as of course you know) is or was at Cefalu, Sicily. Can you give me a description of him *recently*? Or a drawing? Especially his *head*? I rather hesitate putting this through the post, but how else can I ask you these very necessary queries?

APPENDIX 2   159

The "illustrative notes"
Italian original:

Note illustrative

I fogli notizie di cui è fatto cenno nella 1° lettera sono conferenze sul Marxismo e sulla psicologia, ed in questi fogli viene nominato il Colonnello Delahaye.
  Nel foglio 2° viene riprodotta una lettera del Sig. Baker White, indirizzata all'informatrice.
  Il Sig. Baker White è il Segretario della Lega Economica di Londra, potente organizzazione contro il comunismo. P[adre] L[edit] conosce personalmente detto Signore e lo stima come un organizzatore di primissimo ordine.
  L'informatrice alla quale il Segretario della Lega Economica di Londra si rivolge è pure personalmente conosciuta da P[adre] L[edit] che la stima come persona di valore e coraggio. Ha scritto, detta informatrice, un libro su Mussolini molto apprezzato ed è attualmente in sospetto per le sue idee filofasciste.
  P[adre] L[edit] desidera che su detto nominativo venga mantenuto l'incognito temendo che la rivelazione del suo nome possa procurarle dei seri fastidi.
  P[adre] L[edit] è meravigliato dell'indirizzo segnalato nei riguardi del Dr. Vittorio Bauer che è il noto Capo del Partito Social-Democratico in Vienna.
  Nel foglio 3° è giustificata la richiesta della fotografia del famoso *Abister* [*sic*].
  P[adre] L[edit] ignora se detta persona sia oggi a Cefalù in Sicilia, ma prega di avere, se possibile, indicazioni ed anche una fotografia.

Roma, 2 giugno 1936–XIV°

[Added in pencil:] Colloquio P[adre] L[edit] ambasciatore inglese presso la S. Sede.

Reazione cattolica inglese al discorso del Papa.

English translation:

Illustrative notes

The pages of notes that are referred to in the 1st letter are lectures on Marxism and psychology, and in these pages Colonel Delahaye is mentioned.
  On the 2nd page a letter from Mr Baker White is reproduced, directed to the [female] informant.
  Mr Baker White is the Secretary of the Economic League of London, a powerful anti-communist organization. P.L. [Father Ledit] knows the aforesaid gentleman personally and esteems him as an organizer of the highest degree.
  The informant to whom the Secretary of the Economic League of London addresses himself is likewise personally known to P.L. who esteems her as a person of valour and courage. Said informant has written a much-appreciated book on Mussolini and is currently under suspicion for her pro-fascist ideas.
  P.L. wishes her to remain incognito, fearing that the revelation of her name might lead to serious inconvenience.

P.L. is astonished at the address given with reference to Dr Vittorio Bauer, who is known as the head of the Social-Democratic Party in Vienna.

On the 3rd page the request for the photograph of the famous *Abister* [sic] is justified.

P.L. ignores whether said person is in Cefalù in Sicily today, but asks, if possible, to be given information and also a photograph.

Rome, 2 June 1936–XIV°

[Added in pencil:] Interview of P.L. [Father Ledit] with the English ambassador to the Holy See.

English Catholic reaction to the Pope's address.

Letter from the Police Commissioner of Palermo to Police Chief Arturo Bocchini
Italian original:

Il Questore di Palermo   Palermo, 6 Giugno 1936–XIV.
A S.E. il Senatore
Cav. Gr. Croce Dr. Arturo Bocchini
Capo della Polizia
Ministero dell'Interno
Roma

Eccellenza,

l'individuo del quale è cenno nell'appunto da V.E. consegnatomi *brevi manu* è il suddito inglese Crowley Alistair Eduard Alexander di Emily Bishop, nato a Lemingtoer [sic] Warwihstire [sic] il 12-10-1875, il quale dimorò per circa cinque anni in una villa, nelle vicinanze di Cefalù, e fu espulso dal Regno giusta ordinanza Ministeriale in data 13 aprile 1923, essendosi accertato che nella sua villa si svolgevano riti basati su pratiche di oscenità e pervertimento sessuale, alle quali partecipavano tre straniere con lui conviventi more-uxorio, nonché altri stranieri che di tanto in tanto si recavano a trovarlo.

In proposito richiamo i rapporti di questa Prefettura: N° 2815 in data 25 Luglio 1922, responsivo al telespresso N° 17011 del 23 Giugno precedente; N° 1260 del 26 Marzo 1923, responsivo della nota N° 6782 del 5 stesso mese; N° 2150 del 1° Maggio 1923, responsivo alla nota N° 9626 del 16 Aprile precedente.

Successivamente all'espulsione del Crowley, codesta Div. Pol. Politica, con nota N° 500/5883 del 27 Giugno 1927, segnalò che dalla casa del Crowley in Cefalù si irradiavano notizie diffamatorie sulle condizioni dell'Italia Fascista, notizie che venivano raccolte dal servizio speciale di spionaggio del Ministero degli Esteri d'Inghilterra e fatte pubblicare da alcuni giornali. Con lettera N° 14278 del 18 Settembre successivo questa Prefettura rispose che la cennata segnalazione era insussistente poiché dopo la partenza del Crowley, era rimasta a Cefalù solo una delle sue donne – suddita francese – la quale viveva di stenti e non aveva rapporti con alcuno.

Nell'Aprile del 1934 i giornali pubblicarono corrispondenze da Londra circa una causa per diffamazione intentata dal Crowley alla scrittrice Nina Hannet [sic], la quale in un suo libro "Il torso che ride" lo aveva presentato come cultore di magia nera, mentre egli aveva dedicato "tutta la sua fatica e la notevole fortuna lasciatagli dal padre – due o tre milioni di lire – allo studio della magia bianca".

Negli atti non esiste la fotografia del Crowley, ma vi sono i connotati, che trascrivo: alto, robusto, colorito roseo, occhi castani, calvizie centrale con piccolo ciuffo mediano sulla linea di inserzione dei capelli, barba e baffi rasi, piccola cicatrice sulla guancia sinistra, sotto lo zigoma [sic].

Voglia gradire, Eccellenza, i miei deferenti ossequi e credermi

Dell'E.V. Devotissimo
[illegible signature]

English translation:

Police Commissioner of Palermo   Palermo, 6 June 1936–XIV.

To His Excellency the Senator
Dr Arturo Bocchini, Knight Grand Cross
Chief of Police
Ministry of the Interior
Rome

Excellency,

The individual to whom reference is made in the note from Your Excellency that was personally handed to me is the English subject Crowley Alistair Eduard Alexander, son of Emily Bishop, born in Lemingtoer [sic] Warwihstire [sic] on 12-10-1875, who lived for about five years in a villa in the vicinity of Cefalù, and was expelled from the Kingdom following Ministerial order on 13 April 1923, it having been confirmed that rites were taking place in his villa based on obscene and perverse sexual practices, in which three female foreigners participated who were living with him as if married, besides other foreigners who came there from time to time to meet him.

In this regard I will list the reports of this Prefecture: No. 2815 dated 25 July 1922, responding to telegram No. 17011 from 23 June preceding; No. 1260 of 26 March 1923, responding to note No. 6782 of the 5th of the same month; No. 2150 of 1 May 1923, responding to note No. 9626 of 16 April preceding.

Subsequent to Crowley's expulsion, the Political Police Division, in note No. 500/5883 of 27 June 1927, indicated that defamatory statements regarding conditions in fascist Italy were being distributed from Crowley's house in Cefalù, statements that were being collected by the special espionage service of the British Foreign Ministry and were published by some newspapers. In letter No. 14278 on 18 September following, this Prefecture responded that the aforementioned allegation was unfounded because after Crowley's departure, only one of his two women remained in Cefalù – a French citizen – who lived in poverty and had no relations with anybody.

In April 1934 the newspapers published reports from London about a defamation suit brought by Crowley against the writer Nina Hannet [sic], who in her book "Laughing Torso" presented him as a follower of black magic, whereas he had dedicated "all his effort and the considerable fortune left to him by his father – two or three million lire – to the study of white magic".

In the documents in our archive there is no photograph of Crowley, but his features are described as follows: tall, robust, rosy complexion, brown eyes, balding on top with small lock of hair at the middle near the hairline, beard and moustache shaved, small scar on the left cheek, under the cheekbone.

Please accept, Excellency, my humble respects and consider me

Your Excellency's most devoted
[illegible signature]

Notes

Introduction
1. Scholem (1995: 2, 353, n. 3). Scholem offers similar judgements, also extending to other French and English occultists, in Scholem (1969). It seems evident that Scholem was well informed about Crowley's activities and publications even before the Second World War. On this, and more generally about Scholem's interest in occultism, see Burmistrov (2006, esp. 27–8). Interestingly, in November 1945 (thus, when Crowley was still alive) Scholem received a full report on Crowley from the biblical scholar Morton Smith, with whom he would correspond for almost forty years. Smith's information was based on the early monograph on Crowley written by P. R. Stephensen (1930). In view of Smith's long-standing interest in a "libertine" tradition with possible homoerotic connotations within early Christianity, the controversies surrounding his discovery of a secret gospel of Mark and his interpretation of Jesus as a "magician", it is interesting to note his early fascination for a figure such as Crowley. See Smith and Scholem (2008: 10–11).
2. A pioneering study in this field was written by J. Gordon Melton (Melton 1983). Fundamental contributions were subsequently made by Massimo Introvigne, who has offered useful analyses of Crowley's work and personality in the context of magically oriented new religious movements. See in particular Introvigne (1990: 268–76 and *passim*; 2010: 201–10 and *passim*). In this last text, Introvigne, although emphasizing the debt owed to Crowley by contemporary Satanism, argues against defining him as a "Satanist", which has been done too often in the past in an overly simplistic fashion. On Crowley and Satanism see also Dyrendal (2012).
3. A fundamental role in the promotion and development of this new field of study has been played by Antoine Faivre, who, until his retirement in 2002, was Chair of History of Esoteric and Mystical Currents in Modern and Contemporary Europe at the École Pratique des Hautes Études in Paris; and by Wouter J. Hanegraaff, who has been Chair of the similarly oriented centre for the History of Hermetic Philosophy at the University of Amsterdam since this centre was created in 1999. On the history of this field, see in particular Hanegraaff (2004), and the bibliography therein. See also Faivre and Hanegraaff (1998), especially the introduction. At present, at least five valuable introductions to the history of Western esotericism are available in English, each taking a different approach to the matter (Hanegraaff 2013; Faivre 2010; Goodrick-Clarke 2008; Versluis 2007; Stuckrad 2005a). For deeper analyses of authors and currents see also the standard reference work, Hanegraaff *et al.* (2005). Scholem's approach to the adaptations of Kabbalah in non-Jewish contexts is discussed by Kilcher (1998). In this book, Kilcher brings to light the risk of essentialism inherent in Scholem's approach (see esp. *ibid.*: 23–6).
4. See for instance the French journal *Politica Hermetica*, published since 1987 and directed by Jean-Pierre Laurant. Its central focus is precisely the relationship between politics and esotericism.
5. Mosse (1964).
6. See Webb (1971, 1976). The two books are complementary: in the first, Webb covers the nineteenth century and early years of the twentieth, while in the second he explores the subsequent period, up to the 1960s.
7. Webb (1976: 8).
8. *Ibid.*: 7.
9. See Laurant (1992) and Godwin (1994).
10. See Godwin (1994: 204, 315–17). The distinction has been recently used by Wouter J. Hanegraaff in his *Esotericism and the Academy* (see Hanegraaff 2012: 243–4). However, as I have argued in a review of the book, I find his application of it problematic (see Pasi 2013: 204–205).
11. Particularly Galli (1989, 1995).
12. Legends had already begun to form while he was still living. Significantly, Stephensen's apologetic book, to which I have already referred (see n. 1 above), bore the title *The Legend of Aleister Crowley*. Stephensen was not a disciple of Crowley's but one of his publishers. A later edition of the book, with an introduction by Israel Regardie, has been in print for some time since 1970. Now see the new, recent edition with an introduction by Stephen J. King and other interesting biographical material (Stephensen and Crowley 2007).

13. The departure point for my analysis has been Galli (1989), especially chapter 8: "Volo in Inghilterra" (187–214).
14. *Inferno*, V, 56.

1. An unspeakable life

1. For an initial introduction to Crowley's life and works, see my entries in two standard encyclopaedias of esotericism, one in French and one in English (Pasi 1998a, 2005a). The second is more thorough, and obviously more up to date, than the first.
2. In fact, on this last point, the question was purely theoretical, because Crowley, having declared bankruptcy in 1935, no longer owned the rights to his own writings, which had passed to the British state. Any proceeds from his writings, as is usual in such cases, would have been passed on by the state to Crowley's numerous creditors until extinction of the outstanding debts.
3. The first edition was *The Great Beast: The Life of Aleister Crowley* (Symonds 1951). The second was *The Great Beast: The Life and Magick of Aleister Crowley* (Symonds 1971); this second edition included some new chapters that had been previously published in another of Symonds's works, specifically dedicated to Crowley's magical practices: *The Magic of Aleister Crowley* (Symonds 1958). The third edition was *The King of the Shadow Realm: Aleister Crowley, His Life and Magic* (Symonds 1989). This edition also had some new chapters. The fourth and most recent edition is *The Beast 666: The Life of Aleister Crowley* (Symonds 1997). With a few exceptions, this last edition does not vary significantly from the preceding one. See also Pasi (2003: 228, n. 12). In the present book, I will mostly refer to *The King of the Shadow Realm*, which remains in my view the most complete and correct edition, and has had a much broader circulation than the following one.
4. Symonds (1989: 287).
5. See Crowley (1989). For references to Freud, see pp. 45, 59–60, 72, 157, 237, 257, 554, 593, 699. There is a reference to Jung on p. 809. This autobiography was written in the early 1920s and its narrative stops in 1923, 24 years before Crowley's death. It was planned for publication in six volumes, but only the first two were released during Crowley's lifetime, in 1929. Symonds knew it very well, because he, along with Kenneth Grant, edited and abridged it for publication in a single volume in 1969. Naturally, Symonds made extensive use of this work (among others) as a source for his biography.
6. The article "An Improvement on Psychoanalysis" can now be found in Crowley, *The Revival of Magick* (1998b: 76–81). Here, Crowley endeavours to explain the differences between Freud's and Jung's methods, demonstrating a certain familiarity with the works of both authors.
7. See what Colin Wilson wrote in his biography of Crowley (Wilson 1987: 7): "Like all the previous writers on Crowley, I owe a major debt to my friend John Symonds; there is a tendency among modern Crowley disciples to denigrate *The Great Beast* for its attitude of genial scepticism; yet it is hard to imagine how it could ever be replaced as the standard biography". On the relationship between Symonds's book and the recent flurry of Crowley biographies, see my discussion in Pasi (2003: 224–45, esp. 226–9).
8. See Regardie (1993: 5ff.). A good biographical study of Regardie still has to be written. However, useful information on his life, thought and works can be found in Suster (1990), Tereschchenko (1985) and Hyatt (1985).
9. See Regardie (1937–40). The importance of this initiatory order in the history of contemporary Western esotericism has been emphasized among others by Massimo Introvigne: "[The Golden Dawn's] magical system – above all via Israel Regardie's published documents – influenced tens of thousands of people, and its themes deeply pervaded the entire *milieu* of the new magical movement, within which the Golden Dawn acquired a fame that it would be no exaggeration to describe as legendary" (Introvigne 1990: 264). The literature on this subject is now fairly extensive and includes some authoritative works. For a brief introduction, see Gilbert (2005) and Pasi (1998c). For a comprehensive overview of the context in which the Order was born, its history, its importance and its significance, see Introvigne (1990: 257–66 and *passim*) and (with some reservations) King (1989, *passim*). The history of the Order now considered "classic" is Howe (1985). There are also interesting elements and information in Gilbert (1983, 1997b), as well as in the collection of documents (with ample introduction) edited by the same author: Gilbert (1986). Finally, Greer (1995) is an interesting, well-documented study devoted to the women of the Order, who played highly significant roles throughout its history.
10. Regardie explains his intent in the preface: "There is a time to speak and a time to remain silent. For me the time has come now to raise my voice in the interest of clarifying the record of Aleister Crowley. He was one of the greatest mystics of all time, although a very complicated and controversial person." And further on: "John Symonds, his major biographer, evinces throughout his narrative a totally contemptuous attitude toward Crowley. This hostility altogether invalidates his attempt at biography. ... Crowley had appointed him executor of his literary estate, and because of this, Symonds had a unique opportunity to set the record straight once and for all. However his personal prejudices got in the way. His writing is cynical, showing no glimmer of insight or the slightest trace of sympathy" (Regardie 1993: xxiii).
11. See Suster (1988). In his preface, he also gives his opinion of Symonds's work: "John Symonds' biography, *The*

Great Beast, written over 35 years ago ... is dated in its Victorian attitudes and marred by prejudice, hostility, fictionalized sensationalism; by its refusal to expound the essence of Crowley's thought; and even by plain inaccuracy. A fresh approach is sorely needed for the eighties and after" (*ibid.*: 7). It should be noted that Suster also wrote the entry on Crowley for the prestigious *Dictionary of National Biography*, which covers the lives of all the illustrious people of Britain. Crowley was initially not included in the edition of the dictionary published after his death, but was finally given an entry in the special supplement issued in 1993, which included persons neglected in the preceding volumes (Suster 1993). Suster, as mentioned earlier, also wrote a biography of Regardie.

12. Introvigne (1990: 257).
13. The most significant books with regard to Crowley are his early works: Grant (1972, 1973). See also Grant (1991), in which he recalls the relatively brief period during which he was Crowley's secretary. Kenneth Grant's oeuvre is however rather vast and references to Crowley are present in most of his works. For a bibliography, see Bogdan (2003).
14. The history of the OTO and its many branches, with varying claims to authenticity and succession, is extremely complex and cannot be tackled here, even in broad terms. Many questions regarding its history remain controversial, and several groups, at one moment or another, have claimed a legitimate succession. In the last twenty years the group that has emerged as the most structured and widespread is undoubtedly the one that took shape originally in America in the 1970s and has been often referred to as the "Caliphate". Today, this is the group that most persons would call "OTO" without further qualifications. It is also the group that has proved to have, through several court litigations in different countries, a legitimate claim to Crowley's own copyright. The literature on the OTO is now quite extensive, but of varying quality and often difficult to access. A sufficiently thorough introduction, offering new information on some of the more obscure aspects of this organization's history, and including a comprehensive bibliography, can be found in my entry "Ordo Templi Orientis", in the *Dictionary of Gnosis and Western Esotericism* (Pasi 2005b). For those wishing to delve deeper, I would refer (with the reservations mentioned below) to Koenig (1994b; republished in an extended and revised edition in 2001; and then again in a further expanded edition in three vols in 2011). See also the enormous collection of documents in Koenig (1994a, 2000). Important documents on the Order's history, including rituals and teachings reserved for sexual magic, have been published in King (1973) and in Reuss and Crowley (1999). Koenig has also set up an internet site devoted to the OTO, making his studies and the materials he has gathered over the years openly accessible (*The Ordo Templi Orientis Phenomenon*, available at www.parareligion. ch). Even if the wealth of material made available by Koenig can be quite useful, it should also be noted that his books hardly meet any acceptable scholarly standard, being marred not only by a strong anti-cult bias but also by an extremely chaotic arrangement and discussion of the material itself. The Caliphate OTO has also presented its own version of the history of the Order, with contributions by various authors and a good deal of documentation (see Hymenaeus Beta 1986). Interesting elements also in Bouchet (1998: 121–72). R. Kaczynski has published an important study on the origins of the Order, based on impressive archival research, which has brought to light little known details (Kaczynski 2012). The book is also useful for its rich set of illustrations. A very interesting work on the early years of the English branch of the Order led by Crowley, including previously unpublished information, is Gilbert (1997a). Also generally on the history of the Order, but focusing more on developments in North America is Starr (2003).
15. In particular, see Crowley's autobiography, *The Confessions* (1989) and the compilation of his magical writings *Magick* (Crowley 1973a).
16. Symonds (1989: xii).
17. See especially Grant (1991).
18. Cammell (1951), King (1987), Wilson (1987), Hutchinson (1998), Booth (2000), Sutin (2000), Kaczynski (2003, 2010) and Churton (2011). The sensationalist Mannix (1959) and the fictional Roberts (1978) offer no interesting elements for the scholar, and can therefore be set aside.
19. See Wilson (2006: ch. 7, "The Beast Himself", 457–91).
20. For example, Wilson (1987: 164–5) states that two of the formulas that express the essential principles of the Thelemic creed (on which see n. 53 below), namely "Do what thou wilt shall be the whole of the Law" and "Love is the law, love under will", are not found in *The Book of the Law*, which is clearly erroneous. See Crowley (1938: ch. I, verses 40 and 57, respectively).
21. Pasi (2003).
22. Kaczynski (2010).
23. Churton (2011: 7–8).
24. Spence (2008). Spence had previously published an article on the same subject (Spence 2000).
25. Hutin (1973). Another French biography was published two years later (Waldstein 1975). It is fictionalized, sensational and worth mentioning only for the great number of inaccuracies it contains.

26. Tegtmeier (1989).
27. Vermeer (2004). This book has also been translated into German in 2005.
28. On Anger, see especially the "unauthorized" biography by Landis (1995), and on his films, see Hutchison (2004).
29. By Hymenaeus Beta/William Breeze; e.g. see his edition of Crowley's *Magick* (1994, 1997).
30. In my article cited above (Pasi 2003: 237), as well as in the Italian edition of the present work (Pasi 1999), I erroneously associated Starr's name with the OTO, from which he considers himself totally independent. In 1985 Starr created the Teitan Press, a publishing house specializing in reprinting Crowley's works, which was based in Chicago. The imprint was sold in 2006 to Weiser Antiquarian Books. Apart from various introductions to the Teitan Press books, and a number of important articles (Starr 1995, 2006), see also the already mentioned study of the history of the Ordo Templi Orientis in North America (Starr 2003).
31. Bouchet (1988, 1998). The doctoral thesis was defended at the Université Paris Diderot-Paris 7 in 1994. A new edition has been published in 2011 with a different title and a new foreword (Bouchet 2011). Bouchet has also published a brief introduction to Crowley, in which he has summarized the content of his preceding works (Bouchet 1999).
32. Bogdan and Starr (2012). The book includes both essays previously published elsewhere and essays written especially for the occasion.
33. A significant number of articles on Crowley have been published in peer-reviewed scholarly journals such as *Nova Religio*, *Aries*, *The Pomegranate*, *Esoterica* and others.
34. The sect was founded in 1830 by John Nelson Darby. Concerning the Darbyite movement, see Séguy (1990: 68–70) and the entry "Darby, John Nelson" in Melton (1986). Information about the movement's history can be found in Coad (1968) and Ironside (1985).
35. See Crowley (1989: 35, 39).
36. *Ibid.*: 44.
37. Rev. 13:11-18; Rev. 17:1-6.
38. Crowley (1989: 53). Young Crowley respected and intensely admired his father. He describes this relationship in the *Confessions* as follows (*ibid.*: 49): "[Crowley's psychology] was probably determined by his admiration for his father, the big, strong, hearty leader of men, who swayed thousands by his eloquence". Note that in this part of his autobiography Crowley refers to himself in the third person. He does that only in the first few chapters of *The Confessions*; after the point where he describes his father's death, he begins referring to himself in the first person. This is evidence of the great importance this event held for him, and of the turning point it represented in his life. Although Symonds does not point this out, the real problem was that after his father's death, some relatives of Crowley's mother, whom the boy detested, took control of the situation. To make matters worse for him, at that moment his mother began to intensify her religious devotion, which must have been already quite strong even before her husband's death. Crowley did not mince his words, describing his mother plainly as a "bigot" (*ibid.*: 58).
39. "I ... began to behave like a normal, healthy human being. The nightmare world of Christianity vanished at the dawn. ... The obsession of sin fell from my shoulders into the sea of oblivion" (*ibid.*: 75).
40. *Ibid.*: 76. See Genesis 3:5.
41. *Ibid.*: 121.
42. See d'Arch Smith (1987: 29).
43. See Crowley (1989: 105).
44. Arthur Edward Waite was an occultist and one of the most famous writers on esotericism during the late nineteenth and early twentieth centuries. He wrote on various subjects such as Freemasonry, Rosicrucianism, Kabbalah and ceremonial magic. He was a member of the Hermetic Order of the Golden Dawn and various other occultist groups.
45. Regardie (1993: 38). About this episode and the influence of Eckartshausen's work on Crowley, see Faivre (1969: 617–18).
46. On Mathers, see Pasi (2005c) and the appended bibliography. The only book-length biography is Colquhoun (1975).
47. On the Golden Dawn and its history, see n. 9 above.
48. Introvigne (1990: 259). On Bennett, see Harris (1998) and Crow (2009).
49. Namely, the so-called Abramelin system of magic, based on a grimoire that Mathers had found in the Arsenal Library in Paris and had then edited and republished (Mathers 1976, originally published in 1898). Regarding this book, see its recent edition with extensive introduction and commentaries by Georg Dehn (2006). Regarding the use of this text in twentieth-century occultist circles, see the compilation of documents edited by Peter-Robert Koenig (1995). About Crowley in particular, see Pasi (2011). Regarding this particular tradition of magic, see also Roling (2002: esp. 244–9). Crowley, due to his involvement in the internal conflicts of the Golden Dawn, did not complete the series of rituals.

50. Insider authors Ruggiu and Tereshchenko (2009) have noted that the initiation ritual (which was particularly complex) is not mentioned in the minutes of the record book of the Paris Ahathoor Temple, where it is supposed to have taken place. Consequently, they argue that, if the initiation ever took place at all, it was probably performed rather informally.
51. The peak was finally reached for the first time in 1954, by an Italian expedition led by Ardito Desio.
52. Maugham later wrote a novel, *The Magician* (1908), portraying an atmosphere modelled on the circle of artists he and Crowley frequented during this Parisian period, in which the main character, the ruthless Oliver Haddo, was inspired by Crowley himself. In a new edition, almost fifty years later, Maugham added a preface recounting his relationship with Crowley (Maugham 1956). On Crowley and Maugham, see Freeman (2007).
53. Thelema, meaning "will" in ancient Greek, is essentially the keyword for Crowley's beliefs. In his view, each great religion had a sacred word that had been pronounced in the beginning by its founder, which expressed the essence of that religion in the most immediate manner, for example "Anatta" for Buddhism and "Allah" for Islam (see Crowley 1994: 688). In this sense, he intended "Thelema" to be the keyword for the religion he founded. Those who accept the "Law" of Thelema describe themselves as "Thelemites". The Law of this new revelation consists above all in three Thelemic principles: "Do what thou wilt shall be the whole of the Law", "Love is the law, love under will" and "Every man and every woman is a star". The text of *The Book of the Law* has been published in countless editions and translations. For an edition including Crowley's most important comments on the text, see Crowley's *The Law is for All* (1993b).
54. Concerning Crowley's relationship to Freemasonry, see Starr (1995).
55. The peak of Kangchenjunga was finally conquered in 1955 by an English expedition led by Charles Evans.
56. The ritual ended in December 1906, after Crowley's return to England, with some rituals practised in the company of George Cecil Jones (Crowley 1989: 530–33). About the ritual and its context, see also Pasi (2011).
57. Crowley (1989: 529). The system of the Golden Dawn included ten degrees, grouped into three Orders (plus a preliminary sub-degree). There was the Outer Order, which was the actual Golden Dawn itself; the Internal or Second Order, called the *Roseae Rubeae et Aureae Crucis*; and the Third Order, the highest and most secret. The ten degrees, and the three Orders that encompass them, had an ideal relationship to the Kabbalistic "Tree of Life", with its ten *Sephiroth* (ten aspects or emanations of God) and twenty-two "paths" connecting them. What the citation above means, therefore, is that Crowley was now preparing himself to leave behind the highest degree of the second Order, namely that of *Adeptus Exemptus*, and attain the first degree of the third Order, that of *Magister Templi*. In order to pass from the Second Order to the Third, it was necessary to overcome a particular ordeal: the "crossing of the Abyss". Crowley states that it took him three years to pass through this ordeal, and only in 1909 was he able to "enter" the new degree definitively.
58. According to Symonds (1989: 102), however, Fuller was also the only contestant.
59. On Neuburg, especially his relationship to Crowley, see the biography by Jean Overton Fuller (1990), (no relation to J. F. C. Fuller).
60. On Mudd, see Symonds (1989: 331–7 and *passim*) and Kaczynski (2010: 175 and *passim*).
61. The A∴A∴ has sometimes been confused with the OTO. But in fact, both the histories and the goals of the two orders are very different. The differences are well summarized by Regardie (1993: 454ff.), where the contrast between the "individualist" A∴A∴ and the "universal" OTO is made evident. This aspect, as we shall see later, is highly interesting; see p. 27.
62. Frank Harris, a writer of Irish origin and a friend of Oscar Wilde and George Bernard Shaw, was at the time director of *Vanity Fair*. He had at least two things in common with Crowley: a bad reputation as an exhibitionist and an eccentric (due in great part to his own autobiography, *My Life and Loves*) and the accusation of having spread pro-German, or at least anti-British, propaganda in the United States during the First World War.
63. The "Enochian system" was one of the most important components of the teachings of the Golden Dawn. According to Regardie (1993: 203), it was "the crown of the Order Work. All training systems of every kind were amalgamated and synthesised into this Enochian system". The system was derived from a series of "angelic communications" received by the famous English mathematician and erudite John Dee (1527–1608) through his seer Edward Kelley (1555–97). On Crowley's interpretation of the Enochian system, see Asprem (2012: esp. 85–101). Crowley explored the astral regions connected with this system (the so-called Æthyrs or Aires) in the course of a series of visions. The result was the extraordinary and impressive account that is "The Vision and the Voice", first published in *The Equinox* I(5). It can also be found in *Gems from the Equinox*, edited by Israel Regardie (1986: 431–591). On the magical rituals at the basis of the "Vision and the Voice" and the related visions, see Owen (2012).
64. See n. 56 above.
65. On Reuss, see the biography by Möller and Howe (1986). See also the article in English by the same authors (Möller and Howe 1978) and Kaczynski (2012: 33–48). For Reuss's own writings, see the two anthologies of texts edited by Peter-Robert Koenig (1993, 1997). Documents and studies on Reuss can also be found on

Koenig's internet site (www.parareligion.ch). Reuss, after a brief career as an opera singer in Germany (he was then close to Wagnerian circles), devoted himself to journalism, worked as an opera impresario and pursued various Masonic and occultist activities, of which the OTO can be considered the most successful. He often resided in London, moving primarily in socialist, anarchist and theosophical circles. He was also a member of the Socialist League of William Morris and Eleanor Marx (Karl's daughter), but was expelled in 1886 on suspicion of having passed information to the German police about German political fugitives in England. He was continually engaged in the causes of feminism and sexual freedom, publishing pamphlets and delivering lectures. In the final years of his life, he was close to the famous idealistic colony of Monte Verità, near Ascona, becoming one of this community's most prominent members. Concerning his activity as a police informant, his biographers have not found documents proving the fact definitively, but they do consider it probable that Reuss collaborated with the German secret service, both during his London period and later during the First World War. In 1936 Reuss, though already dead for over a decade, was at the centre of a series of violent attacks appearing in the German anti-Semitic journal *Der Judenkenner*, which was particularly aggressive towards other representatives of German contemporary esoteric movements as well, such as Rudolf Steiner (also deceased by that time).

66. On Crowley's *Rites of Eleusis* see Brown (1978), Van Kleeck (2003) and Tupman (2003).
67. Even his funeral ceremony resulted in a scandal. See Marlow (1992: 51).
68. On Crowley's views on, and attitudes towards, Christianity, see Pasi (1998d).
69. The Scarlet Woman is one of the two main archetypal figures of Thelema, together with the Great Beast (incarnated by Crowley himself). She is mentioned in several passages of *The Book of the Law* (I, 15; III, 14; and III, 43) and is obviously related to the feminine figure appearing in the Book of Revelation in the passage quoted above (Rev. 17:4). See also Pasi (2005a: 286).
70. See S. J. Taylor (1990: 36ff.).
71. See Crowley (1989: 745).
72. *Ibid.*: 779.
73. Symonds does not mention this aspect, which I see as essential for understanding Crowley's psychology and therefore for interpreting his ideas and behaviour. Crowley gives three different versions of his American period in his autobiography, focusing in each of them on different aspects of his American experience. The first version can be found in the text of a pamphlet he wrote in the early 1920s, entitled "The Last Straw". This text appears in chapter 76 of *The Confessions* (heavily abridged in the Symonds and Grant 1969 edition) and is mostly a defence from the accusation of being involved in German propaganda. The second version, appearing in chapters 77–80, simply describes the "external" story of the American period, i.e. his journeys, his love affairs, the works he produced and his meetings and experiences in general. These two versions are both "autobiographical" in the generally accepted sense of the term. But the third version, in chapters 81–6, deals with the "subtle" aspects of his life in the same period and relates his stages of initiation to the degree of *Magus*. Of the three versions, the third is doubtless the one that describes the events that Crowley considered as the most important for him. From his point of view, it offers the key for understanding his behaviour and experiences as told in the other two.
74. See Crowley (1989: 848ff.).
75. The March on Rome (27–30 October 1922) was organized by Mussolini in order to put pressure on the King of Italy, Victor Emmanuel III, and force him to appoint him as prime minister of a new government. After this event, Mussolini and his fascist party gradually established their dictatorial regime, which would last more than twenty years.
76. Interestingly enough, the British consul in Palermo at the time was Reginald Gambier Macbean (1859–1942), who was an important member of the Italian branch of the Theosophical Society and in 1921 had been elected Grand Master of one of the offshoots of the Egyptian Masonic Rite of Memphis (see Introvigne 1990: 168ff.; Pasi 2010: 588–9). It is hard to imagine that Macbean could ignore that Crowley was an important figure in another offshoot of the Rite of Memphis (together with the Rite of Misraim) via the Yarker–Reuss line. On the other hand, if Crowley knew about the status of Macbean, he did not say it, either in his diary or in his autobiography. On the complicated story of the Egyptian rites of Memphis and Misraim and their various offshoots, see Caillet (2003), Ventura (1991a) and Galtier (1989). It is not clear whether Macbean played any part in the episode of Crowley's expulsion from Italy a few months later.
77. On this subject, see Schüller (1997).
78. The campaign was mainly conducted through a series of "tracts" and leaflets, printed and distributed by Crowley and his followers. See Kaczynski (2010: 423–5). The Mandrake Press (Thame) has reprinted a few of these leaflets and released them in a collection without any title or further information (in the catalogue of this publishing house, it is listed as Aleister Crowley, *Pamphlets*).
79. John Symonds mentions only one visit of Crowley to Gurdjieff's Prieuré on 10 February 1924, when Gurdjieff

was absent (Symonds 1997: 291). His source is Crowley's own diary. Despite Gurdjieff's absence, Crowley had a very positive impression of Gurdjieff's community of disciples and of his teachings. Other authors mention however a second visit, during which Crowley met indeed with Gurdjieff. The main source for this episode is one of Gurdjieff's pupils, Charles Stanley Nott (1887–1978), who was a direct witness and writes about it in his memoir (Nott 1961: 122). According to Nott, Crowley was received by Gurdjieff and the two talked for some time with each other. Apart from some apparent tension between the two, nothing special seems to have happened on that occasion. Nott is not very precise in his chronology, but this seems to have happened in 1926. James Webb mentions this second visit in his comprehensive study of Gurdjieff, *The Harmonious Circle* (Webb 1980: 314–15), but he also relates another version of it. According to this version, Crowley spent a whole weekend at Gurdjieff's Prieuré and was received at first as any other guest, without hostility. But when he was about to leave, Gurdjieff, who thought his duties of hospitality absolved, treated him contemptuously, calling him "filthy" and "dirty inside" and telling him never to set foot in his house again. Unfortunately, Webb does not give any reference for this version, but it can be inferred that his anonymous source must have been someone from among Gurdjieff's circle of pupils (Webb interviewed several of them for his book). Some later biographers of both Gurdjieff and Crowley have related uncritically this second version of the story (see for instance Moore 1991: 219–20; Wilson 1987: 149). The two versions (Nott's and Webb's) are so different that it would not be illogical to think that they refer to two different episodes, which would bring the total number of visits of Crowley to Gurdjieff's Prieuré to three. However, it is also possible to think that the person who related this story to Webb may have embellished the events so that the contrast between the two spiritual teachers would appear stronger, with Gurdjieff clearly taking distance from a notorious "black magician". It should also be pointed out that a sympathetic biographer of Crowley, G. Suster (1988: 92), tells yet another version of the story: "It was Yorke who gave me an accurate account of the meeting between Crowley and another celebrated magus, G. I. Gurdjieff, for he was the only other person present. There are a number of false versions, one of which Colin Wilson repeated in his elementary introductory work, *The Occult*. According to Yorke, Crowley and Gurdjieff met in Paris for about half an hour and nothing much happened other than a display of mutual male respect: 'They sniffed around one another like dogs, y'know. Sniffed around one another like dogs,' Yorke chuckled." Even if Nott does not refer to any person accompanying Crowley during his visit, it is interesting to note that Nott's and Yorke's versions seem to be quite compatible and very probably refer to the same episode. On all these episodes and versions, see also Kaczynski (2010: 406–7), Sutin (2000: 317–18), and especially Mistlberger (2010: 386–99), who offers the most extensive discussion, with interesting comments on the possible psychological aspects of the meeting between the two "Magi". Mistlberger's book as a whole is a comparative study of Gurdjieff, Crowley and Osho, a.k.a. Bhagwan Shree Rajneesh (1931–90). For another in-depth comparative study of Crowley and Gurdjieff, written before but published after Mistlberger's, see Hall (2012).
80. See Starr (2003: 148–50).
81. A reconstruction of these events can be found in Flowers (1994: 15ff.). See also King (1987: 149ff.). John Symonds (1991) reconstructs this period of Crowley's life in *The Medusa's Head*, a strange novel, mixing fact and fiction.
82. One version is given in Regardie (1993: 10ff.). According to Regardie, one of the persons responsible for the expulsion was Regardie's own sister, even before he left America to join Crowley. Apparently concerned about what might become of her brother in the company of such a sinister individual, she went to the French consul in Washington to prevent him from being granted a visa. But the visa having already been issued, the consul could only promise her that an investigation would be made in Paris. This is confirmed by a letter from Regardie's sister, Sarah Regardie, from 24 August 1935 to the British Minister of the Interior (RP), in which she also explains the difficult situation (from an administrative point of view) in which her brother found himself after Crowley's expulsion from France, and asks for help in getting him a visa to return to America. These events overlapped with a lawsuit brought against Crowley in December 1928 by one of his literary agents, Carl De Vidal Hunt (b. 1869), who denounced Crowley to the police because of financial disagreements. Ultimately, it is also possible that Crowley's role as international head of the OTO, an organization of German origin, led the French authorities to suspect him of being a spy in the pay of the Germans. On these events, see also Kaczynski (2010: 431–40) and Spence (2008: 197–9).
83. About Stephensen, see Munro (1984). On Crowley and Stephensen see King (2007). Stephensen, nicknamed "Inky", was born in Australia. His relationship to Crowley would deserve further investigation, since politics played an important role in his life. He was a passionate reader of Nietzsche and Bakunin, and saw his publishing activities as part of a bitter fight against bourgeois mentality. He was involved in various radical political movements, both of the extreme left (he was a member of the Communist Party during his studies at Oxford in the mid-1920s) and, later in his life, of the extreme right. As was the case with several of Crowley's acquaintances, he paid a high price for his political activities. During the Second World War he was imprisoned for his pro-Nazi activities in Australia, where he had returned to a few years previously. Doubtless he saw Crowley as a

kindred spirit, who shared at least his strong anti-bourgeois sentiments with him; this can explain the sympathy he showed toward Crowley, and the decision to publish his works.
84. Stephensen (1930). Given Stephensen's long-standing interest for politics and activism, it is not surprising that he devotes special attention to the political aspects of Crowley's work in his book.
85. On Crowley and painting, see Pasi (2008) and Hymenaeus Beta (1998).
86. Crowley and Huxley were introduced by a mutual friend, the mathematician John W. N. Sullivan (1886–1937), with whom Huxley was briefly living in Berlin during this period. According to Symonds (1989: 458), Crowley included a portrait of Huxley in the exhibition of his paintings that he held in Berlin shortly after his Portuguese escapade. Symonds also gives this quote from Crowley without indicating the source: "I thought he had a lot of money and painted him like this to flatter him." It is likely that the relationship between Crowley and Huxley was more interesting than how Symonds describes it. In Crowley's diary from 1930, a typewritten copy of which exists in the Yorke Collection (YC, mss. I, H5), there are some references to the meetings Crowley had with Huxley in the month of October. It is also interesting to see what J. Webb has to say about their relationship: "There is firsthand evidence that Crowley introduced Aldous Huxley to mescaline in pre-1933 Berlin" (Webb 1976: 439). Regarding this piece of information, Webb states that "The source is a former disciple of Crowley" (*ibid*.; in all probability, the source is Gerald Yorke). Webb continues: "This is interesting and significant for it indicates that Huxley's wide reading in mystical matters was supplemented by practical experience before he arrived in the United States in 1937" (*ibid*.). He then adds, in a footnote: "As his correspondence shows, Huxley kept in touch with almost every prominent member of the mystical underground. At first there were Gerald Heard and Christopher Isherwood, later Alan Watts and Timothy Leary" (*ibid*.: 482, n. 40). As we have seen, Crowley also associated with Isherwood during his time in Berlin. Finally, the Yorke Collection includes a letter dated 9 December 1932, and two postcards, undated but with postmarks from 1 March and 14 July 1933 (YC/OS, E21), sent by Huxley to Crowley. See also "Aldous Leonard Huxley" in Cornelius and Cornelius (1996: 73–5) and Kaczynski (2010: 448–9).
87. On him and his relationship with Crowley, see pp. 83–8.
88. It is interesting to note that one of Crowley's biographers, Gerald Suster, has claimed that this was not the case. He wrote: "Crowley kept moving during the years 1936–9. He paid a number of visits to Nazi Germany. There … was a successful exhibition of his paintings in Berlin, where he encountered Aldous Huxley" (Suster 1988: 73). It would be remarkable to prove that Crowley went to Germany in those years, but if there is one thing on which all other biographers agree (and which is confirmed by the available evidence), is that he never left England again after 1932. The events to which Suster refers did indeed occur in Germany, but this was (as I have just pointed out) in 1931. Moreover, it is difficult to imagine Crowley holding an exhibition of his paintings in Berlin during a later period, if one considers the limited sort of artistic production that was tolerated in Germany during the Nazi regime. Suster himself appears to have reconsidered his statement, if – as it seems evident – it is he to whom Ralph Tegtmeier is referring in the following passage: "statements in the literature [on Crowley's life] are often very imprecise, and sometimes even contradictory. In one instance (Crowley's travels in the Third Reich), they are given by only one of his biographers, who later, in a personal conversation, expressed doubt about his own account" (Tegtmeier 1989: 35).
89. Cammell (1951: 7–8).
90. Hamnett (1932).
91. Crowley was obviously aware of the situation of his initiatory organizations in Germany. Although Germany had been one of the countries in which the Crowleyan movement was most lively and active, not much of it remained after the Nazi persecution.

2. Magical politics

1. Indeed, he often described himself, using a favourite expression of his beloved Shelley, as a "Wanderer of the Waste". See for example Crowley (1989: 228, 334, 415).
2. In a footnote of his classic study, *The Romantic Agony*, Mario Praz lists Crowley among the English decadents who were inspired by "satanic currents". See Praz (1970: 413).
3. The historian Frank M. Turner has suggested that for the nineteenth-century English context "scientific naturalism" is a better term than positivism, which was more specifically French and mostly inspired by Auguste Comte's (1798–1857) ideas. See Turner (1974: 11). What is referred to by the term is the scientific, agnostic and secular current of thought that was particularly influential in England (but also, in different forms, in other European countries) during the second half of the nineteenth century.
4. Just to give an example: "The result of any election, or for the matter of that any revolution, is an almost wholly insignificant component of those stupendous and inscrutable Magical Forces which determine the destinies of the planet" (Crowley 1973b: 463). For an explicit reference to the subordination of the material plane to the spiritual, see also *The Confessions* (Crowley 1989: 124–5). This is also how we should view Crowley's idea that

each new edition of *The Book of the Law* would cause reverberations on the subtle plane, which in turn would lead to wars affecting the whole world on the material plane. See Crowley's *Magick* (1973a: 233; 1997: 218–9); and also the pamphlet released by Crowley around 1938, and reproduced by Grant (1973: 86–7).
5. "Die Auflösung der Moral führt in der praktischen Consequenz zum atomistischen Individuum und dann noch zur Zerteilung des Individuums in Mehrheiten – absoluter Fluß" (Nietzsche 1988: 140, fr. 4.83). Alex Owen's book *The Place of Enchantment* (2004) has focused precisely on the quintessentially modern forms of exploration and construction of the self in which occultists engaged at the turn of the twentieth century. Significantly, a chapter (originally a separate article) is devoted to Crowley (186–220). The essay has been later republished in Bogdan and Starr's anthology (Owen 2012).
6. Crowley (1989: 460).
7. *Ibid.*: 559–60.
8. It has been suggested more generally that "mythologies of consistency" should be mistrusted on principle in the history of ideas. Quentin Skinner has famously insisted on this point, see Skinner (1969: 16–22).
9. Crowley attributed a very specific meaning to the word "mysticism". The first part of *Book Four*, entitled "Mysticism" (Crowley 1997: 5–44), deals specifically with this subject. The mystical experience, according to Crowley, may variously be called "vision of God", "union with God", or "samadhi", but essentially these are all the same thing (*ibid.*: 14, 37, 42). This experience brings about a superior state of consciousness, through which the individual achieves union with a transcendent principle, which might be called "the Infinite, the Absolute, God, the Oversoul" (*ibid.*: 42), depending on the tradition to which one refers. In order to achieve this result, Crowley claimed to possess a method that was "based only on the ascertained facts of anatomy, physiology, and psychology" (*ibid.*). This "method" was based essentially on the practice of yoga techniques, which – as I have mentioned in Chapter 1 – Crowley had learned and tested in Ceylon between 1901 and 1902, in the company of Allan Bennett. On Crowley and yoga see also Pasi (2001a, 2011).
10. Regardie (1993).
11. It should be remembered that Regardie, after breaking off relations with Crowley and subsequently abandoning the world of occultism, devoted himself to psychoanalysis. After several years of study and training, he began practising in the profession as a therapist of the Reichian school.
12. See Chapter 1, n. 57.
13. Regardie (1993: 414).
14. *Ibid.*: 445. Alex Owen's essay on Crowley (Owen 2004: 186–220), to which I have already referred above in n. 5, focuses mostly on this experience. Interestingly enough, Owen's interpretation of Crowley's magical adventure in the Sahara seems close enough to that of Regardie, even if she does not refer to his book. According to her, this experience could help explain certain aspects of the psychological evolution seen in occult practices during this era, particularly at the hands of authors such as Crowley. See also my own discussion in Pasi (2011). Similarly to Regardie, Owen claims that, "in magical terms, Crowley's work was fatally flawed" (Owen 2004: 219). This poses however a problem: whereas such a judgement is understandable and legitimate from an occultist such as Regardie, it is not clear how it can be appropriated by a scholar working from a historical, critical perspective.
15. "I have reflected long on this early observation of mine and have concluded that it should be modified" (Regardie 1993: 460, n. 4). This note was evidently added in a later edition of the book.
16. For a recent edition see Crowley (1991a).
17. For a recent edition see Crowley (1990).
18. For a recent edition see Crowley (1992c).
19. The first edition of the first part (on mysticism) is from 1912 (but the date is not certain: see d'Arch Smith 1987: 21); the first edition of the second part (on magic) is from 1913. Both parts were later included in *Magick in Theory and Practice*, published between 1929 and 1930.
20. All ten issues of this first volume have gone through multiple reprints; see for instance Crowley (1993a). The second volume was not published (it was supposed to be a "silent" one), and only the first issue of the third volume was published in 1919. It is known as the *Blue Equinox* due to the colour of its cover. In this issue there is a preponderance of texts of Thelemic inspiration. For a reprint, see Crowley (1992b).
21. Regarding the degree of *Magus*, Crowley wrote: "The Magus is … not a person in any ordinary sense; he represents a certain nature or idea. To put it otherwise, we may say, the Magus is a word. He is the Logos of the Aeon which he brings to pass" (Crowley 1989: 795).
22. "Most of my time in 1912 was taken up by the OTO. The Order was a great success and ceremonies of initiation were of almost daily occurrence" (*ibid.*: 689).
23. Regardie (1993: 454–6; emphasis added). It should be noted that this is not merely an interpretation by Regardie. Crowley, in the last years of his life, when explaining the difference between the A∴A∴ and the OTO, wrote: "Here's the essential difference *ab ovo usque ad mala*: the A∴A∴ concerns the individual, his

development, his initiation, his passage from "Student" to "Ipsissimus"; he has no contact of any kind with any other person except the Neophyte who introduces him, and any Student or Students whom he may, after becoming a Neophyte, introduce" (Crowley 1973b: 122).
24. Regardie (1993: 419).
25. See Stephensen and Regardie (1983: 25).
26. Crowley (1989: 120).
27. I am referring here particularly to Crowley's parents, whose influence was stronger in Crowley's formative years. This does not mean however that other members in the family may not have had conservative ideas. Spence mentions for instance the later influence of Crowley's aunt Annie (second wife of his uncle), who had important connections in the Conservative Party and belonged to the Primrose League, an auxiliary group of the Party.
28. *Ibid.*: 40. On this aspect, see also the case of the writer and literary critic Sir Edmund Gosse (1849–1928), a generation older than Crowley but also the son of Darbyites. In his autobiography he records his parents' enthusiastic patriotism during the Crimean war (Gosse 1907: 29–31).
29. See Crowley (1989: 107–8). On the spreading of nationalist and imperialist sentiments in England during this period (between 1886 and 1901), see Ensor (1992: 163, 331–3). It is no coincidence that the term "jingoism", meaning nationalist chauvinism, had appeared just a few years earlier, at the end of the 1860s (*ibid.*: 48).
30. For a comprehensive and detailed reconstruction of the English political events of this period, see Ensor (1992). Ensor's book, the first edition of which came out in 1936, appears somewhat dated today, but still remains an irreplaceable overview of this period of British history, including its social and cultural aspects. Another useful source in this respect is Cevasco (1993). Organized as an encyclopaedia, it is a goldmine of information and details about this period, with many entries that go beyond the strict limits to the 1890s. The book includes also a rather superficial entry on Crowley, by Veronica M. S. Kennedy. For a more general overview of the period in question, from an international perspective, see Hobsbawm (1987).
31. For the details, see Ensor (1992: 91–100, 558–63).
32. Crowley (1989: 120). The poem can also be found in Crowley (1973c: vol. II, 1).
33. "And now, my lord, *in medias res*, / Get rid of all your red Rad fleas" (Crowley 1989: 120).
34. Crowley (1899), republished in Crowley (1973c: vol. I, 136–40).
35. See Crowley (1989: 189).
36. On this subject, see Ensor (1992: 256–7). On the end of "splendid isolation" with the Anglo-Russian Convention, see *ibid.*: 402.
37. "We [i.e. Americans and English] stretch out hands to-day when the white wings / Of Peace are spread beneath you and your foe. / O race of men that slay the slaves of kings!" (Crowley 1973c: 136).
38. "Ye have restored to freedom that fair flower, / Cuba, in her most agonising hour, / And east and west have thundered with red war / … / Priestcraft and tyranny in this defeat / Shake, and the walls of hell with fear resound … " (*ibid.*: 137–8).
39. It was republished with the title "To America" in *The English Review* (October 1914: 273–9). See also Crowley (1989: 717, 750). In these two passages from his autobiography, Crowley erroneously claims that the poem appeared in the November issue of the journal, and that the modification for the 1914 version consisted only in substituting "the traitor Prussian" in a certain verse with "the traitor Russian". In fact, in the version for *The English Review*, the passage in question (verse 38) was simply deleted, along with another three stanzas (stanzas 5–7). These were the stanzas in which Crowley had ranted particularly about France and Russia, which obviously would not have been appropriate in 1914.
40. See Pasi (1998d).
41. The role played by university in the crises of religious faith experienced by many young English intellectuals of the epoch has been keenly described by Frank M. Turner in his collection of essays, *Contesting Cultural Authority* (Turner 1993). See especially his observations on p. 86.
42. On the importance of scientific naturalism and agnosticism at Cambridge University in the epoch during which Crowley studied there, see Brooke (1993: 121–31).
43. As I have mentioned earlier, many of Crowley's writings contain positive references to the writings of Thomas Henry Huxley and Herbert Spencer, whose works were also recommended to aspiring A∴A∴ members (see Crowley 1973a: 309; 1994: 453). It should also be noted that the list of recommended texts included a classic of rationalism: *The Age of Reason* by Thomas Paine (see *ibid.*: 379).
44. For the political and ideological implications of discourses about the "races" that have followed each other on British soil over the centuries (Celts, Anglo-Saxons and Normans) according to the various versions of the British "myth of origin", see Poliakov (1994: 37–53). Unfortunately Poliakov does not discuss the Celtic Revival of the late nineteenth century, which might have offered some interesting material for his study.
45. See Praz (1970).
46. See Ensor (1992: 335–7).

47. Crowley (1989: 121). Gregor Grant, Crowley's elder by six years, had been one of his few childhood playmates, although he was a Presbyterian and therefore an exception to the Darbyite rule (*ibid.*: 46-7). The Jacobite pretender in those days was Maria Theresa of Modena, or Austria-Este (1849-1919), the wife of Ludwig III of Bavaria (1845-1921), who according to Jacobite theory should have become Mary III of England and Mary IV of Scotland, had she acceded to the throne (Webb 1971: 203). Hanover was Queen Victoria's dynasty, and she was its last member to occupy the British throne; Coburg, the dynasty of her consort Albert, took over from Hanover and, in order to eliminate this embarrassing reminder of German heritage, switched to the name Windsor during the First World War. In another passage from *The Confessions*, Crowley calls Victoria a "Hanoverian hausfrau" (Crowley 1989: 343). On Crowley's involvement in the legitimist movements of the day, see also Spence (2008: 24-7).
48. On the history of this movement, see Petrie (1959) and Monod (1988). Unfortunately, Petrie's book concludes with the mid-nineteenth century, and unlike Monod it does not examine the later developments. However, James Webb discusses them in *The Flight from Reason* (Webb 1971: 202-17), exploring in detail the relationships between Jacobite circles, the Celtic Revival and occultist groups in England during the last decade of the nineteenth century and the first few years of the twentieth. On the phenomenon of neo-Jacobitism at the end of the nineteenth century, see also the entry "Jacobitism" by Murray G. H. Pittock in Cevasco (1993: 315-16).
49. See Hutin (1990: 167). More recently, the French historian André Kervella (2002) has presented Jacobitism as one of the key factors in the early development of Freemasonry. See also Kervella and Lestienne (1997), and the thematic issue of the journal *Politica Hermetica* 24 (2010): "La Franc-Maçonnerie et les Stuarts au XVIIIe siècle. Stratégies politiques, réseaux, entre mythes et réalités." It is interesting to note that mystical inclinations were also present in some currents of the French legitimist movement of the first half of the nineteenth century. Webb has also drawn attention to this aspect (Webb 1971: 188-202).
50. Webb 1971: 203.
51. See Crowley (1989: 121).
52. *Ibid.*: 123. Crowley appears to allude to this knighthood in order to explain his habit, in subsequent years, of signing his name *Sir* Aleister Crowley. See also Symonds (1989: 129 and n. 4).
53. On Duncombe-Jewell and his relationship with Crowley, see Kaczynski (2010: 116-18). More generally on Duncombe-Jewell's involvement with the Celtic Revival see Lowenna (2004). See also Crowley (1989: 361). Writing many years after the facts, in his autobiography Crowley describes Duncombe-Jewell's enthusiasm for the Celtic Revival as "childish" if "harmless", but in my view this detached opinion does not reflect Crowley's ideas, or at least attitudes, of twenty years earlier.
54. Duncombe-Jewell had an intense relationship of collaboration with Henry Jenner (1848-1934), who is considered today to be one of the most significant figures in the modern revival of Cornish language and culture. Jenner, who was at the turn of the century a prominent member of the legitimist Order of the White Rose and later also converted to Catholicism, worked as an assistant keeper at the Library of the British Museum, where Mathers, Yeats and other Golden Dawn members spent a lot of their time while researching occult subjects (Kaczynski 2010: 117). On Jenner and Duncombe-Jewell, see Lowenna (2004). More generally on Jenner, see P. W. Thomas (2005).
55. There has been some incertitude about the actual extent of Crowley's participation in Carlist activities and especially in the *Firefly* affair. Webb had already considered his involvement plausible (see Webb 1971: 206), but now evidence has surfaced that seems to prove it beyond dispute (Lowenna 2004: 68).
56. See Yeats (1938: 288). It should be noted that one of the French legitimist factions also considered Don Carlos a pretender to the French throne as the last representative of the House of Bourbon; see Rials (1983: 118-20).
57. Ellic Howe describes Mathers as "obsessed by Jacobite fantasies" (Howe 1985: 16; see also *ibid.*: 112, 114; Colquhoun 1975: 77-80, 88-9). Although Mathers's political engagement within the Celtic and neo-Jacobite movements does not appear to have received particular attention, it seems to have been one of the causes of tension within the Golden Dawn during the time leading up to the schism of 1900. See Howe (1985: 116, 126, 176-7) and Lowenna (2004: 69-70).
58. See Colquhoun (1975: 79-81). Allan Bennett, who was particularly close to both Mathers and Crowley, also adopted the name MacGregor. Moreover, Crowley's decision around the age of twenty to change his name from Alexander to Aleister (a Gaelic form of the name) was an indication of his enthusiasm for things Celtic (see Crowley 1989: 140-41).
59. We should remember that the *Firefly* affair took place in June 1899, and that, according to Howe, Crowley probably met Mathers for the first time in May 1899, when he had already been a member of the Golden Dawn for some months (Howe 1985: 194).
60. See Webb (1971: 204-5).
61. Crowley (1989: 121). Anti-Catholicism should not be confused with anti-Christianity. In this period, Crowley's anti-Christian revolt had not yet fully matured, but he had no need of that to share in the anti-Catholic

prejudices so widespread among most English protestant denominations ever since the 16th century, the Plymouth Brethren certainly being no exception. Concerning Crowley's anti-Christianity and his attitude toward Catholicism, which went through several phases over time, see Pasi (1998d).

62. Bouchet (1998: 20, n. 26) identifies it as one of the small independent churches connected with the *episcopi vagantes* (wandering bishops) who were relatively widespread at the time. It should also be noted that the concept of a historical medieval "Celtic Church" had become particularly popular in Great Britain in the nineteenth century, and there were quite a few attempts at reviving it. See Davies (1992) and Bradley (1999: esp. 119–56).

63. The poem was published in 1901, then republished in Crowley (1973c: vol. I, 214–21).

64. The ruin of England is described in verses of a great expressive force: "O England! England, mighty England falls! / None shall lament her lamentable end! / The Voice of Justice thunders at her walls. / She would not hear. She shall not comprehend! / The nations keep their carnivals: / She hath not left a friend!" (*ibid.*: 215).

65. "No stone of London soon shall stand upon another, / No son of her throughout the land shall know his brother. / I will destroy her who is rotten: from the face / Of earth shall fail the misbegotten, root and race; / And the fair country unto them again I give, Whom in long exile men contemn: for they shall live. Yea, they shall live! The Celtic race! Amen! … " (*ibid.*: 214–15). As mentioned earlier, this contrast between the Saxon or Anglo-Saxon and Celtic "races" formed part of the rhetoric of the Britannic myth of origin; see n. 44 above.

66. Besides England, the nations mentioned are, in this order: France, the German Empire, Austria (Hungary not being mentioned), Russia, Italy, the Ottoman Empire, Greece, Spain and the United States.

67. Crowley alludes to the verdict of Rennes (August 1899), which at the time the poem was written had been the latest episode in the lengthy Dreyfus affair. This verdict condemned Captain Alfred Dreyfus for the second time. In September of the same year he was pardoned, although he was not fully exonerated until 1906.

68. On this subject, see Mosse (1964).

69. Kaczynski has also drawn attention to the references to Carlism in the poem. See Kaczynski (2010: 116–17).

70. "Thou, heart of coin beneath a brazen breast, / Rotten republic, prostitute of gain!" (Crowley 1973c: vol. I, 217).

71. "Thou, murderer of the bravest and the best / That fringed thy southern main!" (*ibid.*).

72. *Ibid.*: 219.

73. "Africa's desperate sons" are the Boers. The reference is explicit in the next and final part of the poem, in which Crowley cites Paul Kruger in a footnote. Kruger was president of Transvaal, one of the two Boer states struggling to avoid falling under British rule. The two states were annexed by the British Empire after their defeat, and a few years later were made part of the South African Union. In this part of the poem Crowley returns to speaking about the war, his words about England becoming harsher: "In Africa women are fighting / Their homes and their freedom to hold / Young children and graybeards, delighting / To die for their country of old! / For the ravenous lion [i.e. England] is smiting / A stroke for their gold" (*ibid.*: 220). The gold is of course that of the rich mines of Transvaal, discovered in the mid-1880s, which were the main indirect cause of the conflict.

74. An Irish Brigade was also formed, which fought the English alongside the Boers. The brigade was commanded by Major John MacBride, who in 1903 married the fiery Irishwoman Maud Gonne (1866–1953), who among other things was W. B. Yeats's muse for many years. Gonne was also a member of the Golden Dawn. See Greer (1995: 229, 276–7). MacBride was one of the organizers of Ireland's Easter Rising of April 1916, for which the English executed him.

75. No wonder that Mathers, who also considered the English his "enemies", was opposed to the war against the Boers. In a letter from 26 April 1900 to a member of the Golden Dawn (Marcus W. Blackden), he makes reference to the "blood of the Highland Regiments … reddening South African earth" that was spilled "in the wrong cause" (see Harper 1974: 217).

76. The date 4 July 1900 appears at the end of the poem, seeming to refer only to this final part rather than to the entire work. Also worth noting is another poem by Crowley dedicated to the anniversary of American independence: *An Hymn for the American People (Independence Day)*. The poem was published in 1910 in the collection *The Winged Beetle* (Crowley 1992d: 151–2). The poem offers no indication of its date of composition; the collection includes other poems that had already been published a few years earlier. With no further reference points, it is impossible to determine whether it was written before or after *Carmen Saeculare*. In any case, it contains no references to the Irish question, and here the tone is that of an American patriot, honouring the memory of the martyrs who fell for the cause of independence and the stars and stripes, an eternal symbol of freedom.

77. "Your stripes are the stripes of dishonour; / Your stars are cast down from the sky; / While earth has this burden upon her, Your eagle unwilling to fly! / Loose, loose the wide wings! For your honour! / Let tyranny die!" (Crowley 1973c: vol. I, 221).

78. The poem originally appeared in the collection *Oracles*, published in 1905. This collection was later reissued *ibid.* (vol. II, 48–9). St Patrick, of course, is the patron saint of Ireland, and his day is 17 March.

79. *Ibid.*

80. "Look not to Europe in your need! / Columbia's [i.e. the USA] but a broken reed! / Your own good hearts, your own strong hand / Win back at last the Irish land" (*ibid*.: 48).
81. "What pity knew the Saxon e'er? / Arise, O God, and slay nor spare, / until full vengeance rightly wrought / Bring all their house of wrong to nought" (*ibid*.: 49).
82. See Crowley (1989: 35).
83. This is also the opinion of R. A. Gilbert (1983: 40). On this subject, see also Sutin (2000: 70-72).
84. See the passage quoted in Howe (1985: 205-7).
85. See Hymenaeus Beta's preface to Crowley and Mathers (1995: xix; see also Stephensen and Regardie 1983: 88-93). In his autobiography Crowley dedicates a few pages to this lawsuit; see Crowley (1989: 638-43). We can also find here a reference to Berridge's questioning of Crowley, with a version that is not too dissimilar from the one given by Berridge during his testimony. Of course, as Hymenaeus Beta notes, the question of Crowley's homosexual tendencies is no longer a mystery or a reason for moral concern, even if Crowley preferred to remain more or less reserved on the subject, depending on circumstances.
86. See Howe (1985: 223).
87. The quote is from a letter dated 25 April 1900, partially reproduced in Symonds (1989: 36). Yeats referred to Crowley again, in the same terms, in letters to Lady Gregory from 28 April and 6 June, and in a letter to George Russell ("Æ") from May 1900. The complete text of the letters can be found in Yeats (1954: 339-46). See also Harper (1974: 27-35).
88. See Howe (1985: 132). Mathers, at the time, was probably afraid that other members of the Order (particularly Annie Horniman) might criticize him for his own political activities, to which I referred above. On this point, see *ibid*.: 126).
89. *Ibid*.
90. Another classic example of this type of conflict, also resulting in a schism, occurred in Anton LaVey's Church of Satan, from which Michael Aquino's Temple of Set split off in 1975. In this case, LaVey's ethic of success in external society as a condition for advancement in the organization went against Aquino's "esoteric" vision (see Pasi 1998b: 90).
91. See Crowley (1989: 176).
92. See O'Donoghue (1912; Crowley appears in appendix A, p. 497, while Yeats is on p. 492). O'Donoghue, for many years, was librarian of University College in Dublin, and was in contact with Yeats at least until the late 1880s (see Yeats's letter to O'Donoghue from May 1888 in Yeats 1954: 73-4). Yeats refers to O'Donoghue's dictionary in one of his autobiographical writings (Yeats 1938: 179).
93. See Donald Read's *Edwardian England 1901–15* (1972) and Alan O'Day's *The Edwardian Age* (1979).
94. About the definition of scientific naturalism, see above, n. 3. For the definition of evangelicalism, see Ensor (1992: 137-40).
95. See *ibid*.: 137.
96. Regarding the crisis of the late Victorian era, see the works of F. M. Turner: *Between Science and Religion* (1974) and *Contesting Cultural Authority* (1993).
97. See Crowley (1989: 216).
98. *Ibid*.
99. See *The Pro-Boers*, edited by Stephen Koss (1973).
100. See Lindqvist (1998: 90).
101. See Webb (1976). Martin Green (1992) paints an interesting picture of this cultural turmoil in Edwardian London, but situates it within a general definition of "New Age" thought, which he also applies to other epochs and connects to our contemporary New Age movement. Although Green's definition is based on a generalization that can be overly vague, his description of the English cultural atmosphere prior to the First World War, with its spiritual unrest, offers interesting details and useful observations.
102. Concerning Crowley's differences with Chesterton and Shaw, see Pasi (1998d: 54-62).
103. On Orage and his journal, see Mairet (1936), Selver (1959), Martin (1967), Gibbons (1973), Steele (1989) and G. Taylor (2000). Interesting remarks on the influence of *The New Age* on contemporary British culture can also be found in Bochinger (1994: 293-9) and Green (1992: 82-3).
104. See Thatcher (1970: 219-68).
105. It is interesting to note that some of the authors mentioned above – Chesterton, Shaw, Orage, and Yeats – played an important role in the initial diffusion of Nietzsche's thought in Britain and in the debate over his personality and ideas in those years (Thatcher 1970, *passim*).
106. Regarding Orage and Gurdjieff, besides Mairet (1936), see Webb (1980: esp. part 2) and P. B. Taylor (2001).
107. We do not know exactly when Crowley and Orage met. According to Beatrice Hastings, who was one of the most important contributors to *The New Age* between 1908 and 1914, Orage was particularly drawn to the world of occultism and had a close relationship with Crowley when she and Orage began working for the

journal (see Hastings 1936: 19). Hastings, writing after her estrangement from Orage and with bitter feelings about it, claims that she had a negative opinion of Orage's occult inclinations and convinced him in taking distance from it. Paul Selver, another contributor to *The New Age* who became involved with the journal a few years later, disputes this, pointing out that John Symonds does not even once mention Orage in his biography of Crowley (see Selver 1959: 95). We could add to that that Crowley himself does not seem to ever mention Orage: neither in his autobiography nor in his other published works. And yet, Selver's objection appears to be unconvincing, because Hastings's testimony is confirmed indirectly by C. S. Nott, who was a disciple of both Gurdjieff and Orage during the 1920s. Orage apparently told Nott he had known Crowley well, often meeting with him while working for the Society for Psychical Research (see Nott 1961: 122; see also Webb 1980: 210-11). Orage had been acting secretary of the SPR around 1905, and the reference is plausible, since it is certain that Crowley associated with psychical research during that period, having made friends with Everard Feilding (1867-1936), one of the most active and important members of the SPR (see Crowley 1989: 639, 681, 744, 755, 791). Moreover, in an article published during the war in *The International*, Crowley mentions having been involved in the production of *The New Age* ("A Noisy Noise Annoys an Oyster", Crowley 1916: 361). In Orage's journal there also appeared some reviews, generally positive, of works by or about Crowley. In an issue from Autumn 1907, Florence Farr, an old colleague of Crowley's from the Golden Dawn who had apparently gotten over the unpleasantness of the schism and internal struggle that had placed them in opposed factions, gave a positive review of J. F. C. Fuller's book *The Star in the West*. Soon after, in February 1908, a review of Crowley's *Konx Om Pax* appeared, signed by the Freudian psychologist David Eder. Crowley read and obviously appreciated both reviews: the text of the first one was reproduced completely in Crowley, *Konx Om Pax*, pp. 10-12 (second pagination, at the end of the volume); the second one was reproduced partially in *The Equinox* I(1) (in the unnumbered pages at the end of the volume). On the first review, see also Crowley (1989: 544). Finally, a few documents confirm the relationship between Crowley and Orage. The first one is a recommendation letter that Orage wrote for Crowley when the latter applied for admission to the Reading Room of the British Museum in March 1908. Very probably, at that moment Crowley intended to study John Dee's papers and the related Enochian material preserved there. Orage's letter is dated 20 March 1908 and is written on *The New Age* letterhead. The application file has been found in the archives of the British Museum by curator Liana Saif, whom I thank for making them available to me. Finally, at least one letter from Orage to Crowley, dated 7 July 1932, is preserved in the Yorke Collection (YC/OS, E21). It can be inferred from the content that Crowley had asked Orage to meet with him in order to discuss some unspecified matters. Orage responded promising to call him to set up an appointment. The letter shows some degree of familiarity between the two.
108. See Thompson (1977) and Bulla (1980). To these names we should add that of Ananda K. Coomaraswamy (1877-1947), who was also a frequent contributor to *The New Age* in that period (before he moved to the US and discovered René Guénon's traditionalist thought). I will return to his relationship with Crowley in Chapter 5.
109. See Thompson (1977: 805).
110. See Webb (1976: 80-86).
111. See for example Crowley (1989: 119-20, 313, 481).
112. Crowley (1991b: xxxvi). On the significance of this book in relation to Crowley's creative work, see Pasi (1998d).
113. On this aspect of Crowley's intellectual development, see Pasi (1998d: 52-4).
114. Some examples: in autumn 1908, during a "magical retreat" in Paris, he noted in his diary "I am an Irishman" (Crowley 1909: 75); in November 1912, in a pamphlet protesting the censoring of sculptor Jacob Epstein's tomb for Oscar Wilde in Père Lachaise Cemetery in Paris, Crowley described himself as a "poète Irlandais" (Crowley 1989: 645); when he travelled to New York in October 1914, after the outbreak of the First World War, he registered himself on the passengers' list as an Irishman (Spence 2008: 51).
115. Crowley (1914a).
116. The song was composed by an anonymous author during the Russo-Turkish War (1877-8), when England sent a naval expedition to the Dardanelles to fight Russia. "By Jingo" at the time was a simple interjection of uncertain origin; but thereafter, the word came to be used to indicate the English variety of nationalist chauvinism, giving rise to the derivatives *Jingoism* and *Jingoist*.
117. Crowley indicates the authors he is imitating only with their initials. Besides those noted above, we can identify, in order, Robert Browning, Percy Bysshe Shelley, William Blake, Owen Seaman (a humourist contemporary with Crowley), Thomas Gray, and Dante Gabriel Rossetti. According to Kaczynski (2003: 220), the initials "F.T." correspond to Francis Thompson. The name of another author, "D. Ch.", remains unidentified.
118. See n. 39 above.
119. See Crowley (1989: 742-5).
120. R. Hutchinson in his biography states that the English police had a file on Crowley going back as far as the time of the schism in the Golden Dawn (1900). See Hutchinson (1998: 76-7).
121. Symonds (1989: 206-9) claims that Crowley was simply a traitor. He supports this judgement with the

testimony of Admiral Guy Gaunt, the leader of the division of British Naval Intelligence in the United States during the war, with whom Crowley claimed to have been in contact while carrying on his pro-German activities. According to Symonds, Gaunt stated that Crowley was motivated solely by his desire for publicity. Gerald Suster (1988: 60–61), on the other hand, appears to give more credit to Crowley's version of the story, although remaining cautious. He points out, quite correctly, that Gaunt's claims should be considered carefully, since it is not unusual for the actions of secret service "collaborators" to be denied by those they worked for – especially when the collaborator's reputation itself is not spotless, as is certainly the case with Crowley. This view is shared by the specialist in the history of espionage, Richard B. Spence (Spence 2000, 2008). Spence throws new light on the events, thanks to documents found in the archives of the US Army's secret service (the Military Intelligence Division, or MID) and a careful analysis of the background of many of Crowley's relations during his period in America. I will return to Spence's contribution to the debate later in this chapter. Other authors, such as Bouchet (1988: 20; 2011: 93–5) suggest on the other hand that Crowley's sympathy with the cause of Irish independence was the real factor that prompted him to collaborate with the pro-German press. Crowley's subsequent defence of his actions would therefore have been motivated only by practical reasons.

122. On Viereck, see Elmer Gertz, *Odyssey of a Barbarian* (1978), and Niel M. Johnson, *George Sylvester Viereck* (1972). Although Johnson's biography was published first, Gertz's was written earlier (a first version dates to the 1930s), but remained unpublished for many years. Both authors give a large amount of space to Viereck's activities during the First World War, but only devote a few lines to Crowley. Gertz (1978: 139) states that Crowley collaborated with Viereck's magazine exclusively to earn money; but according to Johnson (1972: 25), Crowley was a sincere opponent of British imperialism. On Viereck and his relationship with Crowley see also Spence (2008, *passim*).

123. See Symonds (1989: 207).

124. Cited *ibid.*: 206. At least three letters from Viereck to Symonds are preserved at the Warburg Institute (YC/NS, 96). One is dated 22 October 1948, another 8 November 1948. The third is the letter cited by Symonds, but only the last page of it remains, the first page(s) having been lost. Here Viereck states, among other things, that he never personally admired Crowley, and simply used his talents for purposes of propaganda. Viereck later published *Spreading Germs of Hate* (1930), in which he recounted – in a critical manner and, according to him, as objectively as possible – his experiences as a propagandist during the war. Viereck devoted only a few lines to Crowley, and essentially refuted Crowley's version of the story, referring to the testimony of Sir William Wiseman, who was head of Intelligence Services at the British embassy in Washington. We know that Crowley read this book. The copy he owned is at the Warburg Institute (YC, DII 50 [71/3384]). Predictably, he did not appreciate Viereck's statements, and wrote a venomous "response", still preserved in his copy of the book. It consists of two undated typewritten pages, probably not the original version but a copy made by Gerald Yorke. In these, Crowley does not discuss the merits of Viereck's reconstruction, but rather – consistent with his usual style – attacks him personally, calling him narcissistic, immature and a failure. This shows that even in the 1930s, when he presumably read the book, Crowley was still extremely sensitive to the question of his propagandist activity during the war. It is not known whether Viereck ever knew of this response from his former collaborator. But we do know that Crowley and Viereck were in contact during the 1930s. In fact, they met again in London in 1936, and apparently discussed the German political situation. During this period, Viereck was inclined toward Nazism, which led to his trial and imprisonment in 1941 when the United States entered the Second World War. He was released in 1947, and published a few things thereafter, but did not succeed in re-establishing his renown as an author. He died in 1962. Later in this chapter I will discuss Crowley's relationship to Nazism.

125. Crowley's version of the story of his pro-German activity in the United States appears in "The Last Straw", a pamphlet that he included in his autobiography (Crowley 1989: 740–61). As noted earlier, the version in Symonds and Grant's edition is significantly abridged.

126. See Spence (2000, 2008).

127. See Spence (2000: 364).

128. Gaunt's version of the story is cited by Symonds; see above, n. 121.

129. See Sutin (2000: 249–50).

130. See *ibid.*: 248. The articles cited by Sutin are "The New Parsifal" (August 1915) and "The Crime of Edith Cavell" (January 1916). The first article, cited by practically all authors favourable to Crowley as evidence for his defence of himself, is reproduced in its entirety by P. R. Stephensen (see Stephensen and Regardie 1983: 113–16). As for the second article, the grotesque description of it that Crowley provides in his *Confessions* (1989: 752) does not actually match either the tone or the content of the article itself. About this article, see also the remarks of Spence (2008: 116).

131. Crowley 1989: 758.

132. See Regardie (1993: 484–5) and Bouchet (1988: 20–22; 2011: 104–5).

133. Regardie (1993: 485).
134. "The miracle in his life would have been for this Book to have agreed with all that he had been fighting against. But this miracle did not occur. With considerable fervour, the Book echoes Crowley's underlying moral, social, and religious attitudes without equivocation or doubt. Dictated or created, it is his Book" (Regardie 1993: 494). Bouchet (2011: 103) also makes a similar remark.
135. On these three elements, see the following passages from *The Book of the Law* respectively: "With my Hawk's head I peck at the eyes of Jesus as he hangs upon the cross" (Crowley 1938: III, 51); "Also take your fill and will of love as ye will, when, where and with whom ye will" (*ibid.*: I, 51); "Ye are against the people, O my chosen!" (*ibid.*: II, 25).
136. On the history of the various commentaries Crowley wrote on *The Book of the Law*, see Crowley (1994: lxxff.) The principal commentaries can be found in Crowley, *The Law is for All*. The new edition of this book (edited by Wilkinson and Hymenaeus Beta; Crowley 2002) presents a revised version of one of the commentaries, but edits out some of the most controversial passages. In the following, when I cite *The Law is for All* I always use the 3rd edition, edited by Regardie (Crowley 1993b), unless otherwise indicated.
137. See Regardie's introduction to Crowley (1993b: 31). The text of the letter is cited in Symonds (1989: 93).
138. See Crowley (1993b: 98–101, 107–38, 313–16).
139. See *ibid.*: 89, 175–7.
140. See *ibid.*: 176. The reference is to the following passage from *The Book of the Law*: "We have nothing with the outcast and the unfit: let them die in their misery. For they feel not. Compassion is the vice of kings: stamp down the wretched & the weak: this the law of the strong: this is our law and the joy of the world" (Crowley 1938: II, 21). On Nietzsche's influence on Crowley, see Pasi (1998d: 62–4).
141. See Crowley (1993b: 250). In general, Crowley always cites Spencer, as well as Thomas Henry Huxley, with great respect and admiration. For example, in the novel *The Diary of a Drug Fiend* (Crowley 1992a: 113) one of the characters calls Spencer "the genius whose philosophy summarised the thought of the nineteenth century". It is interesting to note that in the *Confessions*, Crowley also refers to Ernst Haeckel (1834–1919) many times. Haeckel was a German biologist and another significant contributor to the diffusion of social Darwinist ideas (Crowley 1989: 401, 494, 746). See also the strange Darwinist creed that appears in that portion of Crowley's diary titled "John St. John" (1909: 129). There is now a great deal of critical literature on social Darwinism. The most recent and up-to-date study is by Hawkins (1997). See especially the sections on Spencer (*ibid.*: 82–103) and Haeckel (*ibid.*: 132–45). It should be noted that there was a strong anti-clerical component in the ideas of both Spencer and Haeckel, which certainly must have appealed to Crowley.
142. See Crowley (1993b: 274).
143. *Ibid.*
144. *Ibid.*: 316.
145. *Ibid.*: 317.
146. Crowley (1938: I, 3).
147. Crowley (1993b: 73).
148. This was produced by Crowley as a single flying sheet in 1941. See Crowley (1997: 689). Crowley calls the document "Rights of Man" in a letter to Gerald Yorke dated 13 September 1941, quoted by William Breeze in his note about the text (Crowley 1997: 788). It is interesting to note that, a few months before his death, Crowley read and liked Ayn Rand's novel *The Fountainhead* ("A Gentleman of Hastings" 2012: 173 and n. 28; I would like to thank Gary Lachman for calling my attention to this passage). Undoubtedly he saw some elements in common between the radical individualism of Thelema and Rand's "Objectivism".
149. See for instance the cautious comments made by the National Grand Master General of the US Grand Lodge of the OTO, Sabazius X° (pseud. of David Scriven 2001).
150. Crowley (1993b: 251).
151. Crowley's commentary to *The Book of the Law* (*ibid.*) quotes a chapter from the *Liber Aleph* ("De ordine rerum") that is quite significant in this respect: "In the Body every Cell is subordinated to the general physiological Control, and we who will that Control do not ask whether each individual Unit of that Structure be consciously happy. But we do care that each shall fulfil its Function, and the Failure of even a few Cells, or their Revolt, may involve the Death of the whole Organism. ... Many Cells fulfil their Destiny by swift Death, and this being their Function, they in no wise resent it. ... Now, O my Son, do then consider deeply of these Things in thine Ordering of the World under the Law of Thelema. For every Individual in the State must be perfect in his own Function, with Contentment, respecting his own Task as necessary and holy, not envious of another's. For so only mayst thou build up a Free State, whose directing Will shall be singly directed to the Welfare of all" (Crowley 1991c: 38).
152. Crowley (1993b: 321).
153. *Ibid.*: 192.
154. *Ibid.*: 192–3.

155. *Ibid.*: 191.
156. *Ibid.*: 89.
157. Crowley (1973b: 293).
158. *Ibid.*: 303. Directly after this, Crowley adds: "Nietzsche may be regarded as one of our prophets; to a much less extent, de Gobineau".
159. See Bouchet (1992: 30). This article forms part of a "Dossier 'Aleister Crowley'", also including an article by Arnaud Guyot-Jeannin and an interview with one of Crowley's French translators, Philippe Pissier. In his article Bouchet offers a "political" interpretation of Crowley's ideas, which is visibly influenced by the former's own involvement in radical politics. Another interpretation clearly coming from the extreme right and connecting Crowley to the idea of the Conservative Revolution has been proposed by Kerry R. Bolton (Frater Scorpio 1996). Based in New Zealand, Bolton is a very active figure in milieus that mix radical right views with occultism, Nordic neo-paganism and Satanism. He is known for having founded the Order of the Left Hand Path around 1990, but has created also a number of other groups, such as the more evidently Crowley-inspired "The Thelemic Society", created in 1996 but which does not seem to have been very active and probably does not exist anymore. More recently, Bolton has published another essay on Crowley and politics, which basically follows up on his earlier interpretation along similar lines, further insisting on the analogies he perceives between Crowley's ideas and perennialist authors such as Julius Evola and René Guénon (Bolton 2010). On Bolton, also in relation to his interest in Crowley, see Goodrick-Clarke (2002: 226–31).
160. For an application to the Italian context, see, for example, Veneziani (1994). There are also some interesting reflections on this question in Nolte (1997), especially regarding the possibility of using a broader definition of "Conservative Revolution" that would include some nineteenth-century European political currents (*ibid.*: 27–31). Concerning the "historical" Conservative Revolution, the classic work is Mohler (1993). See also Breuer (1996).
161. The entry is from 14 June 1917. Crowley's diary for this period, titled "The Urn" or "Liber LXXIII", has not been published in book form but is available online as a PDF document: www.rahoorkhuit.net/library/libers/pdf/lib_0073.pdf (see p. 64).
162. Crowley (1973b: 438).
163. YC/NS, 117. In fact, definitions of this kind were probably not unusual in this period in circles close to those Crowley frequented. In connection with this, it is interesting to note that A. R. Orage's biographer, Philip Mairet, describes Orage's endeavour to unify socialism and Nietzscheanism as "aristocratic socialism" (Mairet 1936: 30–31). This shows that Crowley's idea of presenting his religious system as a new political solution, unifying two apparently irreconcilable elements, owes something to the cultural debates of the Edwardian age to which I made reference earlier.
164. Crowley (1929b: 299).
165. *Ibid.*: 301. The two passages quoted here, appearing in chapter 21 (the third-to-last chapter), may also have been written long after 1916. The novel was not actually published until 1929, and in his *Confessions* (1989: 817), Crowley writes that the first draft from 1916 did not include "the last two or three chapters".
166. Crowley (1989: 911).
167. *Ibid.*: 911–12. On the development of Mussolini's approach to the Catholic Church during those crucial years, see De Felice (1966: esp. 488–98).
168. Nancy Cunard *et al.* (1937). The text of the question posed to the authors read as follows: "This is the question we are asking you: 'Are you for, or against, the legal Government and the People's of Republican Spain? Are you for, or against, Franco and Fascism?' For it is impossible any longer to take no side." (This text appeared on the first page of the compilation, for which the pages are not numbered.)
169. Her name appears among the signatories of the text sent to the authors. Concerning the relationship between Crowley and Cunard, see Symonds (1989: 569). See also Sutin (2000: 365–6), from which we learn that Crowley had already been involved in earlier projects of a similar type with Cunard.
170. As mentioned earlier, the booklet has no page numbers. Within each of its three sections, the responses are arranged alphabetically. Oddly enough, Crowley's name is spelled incorrectly as "Alastair". Interestingly, among the authors contacted was also Arthur Machen, who like Crowley was a former member of the Golden Dawn. Machen, however, appears among Franco's supporters: "Mr. Arthur Machen presents his compliments and begs to inform that he is, and always has been, entirely for General Franco". About Machen's political stance, and its meaning in the context of his literary work, see Pasi (2007: 80–81).
171. Pauwels and Bergier (1960). A recent English edition is Pauwels and Bergier (2001). On "Nazi-occultist" literature, see Hakl (1997). An English translation of Hakl's study is available (Hakl 2000). On the same subject, see also Goodrick-Clark (1985: 217–25).
172. According to Bouchet "Crowley never showed any interest in National Socialism" (Bouchet 1998: 101).
173. Crowley alludes to this letter in his diary from 18 October 1930 (see Symonds 1989: 511). I have not been able

to find the text of this letter; it appears not to be preserved either in the Yorke Collection (YC) or in the Fuller Papers (FP). It is also unknown whether Fuller replied to it, or even received it. The relationship between Fuller and Crowley will be more closely examined in the first section of Chapter 3.
174. On Hopfer, see Kaczynski (2010: 420).
175. YC/NS, 117. Typed copy.
176. See Viereck's letter to Crowley dated 7 July (YC/OS, 21), in which he writes that he will arrive in London at the end of the month and will be available for a meeting. The letter appears to be a response to an earlier card from Crowley.
177. This is made evident by an annotation in Crowley's diary dated 30 July. See Symonds (1989: 503), Sutin (2000: 377–8) and Spence (2008: 244).
178. The letter, from 31 July 1936, is preserved in the OTO Archives. The text is reproduced in Sutin (2000: 378).
179. Crowley also refers to the German anti-Semitic newspaper *Der Judenkenner*, which had published a series of attacks against him in that same year, as well as against Theodor Reuss, as we saw in Chapter 1. I will return to these matters in Chapter 5, situating them within the framework of the great interest the conspiracy press took in Crowley. In an undated letter to Karl Germer, probably from March 1938, Crowley laments the increasingly difficult situation of the members of his organizations in Germany, allowing his sarcasm free rein: "Anything to do with A∴A∴, OTO or those vile communist Jew murderers, the Pansophia mob of cannibal Bolshevists is banned in Germany. Like butter! Official" (typed copy, OA). As noted in Chapter 1, Germer had already experienced this directly, having been arrested in 1935 specifically because of his relationship to these organizations.
180. Crowley probably began to write the letters that would form *Magick without Tears* around 1943, and continued until at least 1945. The work was published posthumously in 1954.
181. See Crowley (1973b: 303–5, 438).
182. See *ibid.*: 303. This anecdote also appears in a letter from Crowley to Germer from 5 December 1939: "You know, Martha [Küntzel] is quite sound on this: she says her 'magical child' has rebuilt the Reich on 93 lines" (typed copy, OA).
183. Crowley (1973b: 304).
184. The French version (*Hitler m'a dit*) was first to be published, in 1939, followed by the English edition later that same year: *Hitler Speaks: A Series of Political Conversations with Adolf Hitler on His Real Aims* (Rauschning 1939). The German version, *Gespräche mit Hitler*, was published in 1940.
185. See Hänel (1984). See also the interesting essay on this subject by Alain de Benoist (Benoist 1985). Before Hänel's critical assessment, the validity of Rauschning's book as a source about Hitler's ideas had been discussed by Theodor Schieder (Schieder 1972). According to Schieder, Rauschning's book was not be used as a primary source on Hitler (i.e. the speeches attributed to him in the book were not to be quoted verbatim by the historian), but it was still an important testimony, and – with some reservations – remained largely dependable. Rauschning's book has been used as a source by such renowned historians as William L. Shirer, Hugh Trevor-Roper, Alan Bullock, George L. Mosse and Joachim C. Fest, among others. Even Nicholas Goodrick-Clarke, in his highly respected study of Nazi Ariosophy, written after the publication of Hänel's work, makes a few references to Rauschning's book (see Goodrick-Clarke 1985: 197, and 261, n. 11).
186. On Rauschning as an essential source for Nazi-occultist mythology, see Turris (1989: 14–15). The question was tackled more recently and thoroughly in Hakl (1997: part 3, 29–30).
187. In fact, a year before publishing *Hitler Speaks*, Rauschning had brought out another book: *Die Revolution des Nihilismus* (1938), in which one can find many of the elements that were later integrated into *Hitler Speaks*. The style of the two books is certainly very different, because *The Revolution of Nihilism* is a cold political analysis of the Nazi phenomenon while *Hitler Speaks* is presented as a report of conversations with Hitler. But the content of the second book often seems to draw upon that of the first. One of the major differences is precisely the insistence of the second book upon the "esoteric" and "secret" element. There is no reason to believe that Crowley read *The Revolution of Nihilism*, as Bouchet (1998: 25) seems to imply.
188. Rauschning (1939, second printing). The Warburg Institute shelf-mark for this book is YC, DHD 350. It is not Crowley's original copy, but one into which G. Yorke copied Crowley's notes by hand. Crowley's original copy, which I have not seen, is in OA.
189. Rauschning (1939: 96).
190. Crowley (1938: I, 61).
191. Rauschning (1939: 96; YC, DHD 350.
192. Symonds (1989: 411). Sutin (2000: 375–7) essentially agrees with him.
193. Letter from Martha Küntzel to Crowley, 19 November 1935, typed copy (YC/OS, EE2).
194. *Ibid.*
195. *Ibid.*
196. *Ibid.*

197. The letter was transcribed by Yorke in his copy of Rauschning's book, cited above. The text is cited by Francis King (1987: 162). See also Sutin (2000: 375–6). It should be remembered that Küntzel died in 1941.
198. *Ibid.*: 380. Sutin insightfully observes that this promotional activity, directed at all kinds of regimes and political forces, "casts retrospective light on his World War One activities as well: Crowley was perfectly capable of playing two political hands at once" (*ibid.*).
199. YC/NS, 94 (18), p. 3. The untitled typewritten text bears an annotation by Crowley in which he says that it was written in October 1936 and sent to a functionary of the British government on 27 January 1937. The passage is also cited in Sutin (2000: 380). According to Sutin, the functionary in question was Alfred Duff Cooper, then secretary of the British Ministry of War.
200. There are in this respect at least three significant letters from Germer to Crowley written on 10 February, 13 March and 16 March 1938 (nos. 405, 406 and 407 in the typewritten copy of the Crowley–Germer correspondence, OA).
201. Letter from Crowley to Germer, 5 October 1938 (typewritten copy, OA).
202. Letter from Crowley to Germer, 14 March 1938 (typewritten copy, OA).
203. Letter from Crowley to Germer, 27 October 1938 (typewritten copy, OA).
204. *Ibid.*
205. Letter from Crowley to Germer, 15 October 1938 (typewritten copy, OA).
206. "Therefore the kings of the earth shall be Kings for ever: the slaves shall serve". Crowley later explained his point of view in another letter to Germer, cited earlier (see n. 182), from 5 December 1939. Here he declares that if Hitler has truly modelled the Third Reich on the principles of Thelema, as Küntzel wished or thought he had, then "he has not understood the rights of the individual, and so made a tyranny in a servile state, which is the opposite of the free alliance of kings – which a *true* democracy would be" (typed copy, OA).
207. Crowley (1938: I, 3). This is one of the three fundamental principles of Thelema (see Pasi 2005a).
208. Letter from Crowley to M. Küntzel, 10 May 1939 (YC/OS, EE2).
209. See Symonds (1989: 512). According to Symonds, the letter was written just after the beginning of the war. I have not been able to find a copy of this letter.
210. Crowley (1938: 31).
211. *Ibid.*
212. Such verses appeared in *Thumbs Up!*, a booklet printed privately in London in 1941. It contained the poem *England, Stand Fast!*, dedicated "To Winston Spencer Churchill, for my people". The booklet also contained a kind of warning to "Adolf Schicklgruber" (i.e. Hitler) in the form of a list of persons, mostly deceased, who had allegedly paid dearly for their hostile behaviour toward Crowley. The work almost comes across as a public "malediction" or curse of Hitler, placing it within the larger context of the "occult" war against Nazism, in which another key player was Crowley's famous occultist colleague, Dion Fortune (see Fortune 1993).
213. The folder EE2 of the YC/OS contains various documents of this kind, including a letter dated September 1939, probably the first in which Crowley offers to collaborate with the Naval Intelligence Department. The dossier contains various responses from the Department to Crowley's offers, mostly negative. Among these documents there is also a draft of a strange manifesto promoting army enlistment inspired by the principles of Thelema: "Do what thou wilt shall be the whole of the Law. What is your true will? Probably you do not know it yourself. But – It is sure that every one has the root-will to make the best of himself … Also he has the will to do this in peace and safety, without fear of disturbance from others. … To do your own true will – join the Army!"
214. See below, pp. 93–4.
215. Crowley (1973b: 304). The fact that Crowley refers to Hitler in the past tense would seem to suggest that the passage was written after the war's end.
216. I discussed the Crowleyan concept of magic more thoroughly in Pasi (2004: ch. 7, "Aleister Crowley"). See also Pasi (2005a, 2011).
217. Note here that Crowley used a particular spelling for the word "Magick". This was the spelling commonly used in England until the seventeenth century, but for Crowley, its reintroduction was not simply a matter of style. As Timothy d'Arch Smith explains (1987: 14, n. 5), "Crowley's spelling is not only an archaism 'to distinguish the Science of the Magi from all its counterfeits': the six-letter word balanced against the orthodox five is the balance of the hexagram and the pentagram. 6+5=11, 'the general number of magick, or energy tending to change'. 'K' is the eleventh letter in the alphabet. It is the initial letter of *kteis*, which, with *phallos*, is the most important weapon in Crowley's magical armoury." *Kteis*, in Greek, means vagina. This spelling reintroduced by Crowley has been extensively adopted by various post-Crowleyan occultist and neo-pagan movements – especially, as we have seen, in English-speaking countries.
218. Eckartshausen (1896).
219. Regardie (1993: 399). Shortly afterwards, Regardie writes: "All through the Golden Dawn years, this had been

the guiding star of his aspiration. As he became more sophisticated, the vision dimmed a little; *eventually it was discarded, as we have already seen, as fanciful and unreal*" (ibid.; emphasis added).
220. On the idea of the Masters in Blavatsky's Theosophical Society – which had an enormous influence over successive esoteric movements, and was in turn derived from a particular tradition of esotericism – see the study by K. Paul Johnson, *The Masters Revealed* (1994). The connections and interrelations between the Theosophical Society and the Golden Dawn has been the object of some attention by scholars. There is no doubt that the link was important, especially considering that various eminent members of the Golden Dawn, including W. W. Westcott, S. L. Mathers and W. B. Yeats, knew Blavatsky personally and took part in the activities of the first Theosophical Society group in England. See in particular Gilbert (1987a) and Godwin (1996: 369–78).
221. According to Crowley, Aiwass, the entity who dictated *The Book of the Law* to him, was one of the "Secret Chiefs". In Crowley's view, contact with Aiwass implicitly bestowed authority upon him.
222. Symonds (1989: 161).
223. Crowley (1973b: 124). Curiously, on the same page, Crowley writes about his opposition to keeping the mysteries secret: "I am, and always have been, the leader of the Extreme Left in the Council-Chamber of the City of the Pyramids." The City of the Pyramids is the place (astral or physical, or perhaps both) in which the Secret Chiefs reside. Crowley, who as we have seen was initially preoccupied with establishing direct contact with the Secret Chiefs, later became convinced that he was one of them. A fairly concise description of a session of this Council can be found in *The Confessions* (Crowley 1989: 838ff.).
224. Symonds claims that the publication dates given for both the first and second parts of *Book Four* are incorrect. According to him, the first part was published in 1911 and the second in 1912 (see Symonds 1989: 152). In fact, Crowley wrote the first three of the projected four parts in 1912. The first part (devoted, as we have seen, to yoga and mysticism) was published in 1912; the second (on ceremonial magic) was published in 1913; and the third was not published, but later formed the core of *Magick in Theory and Practice*, which was published in 1930. On this, see d'Arch Smith (1987: 21) and Crowley (1989: 680–81).
225. *Ibid.*: 681).
226. Crowley (1973a: 130; emphasis added).
227. For this definition of occultism, see Pasi (2005e).
228. For an extensive and articulate discussion focusing on English nineteenth-century esotericism, see Godwin (1994). For an understanding of the manner in which contemporary esotericism interacts with scientific culture – on the one hand to legitimize its message, on the other hand to critique its perceived materialistic excesses – essential readings are Hanegraaff (1996), Hammer (2001) and Asprem (2013). For an interesting discussion of the relationship between esotericism and science, see Laurant (1993: part 2).
229. Crowley (1973a: 128). It is worth mentioning that Frazer was teaching at Trinity College, Cambridge while Crowley was a student there; in fact, Frazer spent most of his academic career at Cambridge. Crowley never mentioned having met him or attended his lectures, but of course this does not exclude such a possibility. The passage quoted above is from Frazer (1911: 220).
230. Crowley (1973a: 129). See also Frazer (1911: 221). Curiously, Wittgenstein was probably referring to this same passage when he wrote, in his commentary on Frazer's work: "simple though it may sound, we can express the difference between science and magic if we say that in science there is progress but not in magic. There is nothing in magic to show the direction of any development" (Wittgenstein 1979: 13). As we will see, Crowley's interpretation is diametrically opposed: since there is progress not only in science but also in magic, there is no difference between them.
231. These are the degrees of *Magister Templi*, *Magus* and *Ipsissimus*. As we saw in Chapter 1, Crowley claimed to have reached both the first and the second. In his diaries he claimed to have reached the third in 1921, but also swore that he would never make this publicly known. See Symonds (1989: 281) and Suster (1988: 15, 66).
232. Crowley, *Magick* (1973: 140; my italics).
233. Comte de Fenix, *The Scientific Solution to the Problem of Government* (Crowley 1936): "The problem of Government is … to find a scientific formula with an ethical implication. … The formula is given by the Law of Thelema" (the pamphlet contains 4 unnumbered pages; this quote is on the last page).
234. Crowley (1973b: letter 31, 218).
235. *Ibid.*
236. *Ibid.*
237. *Ibid.* Significantly enough, the final quote is from Thomas Henry Huxley.
238. *Ibid.*: 219.

3. Dangerous liaisons
1. Webb (1971, 1976).
2. Webb (1976: 13).

NOTES 183

3. Webb describes him thus: "An undoubted Fascist, Fuller was also an undoubted illuminate, and he gravitated to illuminated circles" (*ibid.*: 127).
4. For biographical information on Fuller I generally refer to Anthony J. Trythall's *"Boney" Fuller* (1977). See also Brian Holden Reid's *J. F. C. Fuller* (1987). This, however, is more an intellectual biography than a biography in the strict sense of the word, and it provides no information on Fuller's relationship with Crowley besides what is already presented by Trythall.
5. Trythall (1977: 3).
6. *Ibid.*: 20.
7. Crowley's first letter to Fuller is dated 26 June 1905 and was written in Darjeeling (FP, IV, 12, 1). From the letter we gather that it was a response to an earlier letter from Fuller (probably the very first in the correspondence between the two) from 17 May of the same year. On the relationship between Crowley and Fuller, see also the account given by the latter in the introduction to his catalogue of Crowleyan books and documents (Fuller 1966b).
8. See Symonds (1989: 101–2).
9. J. F. C. Fuller, *The Star in the West* (1907). The title of the book makes an obvious reference to the star of the East that guided the Magi to the birthplace of Jesus, as told in the Gospel of Matthew (2:1-4). The title implies that the new messiah (i.e. Crowley, of course) will, unlike Jesus, rise in the West. It should be noted that another reference to this typical Christian trope, but this time without inverting the original geographical orientation, can also be found around the same time in theosophical milieus. In fact, Annie Besant established in 1911 the "Order of the Star in the East" as an organizational support for Krishnamurti, who was presented as the next "World Teacher". On several occasions Crowley expressed himself violently against this theosophical project and in 1925 he launched his "World Teacher Campaign" against it (see above, pp. 17–18 and n. 78).
10. Crowley (1989: 538).
11. Neuburg contributed to the *Agnostic Journal*, especially between 1903 and 1907, and also served as assistant editor for a while. He was very close to William Ross Stewart (1844–1906), one of the key figures in the movement, and it was at Stewart's house that he met Fuller for the first time, independently from Crowley. On this, see J. O. Fuller (1990: 108–13, 127). In 1907 Neuburg enrolled at Cambridge University and immediately joined the student group of freethinkers, known as the Cambridge University Freethought Association. There he met Mudd, who had enrolled in Trinity the same year, and Crowley, who had access to the university as a former student and was regularly invited there by the association (see Symonds 1989: 331). As I mentioned in Chapter 1, Crowley's visits led to friction with the authorities of Trinity College.
12. See J. O. Fuller (1990: 128).
13. Crowley (1989: 539–41).
14. Cited in Trythall (1977: 20).
15. "We saw each other nearly every day and worked together in a perfect harmony" (Crowley 1989: 543).
16. However, a few letters preserved in the Fuller collection lead us to believe that conflicts were present within the A∴A∴ even before the Jones case and the attacks by the press, and that the atmosphere in this group of Crowley's disciples was anything but harmonious. A source of tension appears to have been a difference in opinions regarding the organization of the Rites of Eleusis. On this subject, for example, there is a significant letter to Fuller from Meredith Starr (regarding Starr, see below) from 12 October 1910 (FP, IV, 12, 57), as well as Crowley's letter to Fuller from 28 October 1910 (FP, IV, 12, 58). This last letter is particularly interesting in that Crowley begins it "My dear ..." and then, instead of writing Fuller's name, draws a swastika. At the bottom of the letter, in place of his signature, there is a five-pointed star. This leads one to assume that Fuller identified himself, to a certain extent, with the symbol of the swastika, which at the time had not yet been "contaminated" in the popular imagination with the use Nazism later made of it. It had, however, begun to be used with political connotations in Germany in connection with the *völkisch* movement. On this subject, see Goodrick-Clarke (1985: 82–6, 191) and Godwin (1996: 50–51, 145–9). Outside Germany, also in the same period, the swastika had begun to take on political meaning as the archetypal symbol of an alleged "Aryan" or "Hyperborean" traditional heritage. See the examples concerning France and Russia in Godwin (1996: 51–2, 54–6). More generally on this question, see Malcolm Quinn, *The Swastika* (1994). The swastika also often appears in the devices and symbolism of the Golden Dawn, along with other elementary symbols, such as the cross or five-pointed star. In connection with this it is interesting to note that in the Golden Dawn, the swastika was also referred to as "Thor's hammer". This is stated by Crowley in one of his notes in the margins of Rauschning's book, *Hitler Speaks* (YC, DHD 350, annotation on the inside front cover). As Sutin has noted, in another annotation in the same book, Crowley goes so far as to claim that Hitler "almost certainly got the [symbol of the swastika] from us", where "us" refers to the group of occultists formed around the Golden Dawn (Sutin 2000: 377; see also YC, DHD 350, p. 212). Crowley states further on that he suggested the use of the symbol to none other than General Erich Ludendorff in 1925 or 1926, "when he started talking about reviving Nordic Theology" (Sutin 2000: 377).

Sutin rightly observes that if Crowley really did meet Ludendorff in person in those years, "he was conveying no new information, as the swastika had already been used as a symbol by other postwar German nationalist groups" (*ibid.*).

17. For the first reason, see Symonds (1989: 133–4); the second is given by Crowley himself in *The Confessions* (1989: 635). Symonds (1989: 133–4) also reproduces the text of what was supposedly Fuller's last letter to Crowley, from 2 May 1911, commenting: "It was Fuller's last word to Crowley, and all Crowley's subsequent communications to Fuller, most of which were of a fervent kind, were unanswered."
18. Trythall (1977: 24).
19. *Ibid.*: 70.
20. *Ibid.*: 107.
21. Fuller (1926).
22. See Trythall (1977: 170). Trythall cites the following passage from a 1931 book by Fuller, *India in Revolt*: "[Authority] implies the control of the majority by the minority, because intelligence is a rare and stupidity a plentiful quality in humankind. The masses must be controlled by some myth, some ideal which enslaves their animal instincts and emotions ... which creates order, and which restricts their animal appetites ... The masses must have a religion, that is a mythology, a Holy Grail."
23. On Mitrinovic, see Rigby (1984, 1999, 2006) and Passerini (1999: 105–48). James Webb and Martin Green also devote a few pages to Mitrinovic and his movement (Webb 1976: 191–5; Green 1992: 106–7). For an anthology of Mitrinovic's writings, see Mitrinovic (1987). After Mitrinovic's death in 1953 the New Atlantis Foundation was created to ensure the continuation of his work and preserve his papers and his large collection of books. The collection was later donated to the library of the University of Bradford. In 2010 the New Atlantis Foundation changed its name and became the Mitrinovic Foundation.
24. Alfred Adler (1870–1937) was an Austrian psychoanalyst and student of Freud. In 1911 he left the Freudian school to establish his own psychological society. Adler placed a great deal of importance on the aspect of education. In his view, education was in fact the origin of neuroses, which ultimately were of cultural and social origin. For this reason, Adler is seen as the precursor of the successive "revisions" of psychoanalysis in light of Marxist theory.
25. Passerini (1999: 126–37).
26. Rigby (2009: 109).
27. Webb (1976: 193).
28. Passerini (1999: 142–3) and Webb (1976: 193). The New Europe Group and the New Britain movement published a journal that took on different names in different moments, such as *New Britain*, *New Albion*, *New Atlantis* and *New Europe*. As is clear, the name invariably emphasized the "novelty" of the political, but also spiritual, message of the movement embodied in a particular geographical space, be it real or mythical.
29. I will return to this point in Chapter 5 (see pp. 125–6).
30. There is a reference to Mitrinovic in a note in Crowley's diary dated 16 August 1930 (YC/NS, 20). Crowley was in Berlin at the time, soon to leave for Portugal to meet with Fernando Pessoa. On the same day Crowley noted that he had met Alfred Adler and "Mitrinowitch [*sic*] philosopher".
31. Passerini (1999: 105–19) and Rigby (2006: 60–88). For a time, in the years 1920–21, Mitrinovic and Orage even signed a weekly column together in *The New Age* with a joint pseudonym ("M. M. Cosmoi").
32. Trythall (1977: 181).
33. On the development of Mosley's ideas and the formation of the BUF, see Thurlow (2009) and Linehan (2000). On British fascism see also Benewick (1972), Cross (1961) and Griffith (1983).
34. See the description in file XOMN/B/7/4 in the "Oswald Mosley Papers" collection, preserved in the Special Collections Department at the University of Birmingham. The file contains the Fuller-Mosley correspondence from the years 1934–6. Unfortunately I have not accessed this file directly. Thanks to William Breeze for drawing my attention to these documents.
35. The BUF had strongly anti-Semitic tendencies. In this regard it differed from Italian fascism (the model that inspired Mosley) and was closer to German national socialism (Nazism). Mosley, however, always denied being an anti-Semite. According to him, the BUF did not attack Jews for "what they were" (from a racial or religious point of view), but for "what they did". In any case, the BUF never developed any "racial" theory, and the reasons for its anti-Semitism always remained quite vague. With the coming of the war, the BUF fell increasingly under the influence of German Nazism, and their anti-Semitic campaign intensified. On the BUF's anti-Semitism, see Benewick (1972: esp. 151–8).
36. Webb (1976: 220).
37. Trythall (1977: 221; emphasis added).
38. See Sutin (2000: 291–2). Sutin incorrectly gives Townshend's initials as "M. E.". On the relationship between Fuller and Townshend, see Trythall (1977: 39–40).

39. The originals of three letters from Townshend to Fuller, from 4, 19 and 28 April 1921, are preserved at the Harry Ransom Center of the University of Texas at Austin, which acquired the greater part of the collection of Crowleyan documents that Fuller sold in 1966. The letters do not touch upon political matters, except for the first one, in which Townshend reports Crowley's justifications for his activities in pro-German propaganda in America during the First World War. The justifications are the same as those Crowley gives in his autobiography, which I have discussed in Chapter 2.
40. See n. 173 for Chapter 2, above.
41. Cammell (1951: x).
42. Letter of J. F. C. Fuller to E. N. FitzGerald dated 17 September 1949. The letter is described, together with some excerpts, in catalogue 13 of Weiser Antiquarian Books (February 2007), which has been available for a certain time at www.weiserantiquarian.com/catalogthirteen/ (accessed 2 August 2008). The URL however does not appear to be active anymore.
43. Trythall (1977: 242). We should also note that Fuller continued until his death to acquire, and presumably read, works by and about Crowley, as is proven by the catalogue of his Crowleyan collection (see Fuller 1966a). His collection of books has also been acquired by the Harry Ransom Center (see above, n. 39).
44. On Driberg, see Wheen (1990). See also Blake and Nicholls (1986), *sub voce*.
45. See Symonds (1989: ch. 31, "Thomas Driberg"). In this added chapter there is however no reconstruction of the events that occurred between the moment when Driberg expressed the desire to become Crowley's disciple and the moment when he changed his mind and the two decided to be only friends. Based on Driberg's letters to Crowley, preserved in the Yorke Collection, I shall attempt here to fill this lacuna.
46. See Symonds (1989: 411ff.). Symonds, however, did not quote all of Driberg's letters; I have found a few others, still unpublished, in the Yorke Collection (YC/OS, E21).
47. The letter is reproduced in its entirety in Symonds (1989: 411).
48. Crowley (1992a: 246).
49. See the letter from February 1926 (YC/OS, D8), in which Crowley asks Driberg to send him a telegram with the exact date of his arrival. Crowley also warns his aspiring disciple of an alleged "conspiracy" involving an attempt to spread false information about him in order to dissuade young people from coming into contact with him.
50. YC/OS, E21.
51. Part of the letter is quoted in Symonds (1989: 413). I am however quoting from the original here (YC/OS, E21).
52. YC/OS, E21 (emphasis added).
53. YC/OS, E21.
54. No date. YC/OS, E21.
55. In YC/NS, 5, there are three letters from Crowley to Driberg: the first from December 1926, the second from 18 January 1927, the third undated but from the same period, surely after the events related above. The letters mostly consist of reprimands to Driberg for not having been able to keep his appointments to meet Crowley. There are no further references to Driberg's contacts in the Communist Party. There is also a letter from Crowley with no indication of the date or even of whom it is addressed to, but the content leads us to believe it was probably intended for Driberg: "I think it is no part of your business to be an idealist. That is the business of youth which I should like you to shake off. ... Never forget that Lenin was an aristocrat of the aristocrats. He destroyed the so-called Aristocracy of Russia, because there were no aristocrats. They were apes, mocking the aristocratic tradition. Lenin was a King of Men. For the meaning of king, refer to the compound letter GN, which is the root of the ideas "to know" and also 'to beget'" (YC/OS, D5).
56. See Symonds (1989: 414).
57. *Ibid.*
58. Of course, Symonds, a little less magnanimously, did not neglect to make a copy of the note, in order that he might publish its content when the right time came. This, as we have seen, was after Driberg's death in 1976.
59. As we saw in Chapter 1, Crowley also had a connection to Huxley at the beginning of the 1930s.
60. On the Driberg–Knight relationship and the recruiting of Driberg by MI5, see Masters (1984, and esp. ch. 9, "Knight as Prophet: 1940–1943").
61. *Ibid.*: 172. Knight was also a homosexual.
62. On the Apostles' Club, see Richard Deacon (pseudonym of Donald McCormick), *The Cambridge Apostles* (1985). On Blunt's group, see *ibid.*: 104–11.
63. What might appear as a branch of the Apostles' Club run amok was in fact simply the most extreme consequence of a combination of leftist radicalism and rationalism, both of which were unquestionably important parts of Cambridge tradition, particularly at Trinity College. It is no coincidence that this college – one of the oldest and most prestigious at Cambridge – was in the front line in the battle for the university's secularization. On this, see Brooke (1993: 7–9, 13–14, 99–106). This tradition was supported by the Apostles' Club, and it is no surprise to learn that between the two world wars, a period when politics was going through an evident process

of radicalization, a few of the members espoused Marxist and communist – and consequently pro-Soviet – positions, as in the case of Blunt's group. We have also seen how Crowley, while a student at Trinity in the 1890s, was influenced by these rationalist and "progressive" traditions.

64. Driberg's biographer, F. Wheen, disagrees with the current version of the story, also told by Masters, according to which Blunt discovered Driberg's identity as an informer when he found a reference to a book by Driberg among Knight's papers (see Wheen 1990: 159–68). Wheen observes in fact that Driberg had not yet published any books at the time. He deems it plausible, however, that Blunt, who had no sympathy for Driberg, might have been at the origin of his expulsion from the party.
65. Masters (1984: 178).
66. Ibid.
67. In his memoirs, published posthumously, Driberg places emphasis on his relationship to Crowley, but in a fairly tendentious manner. He claims, in fact, that it was Crowley who contacted him, and makes no mention of their correspondence – which, as we have seen, he initiated. Naturally, there is also no mention of his "magical oath" (Driberg 1978: 82ff.). Driberg's biographer, F. Wheen, does little more than repeating Driberg's version of the facts (Wheen 1990: 54–5). It should also be noted that Driberg gives another tendentious version of the story of his relationship with Crowley in a review of the 1969 edition of Crowley's *Confessions*. The review was published in *The People*, 23 October 1969 and is quoted in Israel Regardie's preface to Stephensen and Regardie (1983: xii–xiii). Regardie does not appear to have been aware of the particular relationship between Crowley and Driberg.
68. Another author who has made reference to the Crowley–Driberg relationship is W. F. Ryan (Ryan 1992). Ryan, a scholar of Russian literature and culture, writes: "[Driberg] fell in love with Crowley, and promised to put him in touch with the Theosophist and Communist leaders in Britain, Driberg being at that time of both, if not more, persuasions. How far this went is not known, but some time after the [Russian] Revolution it is claimed that Crowley tried to get a message to Stalin with a view to setting up an antireligion" (*ibid*.: 156). As Will Ryan, then librarian of the Warburg Institute, told me during a personal conversation in May 1993, the source of this last piece of information is a letter he received from Gerald Yorke, but does not seem to be supported by any extant original document by Crowley. The alleged attempt by Crowley to make contact with Stalin is probably a distorted memory of the idea Crowley had in 1923 to get in touch with Trotsky "to suggest that I be put in charge of world-wide campaign to eradicate Christianity" (Kaczynski 2010: 399).
69. About Duranty, see Sally J. Taylor's biography (Taylor 1990).
70. Ibid.: 3.
71. Shirer (1960).
72. On this episode, see S. J. Taylor (1990: 168ff.).
73. Ibid.: 171.
74. Ibid.: 45.
75. Ryan (1992: 155). In recent years, even *The New York Times* has cast doubt upon the professional behaviour of its illustrious correspondent. Among the most controversial aspects of Duranty's activity as Moscow correspondent was his coverage of the great famine of 1932–3 in the Ukraine, which resulted in millions of deaths. In his articles, Duranty denied that the effects of the famine had been so devastating, sticking uncritically to the Kremlin's version of the story. In 2003 pressure groups linked to the Ukrainian diaspora in the United States launched a campaign to take away Duranty's Pulitzer Prize posthumously. The campaign contributed to discrediting Duranty's name, but the Pulitzer was not revoked. On these events, see McCollam (2003).
76. S. J. Taylor (1990: 5).
77. Ibid.: 30.
78. See Crowley (1989). The first passage is on p. 599. Crowley describes a meeting with Chéron that took place in Paris in January 1920: "I wanted to see the man with whom she was living, who had not yet returned from Russia; I wanted to make love to her, and I wanted to smoke a few pipes of opium with her, she being a devotee of that great and terrible god". Evidently, "the man with whom she was living" was Duranty. Crowley adds, for the record, that during his visit he did not achieve any of his three goals. The other passage is on p. 722 and refers to the period of *Paris Working*, namely 1914: "During the operation I had a bad attack of influenza, which settled down to very severe bronchitis. I was visited one evening by an old friend of mine and her young man, who very kindly and sensibly suggested that I should find relief if I smoked a few pipes of opium". The "old friend" was undoubtedly Chéron, and her "young man" must have been Duranty. Opium appears to have been a constant presence in their meetings. A fleeting reference to Chéron, Duranty and their evenings spent smoking opium together appears in Crowley's novel *Moonchild* (1929b: 245). Finally, in *Magick without Tears* (1973b: 180, 336, 478), Crowley offers a few anecdotes about Russia drawn from a work by Duranty (1935).
79. Edwin Ray Lankester (1847–1929) was an English zoologist and had been a student of Thomas Henry Huxley.

Crowley probably had Lankester on his mind because he had died in August of that same year. Lankester is here cast as the archetypal agnostic and positivist thinker, which Crowley tended to view favourably.
80. A carbon copy of the original is in YC/OS, D3.
81. On the history and the ritual of the Gnostic Mass, see Apiryon and Helena (2001).
82. Crowley began to take a particular interest in Russia after his journey to Moscow in 1913. He subsequently wrote at least two essays on Russia: "The Heart of Holy Russia", published in the American magazine *The International* in January 1914, and "The Realism of Russian Literature", written in the same period but unpublished (see Ryan 1992: 150ff.).
83. See n. 68 above.
84. The text is reproduced by Ryan (1992: 156). The notes in square brackets are Ryan's. I do not know where the original is located; a copy of it was given to Ryan by the American scholar Martin P. Starr. The "Manifesto", which Ryan describes as not extant, is very probably the leaflet "To Man", which Crowley released from Tunis in October 1924 during his "World Teacher Campaign". See above, Chapter 1, n. 78.
85. I have no further information about this disciple (or at least sympathizer) of Crowley's, who does not appear to be mentioned by any of Crowley's biographers. But there is at least one letter from Crowley to one David Sturgis, located in New York, who is very probably the same person. The letter is dated August 1924, and in it Crowley offers news about himself and his disciples and discusses his plans to turn international public opinion against his expulsion from Italy (see YC/OS, D8).
86. A short excerpt of the letter is cited by S. J. Taylor (1990: 250). The original is in YC/OS, E21.
87. There is a carbon copy of the original at the Warburg Institute (YC, mss II, 13).
88. On this, see Claudio S. Ingerflom's introductory essay, "Communistes contre castrats (1929–1930)", in Volkov (1995: esp. xl–xlv).
89. Typewritten copy, OA.
90. See Symonds (1974).
91. See Bouchet (1998: 90).
92. Isherwood (1935).
93. Isherwood (1977: 64). This book is particularly interesting because, besides describing Isherwood's Berlin period – which, incidentally, coincided exactly with the period in which Crowley also resided there – it also enables us to see his two earlier Berlin novels (*Mr Norris Changes Trains*, 1935, and *Goodbye to Berlin*, 1939), and the experiences that served as subject matter for them, from another perspective. This helps us to gather some useful biographical details that remain in the background in these works.
94. See Isherwood (1977: 61).
95. A critical biography of Hamilton still waits to be written. For biographical information on him, I can only refer to his own autobiographical books (Hamilton 1937, 1956, 1969). Considering Hamilton's personality, the information provided by him in his books must be taken with a large grain of salt.
96. Hamilton (1956: 33). Later, Hamilton often had second thoughts about Catholicism, but always ended up converting back to it (*ibid.*: 53–4).
97. Isherwood (1977: 63).
98. The first entry regarding Hamilton is from 11 October 1931 (Sunday): "Hamilton London *Times* rang up to see me personally. Appt. Tues. 4." Then, on the 13th (Tuesday): "Hamilton Berlin correspondent of *Times* called with his boy. An old friend!" (YC/NS, 20). The "boy" that went with Hamilton to Crowley's house was none other than Christopher Isherwood. In fact, in his last volume of autobiographical memoirs, Hamilton claims that it was Isherwood's idea to visit Crowley, and that his curiosity had been sparked by Crowley's exhibition of paintings then running in Berlin (Hamilton 1969: 55). Hamilton and Isherwood were both homosexuals, but Isherwood, in his autobiography, describes his relationship with Hamilton as nothing more than a friendship. It is not clear whether the "old friend" reference means Hamilton or Isherwood. In the same book Hamilton claims that he had never seen Crowley before (Hamilton 1969: 55).
99. Hamilton (1956: 126ff.).
100. Isherwood (1977: 63). It should be noted that in his memoir Isherwood writes about himself in the third person, using his first name. Sutin quotes a not particularly flattering evaluation of Crowley by Isherwood: "The truly awful thing about Crowley is that one suspects he didn't really believe in anything. Even his wickedness. Perhaps the only thing that wasn't fake was his addiction to heroin and cocaine" (Sutin 2000: 361). The quotation comes from Isherwood's *Diaries*, published after his death (Isherwood 1997: 550). This appears to be the only passage in which Isherwood explicitly mentions Crowley's name. It remains difficult to determine the reason why he preferred to avoid mentioning Crowley in his writings intended for publication. The character Anselm Oakes in Isherwood's story "A Visit to Anselm Oakes", in the collection *Exhumations* (Isherwood 1984), seems to be partly modelled on Crowley; but even on this occasion Isherwood avoids referring explicitly to him in the brief introduction. Oakes, with his sadism and perfidy, is reminiscent of Oliver Haddo's character in Maugham's *The*

Magician. On the relationship between Crowley and Isherwood, see also "Christopher Isherwood" in Cornelius and Cornelius (1996: 40–42).
101. This is confirmed by Crowley's diary as well as through Symonds' conversations with Hamilton. Crowley, in his diary from 22 January 1932, writes: "Hamilton came to stay" (YC/NS, 20). The following day, Crowley consulted the I Ching, an ancient Chinese divination system, concerning the development of his relationship to Hamilton. The response was: "V[ery] good after preliminary struggles. But it is not permanent: if the good luck (when it comes!) turns bad, don't try to keep on" (*ibid.*). Hamilton told Symonds that he had been "a paying guest for about six months at Crowley's apartment in Berlin" (Symonds 1974: 167).
102. Symonds (1989: 480; see also Spence 2008: 216–17).
103. This seems to be confirmed by Donald McCormick in his biography of Ian Fleming (to whom I will return in the next section). McCormick adds an interesting detail: according to him, the liaison between the British secret service and Crowley, when the latter was sending his reports about Hamilton, was none other than Tom Driberg, who had gotten involved in intelligence networks (McCormick 1993: 45, 94). According to Spence, on the other hand, Crowley's liaison in this period, and particularly for information concerning Hamilton, was Col. John F. C. Carter. One possibility of course does not exclude the other. Col. Carter was an Assistant Commissioner of Scotland Yard's Special Branch, specializing in anti-communist intelligence. He had been given the task of investigating Crowley after his expulsion from France in 1929. He subsequently became friends with him and was for a while his liaison to the English secret service (see Symonds 1989: 437; Spence 2008: 210–13; 216–17). He probably even facilitated Crowley's return to England. There is clear evidence that Crowley passed information to the English via Carter during his Berlin period. There is for instance an interesting letter from Colonel Carter to Gerald Yorke from 25 March 1932 (YC/OS, EE2), where Carter asks Yorke to make Crowley stop sending him "long letters" containing confidential information about Germany. Carter justifies his request by claiming that he has stopped working for the secret service and can therefore no longer serve as Crowley's liaison.
104. Trebitsch Lincoln, an adventurer, secret agent, master of the double bluff and of the most varied forms of intrigue, had plenty of things in common with Hamilton. There is a very thorough and well-documented study of his life by Bernard Wasserstein (1988). On the meeting between Hamilton and Trebitsch Lincoln, see Hamilton (1956: 140–41) and Symonds (1974: 96–7). Wasserstein ignores this episode. See also Spence (2008: 96–7).
105. See the two letters from Guénon to Renato Schneider, from 13 September 1936 and 4 September 1938, cited by Robin (1986: 275, 281).
106. Wasserstein makes no mention of Crowley in his biography of Trebitsch Lincoln and there is no evidence of a contact or meeting between the two.
107. In this period he continued associating with Crowley. In fact, for some time, the two even shared an apartment again in London (see Symonds 1989: 518, 521, 553–5, 566–7).
108. See Hamilton (1956: 151ff.). Hamilton also mentions Admiral Wolkoff, a Russian exile in London and the father of Anna Wolkoff, one of the most notorious and colourful characters of the extreme right in England during the 1930s. We will also meet her again in the next section.
109. See Benewick (1972: 29–33, 41) and Lee (2005). Among her books, the best known are *The French Revolution: A Study in Democracy* (Webster 1922a), *World Revolution: The Plot against Civilizations* (Webster 1922b) and *Secret Societies and Subversive Movements* (Webster 1924).
110. Symonds (1974: 93–4).
111. Crowley is mentioned in *Secret Societies and Subversive Movements* (Webster 1924: 314–15).
112. For information on him I am referring to A. Masters's biography (1984).
113. On the affair, see Clough (2005) and Masters (1984: 82ff.). See also Costello (1991: 101–27, 479–80). Costello's book throws interesting light upon Hess's flight to Scotland in May 1941, to which I will return later in this section. Costello was able to gain access to documents kept in the archives of the Soviet and US secret services that had been inaccessible until that time. With the help of these files and other solid documentation, Costello minutely reconstructs various moments from the British political and military situation between 10 May 1940, the day Winston Churchill became prime minister, and 10 May 1941, when Hess fled.
114. Knight was also responsible for the arrest of Mosley and the members of the BUF. In his report on the Tyler Kent case, he stated that Ramsay and Mosley were in cooperation with one another, which was not true (see Masters 1984: 89). As we saw earlier, General Fuller was almost the only prominent member of the BUF who did not end up in prison. Even if this was probably determined by Churchill's personal intervention, because of his admiration of Fuller, we should note that Knight associated with Crowley in this same period, and that the latter had never stopped profoundly admiring his ex-disciple.
115. According to Costello, the Tyler Kent affair, of which Churchill was aware, was used to make things difficult for the American ambassador in London, Joseph Kennedy, father of the future president of the United States, John Fitzgerald. Joseph Kennedy's position was strongly isolationist, and he was therefore completely opposed

(unlike Roosevelt) to the idea of the United States entering the war to help a sorely troubled Great Britain. Rather, as one might expect, he favoured a negotiated peace between the British and the Germans. See Costello (1991: 56ff., 120ff., *passim*).
116. On Dennis Wheatley (1897–1977), see Baker (2009). In 1934 Wheatley published *The Devil Rides Out*, the first of his novels in which the theme of black magic appears; its main character is partly modelled on Crowley (Wheatley 1934). The descriptions of magical rites in Wheatley's novels were inspired in part by Crowley's writings, as well as by information Crowley provided personally, as Wheatley himself confirms in his memoir *Drink and Ink* (1979: 131): "My friend, Tom Driberg, who then lived in a mews flat just behind us in Queen's Gate, proved most helpful. He introduced me to Aleister Crowley … . We had Crowley to dinner several times. His conversation was fascinating. He gave me much useful information and several of his books, but never attempted to draw me into his occult activities". It is interesting to learn that it was Tom Driberg who introduced Crowley to Wheatley. This speaks to the complexity of the relationships that formed between the various persons to whom this chapter has been devoted. Politically, Wheatley was a conservative; he was dismayed at the abdication of Edward VIII, and admired Mussolini and Franco. Nazism, however, was too bloody for him to grant his sympathies (*ibid*.: 142, 166–7).
117. Baker (2009: 350–53, 389–91, and *passim*).
118. On Knight's interest in reincarnation, see Masters (1984: 62). On Wheatley's, see his own memoir (1979: 152). On astral projection, see Masters (1984: 132) and Baker (2009: 405–6).
119. Masters (1984: 68). Wheatley claims, however, that he never participated in magical rites (Wheatley 1979: 131). Baker prefers to follow Wheatley's claim about this (Baker 2009: 353).
120. At the margin of these events, we might observe that Gerald Yorke was a very close friend of Ian Fleming's brother Peter. On Crowley and Fleming, see Spence (2011).
121. Schmidt (2000). Schmidt in part comes to a conclusion similar to that of Costello. In addition to Schmidt's book, the "classic" bibliography on the affair should include Douglas-Hamilton (1971), Irving (1987) and Allen (2004). James Douglas-Hamilton is the son of Douglas Douglas-Hamilton, Duke of Hamilton – the person to whom Hess intended to present his proposal for peace. Irving's book, which is very sympathetic towards Hess, concentrates primarily on his period of incarceration in Britain until the end of the war, but also offers a reconstruction of his career in the Nazi party and of the reasons that led him to flee. There is of course also a number of novelized renditions of the event: see, for instance, Leasor (1962). Leasor, like Irving, is persuaded that, by rejecting Hess's peace offer, Britain (and more generally the West) missed the opportunity to give Germany a free hand in Russia, and consequently to eliminate the communist threat once and for all.
122. This aspect is taken into consideration rather offhandedly by both Douglas-Hamilton (1971: part 2, ch. 4) and Irving (1987: ch. 6). According to Irving, the secret service had known about Hess's plan and had endeavoured to support his efforts in order to lure him to Great Britain and capture him.
123. See Costello (1991: 19, ch. 17).
124. Masters (1984: 126).
125. *Ibid*.: 127. This type of operation was far from unusual during the war. Indeed, the British secret service had a whole department devoted to such undertakings, which were known as "black". As an example, Ellic Howe (whom we have already encountered as the historian of the Golden Dawn) refers to these operations; he worked in this department during the war (see Howe 1967, or the revised edition, Howe 1984). It is not beyond the realm of possibility that some of the projects Howe worked on may have formed part of the plan to lure Hess, considering that in at least one case, his work involved creating a fake issue of a German astrology journal. This possibility is mentioned by McCormick in his biography of Fleming (1993: 87–8).
126. Masters (1984: 127).
127. *Ibid*.: 128. The SIS (Secret Intelligence Service), later MI6, was primarily occupied with espionage, while the main purpose of MI5 was counter-espionage. It would be worth conducting further research in this area. Masters unfortunately does not indicate the sources of his reconstruction.
128. Albrecht Haushofer was first arrested on Hitler's orders immediately after Hess's flight, but later released. He was arrested again in December 1944 in the course of the persecutions launched following Stauffenberg's failed plot to assassinate Hitler, and was finally shot by the SS in April 1945, a few days before Berlin fell before the Soviet advance. See J. Douglas-Hamilton (1971: part 3). Masters's book does not mention Haushofer's role in these events.
129. See Costello (1991: 410).
130. See *ibid*.: 411–12.
131. The secret service, or rather the section of it that led such operations, may not have informed Churchill because he would surely have been opposed to it. Operations of this kind, encouraging German hope (albeit only for strategic reasons), might have damaged the tough image that Churchill had taken such pains to construct. See Costello (1991: 19, 412–13).

132. Masters (1984: 128).
133. On the Ben Greene case, see *ibid.*: 141ff.
134. One version of the events very similar to Masters's, including the involvement of Fleming, Knight and Crowley, appears in Donald McCormick's biography of Fleming cited above. McCormick's book (1993) is more recent than that of Masters (1984), but McCormick never refers to Masters. McCormick has written several books on the history of the secret service, and worked with Fleming for many years both during and after the war. For the sake of completeness it should also be added that there is no reference to either Fleming or Crowley in the books of Hamilton, Irving, Costello, Allen or Schmidt.
135. Pearson (1989: 144). The first edition is from 1966, long predating Masters's book of 1984. Pearson does not speak of Hess's flight as the result of a secret service operation, and does not attribute any role to Fleming in the events other than his suggestion that Crowley might serve as an interrogator.
136. YC/NS, 14; the letter is reproduced in part by Pearson (1989). Here I have only omitted the addresses of the persons Crowley mentions. It appears that Gerald Yorke subsequently asked Donald McCormick to throw some light on these events. McCormick responded with some information in a letter from 10 May 1967, a typewritten copy of which is in the Yorke Collection (YC/NS, 117, p. 55). McCormick writes: "oddly enough Ian Fleming, under whom I worked in the Foreign Department of the *Sunday Times* for many years, had a vague theory about this. ... He wanted Crowley to interview Hess when the Nazi leader landed in Britain; it never came off and the very idea must have horrified the Admiralty. But there was an exchange of letters on the subject ...". The photocopy of Crowley's letter, kept in the YC, includes an annotation by Gerald Yorke, which reproduces the content of McCormick's letter.
137. See Galli (1989).
138. *Ibid.*: 121-3.

4. The Mouth of Hell

1. Several biographies of Pessoa are available. The standard one remains Gaspar Simões (1991), first published in 1950. More recent ones include Crespo (1997; originally in Spanish) and Bréchon (1996; in French). For the rest, the bibliography on Pessoa is now immense, and I will simply refer to relevant titles in the following footnotes. For a general bibliography on Pessoa, see Blanco (2008).
2. There is a large literature today on the political aspects of Pessoa's work, but most of it is in Portuguese. At least two books have been published on the subject (Morodo 1997; Tavares 1998) and several articles or chapters in collective volumes. See the bibliographies in Morodo (1997) and Tavares (1998) for further information on this literature.
3. Tabucchi (1990: 16).
4. Pessoa (1928). On the publication of the pamphlet and its historical context, see Barreto (2012b). It should be noted that later, especially during the last few months before his death, Pessoa grew strongly critical of Salazar and his regime, expressing his discontent in a number of poetic compositions and other texts, which he left unpublished (see Tavares 1998: 128-47; Barreto 2008). The texts and poems about Salazar and the "Estado Novo" can be found in Neves (2009).
5. The first author to point out this reference in Guénon's letter was Gianfranco de Turris, in an editor's note in the Italian edition of John Symonds's biography (Symonds 1972: 444). De Turris later published the letter integrally in an article (Turris 1986: 123ff.). More recently, it was reproduced by Renato Del Ponte in his edition of the Guénon-Evola correspondence (Guénon 1996: 105-13). De Turris calls Guénon's statement regarding Crowley "a disturbing hypothesis that ought to be verified concretely" (Turris 1986: 125, n. 7). Marco Rossi, a historian specializing in Evola and other Italian traditionalist thinkers of the fascist era, gives a certain degree of credit to Guénon's inference, thus confirming its suggestive power (Rossi 1989: 323).
6. Most of Pessoa's esoteric writings have been published over the years by Yvette K. Centeno and Pedro Teixeira da Mota (see in particular Centeno 1985a, 1985b, 1988; Pessoa 1988a, 1988b, 1989a, 1989b). Also important, especially because of its introduction, is the collection of Pessoa's esoteric writings edited by António Quadros (Pessoa 1986a). The critical edition of Pessoa's poem *Mensagem*, edited by José Augusto Seabra, should be mentioned here as well (Pessoa 1993). The book also includes the other esoteric poems by Pessoa; an important essay by Y. K. Centeno on Pessoa's esoteric thought (Centeno 1993), and a useful bibliography. On Pessoa's esotericism, the first comprehensive study is the pioneering work of Dalila L. Pereira da Costa (Costa 1987; originally published in 1971); however, this book is based primarily on Pessoa's poetic works and ignores the many unpublished fragments that emerged after its first publication. Other significant monographic studies include the (still unpublished) doctoral thesis of Ana Maria Binet (1996), Teixeira (1997), Matos (1997), Centeno (2004), Seabra (2004), Anes (2008) and Coyné (2011).
7. Quadros (1986a: 14).
8. Daniel 2:44.

9. There is an abundant literature on Father Vieira, the influence of Sebastianism, and the myth of the Fifth Empire in Portugal. As an introduction see Azevedo (1984; originally 1918), Bercé (1990: 17–81), Coyné (1996: 57–86) and Bigalli (2002).
10. Mutti (1994: 101–2). More generally, on the "hidden King" myth, see Bercé (1990) and Politica Hermetica (2000). Curiously, Crowley, whose youthful interest in Jacobite legitimism I have already discussed, refers to a similar legend concerning King James IV of Scotland (reigned 1488–1513). History tells us that James died in the Battle of Flodden Field against the English, but legend has him remaining hidden and suspended in an immortal state, waiting to return to his people. Crowley refers to S. L. Mathers, who (according to Crowley) claimed that he himself was James IV, living in secret. See Crowley (1973c: vol. 1, 207, col. 1, n. 2). On the legend of James IV as "hidden king", see Bercé (1990: 203–5, 214–15).
11. See Quadros (1986b: 25).
12. On Pessoa and Sebastianism, see Quadros (1986b), De Cusatis (2005) and Uribe and Sepúlveda (2011, 2012).
13. A large selection of Pessoa's political writings, which includes also the texts on Sebastianism and the Fifth Empire, can be found in two volumes of the famous Ática series of Pessoa's collected works (Pessoa 1979a, 1979b), both with important introductions by Joel Serrão. Another edition of Pessoa's political writings is the two-volume one by António Quadros, also with useful introductions by him (Pessoa 1986c, 1986d). In this series, on the other hand, the texts on Sebastianism and the Fifth Empire are collected in a separate volume (Pessoa 1986b).
14. Tabucchi (1977: 34).
15. See, especially, "O Império Espiritual" in Pessoa (1986b: 76) and "O Império Português" in Pessoa (1986b: 171). For a new, critical edition of Pessoa's texts devoted to Sebastianism and the Fifth Empire, see Pessoa (2011).
16. This document is reproduced in Pessoa (1986e: vol. III, 1427–9). The version appearing as an appendix in Simões (1991: 608) is abridged. See also Barreto (2008: 202–4).
17. On the relationship between esotericism and politics in Pessoa's thought, see De Cusatis (2005).
18. The list can be found in Pessoa (1986d: 195ff.).
19. Victor Marsden's 1934 English translation has been recently republished (Protocols 2011). There is now a relatively large critical literature on the *Protocols*, whose beginnings date already to before the Second World War, especially with the ground-breaking study by Henri Rollin (1939). Subsequent important studies include Cohn (1967), Taguieff (1992), De Michelis (2004) and Hagemeister (2008).
20. Along with the list of projected publications for Olisipo, which includes the title of the *Protocols*, there is also a more specific list of publications connected with the theme of Judaism. Here the projected edition of the *Protocols* is described; it was intended to include commentaries proving the text's authenticity. Then there are two other titles: *O Judeu, Sociologicamente Considerado* (*The Jew, Sociologically Considered*), and *Aviso: um estudo sumário dos fundamentos da civilização europeia, e das forças que a sustentam e das que a dissolvem* (*Warning: A Summary Study of the Foundations of European Civilization, the Forces that Sustain It and Those that Dissolve It*). Pessoa planned to be the author of these last two works. The curious thing is that Pessoa was also of Jewish descent, which he proudly asserted. In the 1935 memorandum I have already referred to he describes his lineage as a "mixto de fidalgos e de judeus" ["an assortment of nobles and Jews"] (Barreto 2008: 202–3).
21. See Centeno (1988: 119ff.). The major problem with these fragments, as with most of Pessoa's unpublished material, is that they are not dated. Unfortunately, Centeno does not address this problematic point in her introduction.
22. Pessoa had in his private library at least two books related to Rathenau (Rathenau 1921; Raphaël 1909). See Pizarro *et al.* (2010: 152).
23. On this point (also in reference to Rathenau's assassination), see Cohn (1967: 144, 203) and Michalka (2006). Rathenau had mentioned the elite of three hundred men in an article for the *Neue Freie Presse*, "Unser Nachwuchs", published on 25 December 1909. The article was later included with a slightly different title ("Geschäftlicher Nachwuchs") in a book Rathenau published in 1912, *Zur Kritik der Zeit* (Rathenau 1912), which was quite successful and was subsequently reprinted many times. Here is an English rendering of the original statement made by Rathenau: "Three hundred men, who all know each other, control the economic fortunes of the continent and look for their successors in their own milieu" (Rathenau 1912: 207). It is known that Rathenau had an elitist political vision, the theme of government by an elite having appeared often in his writings. On this aspect, see Struve (1973: 149–85) and Cacciari (1979: 11–16). Interestingly, but not surprisingly, Rathenau's statement was interpreted by conspiracy theorists as confirmation of their theories, coming from someone like him, who was highly knowledgeable in European politics, including their background aspects. In this context, the fact that Rathenau was of Jewish origin was surely not of secondary importance in the eyes of anti-Semite conspiracy theorists. It should be noted however that, even before Rathenau, there was already one precedent for the idea of a hidden elite of three hundred men in anti-Semite literature. In

fact, the French journalist Édouard Drumont (1844–1917) mentioned it as far back as 1889 in his book *La Fin d'un Monde* (Drumont 1889: 230; see also Rollin 1939: 257). Drumont, who was known for his anti-Semitism, pointed out however that these men were not necessarily Jews, but financial magnates.
24. Centeno 1988: 133.
25. *Ibid*.: 129.
26. *Ibid*.: 134. Similar concepts can be found in another text that is highly important for understanding Pessoa's attitude toward Judaism: namely, a preface he wrote to a book of poetry by his friend Eliezer Kamenezky, a Russian Jew living in exile in Lisbon (Kamenezky 1932). In his preface, Pessoa defends Freemasonry from the accusation of being Jewish, denying that it had a "Jewish origin" despite the elements of Kabbalistic symbolism incorporated in it. But, he continues, even if Freemasonry is not of Jewish origin, the Jews have still made use of Freemasonry as a means to their end: "[The political action of the Jews] is obvious and natural; they have exploited not only Freemasonry and egalitarian ideology, but anything, be it of Jewish or non-Jewish origin, which could dissolve, when used effectively, the traditional Greco-Roman and Christian civilization of Europe and the Europeanized world. And it is legitimate to take such advantage, for the Jews have the same rights as all other peoples: the right to defence and the right to rule – the former being an absolute right, the latter just as we concede it to others" (Pessoa 1932: 12). Concerning this topic, see also the interesting collection of texts by Pessoa about Freemasonry and the Jews, translated into German and with an important introduction by Yvette K. Centeno (Pessoa 2009).
27. Centeno (1985a: 51).
28. Pessoa worked for the publisher Livraria Clássica, and translated, among other things, Helena Petrovna Blavatsky's *The Voice of Silence* (*A Voz do Silêncio*) and Charles Webster Leadbeater's *An Outline of Theosophy* (*Compêndio de teosofia*). Pessoa's translation of the former book has been recently republished (Blavatsky 1998).
29. On the concept of neo-gnosticism and its applications in various fields, including literature and politics, see Introvigne (1993: 23, 26ff.). Also interesting on this subject, of course, are Pessoa's own reflections on gnosticism: see Pessoa (1986a: 151–2).
30. Pessoa (1999: 346–7).
31. On Crowley's influence on Pessoa's esoteric thought, see Pasi (2001b).
32. Crowley (1989: 559).
33. Pessoa (1979a: 77).
34. Symonds, in the third edition of his biography, expanded the space devoted to Pessoa, adding two of the letters Pessoa sent to Crowley, now kept at the Warburg Institute (YC/OS, E21). Otherwise, he made no changes to his reconstruction of the encounter as described in the first two editions. See Symonds (1989: 445). The letters are reproduced here in Appendix 2. It should finally be noted that practically all subsequent biographers of Crowley after Symonds have basically followed his reconstruction of the events, without adding anything substantial.
35. Pessoa and Crowley (2010). The compilation has been edited by Miguel Roza (pseudonym of Luis Miguel Rosa Dias), who is Pessoa's nephew and was therefore in possession of the documents. About the history of this collection, see Pasi and Ferrari (2012: 285). The first edition of the book (Pessoa and Crowley 2001) showed significant problems from a philological point of view, which have been partly solved in the second edition (Pessoa and Crowley 2010). A German edition of these documents, edited by the German specialist Steffen Dix, has also been recently published (Pessoa 2012).
36. This letter is reproduced in Symonds's biography, and here in Appendix 2. For a complete, detailed listing of the Crowley–Pessoa correspondence, see Pasi and Ferrari (2012: 303–6).
37. His request was never fulfilled, for the other four volumes of the *Confessions* would not come to light until 1969, when the first edition with all six volumes, edited by K. Grant and J. Symonds, was published.
38. The original is at the Warburg Institute; YC/OS, E21. The text was also published in Symonds (1989: 445–6). For a critical edition of the Crowley–Pessoa letters preserved at the Warburg Institute, together with high-resolution facsimiles, see now Pasi and Ferrari (2012).
39. The unnumbered plate appears just before the beginning of the numbered pages in the first volume of the 1929 edition of *The Confessions* (Crowley 1929). It was not included in the single-volume edition (Crowley 1989).
40. YC/NS, 13.
41. See the Pessoa bibliography in Quadros (1992: 309). The books are now preserved in the Yorke Collection at the Warburg Institute, together with documents that shed further interesting light on the Crowley–Pessoa relationship. See Pasi and Ferrari (2012: 288–90).
42. YC/NS, 13.
43. Similarly to Crowley biographers after Symonds, scholars of Pessoa after Gaspar Simões have not deviated much from his "standard" version – when they have discussed the Crowley–Pessoa relationship at all.
44. Simões (1991: 523).

45. Symonds (1989: 452). "Hanni" was Hanni L. Jaeger, the German art student who was Crowley's companion at the time.
46. Pessoa and Crowley (2001: 78).
47. The original letter is at the Warburg Institute, YC/OS, E21. It was first published in Symonds (1989: 446). See now Pasi and Ferrari (2012: 299–300). The full text of the letter appears in Appendix 2 of the present book.
48. Here it is worth noting that Pessoa had relatives in England, which may have been his principal reason for considering a journey there. However, after his return from South Africa in 1906, Pessoa in fact never left Portugal again.
49. A facsimile reproduction of the letter first appeared among the plates in França (1987). Now see also Pessoa and Crowley (2010: 80). See Appendix 2 for the full text of this letter.
50. YC/OS, E20.
51. Three more letters were exchanged between April and May: one from Regardie (on Crowley's behalf) to Pessoa, one from Crowley to Pessoa and one from Pessoa to Crowley. See Pessoa and Crowley (2010: 315–16).
52. See Pessoa and Crowley (2001: 102–3), and Pessoa and Crowley (2010: 317).
53. YC/OS, F1, n15. The text is untitled, dated January 1937. There are ten pages, the last of which bears a note signed by Crowley, saying that the declaration has been "promulgated to all my representatives in the Order". There are also some handwritten annotations by Gerald Yorke, dated 11 February 1948.
54. See above, p. 20.
55. See Regardie (1993: 8). Regardie also reproduces Crowley's statement about him, which according to him "circulated far and wide in the autumn of 1937".
56. On this, Symonds writes: "He arrived back in England on 24 August 1930. The Monster [i.e. Hanni Jaeger] was with him ... Crowley of course kept out of the way of the prowling Marie ... Yorke had found her lodgings in Hampstead, and was doing his best to help her, but all his pleas on her behalf left the Beast unmoved" (Symonds 1989: 452).
57. YC/OS, F1, n15, p. 7.
58. Octavio Paz, in a well-known work on Pessoa from 1961, wrote: "Occultism has its dangers, and one day Pessoa found himself involved in an imbroglio mounted by the police against the English magician and "Satanist" E. A. Crowley-Aleister [*sic*], who is on his way to Lisbon *in search of adepts for his mystic-erotic order*" (Paz 1988: 16; emphasis added). Perhaps thanks to the "inspiration" of which Tabucchi writes in his introduction (Tabucchi 1988: 9), Paz had unknowingly come very close to the truth, without even needing unpublished documents or erudite research.
59. Letter from Crowley to Pessoa, 3 August 1930. See the facsimile reproduction in Pessoa and Crowley (2001: 122) and the transcription in Pessoa and Crowley (2010: 321). The only temporal reference in the letter is given as "die ♂" (i.e. Tuesday). The editor of the volume, Miguel Roza, erroneously interprets the date of the letter as 15 September (Pessoa and Crowley 2010: 104), but from Crowley's diary we can see that the letter was actually written on 3 September.
60. On the tradition of Masonic and occultist Templarism, the fundamental text is Le Forestier (1987), although it stops at the end of the nineteenth century. See also Partner (1982: part 2), Introvigne (1990: ch. 6 and 7), Ventura (1991b) and Mollier (2005).
61. On the ONT, see Goodrick-Clarke (1985: 97). On the OTR, see Introvigne (1990: 237–8).
62. This is the conclusion reached by Binet (1996: 584–9) on which one can easily agree, since evidence to the contrary appears to be lacking.
63. Pessoa (1999: 347). Quadros comments on this passage as follows: "Here we are faced with two enigmas presented to us by Pessoa: What does this statement mean? And what Order of the Temple (of Christ?) became extinct or dormant in 1888 – precisely the date of the poet's birth? Note furthermore that the *Ordre Kabbalistique de la Rose-Croix* was founded in France, also in 1888, by Sor Paladém [*sic*, for Sâr Péladan], Papus and Stanislas de Guaita, among others, the poet Eugénio de Castro being its Consul in Portugal" (Quadros 1986a: 232, n. 4). We could add that 1888 was also the year in which the Golden Dawn was founded in England.
64. "A Fernando Pessoa nascido no ano certo". (Gomes 1934: xi).
65. See Simões (1991: 495). For a very detailed and informative discussion of the idea that Pessoa was born in the "right year", see Pizarro (2012: 193–210).
66. We may note here in passing that Crowley also attributed particular importance to his date of birth (1875), because Eliphas Lévi had died in that year and Crowley believed himself to be Lévi's reincarnation; and also because in that same year, H. P. Blavatsky and Colonel H. S. Olcott had founded the Theosophical Society in New York.
67. See n. 16 above.
68. "Iniciado, por comunicação directa de Mestre a Discípulo, nos três graus menores da (aparentemente extinta) Ordem Templária de Portugal" (Pessoa 1986e: vol. III, 1429). See also Quadros (1986a: 18).

69. See Lopes (1993: 334). Note that Dix (2009: 74–5) proposes a different reading of a word in the fragment, which is indeed convincing. But it seems to me that this does not change the general meaning of it, considering that, even with this alternative reading, Pessoa still claims to have received some form of initiation and declares to be a Portuguese Templar.
70. See, for example, the fragment BNP/E3/54-91, published in Centeno (1985b: 41). For a broader discussion about this point, see Pasi (2001b: 700–704).
71. See Sena (1984: 112). Pessoa owned two copies of the book, one bound in a single volume and the other in the form of four separate pamphlets (see Pasi 2001b: 699, and n. 19). The book was printed in Paris in 1929, but due to lack of funds it was not bound and distributed until the following year, in London. On this, see d'Arch Smith (1987: 22). For this reason, Pessoa, who acquired the first two volumes of the *Confessions* in November 1929, could not have had this book prior to 1930.
72. The appendix is entitled "One Star in Sight". See Crowley (1973a: 325–38).
73. See Pasi 2001b.
74. BNP/E3/54–A-83. The fragment has been published in Pessoa (1988b: 129; see also Pasi 2001b: 709).
75. I have recently published the relevant part of Crowley's diary, which corresponds to the month of September 1930 (Pasi 2012). This part is missing from the typewritten copy at the Warburg Institute (YC/NS, 20), and was therefore inaccessible to me when the Italian first edition of this book was published (Pasi 1999). Symonds, however, must have used it for his biography, since he quotes from it. At least one significant element emerges from reading the diary: the performance of a ritual of initiation for Raul Leal (and possibly Pessoa himself), on which I will return later in this chapter. Furthermore, the diary obviously enables us to follow Crowley's movements and activities during his sojourn in Portugal with great precision. We can see that Crowley and Pessoa met at least three times, spending a whole afternoon together on two occasions. The Portuguese artist Victor Belém has published a study on the Crowley–Pessoa meeting and Crowley's suicide stunt (Belém 1995), using an earlier, unpublished version of the present study as a source. In 1996, Belém also organized an exhibition inspired by the episode: *Fernando Pessoa versus Aleister Crowley*, whose catalogue was published by the Casa Fernando Pessoa (Belém 1996). On the Crowley–Pessoa meeting, see also Castanho (1996), Alves (1997), Binet (1999–2000) and Dix (2009, 2012).
76. Cited in Symonds (1989: 452).
77. See Symonds (1989: 453).
78. *Ibid.*: 455.
79. See Pasi (2012: 259).
80. See Crowley (1979: 113, n. 66).
81. Sutin (2000: 354).
82. Interestingly, Pessoa, in a letter to his fiancée Ophélia Queiroz from 9 October 1929, alluded to the Boca do Inferno as a place for his possible suicide – a year before the orchestration of Crowley's faked suicide. See Pessoa (1990: 188).
83. The text appears in the entry in Crowley's diary from 21 September (Pasi 2012: 269). The letter was reproduced in Augusto Ferreira Gomes's article "O Mistério da Boca do Inferno", published in the magazine *O Notícias Ilustrado* on 5 October 1930. I do not know the meaning of "Hjsos", but "Tu Li Yu", according to Symonds, "is not the name of a Chinese sage or that of one of Crowley's incarnations, but merely 'toodle-oo' or 'good-bye'" (Symonds 1989: 455n.). This is confirmed by a joking letter that Crowley, signing with the pseudonym "Benjamin Q. Knickerbocker", wrote to Pessoa on 14 December 1930. In the letter Crowley was pretending to be an "expert" who had been asked to give an opinion about the affair. Concerning "Tu Li Yu" he observed: "I do not know the Sage Tu Li Yu – but Tooley-oo is jocose London slang for Au revoir" (Pessoa and Crowley 2010: 378). It is clear that Crowley was having fun with the stunt and wanted to make things sound mysterious enough for its intended audience. In fact, in a copy of his farewell note prepared expressly for Pessoa, he stated: "Tu Li Yu – name of a Chinese Sage (B.C. 3321) of whom A. C. claims to be an incarnation" (Pessoa and Crowley 2001: 146; Pessoa and Crowley 2010: 325). Another interesting detail, just to give an indication of how the plan was set up between Crowley and Pessoa: the cigarette case under which Ferreira Gomes found the letter to Jaeger was not Crowley's, but belonged to Pessoa's brother-in-law. Jorge de Sena, in his essay "Pessoa e a Besta", writes: "Crowley's cigarette case, one of the indicators that the police discovered at the location and used to identify the deceased, was … the property of the then Colonel Caetano Dias, brother-in-law of Fernando Pessoa, who had loaned it for the occasion; it was the colonel himself, currently the representative of the poet's legacy, who communicated this information to me" (Sena 1984: 173).
84. Both articles were entitled "Um caso estranho" ("A Strange Case").
85. We know now, on the basis of Crowley's diary, that the police were right: he did indeed leave Lisbon by train and crossed the Portuguese border in the late afternoon of the 23rd (Pasi 2012: 270). Symonds, who had access to Crowley's diary, states that Crowley left the country on the 24th, but he is here probably confused by the fact

that Crowley arrived in Paris only in the morning of that day (1989: 455). It would also appear that Pessoa's statement that he saw Crowley in Lisbon on the 24th was not sincere, and was part of the plan to exploit the stunt for publicity purposes.
86. "The Mystery of the Mouth of Hell".
87. See Symonds (1989: 455).
88. YC/NS, 20, p. 18.
89. YC/NS, 20, p. 20.
90. Pessoa (1982: 58–9).
91. The letter is dated 4 January 1931 (Pessoa 1982: 61).
92. Pessoa (1982: 66).
93. Israel Regardie, referring to the period following Crowley's expulsion from France (his voyage to Portugal took place during this same period), writes: "At this time Crowley was an inveterate reader and connoisseur of detective stories. He devoured them voraciously, partly because much of the time he was bored. Another reason was that he had once essayed a series of detective stories himself, patterned after an idealization of himself – a sleuth named Simon Iff" (Regardie 1993: 22). For the Iff stories, see Crowley (1987). As for Pessoa, Gaspar Simões himself suggested that his passion for detective novels might have inspired him to take part in the organization of the faked suicide: "Fernando Pessoa, a fan of detective stories – some of the few, if not the only, novels that he read with pleasure in his lifetime, "my opium", as he called them – and also the author of various stories in this genre, distributed among friends, saw himself with inner satisfaction as a character in a detective novel" (Simões 1991: 526). And it should of course be mentioned that Pessoa intended to write a novel in English based on Crowley's suicide stunt. Predictably, it would have been titled *The Mouth of Hell*. He wrote large sections of it, but never completed it. The extant parts have been published by Miguel Roza in the same book that also includes the Crowley–Pessoa correspondence (Pessoa and Crowley 2010: 503–64).
94. Turris (1986: 124; emphasis added).
95. Robin (1986: 275). Who was this "Colonel Etherton" or "Ettington" to whom Guénon referred? The only "English colonel" with whom Crowley had any close connection was Fuller, whom we met in Chapter 3. As we have seen, Fuller was actually in contact with Hitler. But the difference between the names in question is too great for us to suspect any confusion on Guénon's part, though he did seem uncertain of the spelling of this colonel's name. In fact, he was probably referring to Colonel Percy T. Etherton (1879–1963), an Englishman who had been the first to interview Hitler after he became chancellor in 1933. Guénon apparently got this information from a book by Henri Guilbeaux, *Où va l'Allemagne* (1933), in which Colonel Etherton (misspelled as "Etterton") is mentioned on p. 267. Guilbeaux claimed that Etherton had been part of the British Intelligence Service, which allegedly played an important role in Hitler's rise to power. Guilbeaux was a communist writer who had lived in Germany for a long time. In his book he endeavours to explain the historical reasons leading to the Nazi acquisition of power, revealing the secret background behind the events. Why Guénon would have connected Etherton to Crowley remains a mystery. In any case, Guénon must have been quite convinced of a Crowley–Etherton–Hitler link, given that he mentions it in at least two different places and over a substantial period of time (before and after the war). As for Trebitsch Lincoln, we noted his meeting with Gerald Hamilton earlier (see above, p. 87), as well as the apparent lack of any contact between him and Crowley. More recently, R. B. Spence (2000: 368, and 2008: *passim*) has also discussed a possible connection between Crowley and Trebitsch Lincoln. Spence notes that Trebitsch Lincoln, who had become a British national and had even been elected to Parliament in 1910, had been involved in anti-British propaganda in America during the war. However, while the British authorities took no particular pains over Crowley after his return, they had Trebitsch Lincoln extradited from the United States (apparently on the basis of false accusations) and imprisoned him for three years.
96. Pasi (2012).
97. This text should have been in the same file that contained the typewritten copy of Crowley's diary from 1926 to 1934 (YC/NS, 20). In the summary, there is the following entry: "Love and adventures in Berlin. 17 Apr 30 to 4 Jan 32. (Original in possession of Germer)". And then a handwritten note by Gerald Yorke saying: "Missing". About Crowley's diaries in general, and how they have reached us, see Pasi (2012: 255–8).
98. Gomes (1934). See also n. 64 above.
99. Simões (1991: 526) and Pessoa (1986c: 165, n. 5).
100. The name of the review, of course, came from Pessoa's poem of the same name. Ferreira Gomes's poem ("Canção absurda – À sir Edward Aleister Crowley") was published in no. 2, June 1938: "Eu ponho o fim no começo / Para melhor explicar ... / Onde é que está a verdade / – P'lo menos a que exponho – / E onde é que a realidade / Se mistura com o sonho? / Deus fez as coisas em fumo / E misturou-se lá dentro! / É ele que é o centro / De tudo a que deu seu rumo! / Mas o rumo é a vertígem / Sempre em plena confusão, / Em tremenda convulsão / Desde o fim até à origem! / Eu ponho fim no começo / Para melhor explicar ...". English translation: "I put an end to

the beginning / To explain it better … / Where is the truth / At least that which I expose – / And where is the reality / Mixed with the dream? / God put things in the smoke / And mixed them around in it! / It's he who is the centre / Of everything whose course he sets! / But the course is vertigo / Forever in complete confusion, / In tremendous convulsion / From the end to the origin! / I put an end to the beginning / To explain it better … ".

101. For biographical information on Leal, I refer to the entry on him in the *Grande Enciclopédia Portuguesa e Brasileira* (Grande Enciclopédia 1936–60, vol. 14: 779). See also Martins (2008).
102. The event is described in Simões (1991: book 2, part 9, ch. 4, "Polémica em Sodoma"). *Sodoma Divinizada* was published by Olisipo, the house founded by Pessoa mentioned earlier. A new edition of the pamphlet has been published in 1999, with the addition of a helpful chronology of events compiled by Aníbal Fernandes, as well as various documents relative to the debate (including the manifesto written by the students and Pessoa's response; Leal 1989). Recently, however, a more scrupulous edition of the texts, including some that were not included in the earlier editions, has been made by José Barreto (2012a).
103. YC/NS, 13.
104. See p. 102 above.
105. The letter is kept at the Warburg Institute: YC/OS, EE2. It consists of five typewritten pages. It is interesting to note that a carbon copy of the same letter is also present in Pessoa's archive: BNP/E3, 113F-62/66. This brings us to think that, when he wrote his letter, Leal also prepared a copy for Pessoa, so that his friend could be aware of developments in his contact with the British occultist.
106. *Ibid.*: "j'ai reconnu que vous êtes une individualité supérieure, sous les points de vue terrestre et astral, dont les doctrines s'approchent beaucoup des miennes, malgré les convictions que vous avez, d'être profondément intégré dans l'Empire de la Bête (Antéchrist-Raison: 666). J'ai donc pour vos opinions la plus haute considération et c'est pour cela que je désire avec ardeur savoir ce que vous pensez de mon poème …".
107. On the continuing influence of Joachim's ideas in the nineteenth and twentieth centuries, see Gould and Reeves (2001). It is interesting to see that Joachimist ideas had a very significant presence in Portugal in the early modern period and influenced Sebastianism since its earliest phases (*ibid*.: 30).
108. "À travers une progressive intensification de la vie des sens qui doit devenir de plus en plus profonde et de plus en plus bestiale" (YC/OS, EE2).
109. "Nous finirons par la diviniser, l'identifiant même avec la fureur créatrice de Dieu, fureur délirante, folle, vertigique" (*ibid.*).
110. "Les audacieux précurseurs du paraclétianisme" (*ibid.*).
111. "L'initiation dans le Monde Occulte n'a été faite que directement par Dieu et par moi-même" (*ibid.*).
112. Curiously, Leal also claims in the same paragraph (*ibid.*) that he "magically persecuted" Germany during the First World War, and that he was the cause of its defeat, "ce qui m'a obligé à subir de formidables chocs de retour consécutifs, presqu'aussi forts que celui qui a provoqué la tragédie du Calvaire" ("which forced me to go through formidable successive return shocks, almost as strong as that which caused the tragedy of Calvary"). Considering Crowley's activities during the war, one can only wonder what he might have thought of such a statement.
113. *Ibid.*: "J'espère que nos relations puissent devenir de plus en plus fraternelles et intenses: alors si un jour vous auriez le désir d'achever mon initiation, jusqu'à présent seulement esquissée, je suivrais avec promptitude vos indications ésotériques. Vous serez ainsi le Maître de la Haute Initiation du Prophète sacré de Dieu et de la Mort".
114. The letter has been published in *Persona*, a journal of Pessoa studies (see Leal 1982).
115. Unfortunately, this second letter from Crowley to Leal has not surfaced yet.
116. Leal (1982: 55): "falei muito sobre magia e ocultismo com *Mestre Therion* (666) (é claro, em francês) e a uma certa altura ele disse-me *que eu devia sair de Portugal porque era um meio muito pequeno para mim*" (emphasis original).
117. Crowley's diary, 9 September 1930 (Pasi 2012: 266). For a further discussion of this passage and its implications, see *ibid.*: 260–61.
118. "Sentir a oposição do meio é o princípio do estímulo da vitória. Isto me deu o Mestre Therion com autorização superior. Criar a desanalogia entre mim e o que me cerca – eis a primeira passada e a vigília que começa. A insatisfação, eis o início. Honra ao Mestre que deu, atravez da ironia do que succede, a verdade que existe para que não suceda. Assim sei que sou quem sou, e terei que o ser separadamente. A alta lição do escarneo alheio alberga astros em seu futuro" (BNP/E3, 299). The note has been published in Pessoa and Crowley (2010: 302–3). I transcribe the text here directly from the original, now preserved in the Espólio.
119. See above, p. 105, and n. 68.
120. " … nessa ocasião deu-se a "fita" *verdadeiramente mágica* da Boca do Inferno e nunca mais o vi, sabendo apenas pelo Fernando [Pessoa] que ele lhe tinha escrito afinal da Alemanha" (Leal 1982: 55).
121. However, the fact that Leal was less enthusiastic about Crowley when he wrote his letter to Gaspar Simões

becomes evident from his mentioning the possibility that a serious illness he had after their meeting, and perhaps even Pessoa's death, might both have been the result of a magical "vendetta" by Crowley, the latter having been displeased with the way Pessoa handled the Boca do Inferno affair after he left Portugal (*ibid.*: 56). It appears that Leal also discussed his relationship to Crowley with another Pessoa scholar: Jorge de Sena. In his aforementioned collection of essays on Pessoa, he writes: "And the very curious figure of Raul Leal, one of the survivors of the ORPHEU group, has provided me with some fascinating revelations concerning his meeting with Crowley in Portugal ... Among these revelations was the correspondence carried on earlier with Crowley, that adventurous promoter of occultism" (Sena 1984: 173).

122. Webb (1976: 182). On Keyserling, see more generally *ibid.*: 181–5. On his family relationship to Ungern-Sternberg, see *ibid.*: 200. See also Struve (1973: 274–316).
123. See Webb (1976: 185). Webb adds: "It seems that ... he took the Nazi regime as symbolic of the spiritual rebirth he had long been awaiting". Giorgio Galli (1995: 163) draws an analogy (convincingly, in my opinion) between the personality of Keyserling and that of Rudolf von Sebottendorff, another "prophet" of Nazism.
124. See Pedro Teixeira da Mota's commentary on the letter Pessoa wrote to Keyserling, in Pessoa (1988a: 43).
125. Keyserling (1919). See also Webb (1976: 183).
126. Pessoa (1988a).

5. Counter-initiation and conspiracy

1. There is now a vast literature on conspiracy theories. The best historical work on the early developments of conspiracy theories in relation to Freemasonry and secret societies remains Roberts (1972). Concerning conspiracy theories and Western esotericism, see also Webb (1976: 213–73), Introvigne (1990: 28–31), Politica Hermetica (1992), Mayer (1999), Taguieff (2005, 2012), Kreis (2011) and Dyrendal (2013). For a very useful anthology of texts, but focusing only on French sources, see also Kreis (2009).
2. Godwin (1994: 167).
3. I use here the term "traditionalism", even if this current, especially in North America, is sometimes also called "perennialism". For a critical, historical account of the current, see Sedgwick (2009). See also Faivre (1999). For the developments in the United States, but also with a useful discussion of the origins of the current, see Houman (2010). For an overview that is quite sympathetic to traditionalist views but offers some interesting insights, see Quinn (1997).
4. See Webb (1976: 129). On Webster, see also Chapter 3, p. 88 and n. 109 above.
5. See Cohn (1967: 25). Cohn refers to a "Jewish world-conspiracy", but then adds that the Jews did not play any role in Barruel's work. Instead, the French abbot's target was Freemasonry. On Barruel, and his book, see also Roberts (1972: 188–202).
6. Cohn (1967: 25).
7. See for instance what Crowley wrote to the German occultist Henri Birven, who had asked him for some information on *The Patriot*, an English right-wing journal (which we shall encounter again shortly) with a particular focus on conspiracy theories: "*The Patriot* is a 'journal d'opinion' of the basest class. It gets subscriptions and subsidies by playing on the fears and prejudices of people who see Jews and Bolsheviks everywhere; as in earlier days they saw witches, heretics or Jesuits" (letter from 8 October 1929; YC/NS, 24).
8. *The Patriot* was founded in 1922 by the Duke of Northumberland. It spread theories of international conspiracy in England (see Webb 1976: 129). Two of the most important figures in the British milieu of conspiracy theory contributed to it: Nesta Webster and Inquire Within (pseudonym of Christina M. Stoddart, or Stoddard). The review also distributed an English edition of *The Protocols of the Elders of Zion* (see Cohn 1967: 168). Various articles in the review were dedicated to Crowley, and some of these articles were also mentioned or quoted by the *RISS* – see especially "Aleister Crowley" in *RISS* 6 (1 June 1929), occultist section, p. 194. I have already mentioned *Der Judenkenner*, in relation to a letter from Crowley to Germer that confirms that the former was aware of these attacks (see n. 179 for Chapter 2). About these articles, Ellic Howe writes: "The appropriate office in Heinrich Himmler's Reichsicherheithauptamt no doubt carefully read the extraordinary series of articles on Theodor Reuss, the G.D. and Crowley that was published in the anti-Semitic periodical *Der Judenkenner* in 1936" (Howe 1985: 285, n. 1). In the series, whose real target was in fact Rudolf Steiner, Reuss was presented as the "grandfather" of Anthroposophy. Some of these articles are reproduced in facsimile in Koenig (1997: 340–44). As we will see in the second section of this chapter, the mid-1930s was also the period in which the Italian police took an interest in Crowley.
9. Massimo Introvigne, albeit in a different context, has also pointed out the attention paid to Crowley by the French anti-Masonic *Revue Internationale des Sociétés Secrètes* (Introvigne 1998: 89).
10. On Jouin and the *RISS*, see the important study by Emmanuel Kreis (2011: 604–919). On Jouin see also Sauvêtre (1936) – a sympathetic biography written by one of his admirers – and James (1981b, *sub voce* "Jouin, Ernest"). Norman Cohn (1967: 165) erroneously indicates 1909 as the date in which the *RISS* was founded.

11. Sauvêtre (1936: 177).
12. M.-F. James (1981b: 158). James adds that "the subject of his beatification has since been raised in Rome by 'the American friends of Monseigneur Jouin'". On the back dust jacket of the *RISS*, a passage was quoted from a Breve (*Præstantes animi laudes*) that Benedict XV dedicated to Jouin: "you have affirmed the rights of the Catholic Church with constancy and courage – not without peril to your life – against the sects enemy of religion, sparing nothing, neither labour nor expense, to distribute your works on these matters to the public …" (this appeared on the back cover of all the issues of the magazine in the 1920s and 1930s).
13. Cohn (1967: 166).
14. See Sauvêtre (1936: 202).
15. Léo Taxil was the pseudonym of Gabriel Jogand-Pagès (1854–1907). On him, see M.-F. James (1981b, *sub voce* "Taxil, Léo"). On the Taxil affair, see Kreis (2011: 229–464) and Introvigne (2010: 139–200). The "classic" Weber (1964) is also still useful.
16. Bersone (1932).
17. On the Bersone affair, see Kreis (2011: 746–9) and Introvigne (2010: 218–28). On the revival of the Taxil–Diana Vaughan case by the *RISS*, see Kreis (2011: 749–52) and Vannoni (1985: 223ff.). Vannoni has also discussed the *RISS* in relation to Italian fascism (Vannoni 1980: 170–75).
18. Here, in chronological order, is the sequence of articles appearing in the *RISS* that were devoted to Crowley, mentioned him or included translations of texts by him: (a) "L'Ordre Equestre du Saint-Sepulcre, M. Wellhoff et les Hautes Loges" by Lancelot, Masonic section, no. 6 (10 February 1929): 156–62; (b) "La querelle des Hauts Grades" by Roger Duguet, Masonic section, no. 9 (3 March 1929): 217–29; (c) "Atlantis et Amis de l'Atlantide", anonymous, Masonic section, no. 12 (24 March 1929): 299–301; (d) "L'OTO. Expulsion de Sir Aleister Crowley" by A. Tarannes, occultist section, no. 5 (1 May 1929): 133–45; (e) "Encore 'Atlantis'", anonymous, Masonic section, no. 20 (19 May 1929): 497–8; (f) "Aleister Crowley", anonymous, occultist section, no. 6 (1 June 1929): 194–6; (g) "Essai sur un symbole double: Quel est donc ce Dragon?" by A. Tarannes, occultist section, no. 7 (1 July 1929): 197–214; (h) "Une nouvelle Haute Loge in Allemagne", anonymous, occultist section, no. 12 (1 December 1929): 376–9; (i) "Les Missionnaires du Gnosticisme" by XX (Lesley Fry), Masonic section, nos. 19–20 (10 and 17 May 1931): 461–88; (j) "Le Manuscrit de Reuss, l'Encyclique et le Féminisme" by Olivier de Fremond, Masonic section, no. 23 (7 July 1931): 609–12; (k) "Aleister Crowley et l'OTO" by A. B., Masonic section, no. 27 (5 July 1931): 705–13; (l) "La Magie en Théorie et en Pratique – Par le Maître Therion", anonymous, occultist section, series appearing in nos. 3 (1 March 1931): 47–57, 4 (1 April 1931): 67–75, 5 (1 May 1931): 87–92, 6 (1 June 1931): 105–18, 7 (July-August-September 1931): 129–36, 8 (October 1931): 160–63; (m) "L'OTO. Les Constitutions" by A. B., occultist section, no. 3 (1 March 1931): 58–65. In the following I will refer to these articles by the letters indicated in this list. Some of the articles have been republished in *Théléma*, the bulletin of the "Société Aleister Crowley" in Nantes, edited by Christian Bouchet. Articles (f) and (g) appeared in no. 1 (1982); article (m) in no. 2 (1983); article (i) in nos. 8 and 9 (1985); and articles (c), (e), (j) and (k) in no. 10 (1985).
19. See article (a). The Equestrian Order of the Holy Sepulchre of Jerusalem is a Roman Catholic order of knighthood that has its origins in the early period of the Crusades, towards the end of the eleventh century. Pope Pius IX reorganized the Order in 1847.
20. Article (a): 160: "L'heure n'est plus, en effet, de dissimuler certains faits révélateurs à personne. Il est temps de rappeler ici à tous que, derrière la Maçonnerie politicienne du Grand Orient et de la Maçonnerie symbolique de la Grande Loge, aussi bien que derrière les Ateliers soi-disant réguliers d'Angleterre et d'Amérique existent, agissent et gouvernent quelques arrière-Loges ou Hautes Sectes, mal connues et d'autant plus redoutables: la vraie Synagogue de Satan, livrée à un Suprême Pouvoir occulte."
21. Article (a): 160: "L'une des machineries de ces coulisses de la Maçonnerie est l'A∴A∴, dont nous étudierons sous peu l'identité, et l'OTO."
22. See article (b).
23. Article (b): 229: "Bref, qu'on le veuille ou non, un Aleister Crowley existe; il est Maçon et chef d'une branche de la Maçonnerie, tout aussi régulièrement maçonnique que le calvinisme est protestant sans être luthérien." This article is also important because it cites *The Equinox*, vol. 3, no. 1; we therefore know that this was one of the sources used by the authors of the *RISS* for their research on Crowley.
24. See articles (c) and (e).
25. In an article in the *Sunday Express*, 26 November 1922, at a time of hot debate concerning the publication of Crowley's novel *The Diary of a Drug Fiend*, the name of the A∴A∴ was interpreted as "Atlantean Adepts" (cited in Stephensen and Regardie 1983: 138). What is the origin of this interpretation? The legend of Atlantis is a theme recurring frequently in literature of theosophical inspiration, beginning with Blavatsky's writings. Although the actual expression "Atlantean Adepts" does not seem to occur in her works, it is found in the text of a lecture given in San Francisco in 1897 by Countess Constance Wachtmeister (1838–1910), a well-known

member of the Theosophical Society and a personal friend of Madame Blavatsky; see Wachtmeister (1897: 8–9), cited in Godwin (1990: 40). I have earlier mentioned the ideal connection between conspiracy theories and the doctrines of Blavatskyan theosophy. Considering the later use of the expression "Atlantean Adepts", it is interesting to note that the context in which it appeared for the first time was theosophical. In fact, Countess Wachtmeister mentions these mysterious "adepts" in order to explain the origin of spiritualism. According to her – and expressing an opinion that had its roots in Blavatsky's own writings – this movement was none other than the result of a plan conceived and put into operation secretly by the Atlantean Adepts in order to draw humanity away from the growing danger of materialism. As Godwin shows in an article published in 1990 (Godwin 1990), these theories, especially regarding the origin of spiritualism, were fairly widespread in certain spiritualist and esoteric circles during the late nineteenth and early twentieth centuries. It is very tempting to interpret them as a "positive" version of the structurally similar ideas that could be found in the literature of conspiracy theories.

26. Crowley meant the true name of his initiatory order to remain secret (see Regardie 1993: 359; Eshelman 2000: 23). Several authors interpret the initials as standing for a Latin name, *Astrum Argentinum* or *Argenteum Astrum* (i.e. "Silver Star"). However, there are some indications that for Crowley the initials stood for a Greek name, even if commentators differ as to its actual form. In his *Aleister Crowley and the Hidden God*, Crowley's ex-disciple and secretary Kenneth Grant stated that "the one place in Crowley's writings where he gives the meaning of the initials A∴A∴ is in his Magical Record (Cefalu, 1921) where it appears as ACTHP APΓOC [Aster Argos]" (Grant 1973: 59). On the other hand, James A. Eshelman, who represents one of the several contemporary filiations of the Order and who has written a very interesting introduction to its history and teachings, observes that "it is AΣTPON APΓON [Astron Argon], not AΣTHP APΓOΣ [Aster Argos] that we find recorded at least twice in Crowley's handwriting (once in a note, and once in an official document). Any other claims regarding the actual name of the Order must take second place to this" (Eshelman 2000: 23). None of the two authors give exact references to the sources they mention. Whatever the case, it should be noted that these Greek versions have the same meaning as the Latin ones (i.e. "Silver Star").
27. Guénon's reviews of articles published in *Atlantis* have been reprinted in Guénon (1986a: 119ff.). Guénon was highly interested in the myth of Atlantis and often engaged in polemical debates with the director of *Atlantis*, Paul Le Cour, whom he rebuked especially for using sources that were not reliable or serious enough. On Charbonneau-Lassay see Salzani and Zoccatelli (1996) and Zoccatelli (1999). The latter contains various unpublished documents by Charbonneau-Lassay, including Guénon's letters to him.
28. See article (d).
29. See article (d): 135.
30. See Tarannes (1929a: 43–68).
31. See Evola (1978).
32. Article (d): 133: "car le régime mussolinien s'accomode à la rigueur, comme on l'a vu pour Evola, d'un certain satanisme, mais à la condition que cet occultisme soit lui-même marqué de l'estampile fasciste".
33. See article (f).
34. *Ibid.*: 196: "selon l'opinion de Crowley, le Christianisme a fini la partie, une ère nouvelle va commencer, l'ère, évidemment, du Culte du Serpent, du culte sexuel, 'rédempteur de l'humanité'! – le Pouvoir de l'Illuminisme et de la domination Judéo-Maçonnique".
35. See article (i).
36. See Fry (1934). Fry's real name was Paquita Shishmarev (born Louise A. Chandor, 1882–1970; her surname in French sources is also spelled as Chichmarev). She was a renowned anti-Semite and conspiracy theory activist during the interwar period, and a staunch supporter of the authenticity of *The Protocols of the Elders of Zion*. On her see Cohn (1967: 70–71, 167), Introvigne (2010: 189) and Kreis (2011: 654). Fry's article was originally published anonymously in the *RISS* and this has caused some confusion about its authorship. The author writing under the pseudonym of Louis de Maistre (2004: 882–3) suggests that the author was Henri de Guillebert des Essars, another *RISS* contributor, but he seems to be missing the fact that Fry later republished the article in her book, which made her authorship obvious.
37. Article (i): 487: "Ne nous y trompons pas, la Russie, pour l'instant, devient un maigre coin de terre gangrené, dont le cancer envahit le monde. Par quoi? Par les sociétés secrètes, aux innombrables vidangeurs, disciples des Reuss e des Crowley, qui s'appellent bolchévistes et judéomaçons."
38. See articles (k), (l) and (m).
39. Hutchinson (1998: 137–62).
40. ACS, PS, AAGR, 1903–49, RG, b. 1, fasc. 20. The file is cited in Mola (1992: 445–6). On the spelling of Crowley's name in the file, see below, n. 63.
41. Born in France, Ledit taught at the Institute from 1929 to 1939. He was also a man of action and worked as a kind of "secret agent" for the Vatican. In 1926, together with another Jesuit father, he was entrusted by the president of the Institute, Michel d'Herbigny (1880–1957), with the mission of establishing a clandestine

Catholic seminar in Soviet Russia. The mission however failed, and he was soon expelled from the country. He was primarily a specialist in the Slavic world and in communism, subjects on which he wrote for the Jesuit journal *Civiltà Cattolica*. In the 1930s he published at least two critical books about communism: *La religione e il comunismo* (Ledit 1937) and *Paradossi del comunismo* (Ledit 1938). He moved to Canada in 1939, and after the war he appears to have taken interest especially in questions of orthodox liturgy (Ledit 1976). On Ledit (especially his mission in Russia), see Poggi (1987) and Stehle (1981: 109). Poggi (1987) has been republished in an Italian version in Poggi (2000: 257–86), which is also useful for the history of the Pontifical Institute for Oriental Studies more in general. On the Institute, see also Farrugia (1993).

42. See Lacouture (1991: vol. 1, 420) and Veneruso (1987: 177–86).
43. There are also references to Ledit in File 21 of the same collection, entitled "Compagnia di Gesù – Lotta contro il bolscevismo" ("Society of Jesus – Fight against Bolshevism"). Despite Ledit's significant role and his contacts with Leto, Fiorentino ignores him in his study on the relationship between fascist intelligence services and the Catholic Church (Fiorentino 1999). The same goes for Canosa's study on the fascist secret police, the so-called OVRA, and their informers (Canosa 2000).
44. Between 1926 and 1939 Baker White was the director of the Economic League, an anti-communist organization founded in London in 1919 by industrialists and conservative politicians. The primary goal of the organization, which remained active until its dissolution in 1993, was to halt the perceived influence of left-wing "subversion" on British society. During the interwar period it collaborated with other right-wing organizations, creating a network that engaged in private intelligence activities with both political and industrial purposes. Its activities included collecting sensitive information about left-wing groups and activists. On Baker White and the Economic League, see Hughes (2012) and Hollingsworth and Tremayne (1989).
45. Pasi (1999, 2006).
46. Spence (2008: 229). It should be remembered that Knight was probably one of the sources of inspiration for the character of "M" in Ian Fleming's James Bond novel series, as even the title of his biography by A. Masters, *The Man Who Was M*, indicates (Masters 1984).
47. It should be added that, if these hypotheses were founded, we would also have to assume that Ledit misleadingly referred to "M" as a woman in order to cover his real identity.
48. I would like to thank Henry van Sanderburg for suggesting her name to me. Among her books from that period, see Godden (1929, 1935, 1937).
49. Godden (1923).
50. In her study on women and fascism in Great Britain, Gottlieb mentions her only cursorily (Gottlieb 2003: 12, 35 n. 3, and 304), but does offer a few interesting details. According to her (referring to a file from the Home Office archives), "Godden was ... responsible for sending the Home Office reports on the activities of the Kibbo Kift Kindred and the Federation of British Youth in 1925" (*ibid.*: 35, n. 3). We learn thus that Godden, ten years before her letters to Father Ledit included in the file we are discussing, was already acting as an informer on "suspect" groups, in this case for the British Home Office. For the rest, I have been able to gather only scant biographical information. For what we can determine from the Registration Birth Indexes for England and Wales, Gertrude Mary Godden was born in Surbiton, Surrey, in 1867. She was the only daughter of William and Mary, as we learn from the 1871 census of England and Wales. The family, who resided in different places in Surrey, south-west of London, is also listed in subsequent censuses for 1881, 1901 and 1911. In 1911, when she was 44, Godden was still single and living with her parents. She seems to have been interested in folklore and anthropology in her youth. A Miss Gertrude M. Godden, from Wimbledon, is in fact mentioned as a member of the Folk-Lore Society in the first issue of the society's journal (*Folk-Lore: A Quarterly Review of Myth, Tradition, Institution, and Custom* I, 1890: 557). She also published several articles in *Folk-Lore*, in the *Journal of the Anthropological Institute*, and in *The Journal of American Folklore* between 1892 and 1899. One of her articles from the latter journal, devoted to tribal cultures in North-East India was also reprinted as a booklet (Godden 1896). From Godden's publications in the 1920s and 1930s we understand that she was a Catholic, although it is difficult to know whether she was born and raised in a Catholic family or converted later in life. In any case she contributed regularly to the British Catholic journal *The Tablet* and published her books with the renowned Catholic press Burns, Oates and Washbourne. She is however not mentioned (apart from one of her books in the bibliography) in the recent study by Tom Villis on British Catholics and fascism (Villis 2013). A letter to the editor of *The Tablet*, published on 12 November 1936, p. 845, tells us that Godden was then living in 49 Grosvenor Street, London. This is around the time when she was corresponding with Father Ledit. The fact that Godden was a Catholic and shared many of Ledit's interests (the spread of communism and the religious situation in the Slavic world under the influence of Soviet Russia, for which see for instance Godden 1929, 1939), and that "M" was the initial of her middle name (Mary), leaves little doubt that she was indeed Ledit's correspondent. From the Death Index of the General Register Office for England and Wales, we learn that Godden died in 1947. It should also be noted that a Miss Gertrude M.

Godden, O.B.E., was president of the Royal College of Nursing, London, from 1956 to 1958, but this must obviously be just a namesake.
51. The first letter from "M" is dated 25 September 1935, the second 20 April 1936 and the third 28 May 1936. The file does not contain the originals, but typed copies, probably made by Ledit himself for passing on to his police contacts. For the complete text of the letters, see Appendix 2.
52. Hughes (2012: 50–68). See also Porter (1992: 165).
53. Hughes (2012: 59). Baker White himself tells the story of his involvement in Makgill's Section D in one of his autobiographical books (White 1970), but as Hughes observes (Hughes 2012: 51), his version of the story is only partly reliable and constantly needs to be checked with independent sources.
54. White (1970: 130). See also Hughes (2012: 61) and Spence (2008: 190).
55. White (1970: 131). See also Hughes (2012: 61).
56. Hughes (2012: 65).
57. See Spence (2008: 218, 224–5).
58. L'Ordre Nouveau was a political and cultural movement founded in Paris in the early 1930s, whose organ was the journal with the same name published between 1933 and 1938. The movement was animated by young intellectuals such as Alexandre Marc, Robert Aron, Arnaud Dandieu and Denis de Rougemont. It was part of that French "non-conformist" galaxy of the 1930s, ideally close to similar "third way" movements that came to life in the same period in various other European countries, and which of course included New Britain. The classic study of these movements in France is Loubet del Bayle (1969). On the connections between New Britain and L'Ordre Nouveau, see *ibid.*: 113, Webb (1976: 194) and Passerini (1999: 127–8). Contacts between movements such as New Britain and L'Ordre Nouveau were not casual or episodic. Both groups felt they were part of a larger European phenomenon, which came close to becoming an actual international network, if one with uncertain and asymmetric boundaries. For instance, unlike New Britain, one of L'Ordre Nouveau's referents in Germany was Otto Strasser's Black Front, a dissident movement ideologically close to Nazism (see Loubet del Bayle 1969: 102–3, 113).
59. See Webb (1976: 139).
60. Concerning the first meeting, see Chapter 3, n. 30. From what Crowley wrote in his diary about this meeting, it appears that on this occasion he tried to "convert" Adler to the religion of Thelema. The passage from the diary to which I refer is cited in Symonds (1989: 451). Regarding the 1931 meeting, see *ibid.*: 470. Symonds also writes that Karl Germer, Crowley's disciple and successor as head of the OTO, was a patient of Adler's for some time in Vienna.
61. Letter of 28 May 1936 from M. to Ledit.
62. The alternative spelling in the parenthesis, which has been clearly added by the person (probably Ledit himself) who typed Godden's letters from the original handwritten version, seems to indicate that, contrary to Godden's supposition, Ledit was not familiar with Crowley's name.
63. This includes Crowley's very name on the file, which appears as the commissioner spells it in his letter.
64. The Italian writer Leonardo Sciascia (1921–89) wrote a curious piece regarding Crowley's expulsion from Italy ("Apocrifi sul caso Crowley", in Sciascia 1973). The tale reconstructs a presumed correspondence between Mussolini, Italian Police Chief De Bono and the police commissioner of Cefalù, leading to the decision to expel Crowley. Sciascia clearly mixes fact and fiction. His sources for the factual part however are not clear. It is possible that he found documents related to the case during one of his frequent research visits to the Sicilian public archives. There is at least one interesting chronological "error" in the tale: Sciascia dates Crowley's expulsion to September 1924, more than a year after the actual event. This, which was probably intended, allows him to attribute to Crowley a dramatic, but indeed apocryphal, quote concerning the murder of Giacomo Matteotti (1885–1924) by a fascist squad. When, during an inspection of the Abbey, the police commissioner inquires about a square stone stained with blood, presumably used for sacrifices, Crowley bursts out: "At least the Honourable Matteotti was not slain here" (Sciascia 1973: 130). On Sciascia's tale and its sources, see also Saja (1998: 77–8).
65. As Symonds correctly points out (1989: 329), the order was only for the expulsion of Crowley, and not of the other members of the Abbey.
66. Letter from the Police Commissioner of Palermo to Police Chief Arturo Bocchini, 6 June 1936, ACS, PS, AAGR, 1903–49, RG, b. 1, fasc. 20. See Appendix 2 for the full text of the letter (pp. 160–2).
67. This was Ninette Shumway, who stayed at the Abbey for some years after Crowley's departure (see Symonds 1989: ch. 28: "In the Hands of the Gods").
68. The work was printed privately in Tunis; it consisted of a single sheet, folded in two and printed on all four of the pages thus formed. Later that same year it was printed in London, also privately, in an expanded edition of fifteen pages. Interestingly enough, the title probably echoes a poem by Algernon Charles Swinburne (1837–1909), an author who was very dear to Crowley and whose style influenced his poetry considerably. In

1867 Swinburne published a *Song for Italy*, dedicated to Giuseppe Mazzini, where he celebrated the accomplishments of the Italian Risorgimento (Swinburne 1867).
69. Crowley (1923: 15).
70. Letter by Norman Mudd, dated 15 September 1923 and with the letterhead of the Tunisia Palace Hotel, Tunis. In YC, EMH 1160.
71. The catalogue of the "Affari Generali e Riservati" section at the ACS dates this file to July 1936.
72. ACS, PS, AAGR, 1903–49, RG, b.1, fasc.16, p. 1: "Massoneria e giudaismo: due potenze che, in ragione del loro carattere internazionale e delle aspirazioni politiche che ne risultano debbono necessariamente essere, come sono, nemiche implacabili d'ogni Stato nazionale internamente saldo, che senta altamente di sè e del proprio onore."
73. *Ibid.*: "ignorano il concetto di 'Patria' e ... in forza dei propri vincoli internazionali, tenderanno sempre a contrastare le aspirazioni e gli sforzi dei popoli, in quanto tali aspirazioni non si accordino coi princìpi, da esse sostenuti, dell'internazionalismo, dell'incondizionata tolleranza, del pacifismo e quindi del marxismo in generale".
74. See De Felice (1993: 249, 551–3).
75. "Se mi occupo anzitutto della massoneria, si è perché ritengo che, data l'eguale situazione che si ha in Italia e in Germania, regnerà pieno accordo circa il modo di affrontare tale problema" (ACS, PS, AAGR, 1903–49, RG, b.1, fasc.16, p. 1). This statement is an indication of the fact that although there were no differences in the views the two regimes took of Masonry, Judaism was not considered as a significant target yet by fascist authorities, although things were certainly in motion. This interpretation is confirmed by R. De Felice (1993: 248ff.). It is worth noting that the author of this report regarded Judaism as a problem in any case, or even as the root of the entire problem. This means, at least, that the author did not share the disinclination to anti-Jewish action that the fascists still had in 1936 (see *ibid.*: 249).
76. The author claims that the coordinating and directing organ of worldwide Freemasonry is the "Suprème Conseil" of the Scottish Rite.
77. On p. 10 of the report, the author states: "Il patto franco-sovietico [sic] è il primo gradino verso la repubblica mondiale giudeo-massonica!" ("The Franco-Soviet pact is the first step toward the worldwide Judeo-Masonic republic!"). Here, the French government at the time is cast as the epitome of the political influence of Freemasonry, while the Bolshevism of the Soviet Union is simply the other side of this same coin. Nothing, then, would make more sense than a pact between these two governments.
78. Doc. p. 11: "logge pansofiche e occultistiche e la teosofia, la quale, attraverso l'*Ordo Templi Orientalis* e la loggia "Droit Humain", è in stretto rapporto con gli altri [sic] gradi della massoneria francese". *Altri*, meaning "other", is probably a misprint for *alti*, meaning "high".
79. There is now a considerable amount of literature on these two traditionalist authors, but much of it is produced by sympathizers. On Guénon, and focusing particularly on aspects relevant for the present study, see Laurant (1975, 1985, 2006) and de Maistre (2004). On Evola: Rossi (1991), Boutin (1992), Lippi (1998), Di Vona (2000), Hakl (2001), Cassata (2003), Chiantera-Stutte (2003) and Furlong (2011). On both: Politica Hermetica (1987), Di Vona (1993) and Sedgwick (2009).
80. See Guénon (1965: 33–42).
81. On the *RISS*-Guénon polemic, see James (1981a, *passim*) and Robin (1986: 269–71). See also the pertinent remarks in Rousse-Lacordaire (1998: 89–92).
82. Letter from Guénon to Charbonneau-Lassay from 30 March 1929, cited in Zoccatelli (1999: 55–7).
83. *Ibid.*
84. Guénon (1986b: vol. 1, 149). Guénon was referring to article (d) from the list in n. 18 above.
85. Guénon (1965: vol. 2, 373).
86. Crowley was initiated into the Anglo-Saxon Lodge, while Guénon became a member of the Thébah Lodge. Both were affiliated with the Grand Lodge of France (see Starr 1995; Rivet 1985).
87. Cited in Robin (1986: 273–4).
88. See above, p. 123 and n. 36. See also Robin (1986: 273, n. 16).
89. In January 1935 Guénon had reviewed Fry's book in *Le Voile d'Isis* (the review was later republished in Guénon 1986b: 102–4). Guénon does not explicitly mention Crowley or the OTO in his review, but he does make reference to Fry's article, to which I have drawn attention earlier (see n. 36 above), as a probable "key" for understanding the reasons behind this later republication of the Taxil debate. L. de Maistre (2004: 882, n. 334), states that it was the simple fact of the article's republication that offered Guénon the "proof" in question.
90. J. Symonds (1989: 389) describes him as a "secondary-school teacher and editor of the periodical *Hain der Isis* of Berlin-Wittenau". See also the interesting letter from Karl Germer to Crowley, cited *ibid.*, in which Birven is mentioned. According to Symonds, this letter reveals the "soteriological hopes that Birven and other European occultists of the 1920s had in the person of Aleister Crowley" (*ibid.*: 439). Birven and Crowley broke off relations in May 1930, as can be seen from their correspondence (see YC/NS, 24).

91. YC/NS, 116: "Guénon dit dans une polémique avec la *Revue Int[ernationale] des Sociétés Secrètes* (*Voile d'Isis*, octobre 1929) que, si vous vous présentiez à la moindre loge d'apprentis, vous seriez éconduit à la porte avec tous les honneurs dûs à votre rang. (!) C'est idiot, mais il prouve, cela aussi, qu'on ne vous connaît pas."
92. "Merci de votre lettre du 21, qui m'est parvenu [sic] hier soir à la campagne. Les singeries de M. la Guenon m'amusent. Qu'elle [sic, for 'Quelle'] combine!" (YC/NS, 24).
93. YC/OS, D 12. Watkins is a London bookshop, still in business, specializing in esotericism.
94. Later, in 1946, a short-lived *Revue des Sciences Secrètes* was founded by Jean Fervan.
95. L. de Maistre (2004: 114, n. 100) cites an unpublished letter written by Guénon on 22 May 1932, shortly after the polemic with the *RISS*. In this letter Guénon again downplays the "magical" and "initiatory" dangers posed by Crowley and the OTO, instead attributing to them a negative influence on the political plane: "Je ne pense pas qu'il faille les [des actions magiques] attribuer à l'OTO, qui n'est guère dangereuse que politiquement; Cr[owley] est surtout un espion doublé d'un escroc et je crois fort peu à ses pouvoirs de magicien" ("I do not think one should attribute magical actions to the OTO, which is hardly dangerous, except politically; Crowley is above all a double agent and a conman, and I have very little belief in his powers as a magician"). Unfortunately, de Maistre does not indicate to whom this letter was addressed.
96. Guénon (1996: 111).
97. Guénon returned to the subject of Crowley, more or less on the same terms, in a review of the famous issue of *Études Carmélitaines* dedicated to Satan (1948), appearing in *Études Traditionnelles* in 1949. See Guénon (1986a: 195).
98. On the differing opinions held by Evola and Guénon concerning Freemasonry, see Julius Evola, *Scritti sulla massoneria* (1984); the book includes an ample introduction by Renato Del Ponte and an appendix of Guénon's writings.
99. On this point see also Appendix 1, by H. T. Hakl.
100. On the Italian Philosophical Rite, see Sestito (2003b). See also Bisogni (1981: 88–103) and the two biographies of Arturo Reghini, which contain useful information concerning these events (Sestito 2003a; Di Luca 2003). It is also interesting to have a look at Frosini's book, where he presents his vision for the renovation of Italian Freemasonry (Frosini 1911). Another collaborator in Frosini's Masonic initiative was Amedeo R. Armentano, an important figure in the Italian esoteric circles of the time. See Armentano (1992: 75–7).
101. A copy of the diploma (which was in the possession of Kenneth Grant), bearing the signatures of Frosini and Reghini, can be found in King (1975: plate 60). The diploma is dated thus: *ab Urbe condita* MMDCLXVI, which corresponds to 1913. Renato Del Ponte (1994: 22) erroneously interprets this date as 1911. On the presence of Frosini's and Reghini's names in the OTO's Golden Book, see R. A. Gilbert (1997a: 21). Regarding this connection, there is also a typed transcription of a letter, undated but datable to around 1913, from Crowley to Frosini. It is simply a recommendation on behalf of a member of the OTO, John Daniel Reelfs, who is about to travel to Italy. See YC/NS, 12, lett. 75, and Koenig (1994a: 36). Finally, there are references to Crowley, Reuss and the OTO in at least two letters dated 1913 from Reghini to Armentano, which are quoted in Sestito (2003b: 122, 129). The irony is that Reghini was led to consider the OTO as a serious initiatic organization because it claimed to be a direct filiation of the Hermetic Brotherhood of Luxor (H.B. of L.), about which Guénon had expressed himself with respect. About Guénon's attitude towards the H.B. of L., see Godwin et al. (1995: 428–30).
102. The only trace of a connection between Crowley and Italian esoteric milieus after that date, which coincides also with his expulsion from Sicily, is with a man who did not belong to the circle of persons involved in the Italian Philosophical Rite, and who were therefore indirectly connected to the OTO. This is Giuseppe Cambareri (1901–72), an eccentric and enigmatic figure in the political and esoteric landscape of interbellum Italy. A detailed biographical account of Cambareri can be found in Corvisieri 2001. Cambareri lived for a long time in South America and was a disciple of Arnoldo Krumm-Heller (1876–1949), a German occultist who had a close relationship with Crowley (especially during his period in Berlin) and founded a Fraternitas Rosicruciana Antiqua related to the OTO, which spread especially in Latin America. Cambareri's biographer Corvisieri notes that Crowley and Cambareri met in London in 1936, and that an inscribed copy of *The Equinox of the Gods* was given by Crowley to Cambareri as a present on that occasion (see Corvisieri 2001: 58). Crowley's diary for 1936 confirms that the meeting took place: on 15 November we find an entry that reads: "Arrival (from Dr Krum Heller) of Giuseppe Cagliostro Cambereri [sic] going to via Pietro della Valle 2 Roma" (YC/NS 21, 1). On Corvisieri's book see also Pasi (2005d).
103. The book is *Wissenschaft und Buddhismus*, published by the company founded by Crowley's German admirers, the Thelema Verlag. This is a German translation of Crowley's *Science and Buddhism* (1903), published in vol. 2 of the *Collected Works* (1973c: 244–61).
104. Recently, the hypothesis has been advanced that Evola was a member of the OTO prior to the Second World War, on the basis of a document, dated 7 April 1930, discovered at the Central Archives of the State in Rome (see Fenili 1997: 294–5). It is an intriguing hypothesis, but one that does not seem to be founded on solid

enough evidence. It is to be noted that the same document contains various other inexactitudes, such as the claim that Crowley was expelled from other countries than Italy and France. This appears to be the typical document of a low-profile police informant, who did not necessarily have other sources of information than the sensationalist press. It is actually even likely that the informant took some of his information from the articles in the *RISS*, where, as I have noted, an indirect connection between Evola and Crowley had already been suggested (see above, p. 122).

105. See, besides the letter already cited, the letters from 18 April, 13 June and 2 August 1949 (Guénon 1996: 65–103). It would be fascinating to read Evola's letters to Guénon, in order to see what approach Evola took to this argument, but unfortunately his side of the correspondence remains unpublished and inaccessible for the time being. See R. Del Ponte's introduction in Guénon (1996: 15–16).
106. See Guénon (1996: 79–80, 93–4).
107. On this aspect, see Montanari (2001). Also, more particularly with reference to Crowley, see *ibid.*: 61–2.
108. See the abridged English translation: Gruppo di Ur (2001).
109. *Liber Aleph* was finally published in 1961.
110. Gruppo di Ur (1955: vol. 3, 437).
111. *Ibid.*: 438.
112. Evola devotes a certain number of pages to Crowley in his *Metafisica del sesso*, first published in 1958 (Evola 1969: 384–9). He returns to Crowley again in *Maschera e volto dello spiritualismo contemporaneo* (Evola 1971: 179–86; the 1st edition is from 1932; the references to Crowley were added to the 1971 edition, which was the third). See also his preface to the Italian edition of J. Symonds's biography (Evola 1972a); and the interview with Gianfranco de Turris, in which he, with some reservations, confirms his view of Crowley as a true initiate (Turris 1985: 337).
113. Roger Lipsey makes no reference to Crowley in his biography of Coomaraswamy (Lipsey 1977). During his period in the United States, Crowley wrote a story as part of the Simon Iff series ("Not Good Enough") in which one of the characters, named Haramzada Swamy, is based on Coomaraswamy. The story was published in the review *The International* in January 1918, and has been included in the collection edited by Martin P. Starr: Crowley, *The Scrutinies of Simon Iff* (1987: 125–50). Crowley subsequently published a review of Coomaraswamy's book *The Dance of Shiva* (1918) in *The Equinox* 3(1) (1919): 292–4. The review was actually a pretext for launching an unusually violent personal attack upon Coomaraswamy. Crowley later devoted a few pages to his relationship to Coomaraswamy in his *Confessions* (1989: 773–6). See also Kaczynski (2010: 298–301, 304, 307–8) and, especially, with a thorough analysis of the episode and the possible motives of Coomaraswamy in his relationship with Crowley, Houman (2010: 157–66).
114. Crowley (1989: 773).
115. Spence (2008: 125–6, 142).
116. From this correspondence, only the letters from Guénon to Coomaraswamy (numbering over a hundred) are available, in the form of an unpublished typed version. I wish to thank Jean-Pierre Laurant for providing me with a copy.
117. See Lipsey (1977: 105–16) and Antliff (2001: 131–2).

Conclusion

1. One clear example is the (now probably defunct) New Zealand extreme right-wing Crowleyan group "The Thelemic Society", which I have mentioned earlier, and whose highly politicized interpretation of Crowley is evident in their publications.

Appendix 1. Some additional remarks on Julius Evola and Aleister Crowley

1. Evola (1932).
2. Emilio Servadio, the "father of Italian psychoanalysis", made the following comment on this subject in an interview concerning his collaboration with the magical initiatory group *UR*: "I helped Evola a little, because I had a better command of English than he did, and so I was also able to help him with the translation of a few articles" (in Errera 1990: 47ff.).
3. Crowley (1961).
4. Evola must already have had the manuscript by 1953, because in his introduction to the excerpts from the *Liber Aleph*, "Prospettive magiche (secondo Aleister Crowley)", in Gruppo di Ur (1955: vol. III, 438), he writes that the book "until now [1953] only exists as a manuscript".
5. Reprinted in *Ultimi scritti* (Evola 1977: 46–55) and in *I testi del Roma* (Evola 2008: 487–9). This volume collects all articles written by Evola for *Roma*.
6. Reprinted in Turris (1985: 332–54; here 347).
7. Dr Herbert Fritsche in *Merlin* 3 (1950): 64.

8. *Gnostika* 11(37) (December 2007): 57ff.
9. A short summary of Birven's life and ambivalent attitude toward Crowley is in Koenig (2001: 101–4). See also the "Afterword" in *Oriflamme Sonderheft* by Dr Clemens Henri Birven (2002: 156–7). This volume is an enlarged (print size) reprint of the article series of the same name from the journal *Oriflamme*, 1971-2.
10. Excerpts from *Magick in Theory and Practice*, *The Psychology of Hashish* and Crowley's *Confessions*, published in Birven's own review, *Hain der Isis*.
11. On this, see the *Ergänzung und Richtigstellung zum Nachruf auf Karl Germer* sent along with a letter to the Psychosophische Gesellschaft, Zurich, on 29 September 1963, as well as the "Vorbemerkung der Schriftleitung" for Birven's series of articles, "Meine Begegnung mit dem 'Meister Therion'", in *Hain der Isis* (August/September 1930): 258.
12. Birven (2002: 139–41).
13. Reduced facsimile in Koenig (2000: 178).
14. Birven (1960: 17; emphasis added).
15. Birven (1953: 76).
16. *Ibid.* (emphasis added).
17. Letter to Hans Thomas Hakl. The letter is printed in Evola (1996: 158).
18. E.g. in Birven (1960: 17, 28, 80, 97, 113).
19. Birven first mentions Evola in writings from after the Second World War.
20. He mentions this review in a letter to Crowley from 21 October 1929.
21. By Ansata publishing house in Munich.
22. In the archives of the Austrian branch of the Pansophic Society (Heinrich Tränker), there is a typed copy of Küntzel's translation in which the text corresponds precisely to the printed version of 2003, but the succession of sections is slightly different.
23. Crowley (2003: 46).
24. In his letter from 28 September 1963 to the Psychosophische Gesellschaft in Zürich, he writes that he has "several individual essays on Crowley's writings at hand, ready to print" and has also written a "comprehensive essay" on him.
25. As Marco Pasi has told me, this was not the first press report about Crowley in Italy. At the Warburg Institute, there is an article about him that was published in 1952 in the right-wing newspaper *Il Borghese*. Evola might have known about this article; soon afterwards, on 1 March 1953, his own first article in that paper was published.
26. In theory it could also have been John Symonds who gave Evola the manuscript of the *Liber Aleph*. In 1972, Symonds's book *The Great Beast* was published in Italian translation with a foreword by Evola. Even if Evola mentioned Symonds for the first time only in 1959 in a newspaper article, he might still have known him earlier. On the other hand, this theory seems unlikely because Symonds was not at all generous in sharing manuscripts.
27. See the facsimile of the report in *Politica Romana* 4(1997): 296.
28. This, at least, emerges from his article "Fu Evola affiliato all'ordine magico di Aleister Crowley?" in *Politica Romana* (Fenili 1997). See also Pasi's discussion above, p. 204, n. 104.
29. The most striking example of this is his non-membership in the magical groups led by Giuliano Kremmerz (Ciro Formisano), whom Evola esteemed highly.
30. Tarannes (1928, 1929a).
31. Tarannes (1929b).The next article in this issue of the journal is a French translation of the OTO's manifesto.
32. Del Ponte (1996: 14).
33. On this, see Koenig (2001: 208ff.).
34. Another police report from 16 months later, dated 11 July 1931, controverts this, stating that Evola is "a person not worthy of respect, and a cocaine addict, who on other occasions has claimed that he had travelled abroad without a passport in order to meet with political persons, and who also boasted of other similar untrue exploits" (Ministero dell'Interno, Direzione Generale Pubblica Sicurezza, Divisione Affari Generali e Riservati, Busta 33 [Evola]: 1930–43).
35. This text is taken from the documentary appendix to Dana Lloyd Thomas's "Il filogermanesimo di Julius Evola: le reazioni dello stato" (1997: 276).
36. Evola (1972b: 100ff.).
37. However, in January 1921, an exhibition of some sixty paintings by Evola took place at the Berlin gallery "Der Sturm". I have not been able to find out whether he was actually in Berlin at that time.
38. Evola (1972b: 137).
39. A transcription of the document can be found in D. L. Thomas (1997: 278).
40. Julius Evola, "Deutsche Treue", *Il Corriere Padano* XI, 19 January 1933, reprinted in Evola (2002: 53–5).
41. Koenig (1998).

42. Mommsen (1998: 317).
43. Hansen (1998).
44. There are numerous references to this in Evola's journal and newspaper articles from the time. Also, in his postwar analysis of the Third Reich, *Fascismo e Terzo Reich*, he mentions the Stahlhelm and the DNVP as the groups that were most significant for him (Evola 2001: 185; I cite this edition of the book because it is the best from a critical and historical viewpoint).
45. On the many spheres of influence of the press and film magnate Hugenberg, see Holzbach (1981).
46. See John A. Leopold's *Alfred Hugenberg: The Radical Nationalist Campaign against the Weimar Republic* (1977: 102ff.) and Theodor Duesterberg's *Der Stahlhelm und Hitler* (1949: 23). Duesterberg was co-leader of the Stahlhelm, so his book is naturally of an apologetic nature. But the letters reproduced therein, from the Stahlhelm leaders to Adolf Hitler, are highly interesting. Theodor Duesterberg's name was also mentioned often by Evola in his newspaper and journal articles, although he mistakenly calls him "Düstenberg". This is a further proof of Evola's not always reliable memory.
47. Leopold (1977: 103).
48. Here it should be noted that contact must have already begun by 1928, since this was the year the first political essay by Evola was published in the German newspaper *Die Eiche*. Its title was "Der Faschismus als Wille zur Weltherrschaft und das Christentum" ("Fascism as Will to World Domination and Christianity").
49. Scaligero (1972: 85–7).
50. See Ravagli (2004: 92ff.). The anthroposophist Werner G. Haverbeck especially discusses Rudolf Steiner's nationalistic side in *Rudolf Steiner, Anwalt für Deutschland* (1989), although all in all this book takes a one-sided approach.
51. "Une nouvelle Haute Loge en Allemagne", *Revue Internationale des Sociétés Secrètes* XVIII(12) (1929): 378.
52. Ministero dell'Interno, Direzione Generale della Pubblica Sicurezza, Divisione Polizia Politica, Fascicolo Personale, Pacco 467, Fascicolo 64: 1930–43.
53. E.g. in Turris (1985: 337).
54. See, for example, an article by the expert on Arturo Reghini, Roberto Sestito (2000–2004).
55. According to Peter-R. Koenig, closer analyses of the text of the Thelemic *Book of the Law* reveal that it was written over a longer period of time. Differences in shades of ink and handwriting in the original manuscript seem to confirm this.
56. Hakl (2001).
57. Thus far, the most thorough analysis of Crowley's concept of magic is in Pasi (2004), a doctoral dissertation in religious studies from the École Pratique des Hautes Études in Paris. More concise and more easily accessible is Pasi's article "Crowley, Aleister" in Wouter J. Hanegraaff's *Dictionary of Gnosis and Western Esotericism* (Pasi 2005a), in which a large space is devoted to the analysis of Crowley's magic.
58. As the diary's editor (Stephen Skinner) notes here, Crowley means he has been pondering politics while taking ether in order to increase his concentration.
59. Crowley (1979: 32).

Bibliography

For a bibliography of Crowley's works, see Will Parfitt and A. Drylie, *A Crowley Cross-Index* (n.p.: ZRO, 1976). It is far from being always reliable and is obviously quite dated now, but it still remains a useful tool for the scholar. Also useful, besides being more recent and up to date, although rather difficult to navigate and also not always reliable, is J. Edward Cornelius and Marlene Cornelius, *The Aleister Crowley Desk Reference* (Berkeley, CA: Red Flame, 1997).

In the following I list only the works by Crowley referred to in the present volume.

Works by Aleister Crowley

1899. *An Appeal to the American Republic*. London: Kegan Paul, Trench, Trubner and Co.
1905–7. *The [Collected] Works of Aleister Crowley*, 3 vols. Foyers: Society for the Propagation of Religious Truth (see also Crowley 1973c).
1909. "John St. John". *The Equinox* 1(1) (in the special supplement).
1909–13. *The Equinox: The Review of Scientific Illuminism* I(1–10). London: various publishers (see also 1993a).
1910a. *The Scented Garden of Abdullah the Satirist of Shiraz, Translated from a Rare Indian MS. by the Late Major Lutiy*. London: Privately printed (see also Crowley 1990).
1910b. *The Rites of Eleusis*. [London]: Privately printed (see also Crowley 1973c).
1910c. *The World's Tragedy*. Paris: Privately printed (see also Crowley 1991b).
1910d. *The Winged Beetle*. London: Privately printed (see also Crowley 1992d).
1913. *Liber CCCXXXIII: The Book of Lies, which is Also Falsely Called Breaks; the Wanderings or Falsifications of the One Thought of Frater Perdurabo Which Thought Is Itself Untrue*. London: Wieland and Co. (see also Crowley 1992c).
1914a. "Chants Before Battle". *The English Review* (August).
1914b. "To America". *The English Review* (October). New edition of *An Appeal to the American Republic*, with some changes.
1916a. "A Noisy Noise Annoys an Oyster". *The International* X(12) (December): 361–2.
1919. *The Equinox: The Review of Scientific Illuminism* III(1). Detroit, MI: Universal Publishing Company (see also Crowley 1992b).
1922. *The Diary of a Drug Fiend*. London: W. Collins Sons and Co. (see also 1992a).
1923. *Songs for Italy*. London: Privately printed.
1929a. *The Spirit of Solitude: An Autohagiography, Subsequently Re-Antichristened The Confessions of Aleister Crowley*, 2 vols. London: The Mandrake Press (see also Crowley 1989).
1929b. *Moonchild: A Prologue*. London: Mandrake (reprint: York Beach, ME: Weiser, 1996).
1929c. *Magick in Theory and Practice*. [Paris]: Privately printed (see also Crowley 1973a, 1994 and 1997).
1936. *The Scientific Solution to the Problem of Government*. N.p.: OTO. Published under the pseudonym "Comte de Fenix".
1938. *The Book of the Law*. London: OTO.
1941. *Thumbs up! A Pentagram: a Pantacle to Win the War*. London: Privately printed.
1961. *Liber Aleph vel CXI: The Book of Wisdom or Folly in the Form of an Epistle of 666 The Great Wild Beast to his Son 777 being the Equinox Volume III No. vi*, M. R. Motta and K. Germer (eds). West Point, CA: Thelema Publications (see also Crowley 1991c).
1969. *The Confessions of Aleister Crowley: An Autohagiography*, John Symonds and Kenneth Grant (eds). New York: Hill and Wang. The first two of the projected six books were published in 1929 (Crowley 1929a); this is the first single-volume edition, significantly abridged, of all six books. See also Crowley 1989.
1972. *The Magical Record of the Beast 666: The Diaries of Aleister Crowley, 1914–1920*, John Symonds and Kenneth Grant (eds). London: Duckworth.

1973a. *Magick*, John Symonds and Kenneth Grant (eds, intro.). London: Routledge and Kegan Paul (1st edn 1929, Paris, titled *Magick in Theory and Practice*, published under the pseudonym "Master Therion"; see also Crowley 1994).
1973b. *Magick without Tears*. St Paul: Llewellyn Publications (1st edn 1954).
1973c. *Collected Works of Aleister Crowley* (3 vols; Les Plaines: Yogi Publication Society). Reprint of *The Works of Aleister Crowley* (3 vols; Foyers: Society for the Propagation of Religious Truth, 1905–7).
1979. *The Magical Diaries of TO ΜΕΓΑ ΘΗΡΙΟΝ, The Beast 666, Aleister Crowley ΛΟΓΟΣ ΑΙΩΝΟΣ ΘΕΛΗΜΑ, 93, 1923*, Stephen Skinner (ed.). Jersey: Neville Spearman.
1987. *The Scrutinies of Simon Iff*, Martin P. Starr (ed., intro.). Chicago, IL: Teitan Press.
1989. *The Confessions of Aleister Crowley: An Autohagiography*, John Symonds and Kenneth Grant (eds). London: Arkana. The first two of the projected six books were published in 1929 (Crowley 1929a); the single-volume edition, significantly abridged, of all six books, was published in 1969, of which this is a reprint.
1990. *The Rites of Eleusis*. Thame: Mandrake (1st edn 1910).
1991a. *The Scented Garden of Abdullah the Satirist of Shiraz, Translated from a Rare Indian MS. by the Late Major Lutiy*. Chicago, IL: Teitan Press (1st edn 1910).
1991b. *The World's Tragedy*. Scottsdale, AZ: New Falcon (1st edn 1910).
1991c. *Liber Aleph vel CXI: The Book of Wisdom or Folly in the Form of an Epistle of 666 The Great Wild Beast to his Son 777 being the Equinox Volume III No. VI*, Hymenaeus Beta [William Breeze] (ed.). York Beach, ME: Samuel Weiser (1st edn 1961).
1992a. *The Diary of a Drug Fiend*. York Beach, ME: Weiser (1st edn 1922).
1992b. *The Equinox: The Review of Scientific Illuminism* III(1). York Beach, ME: Weiser (1st edn 1919).
1992c. *Liber CCCXXXIII: The Book of Lies, which is Also Falsely Called Breaks; The Wanderings or Falsifications of the One Thought of Frater Perdurabo*. York Beach, ME: Weiser (1st edn 1913).
1992d. *The Winged Beetle*. Chicago, IL: Teitan Press (1st edn 1910).
1993a. *The Equinox: The Review of Scientific Illuminism* I(1–10). York Beach, ME: Weiser (reprint of the first volume of the "official organ of the A∴A∴", originally published biannually in 1909–13).
1993b. *The Law is for All: An Extended Commentary on* The Book of the Law, 3rd edn, I. Regardie (ed., intro.). Phoenix, AZ: New Falcon (1st edn, St Paul: Llewellyn Publications, 1975; 2nd edn, Phoenix, AZ: Falcon, 1983; see also Crowley 2002).
1994. *Magick: Liber ABA, Book Four, Parts I–IV*, with Mary Desti and Leila Waddell (ed., annot., intro, Hymenaeus Beta). York Beach, ME: Weiser (1st edn 1929, Paris, titled *Magick in Theory and Practice*, published under the pseudonym "Master Therion"; see also Crowley 1973a and Crowley 1997).
1997. *Magick. Liber ABA, Book Four, Parts I–IV*, with Mary Desti and Leila Waddell (ed., annot., intro., Hymenaeus Beta). York Beach, ME: Weiser Books (revised edn of Crowley 1994; 1st edn 1929; see also Crowley 1973a).
1998a. "An Improvement on Psychoanalysis: The Psychology of the Unconscious (for Dinner Table Consumption)". In Crowley 1998b, 76–81 (originally published in *Vanity Fair*, November 1916, 55 and 134).
1998b. *The Revival of Magick and Other Essays* (*Oriflamme* 2), Hymenaeus Beta and Richard Kaczynski (eds), S. A. Jacobs (afterword). Tempe, AZ: New Falcon–OTO.
2002. *The Law is for All: The Authorized Popular Commentary on* Liber Al vel Legis sub figura CCXX: The Book of the Law, L. Wilkinson and Hymenaeus Beta (eds). Tempe: New Falcon (see also Crowley 1993b).
2003. *Liber Aleph*, M. Küntzel (trans.). Munich: Ansata (German-language edn).
n.d. "Liber LXXIII: The Urn. The Diary of a Magus", www.rahoorkhuit.net/library/libers/pdf/lib_0073.pdf (accessed 8 April 2013).

In collaboration with Samuel Liddell MacGregor Mathers
1995. *The Goetia: The Lesser Key of Solomon the King*. York Beach, ME: Weiser (1st edn 1904, titled *The Book of the Goetia of Solomon the King*, "translated into English tongue by a dead hand … [T]he whole edited, verified, introduced and commented by Aleister Crowley; Boleskine: Society for the Propagation of Religious Truth).

Articles with political content published in The Fatherland, New York
1915a. "Honesty is the Best Policy". Part 1: *The Fatherland* I(23) (13 January): 11–15; part 2: *The Fatherland* I(24) (20 January): 5–6.
1915b. "England on the Brink of Revolution". *The Fatherland* II(24) (21 July): 3–5.
1915c. "A Great Irish Poet's Endorsement of *The Fatherland*". *The Fatherland* III(1) (11 August): 9.
1915d. "The Future of the Submarine". *The Fatherland* III(9) (6 October): 152–3.
1915–16. "Behind the Front". Part 1: *The Fatherland* III(21) (29 December 1915): 365; part 2: *The Fatherland* III(22) (5 January 1916): 383–4.
1916b. "Leaves from a Lost Portfolio". *The Fatherland* IV(5) (8 March): 67–9 (unsigned).
1916c. "Lifting the Mask from England". *The Fatherland* IV(6) (15 March): 85–6.

Articles with political content published in The International, *New York*
1916d. "The Crime of Edith Cavell". *The International* X(1) (January): 24-5.
1917a. "Listen to the Bird-man!". *The International* XI(8) (August): 238-40.
1917b. "1066: A Study of the Ruling Classes of England". *The International* XI(9) (September): 272-6.
1917c. "Sinn Fein". *The International* XI(9) (September): 282-3 (signed "Sheamus O'Brien").
1917d. "Groans from the Padded Cell". *The International* XI(10) (October): 307-9.
1917e. "The Spoils to the Strong! An Appeal to England and Germany". *The International* XI(10) (October): 315-16.
1917f. "Humanity First". *The International* XI(11) (November): 322 (editorial; reprinted in Crowley 1998b).
1917g. "We Stand Above". *The International* XI(12) (December): 354 (editorial).
1918a. "England Speaks". *The International* XII(1) (January): 2 (editorial).
1918b. "The Conversion of Austin Harrison". *The International* XII(1) (January): 17-18.

Articles with political content published in The Open Court, *Chicago*
1915e. "The New Parsifal: A Study of Wilhelm II". *The Open Court* 29 (August).
1916e. "An Orgy of Cant". *The Open Court* 30: 70-79.

Secondary literature
"A Gentleman of Hastings" [Antony Clayton]. 2012. *Netherwood: Last Resort of Aleister Crowley*, Anok Pe [David Tibet] (foreword), Frater Amor Fati [Gary Lachman] and The English Heretic [Andy Sharp] (texts). London: Accumulator Press.
Alleau, René 1989. *Le origini occulte del nazismo*. Rome: Mediterranee. Original French edition: *Hitler et les sociétés secrètes: Enquête sur les sources occultes du nazisme* (Paris: Grasset, 1969).
Allen, Martin 2004. *The Hitler/Hess Deception: British Intelligence's Best-Kept Secret of the Second World War*. London: Harper Perennial.
Alves, Luisa 1997. "Um excêntrico encontro anglo-português: Aleister Crowley e Fernando Pessoa". *Revista de Estudos Anglo-Portugueses* 6: 83-121.
Anes, José Manuel 2008. *Fernando Pessoa e os mundos esotéricos*. Lisbon: Ésquilo (1st edn 2004).
Antliff, Allan 2001. *Anarchist Modernism: Art, Politics, and the First American Avant-Garde*. Chicago, IL: Chicago University Press.
Apiryon, Tau and Helena [J. Edward Cornelius and Marlene Cornelius] 2001. *Mystery of Mystery: A Primer of Thelemic Ecclesiastical Gnosticism (Red Flame 2)*. Berkeley, CA: Red Flame.
Armentano, Amedeo Rocco 1992. *Massime di Scienza Iniziatica*. Ancona: Ignis.
Asprem, Egil 2012. *Arguing with Angels: Enochian Magic and Modern Occulture*. Albany, NY: State University of New York Press.
Asprem, Egil. 2013. "The Problem of Disenchantment: Scientific Naturalism and Esoteric Discourse, 1900-1939". PhD dissertation, University of Amsterdam, Amsterdam.
Azevedo, João Lúcio de 1984. *A evolução do sebastianismo*. Lisbon: Editorial Presença (1st edn 1918).
Baker, Phil 2009. *The Devil is a Gentleman: The Life and Times of Dennis Wheatley*. Sawtry: Dedalus.
Barreto, José 2008. "Salazar and the New State in the Writings of Fernando Pessoa". *Portuguese Studies* 24(2): 168-214.
Barreto, José 2012a. "Fernando Pessoa e Raul Leal contra a campanha moralizadora dos estudantes em 1923". *Pessoa Plural* 1: 240-70.
Barreto, José 2012b. "A publicação de O Interregno no contexto político de 1927-1928". *Pessoa Plural*: 2: 174-207.
Belém, Victor 1995. *O Mistério da Boca-do-Inferno: O encontro entre o Poeta Fernando Pessoa e o Mago Aleister Crowley*. Lisbon: Casa Fernando Pessoa.
Belém, Victor 1996. *Fernando Pessoa versus Aleister Crowley*. Lisbon: Casa Fernando Pessoa.
Benewick, Robert 1972. *The Fascist Movement in Britain*. London: Allen Lane.
Benoist, Alain de 1985. "Un faux-témoin: Hermann Rauschning". *Panorama des idées actuelles* 9 (November): 11-15.
Bercé, Yves-Marie 1990. *Le Roi caché: sauveurs et imposteurs; mythes politiques populaires dans l'Europe moderne*. Paris: Fayard.
Bersone, Clotilde 1932. *L'Élue du Dragon*. Paris: Nouvelles Éditions Latines.
Bigalli, Davide 2002. "António Vieira: profezia, storia, politica". In A. Vieira, *Per la storia del futuro*, 7-40. Località Borgnalle: Éditions L'Eubage.
Binet, Ana Maria 1996. "L'ésotérisme dans l'œuvre de Fernando Pessoa", 3 vols. Dissertation, University of Bordeaux III.
Binet, Ana Maria 1999-2000. "Le 'Suicide' de Maître Therion". *Latitudes* 7: 10-11.
Birven, Henri 1953. *Lebenskunst in Yoga und Magie*. Zürich: Origo Verlag.
Birven, Henri 1960. *Pforte der Unsterblichkeit: Yoga als Weg der geistigen Erneuerung*. Gelnhausen: H. Schwab.

Birven, Henri 2002. *Oriflamme Sonderheft: Aus dem Leben Aleister Crowleys, Die Werke Aleister Crowleys*. Stein: Psychosophische Gesellschaft.
Bisogni, Beatrice 1981. *Sette enigmi di storia massonica*. Foggia: Bastogi.
Blake, Robert and C. S. Nicholls (eds) 1986. *The Dictionary of National Biography, 1971–1980: With an Index Covering the Years 1901–1980 in One Alphabetical Series*. Oxford: Oxford University Press.
Blanco, José 2008. *Pessoana*. Vol. 1: *Bibliografia passiva, selectiva e temática*; vol. 2: *Índices*. Lisbon: Assírio and Alvim.
Blavatsky, Helena Petrovna 1998. *A Voz do Silêncio*, F. Pessoa (trans., notes). Lisbon: Assírio and Alvim.
Bochinger, Christoph 1994. *"New Age" und moderne Religion: Religionswissenschaftliche Analysen*. Gütersloh: Chr. Kaiser.
Bogdan, Henrik 2003. *Kenneth Grant: A Bibliography – from 1948*. Gothenburg: Academia Esoterica Press.
Bogdan, Henrik and Martin P. Starr (eds) 2012. *Aleister Crowley and Western Esotericism*. Oxford: Oxford University Press.
Bolton, Kerry Raymond [see also Frater Scorpio] 2010. "Aleister Crowley as Political Theorist". Part 1: www.counter-currents.com/2010/09/aleister-crowley-as-political-theorist-part-1 (accessed 8 April 2013); part 2: http://www.counter-currents.com/2010/09/aleister-crowley-as-political-theorist-part-2 (accessed 8 April 2013).
Booth, Martin 2000. *A Magick Life: The Biography of Aleister Crowley*. London: Hodder and Stoughton.
Bouchet, Christian 1988. *Aleister Crowley (1875–1947): Approche historique d'un magicien contemporain*. Nantes: Ars.
Bouchet, Christian 1992. "Aleister Crowley, révolutionnaire-conservateur inconnu". *Vouloir* 94–6: 30–32.
Bouchet, Christian 1998. *Aleister Crowley et le Mouvement Thélémite*. Château-Thébaud: Les Éditions du Chaos.
Bouchet, Christian 1999. *Qui suis-je? Crowley*. Puiseaux: Pardès.
Bouchet, Christian 2011. *Aleister Crowley: La Bête 666*. Rosières-en-Haye: Camion Blanc/Camion Noir.
Boutin, Christophe1992. *Politique et Tradition: Julius Evola dans le siècle (1898–1974)*. Paris: Éditions Kimé.
Bradley, Ian 1999. *Celtic Christianity: Making Myths and Chasing Dreams*. Edinburgh: Edinburgh University Press.
Bréchon, Robert 1996. *Etrange étranger: une biographie de Fernando Pessoa*. Paris: Christian Burgois.
Bremmer, Jan N. and Jan R. Veenstra (eds) 2002. *The Metamorphosis of Magic from Late Antiquity to the Early Modern Period*. Leuven: Peeters.
Breuer, Stefan 1996. *Anatomie de la Révolution conservatrice*. Paris: MSH. Original German edn: *Anatomie der konservativen Revolution* (Darmstadt: Wissenschaftliche Buchgesellschaft, 1993).
Brooke, Christopher N. L. 1993. *A History of the University of Cambridge*, vol. IV (1870–1990). Cambridge: Cambridge University Press.
Brown, J. F. 1978. "Aleister Crowley's Rites of Eleusis". *The Drama Review* 22(2) ("Occult and Bizarre Issue"; June): 3–26.
Bulla, Guido 1980. *William Morris: Fra arte e rivoluzione*. Cassino: Garigliano.
Burmistrov, Konstantin 2006. "Gershom Scholem und das Okkulte". *Gnostika* 33: 23–34.
Cacciari, Massimo 1979. *Walther Rathenau e il suo ambiente, con un'antologia di scritti e discorsi politici 1919–1921*. Bari: De Donato.
Caillet, Serge 2003. *La franc-maçonnerie égyptienne de Memphis-Misraïm*. Paris: Dervy.
Cammell, Charles Richard 1951. *Aleister Crowley: The Man : The Mage : The Poet*. London: Richards Press. New edition with different title: *Aleister Crowley: The Black Magician* (London: New English Library, 1969).
Canosa, Romano 2000. *I servizi segreti del Duce: I persecutori e le vittime*. Milan: Mondadori.
Caron, Roger et al. (eds) 2001. *Ésotérisme, Gnoses and Imaginaire symbolique: Mélanges offerts à Antoine Faivre*. Leuven: Peeters.
Cassata, Francesco 2003. *A destra del fascismo: Profilo politico di Julius Evola*. Turin: Bollati Boringhieri.
Castanho, Arlindo J. 1996. "Fernando Pessoa e Aleister Crowley". *Il confronto letterario: Quaderni del Dipartimento di lingue e letterature straniere moderne dell'Università di Pavia e del Dipartimento di linguistica e letterature comparate dell'Università di Bergamo* XIII(25): 315–31.
Centeno, Yvette Kace 1985a. *Fernando Pessoa: O Amor – A Morte – A Iniciação*. Lisbon: A Regra do Jogo.
Centeno, Yvette Kace 1985b. *Fernando Pessoa e a Filosofia Hermética: Fragmentos do espólio*. Lisbon: Editorial Presença.
Centeno, Yvette Kace 1988. *Fernando Pessoa: Os Trezentos e Outros Ensaios*. Lisbon: Editorial Presença.
Centeno, Yvette Kace 1990. *O pensamento esotérico de Fernando Pessoa*. Lisbon: Publicações Culturais Engrenagem.
Centeno, Yvette Kace 1993. "O pensamento esotérico de Fernando Pessoa". See Pessoa (1993), 359–95.
Centeno, Yvette Kace 2004. *Fernando Pessoa: Magia e fantasia*. Lisbon: Asa.
Cevasco, George A. (ed.) 1993. *The 1890s: An Encyclopedia of British Literature, Art, and Culture*. New York: Garland Publishing.
Chiantera-Stutte, Patricia 2003. *Julius Evola: Dal dadaismo alla rivoluzione conservatrice (1919–1940)*. Rome: Aracne (1st edn 2001).

Churton, Tobias 2011. *Aleister Crowley: The Biography: Spiritual Revolutionary, Romantic Explorer, Occult Master – and Spy*. London: Watkins Publishing.
Clough, Brian 2005. *State Secrets: The Kent–Wolkoff Affair*. Hove: Hideaway Publications.
Coad, Frederick Roy 1968. *A History of the Brethren Movement: Its Origins, Its Worldwide Development and Its Significance for the Present Day*. Exeter: Paternoster Press.
Cohn, Norman 1967. *Warrant for Genocide*. New York: Harper and Row.
Colquhoun, Ithell 1975. *The Sword of Wisdom: MacGregor Mathers and the Golden Dawn*. London: Neville Spearman.
Coomaraswamy, Ananda Kentish 1918. *The Dance of Siva: Fourteen Indian Essays*, R. Rolland (foreword). New York: Sunwise Turn.
Cornelius, J. Edward and Marlene Cornelius 1996. *Friends and Acquaintances of Aleister Crowley* (*Red Flame* 3). Berkeley, CA: Red Flame.
Cornelius, J. Edward and Marlene Cornelius 2001. *Mystery of Mystery: A Primer of Thelemic Ecclesiastical Gnosticism* (*Red Flame* 2). Berkeley, CA: Red Flame.
Corvisieri, Silverio 2001. *Il mago dei generali: poteri occulti nella crisi del fascismo e della monarchia*. Rome: Odradek.
Costa, Dalila L. P. da 1987. *O Esoterismo de Fernando Pessoa*. Porto: Lello and Irmão Editores (1st edn 1971).
Costello, John 1991. *Ten Days That Saved the West*. London: Bantam Press.
Coyné, André 1996. "Antonio Vieira et son 'Histoire du futur'". *Politica Hermetica* 8: 57–86.
Coyné, André 2011. *Regards sur Fernando Pessoa (Écosse, Tradition primordiale, Rose-Croix et Rosicrucianisme, Franc-Maçonnerie templière, Imago Templi, l'Empire de la Fin, Hermétisme, René Guénon, Aleister Crowley, Zacharias Werner, Golden Dawn, Ordo Templi Orientis, Prophétie du Portugal, etc.)*. Milan: Archè.
Crespo, Ángel 1997. *La vita plurale di Fernando Pessoa*. Rome: Antonio Pellicani Editore.
Cross, Colin 1961. *The Fascists in Britain*. London: Barrie and Rockliff.
Crow, John L. 2009. "The White Knight in the Yellow Robe: Allan Bennett's Search for Truth". Master's thesis, Department of Religious Studies, University of Amsterdam.
Cunard, Nancy, W. H. Auden *et al*. 1937. *Authors Take Sides on the Spanish War*. London: Left Review.
D'Arch Smith, Timothy 1987. *The Books of the Beast: Essays on Aleister Crowley, Montague Summers, Francis Barrett and Others*. London: Crucible.
Davies, Wendy 1992. "The Myth of the Celtic Church". See Edwards and Lane (1992), 12–21.
Deacon, Roger [Donald McCormick] 1985. *The Cambridge Apostles: A History of Cambridge University's Élite Intellectual Secret Society*. London: Robert Royce.
De Cusatis, Brunello 2005. *Esoterismo, mitogenia e realismo político em Fernando Pessoa: Uma visão de conjunto*. Porto: Edições Caixotim.
De Felice, Renzo 1966. *Mussolini il fascista: La conquista del potere (1921–1925)*. Turin: Einaudi.
De Felice, Renzo 1993. *Storia degli ebrei italiani sotto il fascismo*. Turin: Einaudi (1st edn 1961).
De Michelis, Cesare G. 2004. *Il manoscritto inesistente: I "Protocolli dei savi di Sion"*. Venice: Marsilio (1st edn 1998).
Dehn, Georg (ed.) 2006. *The Book of Abramelin: A New Translation*. Lake Worth, FL: Ibis Press.
Del Ponte, Renato 1994. *Evola e il magico "Gruppo di Ur"*. Borzano: SeaR.
Del Ponte, Renato 1996. "Introduzione". In *Lettere a Julius Evola (1930–1950)*, R. Guénon. Borzano: SeaR.
Di Luca, Natale Mario 2003. *Arturo Reghini: Un intellettuale neo-pitagorico tra Massoneria e Fascismo*. Rome: Atanòr.
Di Vona, Piero 1993. *Evola Guénon De Giorgio*. Borzano: SeaR.
Di Vona, Piero 2000. *Metafisica e politica in Julius Evola*. Padua: Edizioni di Ar.
Dix, Steffen 2009. "Um encontro impossível e um suicídio possível: Fernando Pessoa e Aleister Crowley". In *Fernando Pessoa: O Guardador de Papéis*, J. Pizarro (ed.), 39–81. Alfragide: Texto Editores.
Dix, Steffen 2012. "Die Rationalisierung eines Mysteriums: Detektivroman und esoterische Wahlverwandtschaft bei Fernando Pessoa". See Pessoa (2012), 367–89.
Douglas-Hamilton, James 1971. *Motive for a Mission: The Story behind Hess's Flight to Britain*, A. Bullock (foreword). London: Macmillan. New edition with different title: *The Truth about Rudolph Hess* (Edinburgh: Mainstream, 1993).
Driberg, Tom 1978. *Ruling Passions*. London: Quartet Books.
Drumont, Édouard 1889. *La fin d'un monde: étude psychologique et sociale*. Paris: Savine.
Duesterberg, Theodor 1949. *Der Stahlhelm und Hitler*. Wolfenbüttel: Wolfenbüttler Verlagsanstalt.
Duranty, Walter 1935. *I Write as I Please*. London: Hamish Hamilton.
Dyrendal, Asbjørn 2012. "Satan and the Beast: The Influence of Aleister Crowley on Modern Satanism". See Bogdan and Starr (2012), 369–94.
Dyrendal, Asbjørn 2013. "Hidden Knowledge, Hidden Powers: Esotericism and Conspiracy Culture". In *Contemporary Esotericism*, E. Asprem and K. Granholm (eds), 200–225. Sheffield: Equinox.
Eckartshausen, Karl von 1896. *The Cloud upon the Sanctuary*. London: George Redway. Original German edn: *Die Wolke über dem Heiligtum* (Munich, 1802).

Edwards, Nancy and Alan Lane (eds) 1992. *The Early Church in Wales and the West: Recent Work in Early Christian Archaeology*. Oxford: Oxbow Books.
Ensor, Robert 1992. *England 1870–1914*. Oxford: Oxford University Press (1st edn 1936).
Errera, Giovanni 1990. *Emilio Servadio: Dall'ipnosi alla psicoanalisi*. Florence: Nardini.
Eshelman, James A. 2000. *The Mystical and Magical System of the A∴A∴: The Spiritual System of Aleister Crowley and George Cecil Jones Step-by-Step*. Los Angeles, CA: College of Thelema.
Evola, Julius 1932. *Maschera e volto dello spiritualismo contemporaneo: analisi critica delle principali correnti moderne verso il "sovrannaturale"*. Turin: Bocca Editori.
Evola, Julius 1954. "L'uomo più perverso del mondo: Credevo di conoscere ogni malvagità disse un giudice al satanico Crowley". *Roma* (Naples) (17 April).
Evola, Julius 1959. "Parliamo di Crowley: La "Grande Bestia 666"; Maghi e streghe sono in mezzo a noi". *Roma* (Naples) (14 May).
Evola, Julius 1969. *Metafisica del sesso*. Rome: Mediterranee (1st edn 1958). English translation: *The Metaphysics of Sex* (New York: Inner Traditions International, 1983). New edition: *Eros and the Mysteries of Love: The Metaphysics of Sex*. (Rochester, Vermont: Inner Traditions, 1991).
Evola, Julius 1971. *Maschera e volto dello spiritualismo contemporaneo*, 3rd edn. Rome: Mediterranee.
Evola, Julius 1972a. "Prefazione". See Symonds (1972), 11–12.
Evola, Julius 1972b. *Il cammino del cinabro*, 2nd edn. Rome: Vanni Scheiwiller.
Evola, Julius 1977. *Ultimi scritti*. Naples: Controcorrente.
Evola, Julius 1978. *Imperialismo pagano*. Padua: Edizioni di Ar (1st edn 1928).
Evola, Julius 1984. *Scritti sulla massoneria*. Rome: Settimo Sigillo.
Evola, Julius 1996. *Lettere 1955–1974: L'Epistolario Evoliano raccolto, catalogato e annotato da Renato del Ponte*. Finale Emilia: La Terra degli Avi.
Evola, Julius 2001. *Fascismo e Terzo Reich*. Rome: Mediterranee.
Evola, Julius 2002. *I testi del Corriere Padano*. Padua: Edizioni di Ar.
Evola, Julius 2008. *I testi del Roma*, V. Campagna (ed.). Padua: Edizioni di Ar.
Faivre, Antoine 1969. *Eckartshausen et la théosophie chrétienne*. Paris: Klincksieck.
Faivre, Antoine 1992. *L'ésotérisme*. Paris: Presses Universitaires de France (English translation in Faivre 2010).
Faivre, Antoine 1999. "Histoire de la notion moderne de Tradition dans ses rapports avec les courants ésotériques (xve–xxe siècles)". See *Symboles et mythes* (1999), 7–48.
Faivre, Antoine 2010. *Western Esotericism: A Concise History*. Albany, NY: State University of New York Press (English translation of Faivre 1992).
Faivre, Antoine and Wouter J. Hanegraaff (eds) 1998. *Western Esotericism and the Science of Religion*. Leuven: Peeters.
Farrugia, Edward G. 1993. *The Pontifical Oriental Institute: The First Seventy-Five Years; 1917–1992*. Chicago, IL: Loyola Press.
Fenili, Piero 1997. "Fu Evola affiliato all'Ordine magico di Aleister Crowley?". *Politica Romana* 4: 294–6.
Fichter, Joseph H. (ed.) 1983. *Alternatives to American Mainline Churches*. Barrytown, NY: Unification Theological Seminary.
Fiorentino, Carlo M. 1999. *All'ombra di Pietro: La Chiesa Cattolica e lo spionaggio fascista in Vaticano 1929–1939*. Florence: Le Lettere.
Flowers, Stephen E. 1994. *Fire and Ice: The History, Structure, and Rituals of Germany's Most Influential Modern Magical Order; The Brotherhood of Saturn*. St Paul, MN: Llewellyn Publications.
Fortune, Dion 1993. *The Magical Battle of Britain*. Bradford on Avon: Golden Gates.
França, Isabel Murteira 1987. *Fernando Pessoa na intimidade*. Lisbon: Editorial Presença.
Frater Scorpio [Kerry Raymond Bolton] 1996. *Aleister Crowley and the Conservative Revolution*. Paraparaumu Beach: Renaissance Press.
Frazer, James G. 1911. *The Golden Bough: A Study in Magic and Religion*. Vol. I: *The Magic Art and the Evolution of Kings*. London: Macmillan.
Freeman, Nick 2007. "Wilde's Edwardian Afterlife: Somerset Maugham, Aleister Crowley, and *The Magician*", *Journal of Literature and History* 16(2): 16–29.
Frosini, Eduardo 1911. *Massoneria Italiana e Tradizione Iniziatica*. Sala Bolognese: Ettore Croce (reprint: 1979. Pescara: Forni).
Fry, Leslie (ed.) 1934. *Léo Taxil et la Franc-Maçonnerie: Lettres inédites*. Chatou: British–American Press.
Fuller, Jean Overton 1990. *The Magical Dilemma of Victor Neuburg*. Oxford: Mandrake (1st edn, London: W. H. Allen, 1965).
Fuller, John Frederick Charles 1907. *The Star in the West: A Critical Essay upon the Works of Aleister Crowley*. London: Walter Scott.

Fuller, John Frederick Charles 1925. *Yoga: A Study of the Mystical Philosophy of the Brahmins and Buddhists*. London: W. Rider and Son.
Fuller, John Frederick Charles 1926. *The Foundations of the Science of War*. London: Hutchinson.
Fuller, John Frederick Charles 1931. *India in Revolt*. London: Eyre and Spottiswoode.
Fuller, John Frederick Charles 1966a. *666: Bibliotheca Crowleyana; Catalogue of a Unique Collection of Books, Pamphlets, Proof Copies, MSS., etc. by, about, or Connected with Aleister Crowley*. Tenterden: Keith Hogg (reprint, Edmonds, WA: Sure Fire, 1989).
Fuller, John Frederick Charles 1966b. "Aleister Crowley 1898–1911: An Introductory Essay". See Fuller (1966a).
Furlong, Paul 2011. *Social and Political Thought of Julius Evola*. London: Routledge.
Fuss, Michael A. (ed.) 1998. *Rethinking New Religious Movements*. Rome: Pontifical Gregorian University.
Galli, Giorgio 1989. *Hitler e il nazismo magico: Le componenti esoteriche del Reich millenario*. Milan: Rizzoli (revised edn 1993).
Galli, Giorgio 1995. *La politica e i maghi: da Richelieu a Clinton*. Milan: Rizzoli.
Galtier, Gérard 1989. *Maçonnerie Égyptienne Rose Croix et Néo-Chevalerie: Les Fils de Cagliostro*. Monaco: Éditions du Rocher.
Geertz, Armin W. and Randi Warne (eds) 2004. *New Approaches to the Study of Religion*. Berlin: De Gruyter.
Gertz, Elmer 1978. *Odyssey of a Barbarian: The Biography of George Sylvester Viereck*. Buffalo, NY: Prometheus Books.
Gibbons, Tom 1973. *Rooms in the Darwin Hotel: Studies in English Literary Criticism and Ideas 1880–1920*. Nedlands: University of Western Australia Press.
Gilbert, Robert A. 1983. *The Golden Dawn: Twilight of the Magicians*. Wellingborough: Aquarian Press.
Gilbert, Robert A. 1986. *The Golden Dawn Companion*. Wellingborough: Aquarian Press.
Gilbert, Robert A. 1987a. *The Golden Dawn and the Esoteric Section*. London: Theosophical History Centre.
Gilbert, Robert A. 1987b. *Arthur E. Waite: Magician in Many Parts*. Wellingborough: Crucible.
Gilbert, Robert A. 1997a. *Baphomet and Son: A Little Known Chapter in the Life of 666*. Edmonds, WA: Holmes Publishing Group.
Gilbert, Robert A. 1997b. *The Golden Dawn Scrapbook: The Rise and Fall of a Magical Order*. York Beach, ME: Weiser.
Gilbert, Robert A. 2005. "Hermetic Order of the Golden Dawn". See Hanegraaff et al. (2005), 544–50.
Godden, Gertrude Mary 1896. *Nágá and Other Frontier Tribes of North-East India*. London: Harrison.
Godden, Gertrude Mary 1923. *Mussolini: The Birth of the New Democracy*. London: Burns, Oates and Washbourne.
Godden, Gertrude Mary 1929. *Russia under the Red Flag: A Record of Socialism in Our Time*. London: Burns, Oates and Washbourne.
Godden, Gertrude Mary 1935. *The Communist Attack on Great Britain: International Communism at Work*. London: Burns, Oates and Co.
Godden, Gertrude Mary 1937. *Conflict in Spain, 1920–1937: A Documented Record*. London: Burns, Oates and Co.
Godden, Gertrude Mary 1939. *The Soviets Liberate Poland*. London: Catholic Truth Society.
Godwin, Joscelyn 1990. "The Hidden Hand, Part 1: The Provocation of the Hydesville Phenomena". *Theosophical History* 3(2) (April): 35–43.
Godwin, Joscelyn 1994. *The Theosophical Enlightenment*. Albany, NY: State University of New York Press.
Godwin, Joscelyn 1996. *Arktos: The Polar Myth in Science, Symbolism, and Nazi Survival*. Kempton, IL: Adventures Unlimited.
Godwin, Joscelyn, Christian Chanel and John Patrick Deveney 1995. *The Hermetic Brotherhood of Luxor: Initiatic and Historical Documents of an Order of Practical Occultism*. York Beach, ME: Weiser.
Gomes, Augusto Ferreira 1934. *Quinto Império*. Lisbon: Parceria António Maria Pereira.
Goodrick-Clark, Nicholas 1985. *The Occult Roots of Nazism: The Ariosophists of Austria and Germany 1890–1935*. Wellingborough: Aquarian Press.
Goodrick-Clark, Nicholas 2002. *Black Sun: Aryan Cults, Esoteric Nazism and the Politics of Identity*. New York: New York University Press.
Goodrick-Clark, Nicholas 2008. *The Western Esoteric Traditions*. Oxford: Oxford University Press.
Gosse, Edmund 1907. *Father and Son: A Study of Two Temperaments*. London: Heinemann.
Gottlieb, Julie V. 2003. *Feminine Fascism: Women in Britain's Fascist Movement, 1923–45*. London: I. B. Tauris.
Gould, Warwick and Marjorie Reeves 2001. *Joachim of Fiore and the Myth of the Eternal Evangel in the Nineteenth and Twentieth Centuries*. Oxford: Clarendon Press (1st edn 1987).
Grande Enciclopédia 1936–60. *Grande Enciclopédia Portuguesa e Brasileira*, 40 vols. Lisbon – Rio de Janeiro: Editorial Enciclopédia.
Grant, Kenneth 1972. *The Magical Revival*. London: Frederick Muller (2nd edn, London: Skoob Books, 1991).
Grant, Kenneth 1973. *Aleister Crowley and the Hidden God*. London: Frederick Muller (2nd edn, London: Skoob Books, 1992).

Grant, Kenneth 1991. *Remembering Aleister Crowley*. London: Skoob Books.
Green, Martin 1992. *Prophets of a New Age: The Politics of Hope from the Eighteenth through the Twenty-first Centuries*. New York: Charles Scribner's Sons.
Greer, Mary K. 1995. *Women of the Golden Dawn: Rebels and Priestesses*. Rochester, VT: Park Street Press.
Griffith, Richard 1983. *Fellow Travellers of the Right: British Enthusiasts for Nazi Germany 1933-39*. Oxford: Oxford University Press (1st edn 1980).
Gruppo di Ur 1955. *Introduzione alla Magia*. Rome: Fratelli Bocca.
Gruppo di Ur 2001. *Introduction to Magic: Rituals and Practical Techniques for the Magus*. Rochester, VT: Inner Traditions (English translation of Gruppo di Ur 1955).
Guénon, René 1965. *Le Théosophisme: Histoire d'une pseudo-religion*. Paris: Éditions Traditionnelles (1st edn, Paris: Nouvelle librairie nationale, 1921).
Guénon, René 1986a. *Comptes rendus*. Paris: Éditions Traditionnelles (1st edn 1973).
Guénon, René 1986b. *Études sur la Franc-Maçonnerie et le Compagnonnage*, 2 vols. Paris: Éditions Traditionnelles (1st edn 1965).
Guénon, René 1996. *Lettere a Julius Evola (1930-1950)*, R. Del Ponte (trans., intro., notes). Borzano: SeaR.
Guilbeaux, Henri 1933. *Où va l'Allemagne*. Paris: Mignolet et Storz.
Hagemeister Michael 2008. "The Protocols of the Elders of Zion: Between History and Fiction". *New German Critique* 103(35/1): 83-95.
Hakl, Hans Thomas 1997. "Nationalsozialismus und Okkultismus". Part 1: *Gnostika* (January): 32-42; part 2: *Gnostika* (April): 26-35; *Gnostika* (July): 22-37. Revised English translation of the entire article in Hakl (2000).
Hakl, Hans Thomas 1998. "Julius Evola und die deutsche konservative Revolution". *Criticón* 158: 16-32.
Hakl, Hans Thomas 2000. *Unknown Sources: National Socialism and the Occult*. Edmonds, WA: Holmes Publishing Group.
Hakl, Hans Thomas 2001. "Die Magie bei Julius Evola und ihre philosophischen Voraussetzungen". See Caron *et al.* (2001), 415-36.
Hall, David 2012. *Beelzebub and the Beast: A Comparative Study of the Teachings of George Ivanovitch Gurdjieff and Aleister Crowley*. London: Starfire Publishing.
Hamilton, Gerald 1937. *As Young as Sophocles*. London: Secker and Warburg.
Hamilton, Gerald 1956. *Mr Norris and I*. London: Allan Wingate.
Hamilton, Gerald 1969. *The Way It Was With Me*. London: Leslie Frewin.
Hammer, Olav 2001. *Claiming Knowledge: Strategies of Epistemology from Theosophy to the New Age*. Leiden: Brill.
Hamnett, Nina 1932. *Laughing Torso: Reminiscences of Nina Hamnett*. London: Constable and Co.
Hanegraaff, Wouter J. 1996. *New Age Religion and Western Culture: Esotericism in the Mirror of Secular Culture*. Leiden: Brill.
Hanegraaff, Wouter J. 2004. "The Study of Western Esotericism: New Approaches to Christian and Secular Culture". See Geertz and Warne (2004): vol. 1, 489-519.
Hanegraaff, Wouter J. 2012. *Esotericism and the Academy: Rejected Knowledge in Western Culture*. Cambridge: Cambridge University Press.
Hanegraaff, Wouter J. 2013. *Western Esotericism: A Guide for the Perplexed*. London: Bloomsbury.
Hanegraaff, Wouter J. et al. (eds) 2005. *Dictionary of Gnosis and Western Esotericism*. Leiden: Brill.
Hänel, Wolfgang 1984. *Hermann Rauschnings "Gespräche mit Hitler": Eine Geschichtsfälschung*. Ingolstadt: Zeitgeschichtliche Forschungsstelle.
Hansen, H. T. [Hans Thomas Hakl] 1998."Julius Evola und die deutsche konservative Revolution". *Criticón* 158 (April-June): 16-32.
Hansen, H. T. 2002. "Julius Evola's Political Endeavors". In *Men Among the Ruins: Postwar Reflections of a Radical Traditionalist*, J. Evola, 1-104. Rochester, VT: Inner Traditions.
Harper, George Mills 1974. *Yeats's Golden Dawn*. Basingstoke: Macmillan.
Harris, Elizabeth J. 1998. *Ananda Metteyya: The First British Emissary of Buddhism*. Kandy: Buddhist Publication Society.
Hastings, Beatrice 1936. *The Old "New Age": Orage and Others*. London: Blue Moon Press.
Haverbeck, Werner G. 1989. *Rudolf Steiner, Anwalt für Deutschland*. Munich: Langen Müller.
Hawkins, Mike 1997. *Social Darwinism in European and American Thought, 1860-1945*. Cambridge: Cambridge University Press.
Hobsbawm, Eric J. 1987. *The Age of Empire: 1875-1914*. London: Weidenfeld and Nicolson.
Hollingsworth, Mark and Charles Tremayne 1989. *The Economic League: The Silent McCarthyism*. London: National Council for Civil Liberties.
Holzbach, Heidrun 1981. *Das "system Hugenberg": Die Organisation bürgerlicher Sammlungspolitik vor dem Aufstieg der NSDAP*. Stuttgart: Deutsche Verlags-Anstalt.

Houman, Setareh 2010. *De la philosophia perennis au pérennialisme américain*. Milan: Archè.
Howe, Ellic 1967. *Urania's Children: The Strange World of the Astrologers*. London: Kimber.
Howe, Ellic 1984. *Astrology and the Third Reich*. Wellingborough: The Aquarian Press (new expanded edn of Howe 1967).
Howe, Ellic 1985. *The Magicians of the Golden Dawn: A Documentary History of a Magical Order 1887–1923*. Wellingborough: Aquarian Press.
Howe, Ellic 1988. *The Black Game: British Subversive Operations against the Germans during the Second World War*. London: Queen Anne Press (1st edn 1982).
Hughes, Mike 2012. *Spies at Work*. N.p.: privately printed.
Hutchinson, Roger 1998. *Aleister Crowley: The Beast Demystified*. Edinburgh: Mainstream Publishing.
Hutchison, Alice L. 2004. *Kenneth Anger: A Demonic Visionary*. London: Black Dog Publishing.
Hutin, Serge 1973. *Aleister Crowley: le plus grand des mages modernes*. Verviers: Gérard.
Hutin, Serge 1990. "La frammassoneria". See Puech (1990), 159–84.
Hyatt, Christopher S. 1985. *An Interview with Israel Regardie: His Final Thoughts and Views*. Phoenix, AZ: Falcon Press.
Hymenaeus Beta [William Breeze] (ed.) 1986. *The Equinox: The Review of Scientific Illuminism* III(10) (March). York Beach, ME: Weiser.
Hymenaeus Beta (ed.) 1998. *An Old Master: The Art of Aleister Crowley*. Austin, TX: Ordo Templi Orientis International.
Ingerflom, Claudio S. 1995. "Communistes contre castrats (1929–1930)". See Volkov (1995), ix–lxiii.
Introvigne, Massimo 1990. *Il cappello del mago: I nuovi movimenti magici, dallo spiritismo al satanismo*. Milan: SugarCo.
Introvigne, Massimo 1993. *Il ritorno dello gnosticismo*. Carnago: SugarCo.
Introvigne, Massimo 1998. "Between Religion and Magic: The Case of Mormonism". See Fuss (1998), 81–100.
Introvigne, Massimo 2010. *I satanisti: Storia, riti e miti del satanismo*. Milan: SugarCo (1st edn 1994).
Ironside, Harry Allen 1985. *A Historical Sketch of the Brethren Movement*. Neptune, NJ: Loizeaux Brothers.
Irving, David 1987. *Hess: The Missing Years 1941–1945*. London: Macmillan.
Isherwood, Christopher 1935. *Mr Norris Changes Trains*. London: Woolf.
Isherwood, Christopher 1939. *Goodbye to Berlin*. London: Hogarth Press.
Isherwood, Christopher 1977. *Christopher and his Kind, 1929–1939*. London: Eyre Methuen.
Isherwood, Christopher 1984. *Exhumations: Stories Articles Verses*. London: Methuen.
Isherwood, Christopher 1997. *Diaries Volume One: 1939–1960*. New York: HarperCollins.
James, Marie-France 1981a. *Ésotérisme et christianisme autour de René Guénon*. Paris: Nouvelles Éditions Latines.
James, Marie-France 1981b. *Ésotérisme, occultisme, franc-maçonnerie et christianisme aux XIXe et XXe siècles: Explorations bio-bibliographiques*. Paris: Nouvelles Éditions Latines.
Johnson, K. Paul 1994. *The Masters Revealed: Madame Blavatsky and the Myth of the Great White Lodge*. Albany, NY: State University of New York Press.
Johnson, Niel M. 1972. *George Sylvester Viereck: German–American Propagandist*. Urbana, IL: University of Illinois Press.
Kaczynski, Richard 2003. *Perdurabo: The Life of Aleister Crowley*. Tempe: New Falcon Publications.
Kaczynski, Richard 2010. *Perdurabo: The Life of Aleister Crowley*. Berkeley, CA: North Atlantic Books (revised edn of Kaczynski 2003).
Kaczynski, Richard 2012. *Forgotten Templars: The Untold Origins of Ordo Templi Orientis*. n.p.: Printed for the author.
Kamenezky, Eliezer 1932. *Alma Errante: poemas, com um prefácio de Fernando Pessoa*. Lisbon: privately printed.
Kervella, André 2002. *La Passion Ecossaise*. Paris: Editions Dervy.
Kervella, André and Philippe Lestienne 1997. "Un haut-grade templier dans les milieux jacobites en 1750: L'Ordre Sublime des Chevaliers Elus aux sources de la Stricte Observance". *Renaissance Traditionnelle* 28(112): 229–66.
Keyserling, Hermann 1919. *Das Reisetagebuch eines Philosophen*. Leipzig: Duncker and Humblot.
Kilcher, Andreas 1998. *Die Sprachtheorie der Kabbala als ästhetisches Paradigma: Die Konstruktion einer ästhetischen Kabbala seit der frühen Neuzeit*. Stuttgart: J. B. Metzler.
King, Francis (ed.) 1973. *The Secret Rituals of the OTO*. New York: Weiser.
King, Francis 1975. *Magic: The Western Tradition*. London: Thames and Hudson.
King, Francis 1987. *The Magical World of Aleister Crowley*. London: Arrow Books (1st edn 1977).
King, Francis 1989. *Modern Ritual Magic: The Rise of Western Occultism*. Bridport: Prism Press.
King, Stephen J. 2007. "Mandrake and the Magician: P.R. Stephensen and the 'Legend' of Aleister Crowley". See Stephensen and Crowley (2007), 1–51.
Koenig, Peter-Robert (ed.) 1993. *Der Kleine Theodor-Reuss-Reader*. Munich: Arbeitsgemeinschaft für Religions- und Weltanschauungsfragen.

Koenig, Peter-Robert (ed.) 1994a. *Materialien zum OTO*. Munich: Arbeitsgemeinschaft für Religions- und Weltanschauungsfragen.
Koenig, Peter-Robert 1994b. *Das OTO-Phänomen: 100 Jahre Magische Geheimbünde und ihre Protagonisten von 1895–1994*. Munich: Arbeitsgemeinschaft für Religions- und Weltanschauungsfragen.
Koenig, Peter-Robert (ed.) 1995. *Abramelin and Co*. Munich: Arbeitsgemeinschaft für Religions- und Weltanschauungsfragen.
Koenig, Peter-Robert (ed.) 1997. *Der Grosse Theodor-Reuss-Reader*. Munich: Arbeitsgemeinschaft für Religions- und Weltanschauungsfragen.
Koenig, Peter-Robert 1998. "Rudolf Steiner: niemals Mitglied irgendeines OTO". *Flensburger Hefte* 63 (April): 89–108.
Koenig, Peter-Robert (ed.) 2000. *Noch mehr materialien zum OTO*. Munich: Arbeitsgemeinschaft für Religions- und Weltanschauungsfragen.
Koenig, Peter-Robert 2001. *Der OTO Phänomen Remix*. Munich: Arbeitsgemeinschaft für Religions- und Weltanschauungsfragen.
Koenig, Peter-Robert 2011. *Der OTO Phänomen Reload*, 3 vols. Munich: Arbeitsgemeinschaft für Religions- und Weltanschauungsfragen.
Koss, Stephen (ed.) 1973. *The Pro-Boers: The Anatomy of an Antiwar Movement*. Chicago, IL: University of Chicago Press.
Kreis, Emmanuel (ed.) 2009. *Les puissances de l'ombre: Juifs, jésuites, francs-maçons, réactionnaires ... la théorie du complot dans les textes*. Paris: CNRS Éditions.
Kreis, Emmanuel 2011. "Quis ut Deus? Antijudéo-maçonnisme et occultisme en France sous la IIIe République". PhD dissertation, École Pratique des Hautes Études, Paris.
Lacouture, Jean 1991. *Jésuites: Une multibiographie*, 2 vols. Paris: Éditions du Seuil.
Landis, Bill 1995. *Anger: The Unauthorized Biography of Kenneth Anger*. New York: HarperCollins.
Laurant, Jean-Pierre 1975. *Le sens caché dans l'œuvre de René Guénon*. Lausanne: L'Âge d'Homme.
Laurant, Jean-Pierre 1985. *René Guénon*. Cahier de l'Herne. Paris: Éditions de l'Herne.
Laurant, Jean-Pierre 1992. *L'ésotérisme chrétien en France au XIXe siècle*. Lausanne: L'Âge d'Homme.
Laurant, Jean-Pierre 1993. *L'ésotérisme*. Paris: Éditions du Cerf.
Laurant, Jean-Pierre 2006. *René Guénon: Les enjeux d'une lecture*. Paris: Éditions Dervy.
Leal, Raul 1982. "Carta de Raul Leal a João Gaspar Simões a propósito de *Vida e Obra de Fernando Pessoa* e de Aleister Crowley". *Persona* 7 (August): 54–7.
Leal, Raul 1989. *Sodoma Divinizada: Uma polémica iniciada por Fernando Pessoa a propósito de António Botto, e tamben por ele terminada, com ajuda de Álvaro Maia e Pedro Teotónio Pereira (da Liga de Acçao dos Estudantes de Lisboa)*. Lisbon: Hiena Editora.
Leasor, James 1962. *Rudolf Hess: The Uninvited Envoy*. London: Allen and Unwin.
Ledit, Joseph 1937. *La religione e il comunismo*. Milan: Vita e Pensiero.
Ledit, Joseph 1938. *Paradossi del comunismo*. Milan: Vita e Pensiero.
Ledit, Joseph 1976. *Marie dans la liturgie de Byzance*. Paris: Éditions Beauchesne.
Lee, Martha F. 2005. "Nesta Webster: The Voice of Conspiracy". *Journal of Women's History* 17(3): 81–104.
Le Forestier, René 1987. *La Franc-Maçonnerie templière et occultiste aux XVIIIe et XIXe siècles*, 2 vols. Paris: La Table d'Emeraude.
Leopold, John A. 1977. *Alfred Hugenberg: The Radical Nationalist Campaign against the Weimar Republic*. New Haven, CT: Yale University Press.
Lindqvist, Sven 1998. *Exterminez toutes ces brutes*. Paris: Le serpent à plumes (original Swedish edn: *Utrota varenda jävel*, 1992).
Linehan, Thomas 2000. *British Fascism 1918–39: Parties, Ideology and Culture*. Manchester: Manchester University Press.
Lippi, Jean-Paul 1998. *Julius Evola métaphysicien et penseur politique*. Lausanne: L'Âge d'Homme.
Lipsey, Roger 1977. *Coomaraswamy: His Life and Work*, vol. 3. Princeton, NJ: Princeton University Press.
Lopes, Teresa Rita (ed.) 1993. *Pessoa inédito*. Lisbon: Livros Horizonte.
Loubet del Bayle, Jean-Louis 1969. *Les non-conformistes des années 30: Une tentative de renouvellement de la pensée politique française; Thèse pour le doctorat en Droit présentée et soutenue publiquement le 6 janvier 1968*. Toulouse: Université de Toulouse.
Lowenna, Sharon 2004. "'Noscitur a sociis': Jenner, Duncombe-Jewell and their Milieu". *Cornish Studies* 12: 61–87.
Mairet, Philip 1936. *A. R. Orage: A Memoir*. London: J. M. Dent and Sons.
Maistre, Louis de 2004. *L'Enigme René Guénon et les "supérieurs Inconnus": Contribution à l'étude de l'histoire mondiale "souterraine"*. Milan: Archè.
Mannix, Daniel P. 1959. *The Beast*. New York: Ballantine Books.

Marlow, Louis 1992. *Seven Friends*. Oxford: Mandrake.
Martin, Wallace 1967. *The New Age under Orage: Chapters in English Cultural History*. Manchester: Manchester University Press.
Martins, Fernando Cabral 2008. "Leal, Raul (1886–1964)". In *Dicionário de Fernando Pessoa e do modernismo português*, F. C. Martins (ed.), 395–7.
Masters, Anthony 1984. *The Man Who Was M: The Life of Maxwell Knight*. Oxford: Blackwell.
Mathers, Samuel Liddell MacGregor (ed.) 1976. *The Book of the Sacred Magic of Abra-Melin the Mage, as Delivered by Abraham the Jew unto his Son Lamech, AD 1458*. Wellingborough: Aquarian Press (1st edn 1898).
Matos, Jorge de 1997. *O pensamento maçonico de Fernando Pessoa*. Lisbon: Hugin.
Maugham, William Somerset 1908. *The Magician*. London: William Heinemann.
Maugham, William Somerset 1956. *The Magician: A Novel Together with a Fragment of Autobiography*, 2nd edn, in *The Collected Works*. London: Heinemann.
Mayer, Jean-François 1999. "Doctrine de la race et théories du complot dans les courants ésotériques". *Tangram* (Bern) 6 (March): 13–18.
McCollam, Douglas 2003. "Should This Pulitzer be Pulled?". *Columbia Journalism Review* 6, www.freerepublic.com/focus/f-news/1041902/posts (accessed 8 April 2013).
McCormick, Donald 1993. *17F: The Life of Ian Fleming*. London: Peter Owen.
McMillin, Arnold (ed.) 1992. *Symbolism and After*. London: Bristol Classical Press.
Melton, J. Gordon 1983. "Thelemic Magick in America". See Fichter (1983), 67–87.
Melton, J. Gordon 1986. *Biographical Dictionary of American Cult and Sect Leaders*. New York: Garland Publishing.
Michalka, Wolfgang 2006. "Vernetzt auf unterschiedlichen Ebenen: Walther Rathenau als Krisenmanager und Visionär 'kommender Dinge'". In *Die Kunst des Vernetzens: Festschrift für Wolfgang Hempel*, B. Brachmann et al. (eds), Berlin: Verlag für Berlin-Brandenburg, 235–49.
Mistlberger, Philip Teertha 2010. *The Three Dangerous Magi: Osho, Gurdjieff, Crowley*. Ropley: O-Books.
Mitrinovic, Dimitrije 1987. *Certainly, Future: Selected Writings by Dimitrije Mitrinović*, H. C. Rutherford (ed., intro.). Boulder, CO: East European Monographs.
Mohler, Armin 1993. *La Révolution conservatrice en Allemagne: 1918–1932*. Puiseaux: Pardès. Original German edn: *Die Konservative Revolution in Deutschland: 1918–1932* (1989).
Mola, Aldo 1992. *Storia della Massoneria italiana dalle origini ai nostri giorni*. Milan: Bompiani.
Möller, Helmut and Ellic Howe 1978. "Theodor Reuss: Irregular Freemasonry in Germany, 1900–23". *Ars Quatuor Coronatorum* 91: 28–46.
Möller, Helmut and Ellic Howe 1986. *Merlin Peregrinus: Vom Untergrund des Abendlandes*. Würzburg: Königshausen-Neumann.
Mollier, Pierre 2005. "Neo-Templar Traditions". See Hanegraaff et al. (2005), 849–53.
Mommsen, Hans 1998. *Aufstieg und Untergang der Republik von Weimar 1918–1933*. Berlin: Ullstein.
Monod, Paul 1988. *Jacobitism and the English People 1688–1788*. Cambridge: Cambridge University Press.
Montanari, Enrico 2001. "Spiritualismo moderno e rischi della persona". In *Julius Evola: Un pensiero per la fine del millennio; Atti del convegno di Milano 27–28 novembre 1998, Centro Congressi "Le Stelline"*, P. F. Ronconi et al. (eds), 51–75. Rome: Fondazione Julius Evola.
Moore, James 1991. *Gurdjieff: The Anatomy of a Myth. A Biography*. Shaftesbury: Element.
Moorehead, Alan 1958. *The Russian Revolution*. London: Collins, Hamish Hamilton.
Morodo, Raúl 1997. *Fernando Pessoa e as "Revoluções Nacionais" Europeias*. Lisbon: Caminho.
Mosse, George L. 1964. *The Crisis of German Ideology: Intellectual Origins of the Third Reich*. London: Weidenfeld and Nicolson.
Munro, Craig 1984. *Wild Man of Letters: The Story of P. R. Stephensen*. Carlton: Melbourne University Press.
Mutti, Claudio 1994. *Le penne dell'arcangelo: intellettuali e Guardia di Ferro*. Milan: Società Editrice Barbarossa.
Neves, João Alves das 2009. *Fernando Pessoa, Salazar e o Estado Novo*. Santo André: Fabricando Idéias.
Nicholls, C. S. (ed.) 1993. *The Dictionary of National Biography: Missing Persons*. Oxford: Oxford University Press.
Nietzsche, Friedrich 1988. *Nachgelassene Fragmente: 1882–1884*, vol. 10 of the *Kritische Studienausgabe*, G. Colli and M. Montinari (eds). Munich: dtv.
Nolte, Ernst 1997. *Heidegger e la rivoluzione conservatrice*. Milan: SugarCo.
Nott, Charles Stanley 1961. *Teachings of Gurdjieff: The Journal of a Pupil. An Account of Some Years with G. I. Gurdjieff and A. R. Orage in New York and Fontainebleau-Avon*. London: Routledge and Kegan Paul.
O'Day, Alan (ed.) 1979. *The Edwardian Age: Conflict and Stability: 1900–1914*. Basingstoke: Macmillan.
O'Donoghue, David James (ed.) 1912. *The Poets of Ireland: A Biographical and Bibliographical Dictionary of English Verse*. Dublin: Hodges Figgis.
Owen, Alex 2004. *The Place of Enchantment: British Occultism and the Culture of the Modern*. Chicago, IL: University of Chicago Press.

Owen, Alex 2012. "The Sorcerer and His Apprentice: Aleister Crowley and the Magical Exploration of Edwardian Subjectivity". See Bogdan and Starr (2012), 15–52.
Partner, Peter 1982. *The Murdered Magicians: The Templars and their Myth*. Oxford: Oxford University Press.
Pasi, Marco 1998a. "Aleister Crowley". See Servier (1998), 358–60.
Pasi, Marco 1998b. "Dieu du désir, dieu de la raison: Le diable en Californie dans les années soixante". In *Le Diable: Colloque de Cerisy*, 87–98. Paris: Dervy.
Pasi, Marco 1998c. "Golden Dawn". See Servier (1998), 554–6.
Pasi, Marco 1998d. "L'anticristianesimo in Aleister Crowley". See Zoccatelli (1998), 41–67.
Pasi, Marco 1999. *Aleister Crowley e la tentazione della politica*. Milan: FrancoAngeli.
Pasi, Marco 2001a. "Aleister Crowley e lo yoga". *Arkete* 2(1): 77–87.
Pasi, Marco 2001b. "The Influence of Aleister Crowley on Fernando Pessoa's Esoteric Writings". See Caron *et al.* (2001), 693–711.
Pasi, Marco 2003. "The Neverendingly Told Story: Recent Biographies of Aleister Crowley". *Aries* 3(2): 224–45.
Pasi, Marco 2004. "La notion de magie dans le courant occultiste en Angleterre (1875–1947)". PhD dissertation, École Pratique des Hautes Études, Paris.
Pasi, Marco 2005a. "Crowley, Aleister". See Hanegraaff *et al.* (2005), 281–7.
Pasi, Marco 2005b. "Ordo Templi Orientis". See Hanegraaff *et al.* (2005), 898–906.
Pasi, Marco 2005c. "Mathers, Samuel Liddell 'MacGregor'". See Hanegraaff *et al.* (2005), 783–5.
Pasi, Marco 2005d. "Review of Silverio Corvisieri, *Il mago dei generali*". *Politica Hermetica* 19: 146–52.
Pasi, Marco 2005e. "Occultism". See Stuckrad (2005b), 1364–8.
Pasi, Marco 2006. *Aleister Crowley und die Versuchung der Politik*. Graz: Stocker Verlag. German translation of Pasi (1999).
Pasi, Marco 2007. "Arthur Machen's Panic Fears: Western Esotericism and the Irruption of Negative Epistemology". *Aries. Journal for the Study of Western Esotericism* 7(1): 63–83.
Pasi, Marco (ed.) 2008. *Peintures inconnues d'Aleister Crowley: La collection de Palerme*. Milan: Archè.
Pasi, Marco 2010. "Teosofia e antroposofia nell'Italia del primo Novecento". In *Storia d'Italia: Annale 25: Esoterismo*, G. M. Cazzaniga (ed.), 569–98. Turin: Einaudi.
Pasi, Marco 2011. "Varieties of Magical Experience: Aleister Crowley's Views on Occult Practice". *Magic, Ritual, and Witchcraft* 6(2): 123–62.
Pasi, Marco 2012. "September 1930, Lisbon: Aleister Crowley's Lost Diary of His Portuguese Trip". *Pessoa Plural* 1: 253–83.
Pasi, Marco 2013. "The Problems of Rejected Knowledge: Thoughts on Wouter Hanegraaff's *Esotericism and the Academy*", *Religion* 43(2): 201–12.
Pasi, Marco and Patricio Ferrari 2012. "Fernando Pessoa and Aleister Crowley: New Discoveries and a New Analysis of the Documents in the Gerald Yorke Collection". *Pessoa Plural* 1: 284–313.
Passerini, Luisa 1999. *Europe in Love, Love in Europe: Imagination and Politics in Britain between the Wars*. London: I. B. Tauris.
Pauwels, Louis and Jacques Bergier 1960. *Le Matin des magiciens: introduction au réalisme fantastique*. Paris: Gallimard.
Pauwels, Louis and Jacques Bergier 2001. *The Morning of the Magicians*. London: Souvenir Press.
Paz, Octavio 1988. *Ignoto a se stesso*. Genoa: Il melangolo.
Pearson, John 1989. *The Life of Ian Fleming: Creator of James Bond*. n.p.: Coronet Books (1st edn 1966).
Pessoa, Fernando 1928. *O Interregno: Defesa e justificação da Ditadura Militar em Portugal*. Lisbon: Núcleo de Acção Nacional.
Pessoa, Fernando 1932. "Prefácio". See Kamenezky (1932), 5–21.
Pessoa, Fernando 1979a. *Sobre Portugal: Introdução ao problema nacional*, J. Serrão *et al.* (eds), J. Serrão (intro.). Lisbon: Ática.
Pessoa, Fernando 1979b. *Da República (1910–1935)*, J. Serrão *et al.* (eds), J. Serrão (intro.). Lisbon: Ática.
Pessoa, Fernando 1982. *Cartas de Fernando Pessoa a João Gaspar Simões*. Lisbon: Imprensa Nacional Casa da Moeda.
Pessoa, Fernando 1986a. *A procura da Verdade Oculta*, A. Quadros (ed.). Lisbon: Publicações Europa-América.
Pessoa, Fernando 1986b. *Portugal, Sebastianismo e Quinto Império*, A. Quadros (ed.). Lisbon: Publicações Europa-América.
Pessoa, Fernando 1986c. *Páginas de Pensamento Político 1: 1910–1919*, A. Quadros (ed.). Lisbon: Publicações Europa-América.
Pessoa, Fernando 1986d. *Páginas de Pensamento Político 2: 1925–1935*, A. Quadros (ed.). Lisbon: Publicações Europa-América.
Pessoa, Fernando 1986e. *Obra poética e em prosa*, 3 vols. Porto: Lello and Irmão Editores.

Pessoa, Fernando 1988a. *A Grande Alma Portuguesa: A carta ao Conde de Keyserling e outros dois textos comentados por Pedro T. da Mota*. Lisbon: Edições Manuel Lencastre.
Pessoa, Fernando 1988b. *Moral, Regras de Vida, Condições de Iniciação: Textos estabelecidos e comentados por Pedro Teixeira da Mota*. Lisbon: Edições Manuel Lencastre.
Pessoa, Fernando 1989a. *Poesia Mágica, Profética e Espiritual: Poemas estabelecidos e comentados por Pedro T. Mota*. Lisbon: Edições Manuel Lencastre.
Pessoa, Fernando 1989b. *Rosea Cruz: Textos estabelecidos e apresentados por Pedro T. Mota*. Lisbon: Edições Manuel Lencastre.
Pessoa, Fernando 1990. *Cartas de amor de Fernando Pessoa*, D. Mourão-Ferreira (ed.). Lisbon: Edições Ática (1st edn, ed. M. da Graça Queiroz, Lisbon: Edições Ática, 1978).
Pessoa, Fernando 1993. *Mensagem: Poemas esotéricos*, J. A. Seabra et al. (eds). Madrid: Coleção Archivos.
Pessoa, Fernando 1999. *Correspondência 1923–1935*, M. P. da Silva (ed.). Lisbon: Assírio and Alvim.
Pessoa, Fernando 2009. *Juden und Freimaurerei*, M. Sahr (trans.), Y. K. Centeno (ed., intro.). Leipzig: Leipziger Literaturverlag.
Pessoa, Fernando 2011. *Sebastianismo e Quinto Império*, J. Uribe and P. Sepúlveda (eds). Lisbon: Ática.
Pessoa, Fernando 2012. *Boca do Inferno: Aleister Crowleys Verschwinden in Portugal*, S. Dix (ed.). Frankfurt: S. Fischer.
Pessoa, Fernando and Aleister Crowley 2001. *Encontro "Magick" de Fernando Pessoa e Aleister Crowley*, M. Roza (ed.). Lisbon: Hugin.
Pessoa, Fernando and Aleister Crowley 2010. *Encontro "Magick": Seguido de A Boca do Inferno (novela policiária)*, M. Roza (ed.). Lisbon: Assírio and Alvim.
Petrie, Charles 1959. *The Jacobite Movement*. London: Eyre and Spottiswoode.
Pittock, Murray G. H. 1993 "Jacobitism". See Cevasco (1993), s.v.
Pizarro, Jerónimo 2012. *Pessoa existe?* Lisbon: Ática.
Pizarro, Jerónimo, Patricio Ferrari and Aantonio Cardiello 2010. *A Biblioteca Particular de Fernando Pessoa, Fernando Pessoa's Private Library*, vol 1. Lisbon: Publicações Dom Quixote.
Poggi, Vincenzo 1987. "Joseph Ledit SJ (1898–1986): Journal d'une mission en Russie (1926)". *Orientalia Christiana Periodica* 53: 5–40.
Poggi, Vincenzo 2000. *Per la storia del Pontificio Istituto Orientale: Saggi sull'istituzione, i suoi uomini e l'Oriente Cristiano*. Rome: Pontificio Istituto Orientale.
Poliakov, Léon 1994. *Le mythe aryen*. Paris: Calmann-Lévy (1st edn 1971).
Politica Hermetica 1987. *Politica Hermetica 1: Métaphysique et Politique: René Guénon, Julius Evola*. Lausanne: L'Âge d'Homme.
Politica Hermetica 1992. *Politica Hermetica 6: Le complot*. Lausanne: L'Âge d'Homme.
Politica Hermetica 2000. *Politica Hermetica 14: Le souverain caché*. Lausanne: L'Âge d'Homme.
Politica Hermetica 2010. *Politica Hermetica 24: La Franc-Maçonnerie et les Stuarts au XVIIIe siècle; Stratégies politiques, réseaux, entre mythes et réalités*. Lausanne: L'Âge d'Homme.
Porter, Bernard 1992. *Plots and Paranoia: A History of Political Espionage in Britain, 1790–1988*. London: Routledge.
Praz, Mario 1970. *The Romantic Agony*. Oxford: Oxford University Press (1st Italian edn 1930).
Protocols 2011. *The Protocols of the Meetings of the Learned Elders of Zion*, V. E. Marsden (trans.), T. Marrs (preface), H. Ford (texts). Austin, TX: RiverCrest Publishing.
Puech, Henri-Charles (ed.) 1990. *Esoterismo, spiritismo, massoneria*. Rome: Laterza (1st edn 1977).
Quadros, António 1986a. "Prefácio". See Pessoa (1986a), 11–29.
Quadros, António 1986b. "Prefácio". See Pessoa (1986b), 11–36.
Quadros, António 1986c. "Introdução". See Pessoa (1986d), 13–18.
Quadros, António 1992. *Fernando Pessoa: Vida, Personalidade e Génio*. Lisbon: Publicações Dom Quixote.
Quinn, Malcolm 1994. *The Swastika: Constructing the Symbol*. London: Routledge.
Quinn, William W. 1997. *The Only Tradition*. Albany, NY: State University of New York Press.
Raphaël, Gaston 1909. *Walter Rathenau: Ses idées et ses projects d'organisation économique*. Paris: Payot and C.
Rathenau, Walther 1912. *Zur Kritik der Zeit*. Berlin: S. Fischer Verlag.
Rathenau, Walther 1921. *The New Society*. London: Williams and Norgate.
Rauschning, Hermann 1938. *Die Revolution des Nihilismus*. Zurich: Europa.
Rauschning, Hermann 1939. *Hitler Speaks: A Series of Political Conversations with Adolf Hitler on His Real Aims*. London: Thornton Butterworth.
Ravagli, Lorenzo 2004. *Unter Hammer und Hakenkreuz: Der völkisch-nationalsozialistische Kampf gegen die Anthroposophie*. Stuttgart: Freies Geistesleben.
Read, Donald 1972. *Edwardian England 1901–15: Society and Politics*. London: Harrap.
Regardie, Israel 1932. *A Garden of Pomegranates: An Outline of the Qabalah*. London: Rider and Co.

Regardie, Israel (ed.) 1937–40. *The Golden Dawn: An Account of the Teachings, Rites and Ceremonies of the Order of the Golden Dawn*, 4 vols. Chicago, IL: Aries Press.
Regardie, Israel 1979. *Foundations of Practical Magic, An Introduction to Qabalistic, Magical and Meditative Techniques*. Wellingborough: Aquarian Press.
Regardie, Israel (ed.) 1986. *Gems from the Equinox: Instructions by Aleister Crowley for His Own Magickal Order*. Phoenix, AZ: Falcon Press.
Regardie, Israel 1993. *The Eye in the Triangle: An Interpretation of Aleister Crowley*. Phoenix, AZ: New Falcon (1st edn 1970).
Reid, Brian Holden 1987. *J. F. C. Fuller: Military Thinker*. Basingstoke: Macmillan.
Reuss, Theodor and Aleister Crowley 1999. *OTO Rituals and Sex Magick*. Thame: I-H-O Books.
Rials, Stéphane 1983. *Le légitimisme*. Paris: Presses Universitaires de France.
Rigby, Andrew 1984. *Initiation and Initiative: An Exploration of the Life and Ideas of Dimitrije Mitrinović*. Boulder, CO: East European Monographs.
Rigby, Andrew 1999. "Training for Cosmopolitan Citizenship in the 1930s: The Project of Dimitrije Mitrinovic". *Peace and Change* 24(3) (July): 379–99.
Rigby, Andrew 2006. *Dimitrije Mitrinović: A Biography*. York: William Sessions (2nd edn of Rigby 1984).
Rivet, Édouard 1985. "René Guénon franc-maçon". See Laurant (1985), 324–39.
Roberts, John M. 1972. *The Mythology of the Secret Societies*. London: Secker and Warburg.
Roberts, Susan 1978. *The Magician of the Golden Dawn: The Story of Aleister Crowley*. Chicago, IL: Contemporary Books.
Robin, Jean 1986. *René Guénon: Témoin de la Tradition*. Paris: Guy Trédaniel (1st edn 1978).
Roling, Bernd 2002. "The Complete Nature of Christ: Sources and Structures of a Christological Theurgy in the Works of Johannes Reuchlin". See Bremmer and Veenstra (2002), 231–66.
Rollin, Henri 1939. *L'apocalypse de notre temps: les dessous de la propagande allemande d'après des documents inédits*. Paris: Gallimard.
Rossi, Marco 1989. [Untitled review of books by Piero di Vona, Giorgio Galli and Rudolf von Sebottendorff]. *Storia Contemporanea* 2 (April): 317–23.
Rossi, Marco 1991. "L'avanguardia che si fa tradizione: l'itinerario culturale di Julius Evola dal primo dopoguerra alla metà degli anni trenta". *Storia Contemporanea* XXII(6): 1039–90.
Rousse-Lacordaire, Jérôme 1998. *Antimaçonnisme*. Puiseaux: Pardès.
Ruggiu, Jean-Pascal and Nicolas Tereshchenko 2009. "The Crowley Affair", www.golden-dawn.com/eu/displaycontent.aspx?pageid=113-crowley-affair (accessed 8 April 2013).
Ryan, William F. 1992. "The Great Beast in Russia: Aleister Crowley's Theatrical Tour in 1913 and his Beastly Writings on Russia". See McMillin (1992), 137–61.
Sabazius X° [David Scriven] 2001. "Observations on Liber OZ", http://hermetic.com/sabazius/ozgloss.htm (accessed 24 August 2013).
Saja, Giuseppe 1998. "Aleister Crowley: il personaggio e il suo doppio letterario". See Zoccatelli (1998), 69–81.
Salzani, Stefano and PierLuigi Zoccatelli 1996. *Hermétisme et Emblématique du Christ dans la vie et dans l'œuvre de Louis Charbonneau-Lassay (1871–1946)*. Paris: Archè-Edidit.
Sauvêtre, Joseph 1936. *Un bon serviteur de l'Eglise: Mgr Jouin*. Paris: Maison Casterman.
Scaligero, Massimo 1972. *Dallo Yoga alla Rosacroce*. Rome: Perseo.
Schieder, Theodor 1972. *Hermann Rauschnings "Gespräche mit Hitler" als Geschichtsquelle*. Opladen: Westdeutscher Verlag.
Schmidt, Rainer F. 2000. *Rudolf Heß: "Botengang eines Toren?" Der Flug nach Großbritannien vom 10. Mai 1941*. Düsseldorf: Econ (1st edn 1997).
Scholem, Gershom 1969. *On the Kabbalah and its Symbolism*. New York: Schocken.
Scholem, Gershom 1995. *Major Trends in Jewish Mysticism*. New York: Schocken (1st edn 1941).
Schüller, Govert 1997. *Krishnamurti and the World Teacher Project: Some Theosophical Perceptions*. Fullerton, CA: Theosophical History.
Sciascia, Leonardo 1973. "Apocrifi sul caso Crowley". In *Il mare colore del vino*, L. Sciascia, 125–31. Turin: Einaudi.
Seabra, José Augusto 2004. *Fernando Pessoa: Pour une poétique de l'ésotérisme*. Paris: À l'Orient.
Sebottendorff, Rudolf von 1933. *Bevor Hitler kam: Urkundliches aus der Frühzeit der nationalsozialistischen Bewegung*. Munich: Deukula-Verlag Grassinger and Co.
Sebottendorff, Rudolf von 1987. *Prima che Hitler venisse*. Turin: Delta-Arktos (Italian translation of Sebottendorff 1933).
Sedgwick, Mark J. 2009. *Against the Modern World: Traditionalism and the Secret Intellectual History of the Twentieth Century*. Oxford: Oxford University Press.
Séguy, Jean 1990. "Non-conformismi religiosi d'Occidente". See Puech (1990), 1–76.

Selver, Paul 1959. *Orage and the New Age Circle: Reminiscences and Reflections*. London: George Allen and Unwin.
Sena, Jorge de 1984. *Fernando Pessoa and C^a Heterónima (Estudos coligidos 1940-1978)*. Lisbon: Edições 70.
Servier, Jean (ed.) 1998. *Dictionnaire critique de l'ésotérisme*. Paris: Presses Universitaires de France.
Sestito, Roberto 2000-2004. "Alcune considerazioni in margine al libro di Marco Pasi, *Aleister Crowley e la tentazione politica*". *Politica Romana* 6: 405-16.
Sestito, Roberto 2003a. *Il figlio del Sole: Vita e Opere di Arturo Reghini Filosofo e matematico*. Ancona: Associazione Culturale Ignis.
Sestito, Roberto 2003b. *Storia del Rito Filosofico Italiano e dell'Ordine Orientale Antico e Primitivo di Memphis Mizraim*. Florence: Libreria Chiari.
Shirer, William L. 1960. *The Rise and Fall of the Third Reich: A History of Nazi Germany*. London: Secker and Warburg.
Simões, João Gaspar 1991. *Vida e Obra de Fernando Pessoa*. Lisbon: Publicações Dom Quixote (1st edn 1950).
Skinner, Quentin 1969. "Meaning and Understanding in the History of Ideas". *History and Theory* 8(1): 3-53.
Smith, Morton and Gershom Scholem 2008. *Correspondence 1945-1982*, G. G. Stroumsa (ed.). Leiden: Brill.
Spence, Richard B. 2000. "Secret Agent 666". *International Journal of Intelligence and Counterintelligence* 13: 359-71.
Spence, Richard B. 2008. *Secret Agent 666: Aleister Crowley, British Intelligence, and the Occult*. Port Townsend, WA: Feral House.
Spence, Richard B. 2011. "Aleister Crowley, Sidney Reilly, Basil Zaharoff: Their Influence on the Creation of James Bond and His World". In *James Bond in World and Popular Culture: The Films Are Not Enough*, R. G. Weiner, B. L. Whitfield and J. Becker (eds), 216-27. Newcastle upon Tyne: Cambridge Scholars Press.
Starr, Martin P. 1995. "Aleister Crowley: Freemason!". *Ars Quatuor Coronatorum* 108: 150-61.
Starr, Martin P. 2003. *The Unknown God: W. T. Smith and the Thelemites*. Bolingbrook, IL: Teitan Press.
Starr, Martin P. 2006. "Chaos from Order: Cohesion and Conflict in the Post-Crowley Occult Continuum". *The Pomegranate* 8(1): 84-117.
Steele, Tom 1989. "From Gentleman to Superman: Alfred Orage and Aristocratic Socialism". In *The Imagined Past: History and Nostalgia*, C. Shaw and M. Chase (eds), 112-27. Manchester: Manchester University Press.
Stehle, Hansjakob 1981. *Eastern Politics of the Vatican 1917-1979*. Athens, OH: Ohio University Press.
Stephensen, Percy Reginald 1930. *The Legend of Aleister Crowley: Being a Study of the Documentary Evidence Relating to a Campaign of Personal Vilifications Unparalleled in Literary History*. London: Mandrake Press.
Stephensen, Percy Reginald and Aleister Crowley 2007. *The Legend of Aleister Crowley*, S. J. King (intro.). Enmore: Helios Books.
Stephensen, Percy Reginald and Israel Regardie 1983. *The Legend of Aleister Crowley*, I. Regardie (intro.). Las Vegas, NV: New Falcon Publications.
Struve, Walter 1973. *Elites against Democracy: Leadership Ideals in Bourgeois Political Thought in Germany, 1890-1933*. Princeton, NJ: Princeton University Press.
Stuckrad, Kocku von 2005a. *Western Esotericism: A Brief History of Secret Knowledge*. London: Equinox.
Stuckrad, Kocku von (ed.) 2005b. *The Brill Dictionary of Religion*. Leiden: Brill.
Suster, Gerald 1988. *The Legacy of the Beast: The Life, Work and Influence of Aleister Crowley*. London: Whallen.
Suster, Gerald 1990. *Crowley's Apprentice: The Life and Ideas of Israel Regardie*. York Beach, ME: Weiser.
Suster, Gerald 1993. "Crowley, Alexander Edward". See Nicholls (1993), 162-3.
Sutin, Lawrence 2000. *Do What Thou Wilt: A Life of Aleister Crowley*. New York: St Martin's Press.
Swinburne, Algernon Charles 1867. *A Song of Italy*. Boston, MA: Ticknor and Fields.
Symboles et Mythes 1999. *Symboles et Mythes dans les mouvements initiatiques et ésotériques (xviie-xxe siècles): Filations et emprunts*. Milan: Archè, Paris: La Table d'Émeraude (special issue of *ARIES*).
Symonds, John 1951. *The Great Beast: The Life of Aleister Crowley*. London: Rider.
Symonds, John 1958. *The Magic of Aleister Crowley*. London: Muller.
Symonds, John 1971. *The Great Beast: The Life and Magic of Aleister Crowley*. London: Macdonald and Co.
Symonds, John 1972. *La Grande Bestia: Vita e magia di Aleister Crowley*. Rome: Mediterranee (Italian translation of Symonds 1971).
Symonds, John 1974. *Conversations with Gerald*. London: Duckworth.
Symonds, John 1989. *The King of the Shadow Realm: Aleister Crowley: His Life and Magic*. London: Duckworth.
Symonds, John 1991. *The Medusa's Head: or Conversations Between Aleister Crowley and Adolf Hitler*. Thame: Mandrake.
Symonds, John 1997. *The Beast 666: The Life of Aleister Crowley*. London: Pindar Press.
Tabucchi, Antonio 1977. "Pessoa o del Novecento". *Quaderni portoghesi* (Pisa) 1: 17-36.
Tabucchi, Antonio 1988. "Pessoa: il rumore di fondo". See Paz (1988), 7-11.
Tabucchi, Antonio 1990. *Un baule pieno di gente: Scritti su Fernando Pessoa*. Milan: Feltrinelli.
Taguieff, Pierre-André 1992. *Les Protocoles des Sages de Sion*, 2 vols. Paris: Berg International.

Taguieff, Pierre-André 2005. *La Foire aux illuminés: ésotérisme, théorie du complot, extrémisme*. Paris: Mille et une nuits.
Taguieff, Pierre-André 2012. *L'imaginaire du complot mondial: aspects d'un mythe moderne*. Paris: Éditions Mille et une Nuits.
Tarannes, A. 1928. "Un Sataniste italien". *Revue Internationale des Sociétés Secrètes* XVII(4): 124–9.
Tarannes, A. 1929a. "Le 'Fasciste' Evola et la mission transcendante de l'Église". *Revue Internationale des Sociétés Secrètes* XVIII(2): 43–68.
Tarannes, A. 1929b. "L'OTO – Expulsion de Sir Aleister Crowley". *Revue Internationale des Sociétés Secrètes* XVIII(5): 133–7.
Tavares, José Fernando 1998. *Fernando Pessoa e as estratégias da razão política*. Lisbon: Instituto Piaget.
Taylor, Gary 2000. *Orage and The New Age*. Sheffield: Sheffield Hallam University Press.
Taylor, Paul Beekman 2001. *Gurdjieff and Orage: Brothers in Elysium*. York Beach, ME: Weiser Books.
Taylor, Sally J. 1990. *Stalin's Apologist: Walter Duranty; The New York Times's Man in Moscow*. Oxford: Oxford University Press.
Tegtmeier, Ralph 1989. *Aleister Crowley: Die tausend Masken des Meisters*. Munich: Knaur.
Teixeira, Luís Filipe B. 1997. *Pensar Pessoa: A Dimensão Filosófica e Hermética da Obra de Fernando Pessoa*. Baguim do Monte: Lello Editores.
Tereschchenko, Nicolas 1985. "Israel Regardie (1907–1985) and the 'Golden Dawn'". *Aries* 4: 71–87.
Thatcher, David S. 1970. *Nietzsche in England 1890–1914: The Growth of a Reputation*. Toronto: University of Toronto Press.
Thomas, Dana Loyd 1997. "Il filogermanesimo di Julius Evola: le reazioni dello stato". *Politica Romana* 4.
Thomas, Peter W. 2005. "Jenner, Henry (1848–1934)". *Oxford Dictionary of National Biography* (May), www.oxforddnb.com/view/article/75066 (accessed 2 June 2011).
Thompson, E. P. 1977. *William Morris: Romantic to Revolutionary*. London: Merlin Press (1st edn 1955).
Thurlow, Richard 2009. *Fascism in Britain from Oswald Mosley's Blackshirts to the National Front*. London: I. B. Tauris (1st edn 1987).
Trythall, Anthony J. 1977. *"Boney" Fuller: The Intellectual General*. London: Cassell.
Tupman, Tracy W. 2003. "Theatre Magick: Aleister Crowley and the Rites of Eleusis". PhD dissertation, Ohio State University, Columbus, OH.
Turner, Frank Miller 1974. *Between Science and Religion: The Reaction to Scientific Naturalism in Late Victorian England*. New Haven, CT: Yale University Press.
Turner, Frank Miller 1993. *Contesting Cultural Authority: Essays in Victorian Intellectual Life*. Cambridge: Cambridge University Press.
Turris, Gianfranco de (ed.) 1985. *Testimonianze su Evola*. Rome: Mediterranee (1st edn 1973).
Turris, Gianfranco de (ed.) 1986. "L'iniziazione, la massoneria, la magia: tre lettere di R. Guénon a J. Evola". *I quaderni di Avallon* 10 (January–April): 109–25.
Turris, Gianfranco de 1989. "Introduzione all'edizione italiana". See Alleau (1989), 9–17.
Uribe, Jorge and Pedro Sepúlveda 2011. "Introdução". See Pessoa (2011), 11–44.
Uribe, Jorge and Pedro Sepúlveda 2012. "Sebastianismo e Quinto Império: o nacionalismo pessoano à luz de um novo *corpus*". *Pessoa Plural* 1: 139–62.
Van Kleeck, Justin Scott 2003. "The Art of the Law: Aleister Crowley's Use of Ritual and Drama". *Esoterica* 5: 193–218, www.esoteric.msu.edu/VolumeV/ArtofLaw.htm (accessed 8 April 2013).
Vannoni, Gianni 1980. *Massoneria, Fascismo e Chiesa cattolica*. Rome: Laterza.
Vannoni, Gianni 1985. *Le società segrete dal Seicento al Novecento*. Florence: Sansoni.
Veneruso, Danilo 1987. *Il seme della pace: la cultura cattolica e il nazionalimperialismo fra le due guerre*. Rome: Edizioni Studium.
Veneziani, Marcello 1994. *La rivoluzione conservatrice in Italia*. Carnago: SugarCo.
Ventura, Gastone 1991a. *I Riti Massonici di Misraïm e Memphis*. Catania: Brancato.
Ventura, Gastone 1991b. *Templari e templarismo*. Rome: Atanòr.
Vermeer, Ruud 2004. *Aleister Crowley: De Levensloop van een der grootste magiërs die ooit leefde*. Amsterdam: Uitgeverij Schors.
Vermeer, Ruud 2005. *Aleister Crowley: Eine illustrierte Biographie des bekanntesten und umstrittenen Magiers des 20. Jahrhunderts*. Amsterdam: Iris (German translation of Vermeer 2004).
Versluis, Arthur 2007. *Magic and Mysticism: An Introduction to Western Esotericism*. Lanham, MD: Rowman and Littlefield.
Viereck, George Sylvester 1930. *Spreading Germs of Hate*. New York: Horace Liveright.
Villis, Tom 2013. *British Catholics and Fascism: Religious Identity and Political Extremism between the Wars*. Basingstoke: Palgrave Macmillan.

Volkov, Nikolaï 1995. *La secte russe des castrats*. Paris: Les Belles Lettres.
Wachtmeister, Constance 1897. *Spiritualism in the Light of Theosophy: A Stenographic Report of a Lecture delivered by Countess Wachtmeister at the Northwestern Spiritualists' Camp Meeting, July 23rd, 1897*. San Francisco, CA: Mercury Print.
Waldstein, Arnold 1975. *Aleister Crowley: Le Saint de Satan*. Paris: Culture, Art, Loisirs.
Wasserstein, Bernard 1988. *The Secret Lives of Trebitsch Lincoln*. New Haven, CT: Yale University Press.
Webb, James 1971. *The Flight from Reason: The Age of the Irrational*. London: Macdonald. New edition with different title: *The Occult Underground* (La Salle, IL: Open Court, 1974).
Webb, James 1976. *The Occult Establishment*. Glasgow: Richard Drew.
Webb, James 1980. *The Harmonious Circle: The Lives and Work of G. I. Gurdjieff, P. D. Ouspensky, and Their Followers*. New York: G. P. Putnam's Sons.
Weber, Eugen 1964. *Satan franc-maçon: La mystification de Léo Taxil*. Paris: Julliard.
Webster, Nesta 1922a. *The French Revolution: A Study in Democracy*. London: Constable.
Webster, Nesta 1922b. *World Revolution: The Plot against Civilizations*. London: Constable.
Webster, Nesta 1924. *Secret Societies and Subversive Movements*. London: Boswell.
Wheatley, Dennis. 1934. *The Devil Rides Out*. London: Hutchinson.
Wheatley, Dennis 1979. *The Time Has Come ... The Memoirs of Dennis Wheatley: Drink and Ink 1919–1977*. London: Hutchinson.
Wheen, Francis 1990. *Tom Driberg: His Life and Indiscretions*. London: Chatto and Windus.
White, John Baker 1970. *True Blue: An Autobiography 1902–1939*. London: Frederick Muller.
Wilson, Colin 1987. *Aleister Crowley: The Nature of the Beast*. Wellingborough: Aquarian Press.
Wilson, Colin 2006. *The Occult*. London: Watkins (1st edn 1971).
Wittgenstein, Ludwig 1979. *Remarks on Frazer's* Golden Bough, Rush Rhees (ed.). Denton: Brynmill Press.
Wolff, Robert Lee 1971. *Strange Stories and Other Explorations in Victorian Fiction*. Boston, MA: Gambit.
Yeats, William Butler 1938. *The Autobiography of William Butler Yeats*. New York: Macmillan Company.
Yeats, William Butler 1954. *The Letters of W. B. Yeats*, A. Wade (ed.). London: Rupert Hart-Davis.
Yeats, William Butler 1972. *Memoirs: Autobiography, First Draft; Journal*, D. Donoghue (ed.). London: Macmillan.
Yeats, William Butler 1986. *The Collected Letters of W. B. Yeats, Volume 1: 1865–1895*, J. Kelly (ed.). Oxford: Clarendon Press.
Zoccatelli, PierLuigi (ed.) 1998. *Aleister Crowley: un mago a Cefalù*. Rome: Mediterranee.
Zoccatelli, PierLuigi 1999. *Le Lièvre qui rumine: autour de René Guénon, Louis Charbonneau-Lassay et la Fraternité du Paraclet*. Milan: Archè.

Index

A∴A∴ 14–15, 26–7, 58–9, 62, 67–8, 71, 106, 120–22, 131, 158, 167 (*n*61), 171–2 (*n*23), 172 (*n*43), 180 (*n*179), 183 (*n*16), 198 (*n*21), 198–9 (*n*25), 199 (*n*26)
Abbey of Thelema *see* Thelema, Abbey of
Abramelin system of magic 34, 166 (*n*49)
Abyss (Golden Dawn system of magic) 14, 62, 167 (*n*57)
Adler, Alfred 19, 69, 78, 126, 157–8, 184 (*n*24, *n*30), 201 (*n*60)
Adler Society 69, 126, 157
Aeon of Horus (*also* New Aeon) 50–51, 56–8, 119
Aeschbach, Annemarie 152
Aeschylus 98
Agnostic Journal, The 66, 183 (*n*11)
agnosticism 31, 39, 66, 172 (*n*42)
Aiwass 13, 26, 73, 182 (*n*221)
Albert of Saxe-Coburg and Gotha, Prince Consort 173 (*n*47)
alchemy 23, 96, 99, 100
Allah 167 (*n*53)
Alldeutsche Verband 148
anarchist
  circles 168 (*n*65)
  doctrine 137
  perspective 49
Anatta 167 (*n*53)
androgyny 151
Anger, Kenneth 9, 166 (*n*28)
Anglo-German Fellowship 92
Anglo-Saxon Lodge (Grand Lodge of France) 202 (*n*86)
Anthroposophical Society 149
Anthroposophy 69, 149, 197 (*n*8)
anti-bourgeois attitude and revolt
  in Crowley 37–8, 96, 119, 169–70 (*n*83)
  in P. R. Stephensen 169–70 (*n*83)
anti-Catholicism 173 (*n*61)
anti-Christian
  views and attitudes 37, 47, 52, 67, 99, 119, 122, 138, 173–4 (*n*61)
  politics 83
anti-Christianity 173–4 (*n*61)
anti-clericalism 51, 66, 178 (*n*141)
anti-communism 124–5, 139

anti-communist
  books by G. M. Godden 124
  Crowley as an 53
  intelligence 188 (*n*103)
  organizations 159, 200 (*n*44)
anti-fascist
  propaganda 127
  enthusiasm of Crowley 128
anti-Masonic
  bias 134
  cause 119–21
  groups 120
  periodicals and journals 111, 130, 133
  revelations 120
anti-Nazi resistance in Germany 92
anti-Semitic
  conspiracy theories 191–2 (*n*23)
  propaganda 98
anti-Semitism
  in Crowley 35
  in É. Drumont 192 (*n*23)
  in J. F. C. Fuller 70
  in M. Küntzel 58
  in the British Union of Fascists 184 (*n*35)
  in the *RISS* 122
  in the Right Club 89
  in Thelema 137
antireligion 186 (*n*68)
apocalyptic literature 113
Apostles' Club 76, 185 (*n*62), 185–6 (*n*63)
Aquino, Michael 175 (*n*90)
Ariosophy 180 (*n*185)
Armageddon 58
Armentano, Amedeo Rocco 203 (*n*100, *n*101)
Army
  British 3, 65, 67–8
  Mongol 115
  Red 115
Aron, Robert 201 (*n*58)
Arthurian cycle 97
Aryan
  race 69
  traditional heritage 183–4 (*n*16)
Ascona 167–8 (*n*65)
Ashburnham, Bertram, 5th Earl of 32–3

astrology 23, 91, 93, 96, 99–100, 111, 154, 157, 189 (n125)
Atlantean Adepts 131, 198–9 (n25) *see also* A∴A∴
Atlantis 122, 199 (n27)
Auden, Wystan Hugh 52
Augoeides ritual, the 13
avant-gardes, literary and artistic 24, 52

Badoglio, Pietro 70
Bakunin, Mikhail Alexandrovich 169 (n83)
Bandarra (pseud. of Gonçalo Anes) 105
Barreto, José 196 (n102)
Barruel, Augustin, Abbé 118, 197 (n5)
Battle
  of Al-Ksar el Kebir 96
  of Amiens 68
  of Arras 68
  of Cambrai 68
  of Culloden 32
  of Flodden Field 191 (n10)
Beardsley, Aubrey 11
Beernink, Ernest 157
Belém, Victor 194 (n75)
Benedict XV, Pope 85, 120, 198 (n12)
Bennett, Allan 11–12, 166 (n48), 171 (n9), 173 (n58)
Benoist, Alain de 180 (n185)
Bergier, Jacques 53
Berkeley, George 151
Berridge, Edward 37, 175 (n85)
Bersone, Clotilde 120, 122–3, 198 (n17)
Besant, Annie 17–18, 66, 183 (n9)
Bible 10 *see also* New Testament, Old Testament
Binet, Ana Maria 190 (n6)
Birven, Henri Clemens 95, 132, 142–4, 197 (n7), 202–3 (n90), 205 (n9–11, n19)
Black Front 201 (n58)
Blackden, Marcus W. 174 (n75)
Blake, William 35, 176 (n117)
Blaue Reiter, der 69
Blavatsky, Helena Petrovna 2, 18, 60, 66, 100, 118, 182 (n220), 193 (n66), 198–9 (n25)
Blitzkrieg, German 65
Blunt, Anthony 76, 185–6 (n62–4)
Bô Yin Râ (Joseph Anton Schneiderfranken) 134
Boca do Inferno affair 96, 107–11, 115, 194 (n82–3), 196 (n120), 196–7 (n121)
Bocchini, Arturo 126, 160–61, 201 (n66)
Bode, Johann Joachim 146
Boer War 36, 39, 44, 65
Bogdan, Henrik 9
Boleskine 12, 33
Bolingbroke, Henry Saint-John 66
Bolshevik
  expansion into Europe 70
  religious politics 82–3
  revolution *see* Russian Revolution
Bolsheviks (*also* Bolshevists) 81, 83, 118, 120, 123, 180 (n179), 197 (n7)

Bolshevism 51, 124, 126, 128, 200 (n43), 202 (n77) *see also* communism; Marxism; socialism
Bolton, Kerry Raymond (a.k.a Frater Scorpio) 179 (n159)
Bond, James (character of I. Flemings novels) 90, 200 (n46)
Book of Revelation 10, 168 (n69)
Book of the Law, The 13, 18, 20, 26–7, 47–9, 51, 53–8, 60, 73, 137–8, 142, 165 (n20), 167 (n53), 168 (n69), 170–71 (n4), 178 (n135–6, n140), 182 (n221), 206 (n55)
  anti-democratic and elitist implications of 47–9
  Crowley's commentary to 47–9, 56, 178 (n136, n151)
  manuscript of 14, 25–6, 206 (n55)
Booth, Martin 7
Botto, António 98
Bouchet, Christian 9, 53, 84, 166 (n31), 174 (n62), 177 (n121), 178 (n134), 179 (n159, n172), 180 (n187), 198 (n18)
Bourbon, House of 173 (n56)
bourgeois
  industrial civilization 40
  mentality and conventions 51, 72, 169–70 (n83)
  society 38
  values, morals, ethics 37–8, 40, 48
Breeze, William 9, 166 (n29), 178 (n148), 184 (n34)
  see also Hymenaeus Beta
Bricaud, Joanny 142
British Museum 173 (n54), 175–6 (n107)
British Union of Fascists (BUF) 14, 69–70, 89, 184 (n33, n35), 188 (n114)
Brocket, Ronald Nall-Cain, 2nd Baron 70
Browning, Robert 176 (n117)
Buddhism 11–12, 23, 167 (n53)
Bullock, Alan 180 (n185)
Bund der Aufrechten 149
Burgess, Guy 76
Burns, Robert 32, 35

Cairo 13, 110
Calvinism 121
Cambareri, Giuseppe 203 (n102)
Cammell, Charles Richard 7, 20, 71, 134
Camões, Luís de 96
Carlism 32–3, 174 (n69)
Carlist
  schemes and activities of Crowley 52, 173 (n55)
Carlos, Don, Duke of Madrid 33, 35, 173 (n56)
Carter, John F. C. 94, 188 (n103)
Carus, Paul 44
Casement, Roger 44, 84–5
castrates, Russian sect (*skopcy*) 82
Castro, Eugénio de 193 (n63)
Catholic
  Church 108, 198 (n12), 200 (n43)
  orders 198 (n19)
  press 200 (n50)

INDEX 227

seminar 200 (*n*41)
theology 121
Catholicism 52, 72, 187 (*n*96)
 anti- 34, 173 (*n*61)
 conversion to 33, 84, 173 (*n*54)
 and conspiracy theories 119, 121
 and the Jacobite movement 34
 and fascism 52, 179 (*n*167), 200 (*n*50)
Cefalù (also spelled as "Kephalu") 17, 47, 51, 60, 71, 73, 81, 125-7, 141, 158-61, 199 (*n*26), 201 (*n*64)
Celtic
 Church 34, 174 (*n*62)
 race 35, 174 (*n*65)
 Revival (*also* Movement) 32-4, 41, 172 (*n*44), 173 (*n*48, *n*53, *n*57)
 tradition and lore 31, 173 (*n*58)
Celtic-Cornish Society (Cowetas Kelto-Kernuac) 33
Centeno, Yvette Kace 98, 190 (*n*6), 192 (*n*26)
Ceylon (Sri Lanka) 12, 35, 171 (*n*9)
Chamberlain, Houston Stewart 115
Chandor, Louise A. *see* Fry, Lesley
Charbonneau-Lassay, Louis 122, 130, 199 (*n*27), 202 (*n*82)
Chaucer, Geoffrey 42
chauvinism 29, 46, 172 (*n*29), 176 (*n*116)
Chéron, Jane 78, 186 (*n*78)
Chesterton, Gilbert Keith 40, 175 (*n*102, *n*105)
Chichmarev, Paquita *see* Fry, Lesley
China 13-14, 84, 87
chivalry 34
Christ Church College, Oxford 72
Christian
 civilization 192 (*n*26)
 values, ethics and morality 47, 98, 123
Christianity 2, 10, 15, 31, 47-8, 53-4, 66, 69, 78-9, 82, 122-3, 166 (*n*39), 168 (*n*68), 186 (*n*68) *see also* anti-Christian, anti-Christianity
 early 163 (*n*1)
Church of Satan 175 (*n*90)
Churchill, Winston 58, 70, 87, 89, 91-2, 181 (*n*212), 188 (*n*113-15), 189-90 (*n*131)
 correspondence with Roosevelt 89, 119
Churton, Tobias 7-8, 124
Ciano, Galeazzo 70
cinema 9
City of the Pyramids 182 (*n*223)
civil war 52
 American 35
 Russian 82, 115
 Spanish 52, 57, 70
Civiltà Cattolica 200 (*n*41)
Coburg, House of 173 (*n*47)
cocaine 12, 17, 187-8 (*n*100), 205 (*n*34)
Cohn, Norman 118, 120
Colazza, Giovanni 149
Coleridge, Samuel Taylor 98
collectivism 58
colonialism 36, 39

communism 52-3, 5 5, 57-8, 69, 124, 139, 200 (*n*41), 201 (*n*50) *see also* anti-communism; bolshevism; Marxism; socialism
 aristocratic 50
 in Europe 91, 124
communist
 beliefs and positions 89, 185-6 (*n*63)
 leaders 77, 186 (*n*68)
 movement 74
 regime 52
 students 76
 threat 189 (*n*121)
Communist Party
 of Germany 86-7
 of Great Britain 72-6, 81, 89-90, 169 (*n*83), 185 (*n*55)
 of Soviet Union 76
concentration camps
 British 39
 French 21
 Nazi 20, 57
Conrad, Joseph 39
conservatism 29, 34, 97
Conservative Party of Great Britain 28-9, 125, 172 (*n*27)
Conservative Revolution 50, 179 (*n*159-60)
conspiracy 34, 89, 185 (*n*49)
 Jewish-Masonic 88, 119, 122, 202 (*n*77) *see also* Judeo-Masonry
 theories 3, 88, 90, 98, 117-19, 123, 129-30, 140, 145, 150, 191-2 (*n*23), 197 (*n*1, *n*5, *n*7-8), 198-9 (*n*25), 199 (*n*36)
 theorists 3, 69, 72, 90, 117-21, 123-4, 129-30, 133, 139, 180 (*n*179), 191-2 (*n*23)
contemporary art 137
Coomaraswamy, Ananda Kentish 3, 16, 117, 135-6, 176 (*n*108), 204 (*n*113, *n*116)
Cooper, Alfred Duff 181 (*n*199)
Cooper, Valerie 158
Corriere Padano 148
Costa, Dalila L. Pereira da 190 (*n*6)
Costello, John 90-91, 188 (*n*113), 188-9 (*n*115), 189 (*n*121)
counter-initiation 3, 87, 110, 118, 129-31, 133 *see also* initiation
Crowley, Edward (Crowley's father) 10
Crowley, Emily Bertha, née Bishop (Crowley's mother) 10, 160, 161, 166 (*n*38), 192 (*n*28)
Crowley, Rose Edith, née Kelly (Crowley's first wife) 13
Crusades 198 (*n*19)
Cuba 30-31, 33
Cult of the Serpent 122
Cunard, Nancy 52, 179 (*n*169)

D'Arch Smith, Timothy 181 (*n*217)
D'Herbigny, Michel 200 (*n*41)
Daily Express 75

Dandieu, Arnaud 201 (*n*58)
Daniel (prophet) 96
Dante Alighieri 4
Darby, John Nelson 166 (*n*34)
Darbyites 10, 166 (*n*34), 172 (*n*28) *see also* Plymouth Brethren
Darbyite
  background 33, 59
  boarding school 10
  doctrine 59
  rules 173 (*n*47)
De Bono, Emilio 201 (n64)
De Vidal Hunt, Carl 169 (*n*82)
Deacon, Richard 185 (n62) *see also* McCormick, Donald
Debenham, Marjorie C. 73
decadence 28, 41, 98, 129
Decadent
  movement 23, 31
  occultism 112
decadents, English 43, 170 (*n*2)
Dee, John 167 (*n*63)
Del Ponte, Renato 134, 152, 190 (*n*5), 203 (*n*98, *n*101)
Delahaye, James Viner, Colonel 157
Delhi 12, 36
democracy 35, 47, 49, 58, 67–8, 97, 117, 181 (*n*206)
  liberal 129
democratization of magic, Crowley's 61
Desio, Ardito 167 (*n*51)
Détective 108
Deutschnationale Volkspartei (DNVP) 148, 206 (*n*44)
Diário de Notícias 108
Dias, Caetano, Colonel 194 (*n*83)
Dickie, Francis 107
Dix, Steffen 192 (*n*35)
Domvile, Barry 87, 91
Douglas-Hamilton, Douglas 92, 189 (*n*121)
Douglas-Hamilton, James 189 (*n*121)
Dreyfus, Alfred (*also* Dreyfus affair) 35, 174 (*n*67)
Driberg, James 74–7, 81, 87, 90, 94, 125, 185 (*n*44–6, *n*46, *n*55, *n*58, *n*60), 186 (*n*64, *n*67–8), 188 (*n*103), 189 (*n*116)
Driberg, Thomas, also known as Tom 3, 18, 72
Droit Humain, Le 128
drugs (*also* mind-altering substances, intoxicating substances) 12, 17, 20, 135, 151 *see also* cocaine, heroin, mescaline, morphine, opium
Drumont, Édouard 191–2 (*n*23)
Duesterberg, Theodor 206 (*n*46)
Duguet, Roger 121
Duncombe-Jewell, Louis Charles Richard (a.k.a. Ludovic Cameron) 33, 173 (*n*53–4)
Duranty, Walter 3, 15, 76–83, 186 (*n*69, *n*75, *n*78)

East, the 14, 33, 183 (*n*9)
Easter Rising, Ireland's 40, 174 (*n*74)

Eastern
  religions 120
  doctrines and teachings 135, 151
Eckartshausen, Karl von 11, 59, 100, 166 (*n*45)
Eckenstein, Oscar 11–13, 39
Economic League 125, 159, 200 (*n*44)
Eder, David 175–6 (*n*107)
Edward VIII, King of England 189 (*n*116)
Edwardian
  age 179 (*n*163)
  England 136
  intellectual and literary circles 40, 136
  London 40, 175 (*n*101)
  society 2, 38
egalitarian ideology 192 (*n*26)
Eleventh Hour Group 69, 158
Eliot, Thomas Stearns 52, 75
elite 59–60, 67–68, 112, 117, 151, 191–2 (*n*23)
  Nazi regime's 94
elitism 47, 59, 137, 139, 151, 191–2 (*n*23)
Empedocles 107
Empire
  British 28, 35, 46, 135, 174 (*n*73)
  Fifth *see* Fifth Empire
  German 35, 174 (*n*66)
  of the Beast 112
  Ottoman 174 (*n*66)
Encausse, Gérard *see* Papus
Engel, Leopold 146–8, 150
English Review, The 17, 42, 172 (*n*39)
Enlightenment 2, 32
Enoch 112
Enochian
  material in J. Dee's papers 175–6 (*n*107)
  system of magic 14, 167 (*n*63)
Ensor, Robert 39, 172 (*n*30)
Epstein, Jacob 176 (*n*114)
Equestrian Order of the Holy Sepulchre 120, 198 (*n*19)
Equinox, The (Crowley's journal) 14–15, 26, 59, 62, 67, 123, 158, 171 (*n*20), 198 (*n*23)
Eshelman, James A. 199 (*n*26)
esoteric
  circles (*also* milieus) 15, 94, 113, 117, 198–9 (*n*25), 203 (*n*100), 203 (*n*102)
  culture 94
  currents 141, 163 (*n*3)
  doctrine of Nazism 55, 94
  groups (*also* movements) 1–2, 18, 20, 150, 167–8 (*n*65), 182 (*n*220)
  homosexuality
  orders (*also* brotherhoods) 38, 138
  scene in Europe 100, 134
  traditions 59, 61–2
esotericism 9, 11, 18–19, 40, 59, 66, 95, 111, 117–18, 139, 164 (*n*1), 182 (*n*220, *n*228), 203 (*n*93)
  and conspiracy theories 117–19, 197 (*n*1)
  and politics 1–2, 95, 97–98, 139, 163 (*n*4), 191 (*n*17)

INDEX   229

and science 182 (*n*228)
  in Fernando Pessoa 95–100, 104–7, 190 (*n*6), 191 (*n*17), 192 (*n*31)
  in Raul Leal 112–15
  Jewish 1, 70
  left-wing 2
  right-wing 2
  Western 1–2, 9, 23, 61, 118, 163 (*n*3), 164 (*n*9), 166 (*n*44), 197 (*n*1)
establishment
  Anglican 29
  British 39, 92, 94
Esterwegen *see* concentration camps, Nazi
Etherton, Percy Thomas 110, 195 (*n*95)
Études Carmélitaines 203 (*n*97)
Études Traditionnelles 203 (*n*97)
evangelicalism 39, 175 (*n*94)
Evans, Charles 167 (*n*55)
Everling, Friedrich 148–9
Evola, Julius 3–4, 19, 96, 110, 117, 122, 129–30, 133–5, 141–52, 179 (*n*159), 190 (*n*5), 202 (*n*79), 203 (*n*98), 203–4 (*n*104), 204 (*n*105, *n*112, *n*1, *n*4–5), 205 (*n*17, *n*19, *n*25–6, *n*28–9, *n*34, *n*37), 206 (*n*44, *n*46, *n*48) *see also* Satanist, Julius Evola as a
evolution, Darwinian 39
evolutionism 129 *see also* Darwinism
experience, mystical *see* mystical experience

Faivre, Antoine 163 (*n*3),
Farr, Florence 12, 37, 175–6 (*n*107)
fascism 58, 69–70, 87, 127, 150, 179 (*n*168)
  British 69, 184 (*n*33, *n*35), 200 (*n*50) *see also* British Union of Fascists
  Catholic 52
  Italian 51–2, 184 (*n*35), 69, 127–8, 160–61, 168 (*n*75), 198 (*n*17), 202 (*n*75)
fascist (Italian)
  authorities 202 (*n*75)
  era 190 (*n*5)
  intelligence services 200 (*n*43)
  methods and ideas 128
  party 168 (*n*75), 179 (*n*168)
  regime 17, 124
  squads 202 (*n*64)
Fascist, The 70
Fatherland, The 16, 43–4
Federation of British Youth 200–201 (*n*50)
Feilding, Everard 175–6 (*n*107)
feminism 129, 167–8 (*n*65)
Fenili, Piero 145, 152
Fenandes, Aníbal 196 (*n*102)
Ferrari de Miramar, Maria Teresa (Crowley's second wife) 19, 78, 100, 104, 193 (*n*56)
Fervan, Jean 203 (*n*94)
Fest, Joachim C. 180 (*n*185)
Fifth Empire 96–7, 191 (*n*9, *n*13, *n*15)
Fifth Monarchists 96

Firefly affair 33–4, 173 (*n*55, *n*59)
First World War 1, 8, 15, 26, 28, 31, 39–43, 45, 47–8, 50–51, 54, 58, 65, 68, 70, 76–7, 84–5, 98, 118, 125, 129, 135, 138–9, 149, 167 (*n*62), 167–8 (*n*65), 173 (*n*47), 175 (*n*101), 176 (*n*114), 177 (*n*122), 185 (*n*39), 196 (*n*112)
FitzGerald, Edward Noel 71, 185 (*n*42)
flagellants, Russian sect (*khlysty*) 82
Fleming, Ian 90–93, 188 (*n*103), 189 (*n*120, *n*125), 190 (*n*134–6), 200 (*n*46)
Fleming, Peter 189 (*n*120)
Fortune, Dion 181 (*n*212)
France antimaçonnique, La 130
Franco, Francisco 52, 179 (*n*168, *n*170), 189 (*n*116)
Frater Scorpio *see* Bolton, Kerry R.
Fraternitas Rosicruciana Antiqua 203 (*n*102)
Frazer, James G. 61–3, 182 (*n*229–30)
freedom 32, 50, 172 (*n*38), 174 (*n*73, *n*76) *see also* liberty
  idea of unlimited 49
  sexual 47, 167–8 (*n*65)
Freemasonry, Freemasons 15, 32, 106, 118, 120–21, 124, 128–31, 133, 145, 150, 166 (*n*44), 167 (*n*54), 173 (*n*49), 192 (*n*26), 197 (*n*1, *n*5), 202 (*n*75–7), 203 (*n*98, *n*100) *see also* anti-Masonic; Masonic
  fringe (Masonry) 15, 133
  Luciferian 120
  Satanic 120, 122–3
Fremond, Olivier de 198 (*n*18)
French Revolution 32, 88, 118, 129
Freud, Sigmund 5–6, 8, 164 (*n*5–6), 184 (*n*24)
Friedrich Krupp AG 149
Fritsche, Herbert 142
Frosini, Eduardo 133–4, 203 (*n*100–101)
Fry, Lesley or Leslie (a.k.a. Paquita Shishmarev or Chichmarev, Louise A. Chandor) 123, 132, 198 (*n*18), 199 (*n*36), 202 (*n*89)
Fuller, Jean Overton 167 (*n*59)
Fuller, John Frederick Charles 3, 14–15, 53, 65–72, 118, 125, 139, 144, 167 (*n*57, *n*59), 175–6 (*n*107), 179–180 (*n*173), 183 (*n*3–4, *n*7, *n*11), 183–4 (*n*16), 184 (*n*17, *n*22, *n*34, *n*38), 185 (*n*39, *n*42, *n*43), 188 (*n*114), 195 (*n*95)
Fusco, Sebastiano 142

Galli, Giorgio 2, 94, 197 (*n*123)
Gardner, Gerald 141–2
Gaunt, Guy 45, 176–77 (*n*121), 177 (*n*128)
George VI, King of England 92
German Rosicrucian Movement 18
Germer, Karl 18, 20, 53, 56–7, 83, 94, 108, 180 (*n*179, *n*182), 181 (*n*200–206), 195 (*n*97), 197 (*n*8), 201 (*n*60), 202 (*n*90)
Gertz, Elmer 177 (*n*122)
Gestapo 56
Girasol 108
Gladstone, William Ewart 28–30
Gleichen, Heinrich von 148

Glorious Revolution 32
Gnostic-Catholic Church 142
Gnostic Mass 79–80, 187 (*n*81)
gnosticism 123, 192 (*n*29)
Gobineau, de Arthur 179 (*n*158)
Godden, Gertrude Mary 124–6, 157–8, 200–201 (*n*50), 201 (*n*62)
Godden, Mary 200–201 (*n*50)
Godden, William 200–201 (*n*50)
Godfrey, John 91, 93
Godwin, Joscelyn 2, 117, 198–9 (*n*25)
Goebbels, Joseph 148
Golden Dawn, Hermetic Order of the 6, 11–16, 23, 26–7, 33–5, 37–8, 59–62, 101, 106, 110, 119, 130, 133, 151, 164 (*n*9), 166 (*n*44, *n*47, *n*49), 167 (*n*57, *n*63), 173 (*n*54, *n*57, *n*59), 174 (*n*74–5), 175–6 (*n*107), 176 (*n*120), 179 (*n*170), 181–2 (*n*219), 182 (*n*220), 183–4 (*n*16), 189 (*n*125), 193 (*n*63)
Gomes, Augusto Ferreira 105, 107–8, 111, 194 (*n*83), 195–6 (*n*100)
Gonne, Maud 174 (*n*74)
Goodrick-Clark, Nicholas 180 (*n*185)
Gospel of Matthew 183 (*n*9)
Gosse, Edmund 172 (*n*28)
Gothic Revival 40–41
Gottlieb, Julie V. 200–201 (*n*50)
Grand Lodge of France 13, 121, 131, 202 (*n*86)
Grand Orient of France 121
Grant, Gregor 173 (*n*47)
Grant, Kenneth 6–7, 53, 164 (*n*5), 165 (*n*13), 192 (*n*37), 199 (*n*26), 203 (*n*101)
Gray, Thomas 176 (*n*117)
Great Work 26–7, 49, 56, 75
Green, Martin 175 (*n*101), 184 (*n*23)
Greene, Ben 93, 190 (*n*133)
Greene, Graham 93
Gregory, Lady Augusta 37, 175 (*n*87)
Grünewald, Olga de 149
Guénon, René 2–3, 19, 53, 87, 96, 105, 110–11, 117–18, 121–3, 129–36, 139, 141, 143, 146, 151, 176 (*n*108), 179 (*n*159), 188 (*n*105), 190 (*n*5), 195 (*n*95), 199 (*n*27), 202 (*n*79, *n*81–2, *n*84, *n*86, *n*89), 203 (*n*91–2, *n*95, *n*97–8, *n*101), 204 (*n*105, *n*116)
Guilbeaux, Henri 195 (*n*95)
Guillebert des Essars, Henri de 199 (*n*36)
Gurdjieff, George Ivanovich 18, 40, 168–9 (*n*79), 175 (*n*106), 175–6 (*n*107)
Guyot-Jeannin, Arnaud 179 (*n*159)

Haddo, Oliver (character of W. S. Maugham's novel based on Crowley) 167 (*n*52), 187–8 (*n*100)
Haeckel, Ernst 178 (*n*141)
Hain der Isis 132, 202 (*n*90), 205 (*n*10–11)
Hakl, Hans Thomas 4, 134, 179 (*n*171), 205 (*n*17)
Hamilton, Gerald 3, 19, 78, 83–8, 91–2, 118, 139, 187 (*n*95–6, *n*98), 188 (*n*101, *n*103–4, *n*108), 195 (*n*95)
Hamnett, Nina 20, 162

Hanegraaff, Wouter J. 9, 163 (*n*3, *n*10)
Hänel, Wolfgang 55, 180 (*n*185)
Hanover, House of 32, 173 (*n*47)
Haramzada Swamy 204 (*n*113)
Harris, Frank 14, 17, 139, 167 (*n*62)
Hart, Basil Liddell 65
Harzburger Front 148–9
Hastings, Beatrice 175–6 (*n*107)
Haushofer, Albrecht 92, 189 (*n*128)
Haushofer, Karl 92
Haverbeck, Werner G. 206 (*n*50)
Hawaii 12
Heard, Gerald 170 (*n*86)
Hermes Trismegistus 112
heroin 17, 187–8 (*n*100)
Herrenklub 147–8
Hess, Rudolf 3, 58, 70, 90–94, 188 (*n*113), 189 (*n*121–2, *n*125, *n*128), 189 (*n*135–6)
"hidden King" myth 191 (*n*10)
Himmler, Heinrich 197 (*n*8)
Hirsig, Leah 16–17
Hitler, Adolf 14, 18–19, 52–8, 70–71, 83, 87, 89, 91, 94, 96, 110–11, 119, 133, 135, 138–9, 148, 180 (*n*185, *n*187), 181 (*n*206, *n*212, *n*215), 183–4 (*n*16), 189 (*n*128), 195 (*n*95), 206 (*n*46)
Hohenzollern, August Wilhelm von, Prince of Prussia 149
Hohenzollern, Eitel Friedrich von, Prince of Prussia 149
Hohenzollern, House of 42
Hohenzollern, Oskar von, Prince of Prussia 149
Holy See 120 *see also* Vatican
Holy Spirit, Kingdom of the 113
Home Rule, Irish *see* Irish Home Rule
homosexuality 37, 72, 175 (*n*85)
  esoteric and spiritual 112
Hopfer, Oskar 53–4, 180 (*n*174)
Horniman, Annie 175 (*n*88)
Howe, Ellic 173 (*n*57, *n*59), 189 (*n*125), 197 (*n*8)
Hugenberg, Alfred 148–9, 206 (*n*45)
humanitarianism 48
Hume, David 151
Hutchinson, Roger 7, 124, 176 (*n*120)
Hutin, Serge 9
Hutton, Ronald 9
Huxley, Aldous 19, 52, 75, 78, 170 (*n*86)
Huxley, Thomas Henry 39, 66, 172 (*n*43), 178 (*n*141), 182 (*n*237), 185 (*n*59), 186–7 (*n*79)
Hymenaeus Beta (pseud. of William Breeze) 9, 144, 166 (*n*29), 175 (*n*85) *see also* Breeze, William
Hyperborean traditional heritage 183–4 (*n*16)

I Ching 188 (*n*101)
Iff, Simon (character in Crowley's fiction) 50, 195 (*n*93), 204 (*n*113)
illuminate, illuminated
  circles 3
  politics 65

thought 96
underground 111, 115–16
Illuminati 131, 145–50
  Order of the *see* Order of the Illuminati
Illuminism 122
individualism 47, 58
  absolute or radical 48–9, 178 (*n*148)
Indochina (Vietnam) 13
industrialization 41
Ingerflom, Claudio S. 187 (*n*88)
initiate 55, 59–60, 62, 105, 131, 150, 204 (*n*112)
initiation 13, 16, 25, 62, 105, 113–15, 119, 134, 142, 167 (*n*50), 168 (*n*73), 171 (*n*22), 171–2 (*n*23), 194 (*n*69), 194 (*n*75) *see also* counter-initiation
  pseudo- 133
  Tantric 146
initiatory
  order (*also* group, organization) 15, 101, 105, 133, 164 (*n*9), 170 (*n*91), 199 (*n*26), 203 (*n*101), 204 (*n*2)
  regularity 134
Inquire Within (Christina Mary Stoddart or Stoddard) 197 (*n*8)
intelligence services *see* secret services
International, The 16, 43–4, 175–6 (*n*107), 187 (*n*82)
International Society for Individual Psychology 158
internationalism 128
Introvigne, Massimo 9, 163 (*n*2), 164 (*n*9), 197 (*n*9)
Ireland 28–9, 31–2, 35–6, 39, 46, 84, 174 (*n*74, *n*78)
Irish
  Brigade 174 (*n*74)
  cause 36–7, 43, 84–5
  Home Rule 29
  independence 35, 84, 176–7 (*n*121)
  Nationalist Party 29
  nationalists 29–30, 35–38, 43
  Republic 44
irrationalism 2, 139
irrationality 62
Irving, David 189 (*n*121–2), 190 (*n*134)
Isherwood, Christopher 19, 78, 84–6, 170 (*n*86), 187 (*n*93, *n*98), 187–8 (*n*100)
Isis Urania Temple (Golden Dawn) 11
Islam 167 (*n*53)
Italian Philosophical Rite (Rito Filosofico Italiano) 133, 203 (*n*100, *n*102)

Jacobitism (*also* neo-Jacobite movement, Jacobite legitimism) 32–4, 173 (*n*48–9, *n*57), 191 (*n*10)
Jaeger, Hanni 19, 107, 193 (*n*45, *n*56), 194 (*n*83)
James II, King of England 32, 34
James IV, King of Scotland 191 (*n*10)
James, Marie-France 198 (*n*12)
Japan 12
Jenner, Henry 173 (*n*54)
Jesus Christ 48, 121, 163 (*n*1), 178 (*n*135), 183 (*n*9)
Jewish–Masonic conspiracy *see* conspiracy, Jewish–Masonic

Jews 35, 48, 58, 70, 98, 118, 120, 145, 184 (*n*35), 191 (*n*20), 191–2 (*n*23), 192 (*n*26), 197 (*n*5, *n*7)
jingoism 46, 172 (*n*29), 176 (*n*116)
Joachim of Fiore 113, 196 (*n*107)
John Bull 17
Johnson, Niel M. 177 (*n*122)
Jones, Charles Stansfeld 16, 18, 21
Jones, George Cecil 11, 14–15, 27, 37, 67–8, 167 (*n*56), 183 (*n*16)
Jouin, Ernest 119–20, 123, 130–31, 145, 197 (*n*10), 198 (*n*12)
Judaism 98, 128–9, 133, 191 (*n*20), 192 (*n*26), 202 (*n*75)
Judenkenner, Der 119, 167–8 (*n*65), 180 (*n*179), 197(*n*8)
Judeo-Masonry 120, 123, 128, 202 (*n*77) *see also* conspiracy, Jewish–Masonic
Jung, Carl Gustav 6, 8, 143, 164 (*n*5–6)
Jünger, Ernst 50

K2 12
Kabbalah 23, 96, 111, 163 (*n*3), 166 (*n*44)
Kabbalistic
  ideas 1
  symbolism *see* symbolism, Kabbalistic
  Tree of Life 57, 167 (*n*57)
  writings by Crowley 1
Kaczynski, Richard 7, 9–10, 165 (*n*14), 174 (*n*69), 176 (*n*117)
Kamenezky, Eliezer 192 (*n*26)
Kandinsky, Wassily 69
Kangchenjunga 13, 66, 167 (*n*55)
Karakorum range 12
Kelley, Edward 167 (*n*63)
Kelly, Gerald F. 13, 47
Kelly, Rose Edith (Crowley's first wife) *see* Crowley, Rose Edith
Kennedy, John Fitzgerald 188–9 (*n*115)
Kennedy, Joseph 89, 188–9 (*n*115)
Kent, Tyler 89, 119
Kent affair (*also* Kent-Wolkoff affair) 89–91, 119, 188 (*n*114), 188–9 (*n*115)
Keyserling, Hermann 115–16, 197 (*n*122–4)
Kibbo Kift Kindred 200–201 (*n*50)
King, Francis 7
King, Stephen J. 163 (*n*12)
Kipling, Rudyard 39
Knight, Maxwell 3, 75–6, 87–93, 119, 124–5, 185 (*n*60–61), 186 (*n*64), 188 (*n*114), 189 (*n*118), 190 (*n*134), 200 (*n*46)
Koenig, Peter-Robert 145, 148, 152, 165 (*n*14), 206 (*n*55)
Kremlin 81, 186 (*n*75)
Kremmerz, Giuliano (Ciro Formisano) 134, 205 (*n*29)
Krishnamurti, Jiddu 18, 183 (*n*9), 150
Kruger, Paul 174 (*n*73)
Krumm-Heller, Arnoldo 142, 203 (*n*102)

Krupp, Frau 147–9
Krur 134, 143, 147
Küntzel, Martha 18, 54, 56, 58, 142, 144, 180 (*n*182, *n*193), 181 (*n*197, *n*206, *n*208), 205 (*n*22)

Labour Party 18, 30, 69, 75–6, 93
Lachman, Gary 178 (*n*148)
Lankester, Edwin Ray 79, 186–7 (*n*79)
Lanz von Liebenfels, Jörg 105
Lao-tzu 101
Laurant, Jean-Pierre 2, 163 (*n*4), 204 (*n*116)
LaVey, Anton 175 (*n*90)
Law of Thelema *see* Thelema
Lawrence, David Herbert 40
Le Cour, Paul 122, 130, 199 (*n*27)
Leadbeater, Charles Webster 18, 192 (*n*28)
League of Nations 70
Leal, Raul 98, 102–3, 111–15, 155–6, 194 (*n*75), 196 (*n*101, *n*105, *n*112, *n*115), 196–7 (*n*121)
Leary, Timothy 170 (*n*86)
Leasor, James 189 (*n*121)
Ledit, Joseph 124–6, 157–160, 199–200 (*n*41), 200 (*n*43, *n*47), 200–201 (*n*50), 201 (*n*51, *n*61–2)
left hand path 135
left wing
  esotericism 2
  groups and activists 200 (*n*44)
  intellectuals 52, 139
  radical movements 125, 169–70 (*n*83)
  subversion 200 (*n*44)
Lega dei Diritti dell'Uomo 129
legitimism (*also* legitimist movements and circles) 32–4, 119, 173 (*n*47, *n*49, *n*54, *n*56), 191 (*n*10)
Lenin (Vladimir Ilyich Ulyanov) 73, 77, 81, 88, 185 (*n*55)
Leopold, John A. 149
Lessing-Hochschule in Berlin 147
Leto, Guido 124, 126, 200 (*n*43)
Lévi, Eliphas (pseud. of Alphonse Louis Constant) 61, 151, 193 (*n*66)
Liberal Party of Great Britain 29–30
liberalism 32, 117
libertarian
  perspective, Thelema from a 49
  doctrine, Thelema as basis for 137
liberty 48 *see also* freedom
  American love of 36
  France as fatherland of 35–6
  ideal and principles of 31, 57
  Law of 50
Ligue Franc-Catholique 119
Link, The 89, 91
Lipsey, Roger 204 (*n*113)
Litvinov, Maxim 77
Looking Glass, The 37, 67
Lopes, Teresa Rita 106
Loveday, Raoul 17, 72
Ludendorff, Erich 183–4 (*n*16)

Ludwig III of Bavaria 173 (*n*47)
Lyons, Eugene 77

MacBean, Reginald Gambier 168 (*n*76)
MacBride, John 174 (*n*74)
MacGregor clan 34
Machen, Arthur 179 (*n*170)
MacLean, Donald 76
Macleod, Fiona *see* William Sharp
Magi 181 (*n*217), 183 (*n*9)
magic 15, 19, 26, 55, 61, 70, 96, 99, 114, 143, 150–51, 171 (*n*19), 182 (*n*230)
  Abramelin system of 166 (*n*49)
  black 90, 162, 189 (*n*116)
  ceremonial 12, 23, 27, 166 (*n*44), 182 (*n*224)
  contemporary 134
  Crowley's interest in and ideas on 12–13, 15, 31, 59–64, 181 (*n*216), 206 (*n*57)
  sexual 15–16, 26–7, 60, 63, 151, 165 (*n*14)
  white 162
magical idealism 143
Magick 60–63, 67, 93, 135, 181 (*n*217)
Maglione, Luigi, Cardinal 87
Mahatmas 118 *see also* Secret Chiefs
Mairet, Philip 158, 179 (*n*163)
Maistre, Louis de 199 (*n*36)
Makgill, George 125, 201 (*n*53)
Mandrake Press, The 19, 100, 153–4
Mansfield, Katherine 40
Marc, Alexandre 201 (*n*58)
Maria Theresa of Modena, or Austria-Este 173 (*n*47)
Marsden, Victor 191 (*n*19)
Marx, Eleanor 167–8 (*n*65)
Marx, Karl 79, 91
Marxism 81, 128, 159 *see also* bolshevism, communism, socialism
Marxist
  positions 185–6 (*n*63)
  theory 184 (*n*24)
Masonic
  activities 167–8 (*n*65)
  speculations 100
  Templarism 105, 193 (*n*60)
  underground 121
Masonry *see* Freemasonry
Masters, Anthony 75–6, 90–94, 186 (*n*64), 189 (*n*127–8), 190 (*n*134–5, *n*46)
materialism 67, 98, 129, 198–9 (*n*25)
  Crowley's anti- 53, 139
  Pessoa's anti- 96
Mathers, Samuel Liddell MacGregor 11–12, 15, 33–4, 37–8, 59–60, 166 (*n*46, *n*49), 173 (*n*54, *n*57–9), 174 (*n*75), 175 (*n*85, *n*88), 182 (*n*220), 191 (*n*10)
Matteotti, Giacomo 201 (*n*64)
Maugham, William Somerset 12, 167 (*n*52), 187–8 (*n*100)
McCormick, Donald (a.k.a. Richard Deacon) 185 (*n*62), 188 (*n*103), 189 (*n*125), 190 (*n*134, *n*136)

INDEX   233

Melton, J. Gordon   163 (*n*2)
Memphis Misraim Order   148 *see also* Rites of Memphis and Misraim
mescaline   170 (*n*86)
metaphysics   23
Mexico   12, 35, 39
Meyrink, Gustav   134
MI1c (Military Intelligence, Section 1c, UK)   45
MI5 (Military Intelligence, Section 5, UK)   75–7, 89, 91, 93, 124, 185 (*n*60)
   Section B5(b)   75, 89, 189 (*n*127)
MI6 (Military Intelligence, Section 6, UK)   45, 93, 189 (*n*127)
Michelstaedter, Carlo   151
MID (Military Intelligence Division, US)   176–7 (*n*121)
Middle Ages   41, 113
Miguelism   32
Military Intelligence Division *see* MID
Mitrinovic, Dimitrije   69, 71–2, 78, 125–6, 157–8, 184 (*n*23, *n*30–31)
Mitrinovic Foundation   184 (*n*23)
modern civilization   2, 41–2, 136
modernism, literary   24
modernity   2, 40, 129, 150
Moeller Van den Bruck, Arthur   50
Monte Verità   167–8 (*n*65)
Monteiro, Adolfo Casais   99, 105
Moorehead, Alan   88
morphine   12
Morris, William   40–41, 167–8 (*n*65)
Morton, Desmond   91
Mosley, Oswald   14, 69–70, 87, 89, 184 (*n*33–5), 188 (*n*114)
Mosse, George L.   1, 180 (*n*185)
Mota, Pedro Teixeira da   116, 190 (*n*6), 197 (*n*124)
Mudd, Norman   14, 17, 66, 72, 128, 167 (*n*60), 183 (*n*11), 202 (*n*70)
Museum of Fine Arts in Boston   135
Mussolini, Benito   17, 51–2, 70, 122, 124, 127–8, 146–8, 159, 168 (*n*75), 179 (*n*167), 189 (*n*116), 201 (*n*64)
Mysteria Mystica Maxima (M∴M∴M∴)   27
mystical
   cult   79
   experience   12, 27, 171 (*n*9)
   regeneration   96
   research   6
   societies   38
   techniques   27
   traditions   23
   underground   170
mysticism   11, 26, 61–3, 66, 99, 171 (*n*9, *n*19), 182 (*n*224)
   Christian   100

nationalism   9
   Indian   135

national-patriotic movement, German   35
National Socialism *see* Nazism
Nationalsozialistische Deutsche Arbeiterpartei (NSDAP)   148
Naval Intelligence Division or Department *see* NID
Nazi
   authorities   54
   Germany   48, 57, 170 (*n*88)
   leaders   91, 93, 190 (*n*136)
   occultism (*also* Nazi-occultist literature and mythology)   53, 55, 179 (*n*171), 180 (*n*186)
   party   55–6, 70, 111, 189 (*n*121)
   phenomenon   180 (*n*187)
   regime and government   52–4, 56, 58, 90, 92, 94, 98, 119, 170 (*n*88), 197 (*n*123) *see also* Third Reich
   -Soviet pact   83
Nazism (*also* National Socialism)   3, 51–8, 80, 83, 87, 111, 115, 133, 135, 139, 177 (*n*124), 179 (*n*172), 181 (*n*212), 183 (*n*16), 184 (*n*35), 189 (*n*116), 197 (*n*123), 201 (*n*58)
Nebuchadnezzar, King   96
neo-gnosticism   192 (*n*29)
neo-Jacobite movement, neo-Jacobitism   32, 34, 173 (*n*48, *n*57) *see also* Jacobitism
neo-Nazi movements   48
neo-paganism   1, 25
   Nordic   179 (*n*159)
neo-spiritualism   120
neo-Templar
   orders   106, 114
   tradition   105 *see also* Templarism
Neruda, Pablo   52
Neuburg, Victor   14–15, 66, 72, 78, 167 (*n*59), 183 (*n*11)
Neue Freie Presse   191–2 (*n*23)
New Age   175 (*n*101)
New Age, The   40–41, 69, 136, 175 (*n*103), 175–6 (*n*107), 176 (*n*108), 184 (*n*31)
New Albion *see* New Britain
New Atlantis *see* New Britain
New Atlantis Foundation *see* Mitrinovic Foundation
New Britain   68–9, 71, 125–6, 157, 184 (*n*28), 201 (*n*58)
New Europe   69, 157–8, 184 (*n*28) *see also* New Britain
new religious movements   1, 4, 9, 163 (*n*2)
New Testament   10
New York Times   15, 76, 186 (*n*75)
Nicholas II, Tsar   84
NID (Naval Intelligence Division or Department, UK)   45, 90, 181 (*n*213)
Nietzsche, Friedrich   24, 40–41, 48, 151, 169–70 (*n*83), 175 (*n*105), 178 (*n*140), 179 (*n*158)
Nietzscheanism   179 (*n*163)
Nordic Theology   183–4 (*n*16)
Northumberland, Alan Percy, 7th Duke of   197 (*n*8)
Notícias Ilustrado   108, 194 (*n*83)
Nott, Charles Stanley   168–9 (*n*79), 175–6 (*n*107)

Oakes, Anselm (character of C. Isherwood's story based on Crowley) 187–8 (*n*100)
Objectivism 178 (*n*148)
Observer, The 88
occult, the (*also* the occult world) 65–8, 70–71, 90–91, 98, 113–14, 117 *see also* occultism
occult
  forces and powers 118, 129, 131
  phenomena 7
  tradition 5
  war 181 (*n*212)
Occult Review, The 71
occultism 2, 25, 32, 61, 64, 96, 112, 120–22, 130, 134, 139, 163 (*n*1), 171 (*n*11), 175–6 (*n*107), 179 (*n*159), 182 (*n*227), 196–7 (*n*121) *see also* occult, the
  Anglo-American 6
  German 72
  international 15
O'Donoghue, David James 38, 175 (*n*92)
Olcott, Henry Steel 193 (*n*66)
Old Testament 10, 57
Olisipo, F. Pessoa's publishing house 97–8, 191 (*n*20), 196 (*n*102)
Olsen, Dorothy 17, 72
Onofri, Arturo 149
opium 12, 78, 186 (*n*78), 195 (*n*93)
Orage, Alfred Richard 40–41, 69, 136, 175 (*n*103, *n*105–6), 175–6 (*n*107), 179 (*n*163), 184 (*n*31)
Ordem Templária de Portugal (OTP) 105–6, 193 (*n*68)
order *see* initiatory order
Order of the Illuminati 146–8 *see also* Weltbund der Illuminaten
Order of the Left Hand Path 179 (*n*159)
Order of the Star in the East 183 (*n*9)
Order of the White Rose 173 (*n*54)
Ordo Novi Templi (ONT) 105
Ordo Templi Orientis (OTO) 6, 9, 15–16, 18–21, 26–7, 56, 72, 104–5, 114, 119–21, 123, 126, 129–31, 133, 142, 144–6, 148, 158, 165 (*n*14), 166 (*n*30), 167 (*n*61), 167–8 (*n*65), 169 (*n*82), 171 (*n*22), 171–72 (*n*23), 180 (*n*179), 201 (*n*60), 202 (*n*89), 203 (*n*95, *n*101, *n*102), 203–4 (*n*104), 205 (*n*31)
  Archives 180 (*n*178)
  Caliphate 165 (*n*14)
  Swiss 142
  US Grand Lodge of the 178 (*n*149)
Ordre du Temple Renové (OTR) 105
Ordre Kabbalistique de la Rose-Croix 193 (*n*63)
Ordre Nouveau, L' 126, 158, 201 (*n*58)
Oriflamme 142, 144
Orthodox
  Church (in Russia) 82
  conservative circles 119
  liturgy 199–200 (*n*41)

Osho Rajneesh (a.k.a. Bhagwan Shree Rajneesh) 168–9 (*n*79)
OVRA 200 (*n*43)
Owen, Alex 9, 171 (*n*5, *n*14)
Oxford Mail 108

pacifism 128
Paine, Thomas 172 (*n*43)
Pan-Germanism 150
Pansophia (*also* Pansophic Society) 18, 180, 205 (*n*22)
Papus (Gérard Encausse) 193 (*n*63)
Paracletianism, Raul Leal's 112–13
Paris Working 78, 186 (*n*78)
Pasi, Marco 141–2, 144, 151–2, 205 (*n*25)
Patrick, St 174 (*n*78)
Patriot, The 119, 122, 197 (*n*7–8)
patriotism 8–9, 42, 57, 172 (*n*28)
Pauwels, Louis 53
Paz, Octavio 193 (*n*58)
Pearson, John 93, 190 (*n*135)
Péladan, Joséphin 112, 193 (*n*63)
Penty, Arthur J. 41
perennialism 197 (*n*3) *see also* traditionalism
personalism, French 151
Pessoa, Fernando 3, 19, 24, 65, 78, 83, 95–116, 118, 153–7, 184 (*n*30), 190 (*n*1–2, *n*4, *n*6), 191 (*n*12–13, *n*15–17, *n*20–22), 192 (*n*26, *n*28–9, *n*31, *n*34–8, *n*41, *n*43), 193 (*n*48, *n*51, *n*58–9, *n*63–5), 194 (*n*69, *n*71, *n*75, *n*82–3), 194–5 (*n*85), 195 (*n*93), 195–6 (*n*100), 196 (*n*102, *n*105, *n*114, *n*120), 196–7 (*n*121), 197 (*n*124)
Petrie, Charles 173 (*n*48)
Philby, Kim 76
Philip II, King of Spain 97
Pius IX, Pope 198 (*n*19)
Pius X, Pope 85
Pius XI, Pope 120
Pissier, Philippe 179 (*n*159)
Plymouth Brethren 10, 28–9, 33, 173–4 (*n*61) *see also* Darbyites
Poe, Edgar Allan 98
Poliakov, Léon 172 (*n*44)
Politica Romana 150
Pontifical Institute for Oriental Studies 124, 199–200 (*n*41)
popular culture 137
populism 147
positivism 23, 40, 170 (*n*3) *see also* scientific naturalism
Pound, Ezra 40, 52
Praz, Mario 31, 170 (*n*2)
Presença 109–10
Primrose League 172 (*n*27)
Prieuré, G. I. Gurdjieff's 168–9 (*n*79)
prophecy 96, 105, 111
Protocols of the Learned Elders of Zion 98, 119–20, 191 (*n*19–20), 197 (*n*8), 199 (*n*36)

INDEX 235

Providence 56
psychoanalysis
    Adlerian 69 *see also* Adler, Alfred
    Freudian 164 (*n*6), 184 (*n*24) *see also* Freud, Sigmund
    Jungian 164 (*n*6) *see also* Jung, Carl Gustav
Psychosophische Gesellschaft 205 (*n*24)
Pulitzer Prize 76, 186 (*n*75)
Puritanism 28, 39–40
Pythagorean tradition 133

Quadros, António 96, 111, 190 (*n*6), 191 (*n*13), 193 (*n*63)
Quakers 10
Queiroz, Ophélia 194 (*n*82)
Quinn, John 16
Quotidien, Le 128

race 48, 96
    Anglo-Saxon 35
    Aryan 69
    Celtic 35, 174 (*n*65)
racist
    component in Thelema 137
    politics 98
    statements in Crowley's writings 137
    theory and ideas 115
    undertones in Crowley's judgment of Coomaraswamy 135
radical right 179 (*n*159)
    in England 87, 119
radicalism (*also* radical politics) 49, 51, 57, 137–9, 179 (*n*159)
    leftist 185 (*n*63)
Radicals (wing of the Liberal Party) 30
Ramsay, Archibald 87, 89, 188 (*n*114)
Rand, Ayn 178 (*n*148)
Ratan Devi (pseud. of Alice Richardson) 16, 135
Rathenau, Walter 98, 191 (*n*22), 191–2 (*n*23)
rationalism 2, 67, 139, 172 (*n*43), 185–6 (*n*63)
Rationalist Press Association 66
rationality 2, 62
Rauschning, Hermann 55–6, 180 (*n*185–7), 181 (*n*197), 183–4 (*n*16)
Red Flame 9
Reelfs, John Daniel 203 (*n*101)
Regardie, Israel 6–7, 18–20, 25–8, 47, 59, 72, 78, 100, 104, 108, 122, 132, 163 (*n*12), 164 (*n*8–10), 164–5 (*n*11), 169 (*n*82), 171 (*n*11, *n*14), 171–2 (*n*23), 181–2 (*n*219), 186 (*n*67), 193 (*n*51, *n*55), 195 (*n*93)
Regardie, Sarah 169 (*n*82)
Reghini, Arturo 133–4, 203 (*n*100–101), 206 (*n*54)
Reichssicherheithauptamt 197 (*n*8)
relativism 129
religion 31, 66–7, 80, 82, 184 (*n*22), 198 (*n*12) *see also* antireligion
    contemporary 25
    Crowley's concept of 62–3, 80, 167 (*n*53)
    Crowley's new 13–14, 16, 18, 23, 25–7, 50–51, 61, 63, 80–81, 99, 122, 130, 137–140 *see also* Thelema
    Eastern 120
    Raul Leal's personal 112
    social control by means of 80
    state 78
religiosity 10
    occult-oriented 137
Reuss, Theodor 15, 18, 26, 60, 122–3, 133–4, 145–8, 150, 167–8 (*n*65), 168 (*n*76), 180 (*n*179), 197 (*n*8), 203 (*n*101)
revolution 24, 47, 79, 119, 170 (*n*4) *see also* Conservative Revolution, Glorious Revolution, French Revolution, Russian Revolution
    aristocratic 50
    mental 56
    of Thelema 57
    political 81
    social 66–7
    spiritual 81
Revue des Sciences Secrètes 132, 203 (*n*94)
Revue Internationale des Sociétés Secrètes (*RISS*) 111, 119–23, 129–33, 139, 145–6, 149–50, 197 (*n*8–10), 198 (*n*12, *n*17–18, *n*23), 199 (*n*36), 202 (*n*81), 203 (*n*95), 203–4 (*n*104)
Ribbentrop–Molotov Pact 83
Richardson, Alice *see* Ratan Devi
Right Club 89
right wing (*also* radical or extreme)
    activists and extremists 3, 84, 98, 124, 169–70 (*n*83)
    esotericism 2
    journals 33, 197 (*n*7), 205 (*n*25)
    groups, circles and organizations 89, 91, 119, 200 (*n*44), 204 (*n*1)
Risorgimento, Italian 201–2 (*n*68)
Rites of Eleusis, Crowley's 15, 168 (*n*66), 183 (*n*16)
Rites of Memphis and Misraim 168 (*n*76) *see also* Memphis Misraim Order
Rito Filosofico Italiano *see* Italian Philosophical Rite
Rodin, Auguste 12
Rollin, Henri 191 (*n*19)
Roma 142, 144, 204 (*n*5)
romanticism, late English 31
Rome 70, 124, 141, 149, 198 (*n*12)
    March on 17, 51, 168 (*n*75)
Roosevelt, Franklin Delano 77, 89, 119, 188–9 (*n*115)
    correspondence with Churchill *see* Churchill, Winston Spencer
Rosae Rubeae et Aureae Crucis (Second or Inner Order of the Golden Dawn) 13, 37–8, 167 (*n*57) *see also* Golden Dawn, Hermetic Order of the
Rosebery, Archibald Primrose, 5th Earl of 30
Roselius, Ludwig 147
Rosicrucianism (*also* Rosicrucian tradition) 23, 96, 166 (*n*44)
Rossi, Marco 190 (*n*5)

Rossetti, Dante Gabriel 176 (*n*117)
Rotary Club 128
Rougemont, Denis de 201 (*n*58)
Royalist, The 33
Roza, Miguel (pseud. of Luis Miguel Rosa Dias) 192 (*n*35)
Royal College of Nursing 200–201 (*n*50)
Ruskin, John 41
Russell, George (a.k.a. Æ) 32, 175 (*n*87)
Russian (*also* Bolshevik and Soviet) revolution 53, 77, 79–80, 82–3, 88, 186 (*n*68)
Ryan, Will F. 77, 80, 186 (*n*68), 187 (*n*84)

Sá-Carneiro, Mário de 98
Sabazius X° *see* Scriven, David
sacramentalism 34
Saif, Liana 175–6 (*n*107)
Salazar, António de Oliveira 96, 190 (*n*4)
samadhi 171 (*n*9)
Satan 203 (*n*97)
    adherents of 145
    Church of *see* Church of Satan
    Synagogue of 121
Satanism 1, 11, 122, 146, 179 (*n*159)
    contemporary 163 (*n*2)
Satanist
    Crowley as a 121, 146, 150, 163 (*n*2), 193 (*n*58)
    Freemasons 122
    Julius Evola as a 122, 146, 150
    sect, Ordo Templi Orientis as a 145
Scaligero, Massimo (pseud. of Antonio Sgabelloni) 149
Scarlet Woman 15–17, 19, 72, 78, 100, 168 (*n*69)
Schicklgruber, Adolf *see* Hitler, Adolf
Schieder, Theodor 180 (*n*185)
Schmidt, Rainer F. 90, 189 (*n*121), 190 (*n*134)
Schneider, Renato 110, 131, 133, 188 (*n*105)
Scholem, Gershom 1, 163 (*n*1, *n*3)
School of Wisdom 115
Schwob, Marcel 12
Sciascia, Leonardo 201 (*n*64)
science 62–4, 80, 182 (*n*228, *n*230)
    esoteric 59
    modern 61
    of the Magi 181 (*n*217)
scientific naturalism 23, 31, 38–9, 170 (*n*3), 172 (*n*42), 175 (*n*94)
Scott, Walter 32, 35
Scottish Rite 202 (*n*76)
Scriven, David (a.k.a. Sabazius X°) 178 (*n*149)
Seabra, José Augusto 190 (*n*6)
Seaman, Owen 176 (*n*117)
Sebastian, King of Portugal 96–7, 105
Sebastianism 96–7, 105, 191 (*n*9, *n*12–13, *n*15), 196 (*n*107)
Sebastianist myth 96, 111, 116
Sebottendorff, Rudolf von 197 (*n*123)
Second Nordic Thing 147–8

Second World War 48, 54–5, 57, 65, 69–72, 76, 83, 86–90, 94, 133–4, 139, 163 (*n*1), 169–70 (*n*83), 177 (*n*124), 191 (*n*19), 203–4 (*n*104), 205 (*n*19)
secrecy 29, 59
secret services, police and intelligence 8, 75, 125, 176–7 (*n*121), 190 (*n*134–5)
    British/English 3, 8, 15, 42, 44–5, 58, 75–6, 86–7, 91–2, 123–5, 130, 135, 176–7 (*n*121), 177 (*n*124), 188 (*n*103), 189 (*n*122, *n*125, *n*131) *see also* MI1c, MI5, MI6, NID, SIS
    French 86
    German 15, 86, 167–8 (*n*65) *see also* Gestapo, Reichssicherheithauptamt
    Italian 124, 146, 200 (*n*43) *see also* OVRA
    Soviet 89, 188 (*n*113)
    Tsarist 98
    US 45, 176–7 (*n*121), 188 (*n*113) *see also* MID
Secret Chiefs (*also* Masters) 59–60, 118–19, 182 (*n*221, *n*223), 182 (*n*220) *see also* Mahatmas
Section D, G. Makgill's 125, 201 (*n*53)
secularization 129, 185–6 (*n*63)
Seldte, Franz 148
Selver, Paul 175–6 (*n*107)
Semiramis 4
Sena, Jorge de 194 (*n*83), 196–7 (*n*121)
Serrão, Joel 191 (*n*13)
Servadio, Emilio 204 (*n*2)
sexual magic *see* magic, sexual
Shakespeare, William 98
Shanghai 14, 87
Sharp, William (Fiona Macleod) 32
Shaw, George Bernard 40, 52, 167 (*n*62), 175 (*n*102, *n*105)
Shelley, Percy Bysshe 170 (*n*1), 176 (*n*117)
Shirer, William L. 76, 180 (*n*185)
Shishmarev, Paquita *see* Fry, Lesley
Shumway, Ninette 17, 201 (*n*67)
Simões, João Gaspar 100–101, 109, 111, 113–15, 192 (*n*43), 195 (*n*93), 196–7 (*n*121)
Sing Sing 158
SIS (Secret Intelligence Service, UK) 45, 91, 189 (*n*127) *see also* MI6
Skinner, Quentin 171 (*n*8)
Skinner Stephen 206 (*n*58)
Slade, Vivian 158
Smith, Harry 90
Smith, Morton 163 (*n*1)
Smithers, Leonard Charles 11
social Darwinism 48, 139, 178 (*n*141)
    in Hitler 56
Social-Democratic Party, Austrian 160
socialism 32, 67, 129, 179 (*n*163)
    aristocratic 179 (*n*163)
    English 40
    guild 41
    medievalizing 41
    non-Marxist 40

socialist
  circles in London 167-8 (*n*65)
  culture 40
  ideas in early Italian fascism 51
Socialist League 167-8 (*n*65)
Sociedade Esoterica da Comunhão do Pensamento 113
Société Aleister Crowley 198 (*n*18)
Society for Psychical Research 175-6 (*n*107)
Society of the Divine Wisdom 73
Soviet
  leaders and authorities 77, 80, 87
  menace 70
  regime 54, 79, 82
  religious politics 81-2
  Revolution *see* Russian Revolution
Spanish-American war 30-31, 33
Spence, Richard B. 8, 45, 124-5, 135, 165 (*n*24), 172 (*n*27), 176-7 (*n*121), 188 (*n*103), 195 (*n*95)
Spencer, Herbert 48, 172 (*n*43), 178 (*n*141)
Spender, Stephen 52, 86
spiritualism 66, 98, 120, 198-9 (*n*25) *see also* neo-spiritualism
spirituality 11, 37, 40, 130
Sri Lanka *see* Ceylon
Stahlhelm 147-9, 206 (*n*44, *n*46)
Stalin (Iosif Vissarionovich Dzhugashvili) 77, 81-3, 186 (*n*68)
star of the East 183 (*n*9)
Starr, Martin P. 9, 166 (*n*30), 187 (*n*84)
Starr, Meredith (pseud. of Herbert Close) 68, 71, 183-4 (*n*16)
Stauffenberg, Klaus Schenk von 189 (*n*128)
Steiner, Rudolf 69, 148-9, 167-8 (*n*65), 197 (*n*8), 206 (*n*50)
Stephen III the Great, Voivode of Moldavia 97
Stephensen, Percy Reginald 19, 28, 139, 163 (*n*1, *n*12), 169-70 (*n*83), 170 (*n*84)
Stewart, Robert J. (Bob) 73
Stewart, William Ross (a.k.a. "Saladin") 66, 183 (*n*11)
Stoddart (or Stoddard), Christina Mary *see* Inquire Witihin
Strasser, Otto 201 (*n*58)
Stuart, House of 32, 34
Sturgis, David 81, 187 (*n*85)
subversion 32, 87-8, 117-18, 120, 123, 125, 129, 200 (*n*44)
Sullivan, John W. N. 170 (*n*86)
Sunday Express 17, 198-9 (*n*25)
Suster, Gerald 6, 164-5 (*n*11), 168-9 (*n*79), 170 (*n*88), 176-7 (*n*121)
Sutin, Lawrence 7, 10, 45, 54, 57, 177 (*n*130), 181 (*n*198-9), 183-4 (*n*16), 184 (*n*38), 187-8 (*n*100)
swastika 183-4 (*n*16)
Swinburne, Algernon Charles 43, 201-2 (*n*68)
symbolism
  Christian 122
  Kabbalistic 192 (*n*26)
  of the Golden Dawn 183-4 (*n*16)

Symonds, John 5-7, 10, 13, 44, 50, 56, 58, 60, 71-2, 75, 83, 86, 88, 100-101, 107, 110, 134, 144, 164 (*n*3, *n*5, *n*7, *n*10), 164-5 (*n*11), 166 (*n*38), 168 (*n*73), 168-9 (*n*79), 169 (*n*81), 170 (*n*86), 175-6 (*n*107), 176-7 (*n*121), 177 (*n*124-5), 181 (*n*209), 182 (*n*224), 184 (*n*17), 185 (*n*46, *n*58), 188 (*n*101), 192 (*n*34), 192 (*n*43), 193 (*n*56), 194 (*n*75, *n*83), 194-5 (*n*85), 201 (*n*60, *n*65), 202 (*n*90), 204 (*n*112), 205 (*n*26)
Synagogue of Satan *see* Satan, Synagogue of

Tablet, The 200-201 (*n*50)
Tabucchi, Antonio 95, 97, 193 (*n*58)
Tantra (*also* Tantrism) 135, 151
Tantric initiation rites 146
Tarannes, A. 122-3, 146
Tarot 20, 23
Taxil, Léo (pseud. of Marie Joseph Gabriel Antoine Jogand-Pagès) 120, 123, 198 (*n*15, *n*17), 202 (*n*89)
Taylor, Alan John Percivale (A. J. P.) 88
Taylor, Sally J. 77
Tegtmeier, Ralph 9, 170 (*n*88)
Templar
  ideas and traditions 104-5
Templar Order of Portugal *see* Ordem Templária de Portugal (OTP)
Templarism 96 *see also* neo-Templar tradition and orders
  Masonic and/or occultist 105, 193 (*n*60)
Templars 113
Tennyson, Alfred 42
Thébah Lodge (Grand Lodge of France) 202 (*n*86)
Thelema 13, 17, 25-7, 48-58, 62, 79-80, 82, 95, 106, 135, 137-9, 151, 165 (*n*20), 167 (*n*53), 168 (*n*69), 178 (*n*148, *n*151), 181 (*n*206-7, *n*213), 182 (*n*233), 201 (*n*60) *see also* religion, Crowley's new
  Abbey of 17, 20, 71, 73, 127-8
  ethics of 47
Théléma (bulletin of the Société Aleister Crowley) 198 (*n*18)
Thelema Publishing Company 144
Thelema Verlag 203 (*n*103)
Thelemic Society, The 179 (*n*159), 204 (*n*1)
Thelemites 17, 48-9, 57, 137, 167 (*n*53)
theosophy 2, 100, 120, 129, 198-9 (*n*25)
theosophical
  books and literature 98, 198-9 (*n*25)
  doctrine and teachings 60, 72, 119
  groups, circles and milieus 40, 167-8 (*n*65), 183 (*n*9)
  leaders 73, 186 (*n*68)
Theosophical Society 17-18, 66, 72, 74, 130, 168 (*n*76), 182 (*n*220), 193 (*n*66), 198-9 (*n*25)
Third Reich 1, 56, 76, 115, 170 (*n*88), 181 (*n*206), 206 (*n*44) *see also* Nazi regime
third way 50, 69, 201 (*n*58)

238   INDEX

Thomas, Dylan 14
Thompson, Francis 176 (*n*117)
three hundred men (conspiracy theories trope) 98, 191–2 (*n*23)
Times (London) 85, 187 (*n*98)
Torre, La 147
totalitarian
  ideologies 49, 51, 137, 139
  regimes 48, 51, 53, 57–8
totalitarianism 39, 97, 139
Townshend, F. H. E. 71, 184 (*n*38), 185 (*n*39)
traditional social order 118–19, 123, 129
traditionalism 2–3, 117, 129, 197 (*n*3) *see also* perennialism
  Italian 150
Tränker, Heinrich 18, 205 (*n*22)
transcendentalism 67
Trebitsch Lincoln, Ignácz 87, 110, 188 (*n*104, *n*106), 195 (*n*95)
Trevor-Roper, Hugh 180 (*n*185)
Trinity College, Cambridge 11, 14, 182 (*n*229), 183 (*n*11), 185–6 (*n*63)
Trotsky, Leon (Lev Davidovich Bronshtein) 80, 186 (*n*68)
True Will 48–9, 56, 73, 75, 106–7, 137, 151, 181 (*n*213)
Trythall, Anthony J. 65, 67–9, 71, 183 (*n*4), 184 (*n*22)
Tunis 17–18, 73–4, 107, 127, 187 (*n*84), 201–2 (*n*68), 202 (*n*70)
Tunisia 17, 47, 72, 74
Turner, Frank Miller 170 (*n*3), 172 (*n*41)
Turris, Gianfranco de 142, 152, 190 (*n*5), 204 (*n*112)
Tzara, Tristan 52

Ungern-Sternberg, Roman 115, 197 (*n*122)
United Grand Lodge of England 13, 131
Ur (journal and group) 134, 141, 143–5, 149, 204 (*n*2) *see also Krur*
Urban, Hugh B. 9

Vanity Fair 6, 16, 167 (*n*62)
Vannoni, Gianni 198 (*n*17)
Vatican 24, 51, 84, 87, 124, 199–200 (*n*41) *see also* Holy See
Vaughan, Diana 120, 198 (*n*17)
verdict of Rennes *see* Dreyfus, Alfred
Vermeer, Ruud 9
Versailles, Treaty of 57–8, 149
Vieira, António 96, 191 (*n*9)
Viereck, George Sylvester 16, 42–5, 54, 139, 177 (*n*122, *n*124), 180 (*n*176)
Victor Emmanuel III, King of Italy 168 (*n*75)
Victoria, Queen 32, 38–9, 173 (*n*47)
Victorian
  attitudes 164–5 (*n*11)
  era 31, 38–41, 65, 175 (*n*96)
  England 28, 37

Puritanism 28, 40
  society 2, 38, 41
Vietnam *see* Indochina
Villis, Tom 200–201 (*n*50)
Voile d'Isis, Le 131–2, 143, 202 (*n*89)
völkisch movement, German *see* national-patriotic movement, German
Von Salomon, Ernst 50

Wagnerian circles 167–8 (*n*65)
Waite, Arthur Edward 11, 100, 166 (*n*44)
Wasserstein, Bernard 188 (*n*104, *n*106)
Watkins Bookshop 132, 203 (*n*93)
Watts, Alan 170 (*n*86)
Webb, James 1–2, 65, 70, 115, 163 (*n*6), 168–9 (*n*79), 170 (*n*86), 173 (*n*48–9, *n*55), 183 (*n*3), 184 (*n*23), 197 (*n*123)
Webster, Nesta 88, 118, 124, 188 (*n*109), 197 (*n*4, *n*8)
Weida meeting 18, 72
Weininger, Otto 151
Weishaupt, Adam 146
Wells, Herbert George 40, 52
Weltbund der Illuminaten 146, 150 *see also* Order of the Illuminati
Wendt, Heinrich 142
Westcott, William Wynn 182 (*n*220)
White, John Baker 124–5, 157–9, 200 (*n*44), 201 (*n*53)
Wilde, Oscar 11, 37, 43, 167 (*n*62), 176 (*n*114)
Wilhelm II, Kaiser 85, 149
Wilhelm, Crown Prince of Prussia 147–9
will *see* True Will
William III of Orange, King 32
Wilson, Colin 7, 164 (*n*7), 165 (*n*20), 168–9 (*n*79)
Windsor, House of 173 (*n*47)
Wiseman, William 45, 177 (*n*124)
Wittgenstein, Ludwig 182 (*n*230)
Wheatley, Dennis 90, 189 (*n*116, *n*118–19)
Wicca 141
witchcraft 142
Wolkoff, Nikolai, Admiral 188 (*n*108)
Wolkoff, Anna 89, 188 (*n*108) *see also* Kent affair
World Teacher Campaign 17, 72, 81, 183 (*n*66), 187 (*n*84)

Yarker, John 168 (*n*76)
Yeats, William Butler 12, 32–4, 37–8, 40, 173 (*n*54), 174 (*n*74), 175 (*n*87, *n*92, *n*105), 182 (*n*220)
yoga 12, 23, 27, 65, 68, 171 (*n*9), 182 (*n*224)
Yorke Collection 55, 93, 111, 128, 170 (*n*86), 175–6 (*n*107), 179–80 (*n*173), 185 (*n*45, *n*46), 190 (*n*136), 192 (*n*41)
Yorke, Gerald 19–20, 55, 72, 104, 128, 132, 142, 168–9 (*n*79), 170 (*n*86), 177 (*n*124), 178 (*n*148), 180 (*n*188), 181 (*n*197), 186 (*n*68), 188 (*n*103), 189 (*n*120), 190 (*n*136), 193 (*n*53, *n*56), 195 (*n*97)

Zionism 124